# UNDERSTANDING
# JUVENILE LAW
# THIRD EDITION

# UNDERSTANDING JUVENILE LAW

## THIRD EDITION

**Martin R. Gardner**
*Steinhart Foundation Professor of Law*
*University of Nebraska, College of Law*

 LexisNexis

**Library of Congress Cataloging-in-Publication Data**

Gardner, Martin R.
  Understanding juvenile law / Martin R. Gardner. -- 3rd ed.
    p. cm. -- (Understanding series)
    ISBN 978-1-4224-2955-6 (softbound)
  1. Juvenile justice, Adminstration of--United States. 2. Children--Legal status, laws, etc.--United States. 3. Minors--United States. I. Title
    KF9780.G37 2009
    345.73'08--dc22

                                                                    2008052907

Editorial Offices
744 Broad Street, Newark, NJ 07102 (973) 820-2000
201 Mission St., San Francisco, CA 94105-1831 (415) 908-3200
www.lexisnexis.com

MATTHEW◊BENDER

# Dedication

---

In memory of my goodly parents.

Martin R. Gardner

# *Acknowledgments*

The author wishes to express appreciation for the generous support made available through the Ross McCollum Research Fund at the University of Nebraska College of Law; for the superb research and editorial assistance provided by Jeanette Ericson, Jolene Papa, and Krista Carlson; for the excellent secretarial service performed by Jann Howard, Gretchen Hammon, Marie Mathine, and Vida Eden; and, most of all, for the patience and encouragement of his wife, Anne.

# Preface

This text examines the topic of juvenile law. The book addresses issues of children and the law in the context of common law doctrine, federal constitutional principles, and statutory enactments.

The book discusses these various bodies of law in relation to a fundamental issue permeating the entire field of juvenile law: the extent to which the law should protect young people rather than recognize them as autonomous persons. While the law traditionally adopted a protectionist posture, recent legal developments appear to recognize autonomy rights of adolescents in certain contexts. These developments are praised by some commentators who advocate wholesale rejection of the paternalistic model in favor of a system that treats adolescents as full-fledged persons under the law. This book does not advocate any particular resolution of the current debate about the nature of the rights of young people; rather, it suggests that sensitivity to the issues and arguments entailed in that debate is essential to any true understanding of the present state of juvenile law.

With these concerns in mind, the text begins with a general discussion of the nature of the rights of juveniles and the perception that young people constitute a unique class under the law. This theoretical introduction will serve as a background for subsequent discussion of juvenile law doctrine. The discussion separates aspects of juvenile law arising outside the juvenile justice system (defined in this text as the system of separate courts organized to deal with "delinquents" and "status offenders")[1] from those arising within that system. This division is created as a useful means of organizing the doctrinal material, given the extensive body of rules that govern the juvenile justice system. Moreover, this organization permits the juvenile justice section to stand by itself as an independent text for students in courses that cover only that aspect of juvenile law.

Finally, for readers interested in single sources providing broader attention to juvenile law issues than provided in this text, two multi-volume sources may be useful starting points. Donald Kramer's three-volume second edition to *Legal Rights of Children* offers a well organized treatment of a host of legal issues affecting young people. In addition, the various volumes of *Juvenile Justice Standards* from the Institute of Judicial Administration and the American Bar Association Joint Commission provide useful commentary on a variety of juvenile law issues. Finally, for a treatment of the juvenile justice system, the second edition of Samual Davis's *Rights of Juveniles* provides an excellent source.

---

[1] A separate section (Part Three) is devoted to the delinquency/status offense aspects of juvenile law under the label "juvenile justice system." Sometimes this label is used more broadly to include abuse and neglect jurisdiction or any other matter handled in a separate juvenile court. The label "juvenile justice system" always includes, however, and is often limited to, that system of courts created to deal with delinquents and status offenders.

# Table of Contents

# Table of Contents

# Table of Contents

# Table of Contents

## Table of Contents

# Table of Contents

# Table of Contents

# Table of Contents

## Table of Contents

# Part One
## INTRODUCTION

# Chapter 1

# MINORITY AS A LEGAL STATUS

## § 1.01 OVERVIEW

The phenomenon of childhood is not unique to humans. Most other forms of life also embody a process where infants over time become adult members of the species. However, human infants are unique, at least among the primates, in the extent of their vulnerability and dependence on an extended period of socialization and learning in order to achieve maturity.[1] Thus, childhood for humans is a comparatively long period during which young people gradually acquire the competencies of adulthood.[2]

Because young people are perceived to be vulnerable and dependent upon more competent adults, they are viewed as a distinct class for legal purposes.[3] From Biblical times to the present, the law has imposed disabilities upon, and provided special protections for, young persons.[4]

## § 1.02 DISTINGUISHING MINORS FROM ADULTS

### [A] Chronological Age Rules

#### [1] Common Law

At common law an "infant" was any person who had not attained the age of majority as prescribed by law.[1] The term "infant" retains current usage, but is often replaced by the more modern terms "minor," "juvenile," or "child."[2]

The common law defined the status of minority in terms of chronological age without regard to individualized characteristics such as physical maturity, mental capacity, education, experience, or accomplishment.[3] While the age of majority varied for different classes of people under the early law, the common law eventually settled upon the age of twenty-one as the age at which persons attained

---

[1] D. Richards, *The Individual, the Family, and the Constitution: A Jurisprudential Perspective*, 55 N.Y.U. L. Rev. 1, 20 (1980).

[2] *Id.*

[3] E. Scott, N. Reppucci & J. Woolard, *Evaluating Adolescent Decision Making in Legal Contexts*, 19 Law & Hum. Behav. 221 (1995).

[4] *See, e.g., Deuteronomy* 21: 18–21 ("stubborn and rebellious" sons not "hearken[ing]" to the voices of their parents are subject to stoning at the hands of the "elders"). Some argue, however, that the concept of childhood is a relatively recent social invention, noting that medieval children were typically absorbed in the working world of adults at about age seven. See the summary of the work of Phillipe Aries in B. Hafen, *Children's Liberation and the New Egalitarianism: Some Reservations About Abandoning Youth to Their "Rights"*, B.Y.U. L. Rev. 605, 613 (1976). Hafen questions this view, however, pointing out that the common law's recognition of a longer childhood with the coming of the Renaissance, the Enlightenment, and the Industrial Revolution actually constituted a rediscovery of traditional notions of childhood found in ancient Greek and Roman cultures. *Id.* at 613–14.

[1] *See, e.g.,* Hartwell v. Cooper, 380 P.2d 591, 592 (Alaska 1963).

[2] *Id.*

[3] *See, e.g.,* Baril v. Baril, 354 A.2d 392, 396 (Me. 1976).

full legal capacity for most purposes.[4] The criminal law, however, designated age fourteen as the age at which offenders were fully responsible for their actions.[5] The common law thus created what at first glance appears to be a puzzling situation: while a fifteen-year-old is too young to enter into a contract, the same person is old enough to be held accountable for her criminal conduct.

## [2]  Modern Statutes: Different Ages for Different Contexts

With the passage of the Twenty-Sixth Amendment giving eighteen-year-olds the right to vote,[6] most states reduced the age of majority to eighteen.[7] For a time, many states attempted to treat eighteen-year-olds as adults for all legal purposes and thus, among other things, lowered the legal age for alcohol consumption to age eighteen. Attempts at establishing eighteen as the single age of majority were short-lived, however. In response to influences from the federal government to establish age twenty-one as a uniform national minimum age for permissible alcohol consumption, all states as of 1988 had enacted legislation establishing age twenty-one as the minimum legal drinking age.[8] Thus, while eighteen remains the "age of majority" in most states, being of "legal age" does not assure that one will enjoy all the rights and privileges as adults.

Conversely, states routinely establish a general age of majority but choose to permit young people to engage in some governmentally regulated conduct at an earlier age. For example, states generally permit young people to operate motor vehicles at ages younger than the designated age of majority.[9] As another example, Nebraska establishes the age of majority at nineteen, but allows young people who are eighteen or older to use tobacco.[10] Indeed, the laws of virtually every state consist of a complexity of rules granting privileges and imposing prohibitions on the basis of age levels both greater and lesser than the specified "age of majority."

Some of these apparent anomalies, for example granting driving privileges at an age earlier than the age of majority but restricting drinking past that age, can be explained as early extensions of privileges to young people while retaining residual control over their possible abuse of the privilege granted.[11] This explanation suggests that the law permits young people a period of transition to grow to adulthood by enjoying some, but not all, of the rights and privileges inherent in adulthood.[12]

---

[4]  H. Clark, The Law of Domestic Relations in the United States 309 (2d ed. 1988) (the age of majority for the knightly class historically was age twenty-one, the age at which men were thought strong enough to bear heavy medieval armour). *See supra* § 1.01, note 4.

[5]  *See, e.g.,* F. Ludwig, *Rational of Responsibility for Young Offenders,* 29 NEB. L. REV. 521, 527–28 (1950).

[6]  U.S. Const. Amend. XXVI.

[7]  Clark, *supra* note 4.

[8]  R. Mnookin & D. Weisberg, Child, Family and State 967 (3d ed. 1995).

[9]  *Id.* at 947.

[10]  Neb. Rev. Stat. §§ 28-1418 (1995) ("being a minor under eighteen years" and using tobacco "in any form" is a Class V misdemeanor), 43-2101 (1993) ("persons under nineteen are declared to be minors").

[11]  F. Zimring, The Changing World of Legal Adolescence 26 (1982).

[12]  *Id.*

## [B]   Individualized Standards for Assessing Maturity

Defining legal adulthood solely in terms of chronological age standards is controversial. Arriving at adulthood is a process rather than the occurrence of a particular birthday. While young people grow to adulthood by experiencing increasing degrees of autonomy, not all of them mature and become responsible adults at the same chronological age.[13]

While maturity is clearly a matter of individual variation, some social science data suggests that at the beginning of the period of adolescence (often identified as fourteen years of age) young people routinely employ the same decision-making processes as those utilized by most adults.[14] Reliance on such data has led some to advocate treating the considered choices of competent adolescents as having the same legal effect as similar choices of adults.[15] In this view, an adolescent should legally be permitted to contract, marry, choose a religion, or make enforceable decisions to engage in legally permissible conduct opposed by the adolescent's parents. Such choices could be denied legal effect only if the individual adolescent decision-maker were shown to be incompetent.[16] Proponents of this position reject the traditional method of distinguishing juveniles from adults solely by chronological age standards and instead favor a system presuming adolescents to be adults in lieu of an individualized showing of competence.

## [1]   Manifestations of the Individualized Standard

In contrast to the prevailing chronological age model, a few manifestations of the individualized approach do exist in current juvenile law. Two examples — the "mature minor" doctrine and the process of waiving jurisdiction from juvenile to criminal court — will be briefly noted here.

### [a]   The "Mature Minor" and Medical Treatment

In most states parents possess legal authority to make decisions regarding the medical treatment of their children. However, a few jurisdictions have statutorily permitted minors to determine their own treatment if the individual minor is competent to understand the possible risks and benefits of the proposed medical procedure.[17] Several courts have recognized a similar "mature minor" exception to the general rule that minors lack capacity to make their own treatment decisions.[18] Moreover, the United States Supreme Court has held as a matter of constitutional law that parents cannot veto decisions of their pregnant minor daughters to have abortions so long as the daughter possesses sufficient maturity and understanding to make the abortion decision competently.[19]

---

[13] *Id.* at xi, 127.

[14] *See, e.g.*, G. Melton, Child Advocacy: Psychological Issues and Intervention (1993).

[15] *See, e.g.*, R. Batey, *The Rights of Adolescents*, 23 Wm. & Mary L. Rev. 363 (1982).

[16] *Id.*

[17] L. Weithorn, *Developmental Factors and Competence to Make Informed Treatment Decisions*, in Legal Reforms Affecting Child and Youth Services 85 (G. Melton ed., 1982).

[18] Many of the cases are summarized in W. Wadlington, *Minors and Health Care: The Age of Medical Consent*, 11 Osgoode Hall L.J. 115 (1973).

[19] *See* Planned Parenthood v. Danforth, 428 U.S. 52 (1976); Bellotti v. Baird, 443 U.S. 622 (1979). For further discussion, see *infra* § 6.06[A][1][a].

## [b] Waivers of Juvenile Court Jurisdiction

A second example of the individualized competency approach in determining legal interests of juveniles can be seen by the operation of waiver procedures for transferring jurisdiction from juvenile to adult criminal court. Those procedures, discussed extensively in Part Three of this text,[20] focus on the individual circumstances of young people accused of wrongdoing in determining whether an accused should be tried in criminal rather than juvenile court. Courts in waiver proceedings, *inter alia*, assess *ad hoc* the individual's maturity and capacity for moral accountability rather than simply making the jurisdictional decision on the basis of the chronological age of the accused.

## [2] Social Science and the Process of Maturation: The Nature of Adolescence

Juvenile law is premised on empirical assumptions that young people are vulnerable, dependant, and incompetent.[21] These assumptions are seldom disputed in the context of very young children. However, as the discussion immediately above has illustrated, the assumptions become more controversial when related to adolescents. Indeed, some social science research calls into question basic assumptions of traditional juvenile law as applied to adolescents. Appreciation of the role of the social sciences in shaping policy is thus essential to understanding juvenile law.

The psychological and sociological literature on the subject of adolescence is immense.[22] Even a brief summary of the research is well beyond the scope of this work. A few general observations about the current state of social science research can be made, however.

The majority of empirical research aimed at determining adolescent maturity focuses on issues of informed consent in the context of medical decision-making.[23] While such research supports the claim that adults and adolescents engage in similar decision-making processes in making treatment decisions,[24] some social scientists question whether the data reveal an absence of differences between the decision-making capability of adolescents and adults.[25] Moreover, even if the studies provide evidence that adolescents and adults are equally competent in making important decisions, few studies have belied other traditional assumptions about the differences between juveniles and adults that supposedly support the law's predominantly paternalistic response towards young people. Adolescents in particular are presumed to be more susceptible to peer pressure than adults, to have more of a tendency than adults to attend to immediate rather than long-term consequences, and to be more prone to make risky choices than adults.[26]

Thus, it is safe to say that modern social science has not refuted the traditional perception that as a matter of legal relevance adolescents as a general class are

---

[20] *See infra* §§ 8.03[C], 9.05.

[21] *See supra* § 1.01, note 3.

[22] *See* Zimring, *supra* note 11, at xi.

[23] *See* Scott, Repucci & Woolard, *supra* § 1.01, note 3, at 223–24.

[24] *Id.* at 222.

[25] *Id.* at 224–26.

[26] *See id.* at 230 (summarizing the literature supporting the notions that adolescents are more subject to peer pressure and risky conduct than adults).

distinct from adults. Yet, it is also clear that the presumptions of vulnerability, dependence, and incompetence that support a paternalistic view of juvenile law are less applicable to adolescents than to younger children. As a result, the problem of defining the rights, privileges, and duties of adolescents is perhaps the central problem of juvenile law.[27]

---

[27] *See generally* Zimring, *supra* note 11.

# Chapter 2
# THE RIGHTS OF JUVENILES

## § 2.01 OVERVIEW

Explicating theories of juvenile rights is a complicated matter. The task is particularly difficult given that three sets of interests — the child's, her parents' or guardians', and the government's — routinely coalesce and require accommodation. As will become evident in later chapters of this text, no clear design of constitutional rights appears from the caselaw. The courts tend to proceed in a piecemeal fashion in resolving various conflicts arising between the state and the child, sometimes aligning the parent's interests with the child's, but other times with the interests of the state, or as a separate interest against those of the child and the state. As will be illustrated later, the United States Supreme Court appears to have recognized full-fledged constitutional rights for young people in some contexts but not in others. Matters are slightly clearer outside the context of constitutional law, but even there anomalies caution against identifying a single coherent theory to rationalize the law.

Much of the difficulty in the theory of juvenile law appears as a consequence of the interplay of two often conflicting theories of rights that are both reflected, to a degree at least, in current law. The first, and more predominant of the two is the protectionist theory which entitles young people to paternalistic care. The second theory, herein designated the personhood theory, affords young people rights guaranteed to autonomous persons.

The tension between these two theories of rights will be discussed throughout this text's explication of juvenile law. An introductory overview of the conflict can be illustrated by two United States Supreme Court opinions, *Parham v. J.R.*[1] and *Fare v. Michael C.*,[2] delivered, ironically perhaps, on the same day.

In *Parham*, the Court recognized that minors possess a protected interest in physical liberty that was compromised by confinement in a state mental hospital against the minor's will. This interest notwithstanding, the Court denied that young people are entitled to such procedural protections as judicial hearings and rights to counsel as preconditions of commitment to mental institutions when instigated by the recommendation of parents or guardians. In an important assessment of the nature of childhood, the Court noted that "[m]ost children, even in adolescence, simply are not able to make sound judgments concerning many decisions. . . . Parents can and must make those judgments."[3] Such a view of adolescence clearly reflects the protectionist theory of rights.

Yet in *Fare*, the Court appeared to embrace a view more at home with personhood theory in finding that minors are not entitled to any special protections, such as access to parents or counsel, as preconditions to valid waivers of *Miranda* rights granted to subjects of police interrogation. While age is one factor in the "totality of circumstances" that must be considered in determining valid waivers, the Court found that the same general standard was applicable to both adults and juveniles.

---

[1] 442 U.S. 584 (1979).

[2] 442 U.S. 707 (1979).

[3] Parham v. J.R., 442 U.S. at 603.

This totality-of-the-circumstances approach is adequate to determine whether there has been a waiver even where interrogation of juveniles is involved. We discern no persuasive reasons why any other approach is required where the question is whether a juvenile has waived his rights, as opposed to whether an adult has done so.[4]

In failing to fashion a special rule to protect juveniles, the *Fare* Court implied that young people can function as autonomous persons when making crucial decisions.

*Parham* and *Fare* thus appear at odds with each other. How can it be that minors are incompetent to make treatment decisions in *Parham*, but are potentially competent to relinquish crucial legal rights in *Fare*? If medical treatment decisions are governed by protectionist rights, why are these same rights not applied to waivers of *Miranda* rights, which are decisions equally if not more complex?[5]

Such questions appear particularly pertinent in light of social science research made available after the decisions in *Parham* and *Fare*. As mentioned in Chapter 1, some researches claim that the empirical evidence supports the view that, contrary to the Court's position in *Parham*, adolescents are as competent as adults in making medical treatment decisions.[6] On the other hand, again seemingly at odds with the Court's views in *Fare*, research shows that younger adolescents misunderstand the *Miranda* warnings more readily than do adults and manifest significantly lower comprehension of the nature and significance of the *Miranda* rights.[7] Therefore, the research suggests that juveniles faced with decisions whether or not to waive *Miranda* rights may be in need of special protections, not necessary for adults, to reduce the risk of incompetent decisions.

The following discussion sketches the protectionist and personhood theories, respectively. After presenting "pure" models of the two theories, the chapter concludes with some views about how the theories might be simultaneously accommodated within a system of juvenile law.

## § 2.02   THE PROTECTIONIST THEORY

### [A]   Theoretical Premises

While democratic traditions recognize rights of autonomy and personhood to each individual,[1] children, like women and some racial minorities, historically were not possessors of the full panoply of legally recognized rights. Although legal distinctions based on gender and race have been diminished, if not eliminated altogether, children continue to be denied full equality under the law. The perception of limited mental capacity, which historically for John Locke and other

---

[4]  Fare v. Michael C., 442 U.S. at 725.

[5]  *Parham* and *Fare* are discussed in more detail at *infra* §§ 6.06[A][2][b] and 9.02[B][3][a], respectively. Attempts to explain the denial of rights in *Parham* in terms of avoiding intra-family conflicts between parents who in good faith seek hospitalization of their children and children who resist such action are only partially satisfactory in light of the fact that the *Parham* Court did not require enhanced procedural protections when the state seeks hospitalization of children who are wards of the state. 442 U.S. at 617–20. No intra-family conflicts arise where parents are not parties in instigating hospitalization.

[6]  *See supra* § 1.02, notes 14–19 (and accompanying text).

[7]  *See* T. Grisso, *Juveniles' Capacity to Waive* Miranda *Rights: An Empirical Analysis*, 68 CAL. L. REV. 1134, 1160 (1980).

[1]  *See* Hafen, *supra* § 1.01, note 4, at 610–11.

Enlightenment thinkers eliminated children as autonomous persons under the Social Contract,[2] continues to operate as a barrier to affording juveniles the same rights enjoyed by adults. The perception of vulnerability and dependence, which for John Stuart Mill required the law to protect children "against their own actions as well as against external injury,"[3] endures to this day as a basis for paternalistic legal treatment not applied to adults.

To say that young people do not possess the rights afforded autonomous persons is not to say that juveniles are without rights. They possess rights of protection that include rights to receive care, affection, discipline, and guidance enabling their development into mature and responsible adults.[4] Protection rights also incorporate rights to be supported, maintained, educated, and provided legal remedies consistent with the minor's best interests when obligated caretakers fail to provide the minor the protection to which he is entitled.[5]

## [B] Overview of Private Law

Protectionist theory is embodied in a variety of traditional doctrines unique to juveniles. As mentioned above, the law has historically denied minors capacity to consent to their own medical treatment. Moreover, as will be discussed in detail later in this text, under the common law juveniles are legally incapable of marrying, contracting, making wills, or retaining their own earnings.[6] All of these doctrines, with the exception of the denial of wages, can be explained in terms of protecting young people from being bound by their propensity to make irresponsible choices. The denial of wages doctrine may well have been grounded historically on the feudalistic principle that a father was entitled to the earnings of his children in return for the father's duty of support.[7] However, this doctrine's current vitality may find more support in the protectionist notion that parents or guardians should be entrusted to hold the earnings of minors in their charge until such time as they become sufficiently mature to handle their own finances. The protectionist principle is also clearly manifest in divorce proceedings where courts make child custody and support orders in an effort to promote the "best interests of the child."[8]

---

[2] *Id.*

[3] *Id.* at 612 (quoting J.S. Mill, On Liberty 13–14 (1956)).

[4] *See* H. Foster & D. Freed, *A Bill of Rights for Children*, 6 Fam. L.Q. 343, 347 (1972). While Foster and Freed develop their "bill of rights" from the premise that children are "persons," the rights identified in the text seem much more at home with protectionist rather than personhood philosophy.

[5] The court in *People v. D.*, 315 N.E.2d 466, 469 (N.Y. 1974), offered this summary of protection rights theory:

> Children may not be equated with adults for all . . . purposes . . . . Their natural limitations, varying with age, and the obligation of those, in whose charge they are, to protect, guide, and if need be, discipline them, are recognized in every kind of society. At the same time, in a civilized society it is also recognized that the obligations and powers of those charged with the care of children should be limited by standards shaped by the conditions which require them. Thus, the imposition of authority over children may not exceed the causes which give rise to that authority.

[6] *See infra* §§ 5.03, 5.05, 5.06.

[7] *See* Foster & Freed, *supra* note 4, at 357.

[8] *See infra* §§ 3.02, 3.06.

## [C]   The State as *Parens Patriae*

In addition to litigating disputes between private parties involving children, courts from early times have themselves assumed direct responsibility for protecting the welfare of children under certain circumstances. Through the concept of *parens patriae* (the state as a parent), English courts of equity could declare a child a ward of the Crown when parents or guardians failed to provide adequately for the child's welfare.[9] The *parens patriae* principle has been extended in recent times to support a host of state mechanisms aimed at protecting children in need.[10] When the protection rights of children are not adequately provided by the private parties charged with affording those rights, the state intervenes, sometimes by helping parents or guardians to care for the child, sometimes by modifying the custodial situation of the child, and sometimes by imposing penalties for failure to provide the required protection of the child.[11] Moreover, the *parens patriae* concept provides the philosophical basis for the juvenile justice system, enacted to provide a non-punitive alternative to the criminal law in dealing with youthful offenders.[12]

## § 2.03   THE PERSONHOOD THEORY

### [A]   Overview

While the United States Supreme Court has not clearly articulated a general theory of juvenile rights to determine the proper balance between the interests of children, parents, and the state,[1] some argue that respect as a person and rights to autonomy available to adults should be similarly afforded to adolescents.[2]

The theory of human rights that underlies the Constitution assumes that every person has the capacity for autonomy and the right to equal respect in his pursuit of autonomy.[3] Autonomy is the central aspect of moral personality because of the unique capacity of humans to shape their lives through rational planning.[4] As rational planners, all persons are assumed equally capable of defining the meaning of their own lives.[5] Any individual capable of rational self-rule is entitled to be

---

[9] S. Davis, Rights of Juveniles 1–2 (2d ed. 1996).

[10] While some commentators dispute whether the early Chancery notion of *parens patriae* explains the origins of intervention for the protection of minors, *see* D. Rendleman, *Parens Patriae: From Chancery to the Juvenile Court*, 23 S.C. L. Rev. 205, 210–12 (1971), others see the Latin phrase as a useful term to describe the undisputed power of the state to make such intervention. Clark, *supra* § 1.02, note 4, at 335.

[11] *See* Mnookin & Weisberg, *supra* § 1.02, note 8, at 709.

[12] *See* B. Feld, *The Juvenile Court Meets the Principle of the Offense: Legislative Changes in Juvenile Waiver Statutes*, 78 J. Crim. L. & Criminology 471, 476 (1987).

[1] Richards, *supra* § 1.01, note 1, at 3.

[2] *See, e.g.*, Batey, *supra* § 1.02, note 15.

[3] Richards, *supra* note 1, at 8. While the notion of capacity is central to the traditional theory of rights, some criticize the emphasis on capacity as injecting into the theory "hierarchical" power structures that exclude the powerless and disadvantage those with "different voices." *See* K. Federle, *On the Road to Reconceiving Rights for Children: A Post-feminist Analysis of the Capacity Principle*, 42 DePaul L. Rev. 983, 1025 (1993).

[4] Richards, *supra* note 1, at 8.

[5] *Id.* at 8–10.

treated as a person, which in turn entails freedom from paternalistic interventions against his will.[6]

Persons are entitled to exercise their capacity for autonomy and be treated with dignity and respect. Persons also enjoy a right to be protected from unwanted invasions of personal privacy.[7]

Very young children lack the capacity for rationality and thus possess only a "future interest" in personhood and the rights that flow therefrom.[8] Paternalistic responses are therefore appropriate until such time as the young person develops a capacity for rationality. When that capacity is developed, arguably by adolescent, paternalistic responses are inconsistent with personhood rights.[9]

## [B]  Personhood Rights and Current Law

As mentioned in Chapter 1, reliance on social science studies exploring decision-making by adolescents has led some to the view that this category of young people generally possesses the same capacity for rational choice of adults.[10] According to this view, adolescents are entitled to be treated as autonomous persons free from paternalistic interventions.[11]

The extent to which the law recognizes personhood rights for minors is a theme that will be examined throughout this text. For now it is enough to say that one can arguably identify pockets of personhood protection within an otherwise paternalistic body of juvenile law. The "mature minor" doctrine and the juvenile court waiver mechanism mentioned in Chapter 1[12] may reflect personhood theory. Moreover, in addition to the abortion cases noted in Chapter 1,[13] other Supreme Court cases arguably recognize certain personhood rights under the Constitution. For example, in *Tinker v. Des Moines Independent School District*,[14] the Court extended free speech rights under the First Amendment to school children finding that "students in school as well as out of school are 'persons' under our Constitution . . . possessed of fundamental rights."[15]

---

[6] *Id.* at 18–19; *see also* H. Morris, *Persons and Punishment, in* Philosophy of Law 572, 580–82, 586 (J. Feinberg & H. Gross eds., 1975).

[7] Lawrence Tribe has suggested that a fundamental purpose of our constitutional scheme is the "preservation of 'those attributes of an individual which are irreducible in his selfhood.'" L. Tribe, American Constitutional Law 889 (1978) (quoting Freund, 52 A.L.I. Ann. Meeting 42–43 (1975)). Inherent in such purpose is the protection of an unarticulated "right of personhood" manifested by "the obviously incomplete listing in the Bill or Rights" and woven throughout the "spirit and structure" of the Constitution's "spare text." *Id.* at 893.

Privacy protection is often linked to the right to be treated as a person. *See, e.g.,* E. Bloustein, *Privacy as an Aspect of Human Dignity,* 39 N.Y.U. L. Rev. 962, 974 (1964); Note, *Formalism, Legal Realism and Constitutionally Protected Privacy Under the Fourth and Fifth Amendments,* 90 Harv. L. Rev. 945, 987 (1977) ("The right to privacy [in the Fourth Amendment] deserves primary recognition . . . because of its close connection with uniqueness of the person and human dignity.").

[8] *See* Morris, *supra* note 6, at 583.

[9] Richards, *supra* note 1, at 20.

[10] *See supra* § 1.02, notes 14–15 (and accompanying text).

[11] *See, e.g.,* Batey, *supra* note 2.

[12] *See supra* § 1.02[B][1][a].

[13] *See supra* § 1.02, note 19.

[14] 393 U.S. 503 (1969).

[15] *Id.* at 511.

## § 2.04   ACCOMMODATION OF PROTECTIONIST AND PERSONHOOD THEORIES

Some commentators have argued that the rights of adolescents should be founded on neither protection nor personhood rights exclusively, but on a combination of the two theories. Because the practice of independent decision-making is an integral part of the maturation process, adolescents should be permitted freedom to make important choices.[1] Yet, at the same time, because such choices may not be fully mature, some protection against the consequences of ill-advised choices may be desirable. Therefore, some proponents of this view advocate a model of "semi-autonomy" where adolescents are permitted to learn how to make independent choices, but are at the same time shielded from the full burden of adult responsibilities and consequences that flow from certain of those choices.[2]

The subordination of young people, even adolescents, to adult authority may thus be understood as necessary to the development of young people's autonomy.[3] Parents or other adult authorities may be viewed as instruments through whom children and adolescents experience autonomy in gradually increasing measures as maturation occurs.[4] By decreasing protections and limits as the child matures, parents or guardians permit minors in their charge to grow as semi-autonomous individuals until they are able to assume the full benefits and burdens of personhood.

Rather than a single "age of minority" for all legal purposes, advocates of the theory of the semi-autonomous adolescent suggest that the law adopt one age for "phasing-in" the liberty interests enjoyed by adults and a different age for cutting off special entitlements (*e.g.*, the Job Corps) reserved for minors and for assessing adult responsibility for misdeeds and self-support. Thus, the age of majority for protecting adult liberty interests could be set at eighteen while twenty-one could be the legal age for purposes of denying juvenile entitlements and imposing adult responsibilities.[5]

---

[1] *See* Zimring, *supra* § 1.02, note 11, at 89–96.

[2] *Id.* at 96, 100.

[3] J. Coons, *Intellectual Liberty and the Schools*, 1 J. Legal Ethics & Pub. Pol'y 495, 501–510 (1985).

[4] *Id.*

[5] *Id.* at 111. While defining adulthood in terms of any particular chronological age is admittedly somewhat arbitrary, such a system is arguably preferable to assessing maturity and competency on an entirely individualized, *ad hoc* basis. Zimring, *supra* note 1, at 96, 100.

# Part Two

# OUTSIDE THE JUVENILE JUSTICE SYSTEM*

---

\* As explained in the Preface to this text, the "juvenile justice system" is herein defined as that system of courts created to deal with juvenile delinquents and status offenders.

15

# Chapter 3

# THE CHILD AND THE FAMILY

## § 3.01   GENERAL BACKGROUND

Historically, parents possessed virtually unlimited and unchecked power over their offspring.[1] This recognition of broad parental authority to rear their children acknowledged the family as a basic social, economic, and political unit.[2] For many, protection of these parental prerogatives is an acknowledgment of parental "rights." For a time, parental rights were understood in property terms, with children considered the chattels of their parents.[3] Such property conceptions have now largely been abandoned in favor of theories identifying parental rights as inherent natural rights[4] reflecting the "law's respect for kinship."[5] As such, parental rights to custody and control of minor children prevail over the claims of the state, other outsiders, and the children themselves unless there is substantial justification for interference.[6]

Nevertheless, Anglo-American Law never allowed parents absolute power over their children. Under common law principles still applicable, parents are permitted to assert authority over their children so long as they do so "in a reasonable manner."[7] Thus, whatever the rights of parents, they owe their children a duty of care and protection which can be viewed to form the basis for a corresponding right of children to receive such care from their parents. As mentioned in Chapter 2, when parents neglect, abuse, or abandon their children, the state may exercise its *parens patriae*, power and intervene to protect the children against serious harm.[8]

Rather than deriving protectionist rights from parental duties, some see the rights of children to individualized care and protection as the basic source from which parental rights are derived. For these theorists, parents have rights to raise their children only because they are presumed to be in a better position than anyone else to satisfy the child's projectionist rights.[9]

Whether the rights of children are derived from parental duties or are themselves the source of parental rights, an extensive body of legal doctrine flows

---

[1]   *See* H. Krause, Family Law 225 (3d ed. 1995).

[2]   *See* Hafen, *supra* § 1.01, note 4, at 615.

[3]   *See, e.g.*, Poe v. Gerstein, 517 F.2d 787, 789 (5th Cir. 1975) ("The [common] law did not distinguish between the infant and the mature teenager, treating them both as the property of their parents, who could make all decisions affecting them.").

[4]   *See* Hafen, *supra* note 2, at 616–17.

[5]   *See* B. Hafen, *The Constitutional Status of Marriage, Kinship, and Sexual Privacy — Balancing the Individual and Social Interests*, 81 Mich. L. Rev. 463, 493–94 (1983).

[6]   Hafen, *supra* note 2, at 615–17.

[7]   I. W. Blackstone, Commentaries *451.

[8]   *See supra* § 2.02[C].

[9]   *See* Richards, *supra* § 1.01, note 1, at 28; *see also* J. Dwyer, *Parent's Religion and Children's Welfare: Debunking the Doctrine of Parents' Rights*, 82 Cal. L. Rev. 1371 (1994) (children possess rights necessary to protect their fundamental interest in an intimate, continuous relationship with their parents while parents possess a "privilege" to care for their children in ways not contrary to child's temporal interests).

from the parent-child relationship. In the following discussion, this doctrine is generally discussed in terms of parental duties owed to children.

## § 3.02  SUPPORT AND MAINTENANCE

While it is questionable whether the English common law ever recognized parental support duties,[1] such duties were statutorily imposed from a relatively early date.[2] Indeed, some early American cases denied the existence of support duties unless imposed by statute.[3] This view, however, has been largely repudiated by most courts which now take the view that, whether or not statutorily imposed, parents are legally obligated to maintain and support their minor children.[4] Although historically fathers were primarily liable for support of their children and mothers liable only in cases of paternal failure or refusal to furnish support, today both parents owe equal support duties.[5]

Moreover, current parental support obligations are not contingent on the marital status of the parents. It is questionable whether children "born out of wedlock" enjoyed rights to support from either of their parents under English common law.[6] In contrast, the American cases traditionally imposed support duties on the mother but not the father.[7] These cases thus afforded illegitimate children fewer rights than those enjoyed by children born to married parents who were entitled to support from both parents. The United States Supreme Court eventually held such discrimination unconstitutional under the Equal Protection Clause.[8] Presently, nearly every state imposes statutory support obligations on both parents even if their children are born out of wedlock.[9]

In some situations, biological parenthood does not entail support obligations. Men who father children in adulterous relationships with married women are often not legally responsible for their offspring because the mother's husband is presumed to be the child's father.[10] Moreover, most states have enacted legislation defining paternal rights and responsibilities with respect to children conceived through artificial insemination.[11] The statutes generally dictate that the sperm

---

[1] *See* Clark, *supra* § 1.02, note 4, at 259.

[2] *Id.*

[3] *See, e.g.*, Hunt v. Thompson, 4 Ill. 179 (1841).

[4] *See, e.g.*, Osborn v. Weatherford, 170 So. 95 (Ala. App. Ct. 1936); Addy v. Addy, 36 N.W.2d 352 (Iowa 1949), *overruled on other grounds by* Brown v. Brown, 269 N.W.2d 819 (Iowa 1978). Presently statutes in every state impose a duty of support for minor children upon parents. Mnookin & Weisberg, *supra* § 1.02, note 8, at 245.

[5] Clark, *supra* note 1, at 259.

[6] Mnookin & Weisberg, *supra* note 4, at 238 (while support duties doubtful under common law, parents likely economically responsible for their children under the Poor Laws and under ecclesiastical law).

[7] *Id.* at 241.

[8] Gomez v. Perez, 409 U.S. 535 (1973).

[9] Mnookin & Weisberg, *supra* note 4, at 245.

[10] In many states the issue of paternity can be raised by the child's mother or her husband, the "presumptive father," but not by the biological father. *See* Michael H. & Victoria D. v. Gerald D., 491 U.S. 110 (1989); John M. v. Paula T., 571 A.2d 1380, 1384 (Pa. 1990).

[11] 1 D. Kramer, Legal Rights of Children 169 (2d ed. 1994). The courts have also recently struggled with the issue of parental rights in surrogate mother situations. The cases raise a variety of delicate

donor has no rights or responsibilities with regard to the child and that the mother's husband is the child's legal father so long as he consents to his wife's impregnation with the donor's sperm.[12]

While natural parents generally owe support duties to their children, similar duties are sometimes imposed on persons not biologically related to the child entitled to support. Adoptive parents are obligated to support their adopted children[13] and a few jurisdictions statutorily require stepparents to support their stepchildren so long as the stepparent remains married to the child's natural parent.[14] Under common law, stepparents are not liable for support except where they stand "*in loco parentis*" by voluntarily taking the stepchildren into their families and assuming support duties.[15] Even in those circumstances, however, the stepparent can generally terminate his support obligation at will.[16]

## [A] "Necessary" Support

Parents are ordinarily obligated to provide their minor children with "necessaries."[17] While the law provides no exact definition of the term, the courts have generally held that suitable shelter, food, clothing, medical attention, and an education are necessaries to which the child is entitled.[18] Some courts also include many of the conveniences of modern life as necessaries depending upon the parent's financial situation.[19] The facts and circumstances of each case dictate whether a particular benefit is deemed a necessary or an unentitled extravagance.[20]

## [1] Setting The Amount Of Financial Support

If a child lives with both parents and no evidence of parental neglect exists, the parents will be free to decide how much of their disposable income will be spent on their children.[21] If, however, the parents should separate or divorce, the courts establish the extent of child support. While historically courts exercised broad discretion in determining the amount of support based on individualized assessments of the child's needs and the obligor's ability to provide,[22] today the

---

public policy issues and a variety of judicial responses. *See* W. Wadlington, Domestic Relations 367–465 (3d ed. 1995).

[12] Kramer, *supra* note 11, at 169.

[13] Krause, *supra* § 3.01, note 1, at 206.

[14] S. Friedman, The Law of Parent-Child Relationships 110 (1992).

[15] Clark, *supra* note 1, at 264.

[16] *Id.* In contexts where the stepchild believes the stepparent is his biological father because the stepparent fosters that belief, the courts sometimes apply the doctrine of equitable estoppel to prevent the stepparent from avoiding support. *Id.*

[17] *See, e.g.*, Porter v. Powell, 44 N.W. 295 (Iowa 1890); Colovous v. Gouvas, 108 S.W.2d 820 (Ky. 1937).

[18] 59 Am. Jur. 2d *Parent and Child* § 44 (1987).

[19] *Id.*

[20] *Id.*

[21] So long as necessaries are provided and the standard of minimum care set by neglect and dependency laws is not breached, married parents in intact families need not afford their children a lifestyle consistent with the parents' income and station in life. Krause, *supra* note 13, at 247.

[22] *Id.* The Uniform Parentage Act § 15(e) (2001) summarizes the factors used, within the court's discretion, in establishing support orders:

extent of required support is routinely established pursuant to set formulae taking into account such things as combined parental income, the percentage of such income earned by the noncustodial parent, and the number of children to be supported.[23]

## [2]  Education

The marital status of a child's parents also has important consequences with regard to the issue of educational support. Ordinarily, parent's obligations to assure the education of their children terminate when the children reach the age of majority, typically age eighteen.[24] Thus, children generally enjoy no right to higher education at their parents' expense.

If, however, the parents are divorced, the situation is more complicated. While some courts flatly hold that parents, married or divorced, owe no duty to provide higher education for their children,[25] other courts require that divorced parents, usually non-custodial ones, provide their children the expenses for higher education if, among other things, the children possess the desire and ability to pursue such education and the expenses do not cause an undue hardship to the parent.[26] In deciding whether to impose support obligations, some courts consider other factors such as whether the child would have had a reasonable expectation of having the parent contribute to his education had no divorce occurred, whether the child himself has financial resources, and whether the child's relationship with his parent is sufficiently close so as to justify imposing the costs of postsecondary education on the parent.[27]

Outside the context of secondary schooling, issues of parental responsibility for providing appropriate education have arisen in conjunction with now ubiquitous compulsory education laws. While at early common law, education of children was a private matter entrusted to the discretion of parents, education in America was

---

In determining the amount to be paid by a parent for support of the child and the period during which the duty of support is owed, a court enforcing the obligation of support shall consider all relevant facts including (1) the needs of the child; (2) the standard of living and circumstances of the parents; (3) the relative financial means of the parents; (4) the earning ability of the parents; (5) the need and capacity of the child for education, including higher education; (6) the age of the child; (7) the financial resources and the earning ability of the child; (8) the responsibility of the parents for the support of others; and (9) the value of services contributed by the custodial parent.

[23] Friedman, *supra* note 14, at 109, 179. Historically, when parents separated, child support was usually premised on the custodial parent's reasonable choice of lifestyle and the non-custodial parent's ability to provide for such. *Id.* at 248.

[24] *Id.* at 115. Today, all states determine the amount of child support by using child support guidelines, which are essentially schedules that base the obligor's responsibility for paying child support on the custody arrangements, both parents' incomes, and the number of children in the family. I. Ellman & T. Ellman, *The Theory of Child Support*, 35 HARV. J. ON LEGIS. 107, 109 (2008). Deviations from the guidelines can be made with judicial approval. *Id.* at 112. For examples of state child support guidelines, see Colo. Rev. Stat. § 14–10–115 (2007); Fla. Stat. § 61.30 (West 2005 & Supp. 2009); and Va. Code Ann. § 20–108.2 (2004 & Supp. 2005).

[25] *See, e.g.*, Arce v. Arce, 566 So. 2d 1308, 1313 (Fla. App. 1990).

[26] Kramer, *supra* note 11, at 193–94; Krause, *supra* note 13, at 248.

[27] Kramer, *supra* note 11, at 194.

from the nation's inception perceived to be a function of government.[28] In every state, legislatures have enacted systems of public education, established standards aimed at assuring quality programs, and required that children of particular ages (generally from age seven to age sixteen) attend school.[29]

While parents are not required to send their children to *public* schools,[30] parents who fail to provide a suitable education, public or private, are subject to state imposed sanctions.[31] The courts have allowed several exceptions to compulsory school attendance laws. Certain religious groups, particularly the Amish, are not required to follow statutes mandating education through specified ages falling in the period of younger adolescence because of perceived negative effects of formal education on religious practice.[32] Moreover, exemptions to compulsory education laws have been recognized in cases where children are physically or mentally disabled,[33] or where parents provide adequate instruction at home.[34]

In certain circumstances, parents have been permitted to control the content of what their children are taught in school. Arguably, compulsory sex education classes with no excusal system violate the constitutional rights of parents who view their children's participation in such classes as offensive on moral or religious grounds.[35] Similarly, courts have held unconstitutional condom give-away programs in schools where no "opt-out" provision existed for parents who desired that their children not have access to condoms.[36] On the other hand, the United States Supreme Court has struck down as an unconstitutional establishment of religion a state statute forbidding teachers from teaching organic evolution in order to promote the doctrine of Biblical creationism.[37] Thus, curricular decisions cannot be based on desires to promote particular religious beliefs, however firmly held by a majority of parents.

By imposing duties on parents to educate their children, compulsory education laws recognize corresponding rights of children to an education. Although the United States Supreme Court has denied a federal constitutional right to

---

[28] R. Horowitz & H. Davidson, Legal Rights of Children 517 (1984).

[29] *Id.* at 517–19; Krause, *supra* note 13, at 233.

[30] Pierce v. Society of Sisters, 268 U.S. 510 (1925), discussed in detail *infra* § 6.02, notes 7–12 and accompanying text.

[31] Horowitz & Davidson, *supra* note 28, at 519.

[32] Wisconsin v. Yoder, 406 U.S. 205 (1972), discussed in detail *infra* § 6.03[A][2], notes 19–27 and accompanying text.

[33] *See, e.g.*, Ill. Ann. Stat. Ch. 105, ¶ 5/26-1 (Smith-Hurd 1998). On the other hand, Congress has enacted federal legislation encouraging states to provide special education for physically or mentally handicapped students. The Individuals with Disabilities Act, 20 U.S.C.A. §§ 1401–1461 (West 2000).

[34] *See* Mnookin & Weisberg, *supra* note 4, at 87–88; W. Wadlington, C. Whitebread & S. Davis, Children in the Legal System 109–10 (1983).

[35] *See* Medieros v. Kiyosaki, 436 P.2d 314 (Haw. 1970) (dicta implying that compulsory sex education with no "opt-out" provision might be unconstitutional).

[36] Alfonso v. Fernandez, 606 N.Y.S.2d 259 (N.Y. App. Div. 1993). *Contra* Curtis v. School Committee of Falmouth, 652 N.E.2d 580 (Mass. 1995).

[37] Epperson v. Arkansas, 393 U.S. 97 (1965); Edwards v. Aguillard, 482 U.S. 578 (1987) (Court struck down statute that forbade teaching of evolution unless creation science was also taught). *See infra* § 6.03[A][1].

education,[38] the Court has recognized that certain procedural protections must attend denials of the constitutionally protected "property" and "liberty" interests in education that flow from state compulsory education laws.[39]

Attempts by students to enforce alleged denials of substantive rights against school officials have met with little success. Actions for "educational malpractice" have generally been rejected, often because courts find practical difficulties in proving malfeasance in the educational process.[40] Some courts have, however, awarded damages in situations of educational misfeasance, for example where a school improperly diagnoses a child as mentally retarded and places him in a special program for retarded students.[41]

## [3] Medical Care

Parents are obligated to provide proper medical care for their children.[42] While parental failure to do so can trigger state intervention aimed at assuring attention to the child's medical needs,[43] parents are allowed broad discretion in making medical treatment decisions for their children.[44] As a general rule, informed parental consent is both a necessary and sufficient condition for medical treatment of minors.[45]

Where parents callously neglect their children by failing to provide medical care for no good reason, the state will intervene to protect the health interests of the child.[46] In some cases, however, parents object, often on religious grounds, to particular forms of treatment, thus requiring courts to balance legitimate assertions of parental authority against the perceived medical needs of the child.

## [a] Parental Objections On Religious Grounds

Family members are afforded broad rights to practice their chosen religion within their family.[47] Parents are not entitled, however, to make religiously based objections to medical care for their children where the religiously based objections

---

[38] San Antonio Indep. Sch. Dist. v. Rodriguez, 411 U.S. 1 (1973). Some states, however, recognize education as a "fundamental" right under state constitutional law. *See, e.g.,* Cathe A. v. Doddridge County Bd. of Educ., 490 S.E.2d 340 (W. Va. 1997); Brigham v. State, 692 A.2d 384 (Vt. 1997).

[39] Goss v. Lopez, 419 U.S. 565 (1975), discussed in detail *infra* § 6.06[A][2][a].

[40] *See* Wadlington, Whitebread & Davis, *supra* note 34, at 114–15.

[41] *Id.* at 114–17.

[42] *See, e.g.,* Stehr v. State, 139 N.W. 676 (Neb. 1913).

[43] Krause, *supra* note 13, at 238.

[44] Wadlington, Whitebread & Davis, *supra* note 34, at 893–94.

[45] Mnookin & Weisberg, *supra* note 4, at 533. Parental consent is necessary for the medical treatment provider to avoid tort liability for battery upon the child, who under traditional doctrine lacks capacity to consent. *Id.* at 534–35. See, however, *infra* note 64 and the accompanying text describing the traditional rule that parental consent is unnecessary when a child is in need of "emergency" medical treatment. Moreover, because parents are legally responsible for the care and support of their children, the parental consent requirement protects parents from the financial costs of unwanted or unnecessary medical care and of supporting the child if unwanted treatment is unsuccessful. Mnookin & Weisberg, *supra* note 4, at 536. Parental consent is sufficient, of course, for the child's medical treatment because the parent possesses authority to make decisions regarding the child's welfare.

[46] *See, e.g., In re* Karwath, 199 N.W.2d 147 (Iowa 1972) (court permitted state officials to effectuate tonsillectomy of child in state custody over objection of natural father).

[47] *See, e.g.,* Wisconsin v. Yoder, 406 U.S. 205 (1972). Family rights to religious practice are discussed

to medical care for their children where the child's life is clearly endangered without the medical treatment, particularly if the treatment is itself relatively risk free. Thus, the courts appoint guardians to consent to blood transfusions necessary to prolong the life of children, thereby enabling the state to intervene, even though the parents' religion forbids transfusions.[48] Some authority permits state intervention to override parents' religious objections to medical treatment unnecessary to save their child's life,[49] but other courts limit such intervention to "life-threatening" situations.[50] It is obviously controversial whether a court should substitute its judgment for that of parents who raise religious objections to medical treatment of their children where the treatment promises enhanced quality of life but is not necessary for life itself.[51]

## [b]   Objections On Grounds Of Parental Autonomy

Apart from the religious context, parents often object to proposed medical treatment of their children on the basis that the treatment entails unacceptable risks. As in the religion cases, the courts often defer to the parents if the medical treatment is not necessary to protect the child's life.[52] Again, however, some courts permit intervention in cases not raising issues of life and death where somewhat risky medical procedures offer hope for a longer, or higher quality, life.[53]

Similar issues arise when parents favor nontraditional courses of treatment for their child. The problem is particularly acute in cases where the child has a life-threatening illness for which the parents seek unconventional medical treatment, often in order to avoid the unpleasant side effects of "accepted" treatment. Several cases address situations where parents of children afflicted with cancer reject traditional treatments of chemotherapy and radiation in favor of nutritional and metabolic approaches, often involving laetrile. The decisions do not entirely conform. Some courts order traditional treatment, concluding that the alternative

---

in detail at *infra* § 6.03[A][2], notes 19–27. *See also* Fosmire v. Nicoleau, 551 N.E.2d 77 (N.Y. 1990) (upholding mother's right to refuse on religious ground life-saving blood transfusion where state seeks the transfusion in order to preserve the mother's life for the welfare of her children).

[48]  *See* People *ex rel.* Wallace v. Labrenz, 104 N.E.2d 769 (Ill. 1952). Moreover, parents who pursue prayer as the sole means of protecting their child's health may be liable for homicide if their child dies in a situation where medical care could have preserved life. Walker v. Superior Court, 763 P.2d 852 (Cal. 1988); Commonwealth v. Twitchell, 617 N.E.2d 609 (Mass. 1993).

[49]  *In re* Sampson, 278 N.E.2d 918 (N.Y. 1972). In *Sampson*, the court upheld a lower court order to perform corrective surgery on a fifteen-year-old suffering from severe facial deformities that precluded the young man from having a normal social life. The surgery was a lengthy and dangerous process that required a blood transfusion to which the boy's mother raised religious objection.

[50]  *See, e.g.*, *In re* Green, 292 A.2d 387 (Pa. 1972) (court refused to order corrective surgery for a minor's curvature of the spine where mother objected on religious grounds to the blood transfusion required for the surgery; court specifically noted that child's health was "not immediately imperiled" if surgery was not performed).

[51]  *See* S. Davis & M. Schwartz, Children's Rights and the Law 79–95 (1987).

[52]  *See, e.g.*, *In re* Seiferth, 127 N.E.2d 820 (N.Y. 1955) (court refused to order virtually risk free corrective surgery for a child's cleft palate and hairlip where both the child and his father objected to the surgery).

[53]  *See In re* Phillip B., 156 Cal. Rptr. 48 (Cal. Ct. App. 1979) (court ordered corrective surgery for heart defect of Down's syndrome child whose natural parents objected because they saw the risks of the surgery [5 to 10 percent mortality rate] as being too high — without the surgery the child would die in a period of years).

treatment is inconsistent with good medical practice.[54] Other courts permit the use of unconventional treatment in certain cases, at least where the treating physicians approve its use in conjunction with traditional treatment.[55]

### [c]  Handicapped Newborns

A complexity of legal and ethical problems attend situations where children with severe birth defects risk loss of life unless surgical or other medical procedures are performed. Where the medical procedure offers a realistic prospect that the child will live a relatively normal mental life, the courts have routinely ordered the medical procedure over parental objection even though the child will live with grave physical deformities.[56] Where, however, the child will exist in a state of severe and irreversible mental retardation, parents and attending physicians, until recently, have been free from legal sanctions[57] if they refuse the life-saving treatment and allow the child to die of natural causes.[58]

The situation changed, however, in the 1980s. Triggered by reports of judicial reluctance to interfere with parental refusals to consent to life-saving treatment for a Down's syndrome child who eventually died, federal officials informed federally-funded hospitals that withholding medical treatment for handicapped infants could constitute violations of federal law resulting in loss of federal funding.[59] While the courts eventually held that then-existing federal law did not speak to decisions to refuse treatment for seriously ill infants,[60] Congress enacted new legislation requiring states to provide procedures to allow state intervention to prevent the denial of necessary medical treatment for infants.[61] Under the federal statute and regulations pursuant thereto, medical treatment can be withheld only where the infant is in an irreversible coma, where death will occur quickly whether or not the infant is treated, or where the treatment itself is so extreme and the prospects of life so remote that treatment would be inhumane.[62] Several states also have passed statutes aimed at assuring that medical care for handicapped infants will be provided on the same basis as for other children.[63]

---

[54] *See, e.g.*, Custody of a Minor, 379 N.E.2d 1053, 1056 (Mass. 1978) (court rejected parents' desires to treat their son's leukemia with laetrile, noting that "there is a substantial chance for cure if he undergoes chemotherapy treatment" and that "no evidence of any alternative treatment consistent with good medical practice was offered").

[55] Matter of Hafbauer, 393 N.E.2d 1009 (N.Y. 1979) (court permits laetrile treatments for child's Hodgkin's disease where physicians testified they utilized nutritional therapy in treating some cancer cases while utilizing radiation and chemotherapy in others; court thus finds use of laetrile not "totally rejected by all responsible medical authority").

[56] *See, e.g.*, Application of Cicero, 421 N.Y.S.2d 965 (N.Y. Sup. Ct. 1979) (court ordered corrective surgery for infant afflicted with spina bifida over objection of parent; with surgery child would live with paralysis of feet and absence of sphincter control of bladder and anus).

[57] S. Smith, *Disabled Newborns and the Federal Child Abuse Amendments: Tenuous Protection*, 37 Hastings L.J. 765, 789–90 (1986).

[58] *Id.*

[59] *Id.* at 789–91.

[60] Bowen v. American Hosp. Ass'n, 476 U.S. 610 (1986).

[61] 42 U.S.C.A. § 5101 *et. seq* (West 1995).

[62] 42 U.S.C.A. § 5102(3) (West 1995).

[63] Davis & Schwartz, *supra* note 51, at 84–85.

## [d]  Consent by the Juvenile: The "Mature Minor" Exception

As mentioned above, parental consent is generally necessary if a minor is to receive medical treatment. In cases of emergency medical care, however, parental consent is not required on the theory that the health provider is entitled to assume that if the patient himself were competent and understood the situation, he would consent.[64]

A few courts deviate from these general rules and permit some minors to give valid consent for their medical treatment in nonemergency situations. For example, one court found that a seventeen-year-old "was mature enough" to consent to a skin graft from her forearm to repair an injured finger.[65] Another court overturned a lower court decision that had erroneously found that an eighteen-year-old could not consent to a "simple" surgical procedure to reshape her nose.[66] In these and other cases, courts dispense with the requirement of parental consent and recognize the capacity of some adolescents to understand fully the nature and importance of proposed "minor" or "non-serious" medical procedures to be performed for the benefit of the adolescent.[67]

Some courts have extended the "mature minor" principle to treatment decisions involving issues of life and death. For example, one court held that a seventeen-year-old minor with leukemia could refuse blood transfusions that she and her mother opposed on religious grounds even though the transfusions were thought necessary to preserve the daughter's life.[68] The court found the minor sufficiently mature to make her own health care choices.

As a matter of constitutional law, the United States Supreme Court has held that a "mature minor" must be permitted to make her own decision whether to terminate her pregnancy.[69] Similarly, the Court has held that minors cannot be denied access to contraceptives, some of which are medically prescribed.[70]

Some legislatures have codified a "mature minor" exception to the general rule requiring parental consent. Under one such provision, consent for medical treatment is valid if given by "[a]ny unemancipated minor of sufficient intelligence to understand and appreciate the consequences of the proposed surgical or medical treatment or procedures, for himself."[71] Moreover, legislatures routinely recognize competency to consent to their own medical treatment for minors who are married, serving in the armed forces, emancipated, receiving drug or alcohol treatment, or who have been exposed to a communicable disease.[72]

---

[64]  W. Prosser, Law of Torts 103 (4th ed. 1971).

[65]  Younts v. St. Francis Hosp. & Sch. of Nursing, Inc., 469 P.2d 330 (Kan. 1970).

[66]  Lacy v. Laird, 139 N.E.2d 25, 34 (Ohio 1956).

[67]  Wadlington, *supra* § 1.02, note 18, at 119. The cases do not recognize that "mature minors" can consent to medical procedures for the benefit of third parties. *Id.*

[68]  *In re* E.G., 549 N.E.2d 322 (Ill. 1989).

[69]  *See* Planned Parenthood v. Danforth, 428 U.S. 52 (1976); Bellotti v. Baird, 443 U.S. 622 (1979), discussed in detail at *infra* § 6.06[A][1][a].

[70]  Carey v. Population Serv. Int'l, 431 U.S. 678 (1977), discussed in detail at *infra* § 6.06[A][1][a].

[71]  Ark. Code Ann. § 20-9-602 (7) (2000).

[72]  Davis & Schwartz, *supra* note 51, at 94.

## [4] Unborn Children

The United States Supreme Court has recognized a constitutional right for women to terminate unwanted pregnancies.[73] Such a right is "fundamental" and, while the state has an interest in protecting fetal life, the state may not "unduly burden" the woman's right to choose an abortion prior to the time the fetus becomes "viable" (the point at which the fetus is capable of surviving outside the womb).[74] After viability the state may, if it chooses, prohibit abortions altogether except in situations where the woman's life or health is endangered by continuing the pregnancy.[75]

Outside the abortion context, states sometimes seek to protect fetal life by influencing the behavior of the pregnant woman. Some courts have ordered pregnant women to undergo medical procedures, Caesarian sections requiring blood transfusions for example, in order to protect fetal life, even though the women have objected to the procedure on religious grounds.[76] Other courts honor the religiously motivated decisions of pregnant women to forego such medical measures even though they are deemed necessary for the unborn child.[77] Where the mother's refusal of treatment is not for religious reasons, the justification for state intervention to protect fetal life is arguably more substantial, especially where the medical procedure at stake does not pose significant risks to the pregnant woman.[78]

Aside from cases involving particular medical procedures, states have sometimes sought to influence pregnant mothers to engage in, or refrain from, particular conduct affecting the well-being of their unborn children. Some jurisdictions permit sentencing courts in criminal cases to require pregnant women to follow programs of prenatal care as conditions of probation.[79] Other attempts to protect fetal life through the criminal law have met with less success. For example, courts have generally refused to apply traditional statutes prohibiting delivery of controlled substances or child abuse to pregnant women who use drugs harmful to the child they are carrying.[80] Moreover, medical practitioners as a rule are not required to seek state intervention to override the wishes of competent adult women who refuse prenatal treatment or otherwise fail to follow medical advice aimed at promoting the welfare of the unborn child.[81]

---

[73] Roe v. Wade, 410 U.S. 113 (1973).

[74] *Id.*; Planned Parenthood v. Casey, 505 U.S. 833 (1992). For a summary of state attempts at regulating abortions in the era following *Roe v. Wade*, see Mnookin & Weisberg, *supra* note 4, at 32–28.

[75] Roe v. Wade, 410 U.S. 113 (1973).

[76] Jefferson v. Griffin Spalding County Hosp. Auth., 274 S.E.2d 457 (Ga. 1981).

[77] *In re* Baby Boy Doe, 632 N.E.2d 326 (Ill. App. Ct. 1994).

[78] Mnookin & Weisberg, *supra* note 4, at 45–46.

[79] People v. Pointer, 199 Cal. Rptr. 357 (Cal. Ct. App. 1984).

[80] *See* Mnookin & Weisberg, *supra* note 4, at 47–48; Johnson v. State, 602 So. 2d 1288 (Fla. 1992). *But see* Whitner v. State, 492 S.E.2d 777 (S.C. 1997) (mother guilty of child abuse for illegal drug use during her pregnancy).

[81] Mnookin & Weisberg, *supra* note 4, at 48.

## [B]   Duration of Support

Generally, parental duties of support terminate when the child reaches the age of majority. However, as mentioned above, the context of education presents a situation where parental support obligations sometimes extend beyond the age of majority.[82] Some courts have imposed similar duties for support of adult children who are unable to support themselves because of illness or incapacity.[83] Conversely, in some situations parents are relieved of support duties while their children are still minors under the law. Such termination of parental duties occurs through the doctrine of emancipation and sometimes through actions of minors who refuse to obey parental rules. Finally, support duties may terminate prior to the age of majority upon the death of either the parent or the child.

## [1]   Emancipation

Emancipation is a common law doctrine derived from Roman law.[84] Emancipation terminates parental support duties and corresponding rights to control the life of the child.[85] In addition, upon the child's emancipation, parents lose common law entitlements to the services and earnings of the child.[86]

Common law emancipation occurs while the child is still a minor and is triggered through acts of the child and her parents without any contemporaneous judicial declarations.[87] The question of emancipation subsequently arises when a particular legal issue, generally whether a parent is obligated to pay for an item necessary to the child's support, comes before the courts.[88] Whether a child is deemed emancipated is then a matter of judicial determination based on the particular circumstances of the case.[89] While a set test is not established in the cases, the courts have found minors emancipated in situations where they leave home with their parents' consent or acquiescence and become financially self-supporting.[90] Some courts find emancipation where the minor is still living at home but pays her parents for room and board and generally supports herself.[91] In determining emancipation, the courts also consider whether the parents exercise disciplinary control over the minor, whether the parents permit the minor to retain all her wages, and whether the parent has listed the minor as a dependent for tax purposes.[92]

No single factor is conclusive in determining emancipation. As much as anything, the legal context and the nature of the claim raised may determine whether emancipation will be decreed. For example, the courts tend to liberally

---

[82] *See supra* § 3.02[A][2], notes 24–27 and accompanying text.

[83] Clark, *supra* note 1, at 260.

[84] Horowitz & Davidson, *supra* note 28, at 143.

[85] *Id.*

[86] *Id.*

[87] *Id.* at 144.

[88] *Id.*

[89] Davis & Schwartz, *supra* note 51, at 39.

[90] Accent Serv. v. Ebsen, 306 N.W.2d 575 (Neb. 1981).

[91] Wurth v. Wurth, 322 S.W.2d 745 (Mo. 1959).

[92] S. Katz, W. Schroeder & L. Sidman, *Emancipating Our Children — Coming of Legal Age in America*, 7 Fam. L.Q. 211, 218 (1973).

find emancipation in the context of inter-family torts, but are more reluctant to find it in cases raising the issue of termination of parental support.[93]

Where minors marry or join the military, the situation is more certain. Under common law, marriage or enlistment in the armed forces is sufficient in itself to constitute emancipation.[94]

Some jurisdictions have augmented the common law with legislation allowing juveniles to petition the courts for a declaration of emancipation.[95] Such provisions allow for a clarification of the minor's status in advance of any legal controversy where emancipation may become an issue. The statutes typically dictate a minimum age of sixteen[96] and require a showing that the minor is financially supporting herself while wilfully living apart from her parents with their consent.[97] Some statutory variations require additional findings that the decree of emancipation is "in the best interests" of either the minor, the parents, or both.[98]

While terminating parental support obligations, emancipation may or may not remove certain disabilities traditionally connected with minority. Common law emancipation generally does not enhance the contractual capacity of the emancipated minor,[99] although there are some cases to the contrary.[100] Some statutory emancipation provisions specifically treat the emancipated minor as an adult for purposes of contracting, selling property, litigating in one's own name, and making wills, trusts, or gifts.[101] On the other hand, in no jurisdiction is emancipation itself sufficient to permit the person to vote, to drink alcohol, or to subject the minor to adult criminal responsibility.[102]

## [2]  Disobedience to Parents

While parents' support duties generally are not terminated if their children disobey them or treat them rudely or with disrespect,[103] some cases hold that such duties are terminated if a particular child refuses to adhere to standards of conduct urged by her parents. Thus, one court held that a father no longer owed support duties to his twenty-year-old daughter who, while at college, refused to obey her father's stipulation that she live on campus.[104] Such cases find that a minor forfeits her right to parental support if she blatantly disregards their reasonable rules aimed at governing the family.[105] Other courts reject this view, however, and hold

---

[93]  *Id.* at 223, 225.

[94]  Horowitz & Davidson, *supra* note 28, at 145.

[95]  Davis & Schwartz, *supra* note 51, at 40.

[96]  Horowitz & Davidson, *supra* note 28, at 145.

[97]  Kramer, *supra* note 11, at 682.

[98]  *Id.*

[99]  *Id.* at 669.

[100]  Horowitz & Davidson, *supra* note 28, at 147–48; *see infra* § 5.03[A][5].

[101]  Davis & Schwartz, *supra* note 51, at 40.

[102]  Kramer, *supra* note 11.

[103]  59 Am. Jr. 2d *Parent and Child* § 56 (1987).

[104]  Roe v. Doe, 272 N.E.2d 567 (N.Y. 1971).

[105]  *See* Parker v. Stage, 371 N.E.2d 513, 514 (N.Y. 1977) (parent not obligated to support minor daughter who, contrary to parent's wishes, abandons the family home to live with paramour).

that unless the minor is emancipated, the parent owes a duty of support even where the minor leaves home against the wishes of her parents and lives in ways of which they disapprove.[106]

### [3]  Death of Parent or Child

Traditionally, the parental duty of support terminated upon the death of either the child or the parent.[107] However, some statutes and court decisions have recently extended the duty to support beyond the death of the parent, thus permitting support orders to be entered against the estate of the deceased parent.[108]

### [C]  Theoretical Implications

As is clear from the above discussion, the law defining support and maintenance generally embraces a theory of protectionist rights for children. However, as discussed immediately below, small pockets of this body of law appear to be better understood in terms of personhood theory.

The "mature minor" doctrine in the area of medical treatment seemingly recognizes adolescents as competent decision-makers with sufficient capacity to make important decisions for themselves. Typically, the chosen medical care is often "unnecessary" under the law[109] and thus not essential for the minor's basic well-being. Legal recognition of a minor's right to choose nonessential care is difficult to explain in terms of protectionist theory, but it is clearly at home with personhood theory and its requirement that the choices of competent moral agents be respected.

Similarly, the forfeiture-of-support cases appear at odds with protectionist theory. Minors who disregard parental rules and thereby forfeit their right to support may still require as much support as they did prior to their acts of disobedience. If so, projectionist theory would require continued parental support notwithstanding the rebellious actions of the child. On the other hand, to the extent the rational of the forfeiture cases is premised on a recognition that minors are accountable for their choices — in these cases their choices to disregard the edicts of legitimate parental authority and thereby forego support — the cases seem to reflect principles central to personhood theory.[110]

## § 3.03  PARENTAL NEGLECT

As mentioned above, parents owe a duty of support and care to their children. Breach of this duty may trigger a variety of responses ranging from private tort actions brought by the child to state interventions imposing criminal penalties, temporary removal of custody, or permanent termination of parental rights.

---

[106]  Byrd v. O'Neill, 244 N.W.2d 657 (Minn. 1976).

[107]  J. Gregory, P. Swisher & S. Scheible, Understanding Family Law 269 (2d ed. 1993).

[108]  *Id.*

[109]  *See supra* notes 65–67 and accompanying text.

[110]  *See* Morris, *supra* § 2.03, note 6.

## [A]  Parental Tort Liability

At common law, children theoretically were able to bring tort actions against their parents.[1] Beginning in the late nineteenth century, however, American courts widely adopted a doctrine of parental immunity, thus precluding unemancipated children from bringing actions against their parents for alleged negligence or intentional torts.[2] The immunity rule was premised on the view that intrafamily tort actions posed risks of collusion and disruption of family harmony.[3]

While the parental immunity doctrine is still recognized in some states,[4] the rule has been partially or totally rejected in most states in personal injury cases.[5] Some courts recognize partial immunity when the duty allegedly breached inheres in the parent-child relationship itself, but permit actions based on breach of duties owed to the world at large.[6] Accordingly, a child could not sue his parent for negligent parenting (*e.g.*, carelessly allowing the child to wander into the street and be hit by a passing car), but the child could bring an action for injuries caused by the parent's failure to carefully operate a motor vehicle in which the child was riding.[7] Other courts have abolished the parental immunity doctrine entirely in personal injury cases.[8]

The erosion of the parental immunity doctrine is premised on the perception that collusion is no more likely in intrafamily cases than in any others.[9] Moreover, courts often see the risk of disrupting family harmony by permitting parent-child actions to be outweighed by the advantages of compensating injured children, particularly in light of the fact that parents often carry liability insurance.[10]

While children are now often able to receive compensation for personal injuries caused by the negligent acts of their parents, the courts have not permitted actions premised merely on psychological harm. Thus, in a widely cited Oregon case, the court denied a cause of action to children who alleged emotional and psychological damage caused by the failure of their mothers to perform their parental duties.[11] While the court expressed concern for the child plaintiffs, it feared that permitting an action for emotional damage would be unwise on policy grounds and would expose the courts to a flood of questionable litigation.[12] However, in dicta the court

---

[1]  W. Prosser & P. Keeton, The Law of Torts 904 (5th ed. 1984).

[2]  *Id.*

[3]  *Id.* at 905.

[4]  Kramer, *supra* § 3.02, note 11, at 468.

[5]  *Id.* at 469.

[6]  *See, e.g.,* Gelbman v. Gelbman, 245 N.E.2d 192 (N.Y. 1969); Holodook v. Spencer, 324 N.E.2d 338 (N.Y. 1974); Grivas v. Grivas, 496 N.Y.S.2d 757 (N.Y. App. Div. 1985).

[7]  *Id.*

[8]  *See, e.g.,* Anderson v. Stream, 295 N.W.2d 595 (Minn. 1980). But see the discussion of *Burnette, infra* notes 11–13 and the accompanying text.

[9]  Kramer, *supra* note 4, at 469.

[10]  *Id.* "When insurance is involved, the action between parent and child is not truly adversary [sic]; both parties seek recovery from the insurance carrier to create a fund for the child's medical care and support without depleting the family's other assets." Sorensen v. Sorensen, 339 N.E.2d 907, 914 (Mass. 1975).

[11]  Burnette v. Wahl, 588 P.2d 1105 (Or. 1978).

[12]  The *Burnette* court noted that "there are probably as many children who have been damaged in some manner by their parents' failure to meet completely their physical, emotional, and psychological

left open the possibility of recovery by the children on a theory of intentional infliction of emotional harm by their parents.[13]

## [B]　State Intervention

## [1]　Criminal Actions

Parents who abandon or otherwise fail to support their children may be subject to criminal liability, particularly where the parents do so intentionally or with callous disregard for the welfare of their children.[14] Moreover, special statutes defining and punishing child abuse now exist in most states.[15] The legal issues surrounding the problem of child abuse are extensive and sometimes involve parties outside the parent-child relationship. The topic thus extends beyond the scope of this Chapter and therefore will be given consideration later in a separate Chapter.[16]

Utilizing criminal sanctions in neglect and non-support cases is controversial. Obviously, a parent is unable to provide financial support while incarcerated.[17] This problem is alleviated somewhat by statutes that authorize the court to suspend the sentence on the condition that the convicted parent support his children.[18]

---

needs as there are people." *Id.* at 1111. As an example of the kind of unwise tort claim that might, result if the action in the instant case were permitted, the court cited a possible action by children against their divorcing parents given that "children of divorced parents would almost always [experience] emotional trauma . . . from the legal dissolution of the family and the resultant absence of at least one of the parents." *Id.* at 1111–12.

In a dissenting opinion, Justice Lind argued, among other things, that because the theory of the instant case was premised on parental breach of statutorily imposed duties, the action could be permitted without opening the floodgates of litigation. The courts could simply limit permissible actions to statutory breaches and deny actions premised on breaches of non-statutory parental duties. *Id.* at 1117 (Lind, J., dissenting).

[13]　*Id.* at 1111.

[14]　The following Oregon statutes are representative:

Abandonment of a child. (1) A person commits the crime of abandonment of a child if, being a parent, lawful guardian or other person lawfully charged with the care or custody of a child under 15 years of age, the person deserts the child in any place with intent to abandon it. (2) Abandonment of a child is a Class C felony.

Child neglect in the second degree. (1) A person having custody or control of a child under 10 years of age commits the crime of child neglect in the second degree if, with criminal negligence, the person leaves the child unattended in or at any place for such period of time as may be likely to endanger the health or welfare of such child. (2) Child neglect in the second degree is a Class A misdemeanor.

Criminal nonsupport. (1) A person commits the crime of criminal non-support if, being the parent, lawful guardian or other person lawfully charged with the support of a child under 18 years of age, born in or out of wedlock, the person refuses or neglects without lawful excuse to provide support for such child. . . . (3) Criminal nonsupport is a Class C felony.

Or. Rev. Stat. §§ 163.535, Or. Rev. Stat. §§ 163.545, 163.555 (2001). Model Penal Code § 230.5 (Proposed Official Draft 1962) provides: "A person commits a misdemeanor if he persistently fails to provide support which he can provide and which he knows he is legally obliged to provide to a . . . child. . . ."

[15]　2 D. Kramer, Legal Rights of Children 10 (2d ed. 1994).

[16]　*See infra* Chapter 4.

[17]　Clark, *supra* § 1.02, note 4, at 270.

[18]　Kramer, *supra* note 4, at 200.

## [2]    *Parens Patriae* Limitations on Parental Authority

State laws pertaining to parental neglect afford a basis for state intervention to protect children receiving inadequate care. The statutes typically describe neglected children in broad terms.[19] For example, in the District of Columbia, neglected children are defined as children who are "without proper parental care or control, subsistence, education as required by law, or other care or control necessary for [their] physical, mental, or emotional health, and the deprivation is not due to the lack of financial means of [their] parent, guardian, or other custodian. . . ."[20] Despite the breadth of the statutory language, the courts have upheld such statutes against attacks of unconstitutional vagueness.[21] The open-ended language of neglect statutes affords trial courts broad discretion to make individualized judgments based on the circumstances of each case.[22] If the court finds that a child is neglected, a variety of responses may be employed. The court might permit the child to remain with her present custodians under specified conditions of supervision under the direction of state social service agencies, sometimes including psychological counseling for the parents and/or the child.[23] If the court concludes that the welfare of the child cannot be adequately assured under the present conditions, the court might order a change of custody, often placing the child with foster parents supervised by the state.[24] Such placements are usually anticipated as a temporary mechanism for providing care for the child until such time as she can be reunited with her parents.[25]

While state interventions resulting in even a temporary loss of custody raise issues of deprivation of constitutionally protected parental rights,[26] some courts permit denial of parental custody rights if the state proves neglect by a mere "preponderance of the evidence."[27] On the other hand, other courts require that the state meet the more rigorous standard of "clear and convincing evidence."[28]

---

[19]  Krause, *supra* § 3.01, note 1, at 274.

[20]  D.C. Code Ann. § 16-2301(9)(B) (2001).

[21]  *See, e.g.*, Matter of B.K., 429 A.2d 1331 (D.C. 1981). *But see* Roe v. Conn., 417 F. Supp. 769 (M.D. Ala. 1976) (court finds child neglect statute unconstitutionally vague where court removes a child from the custody of his mother in part on ground that he was white and she was living with a black man — court enjoins enforcement of neglect statute in absence of a showing of physical or emotional harm to the child).

[22]  Krause, *supra* note 19.

[23]  R. Mnookin, *Foster Care — In Whose Best Interest?*, 43 Harv. Educ. Rev. 599, 606 (1973). Model statutes often present a variety of alternatives ranging from such minimal interventions as state wardship with informal supervision to the more drastic alternative of removal of the child from her present home. *See, e.g.*, Institute of Judicial Admin. & American Bar Ass'n, Juvenile Justice Standards Project, Standards Relating to Abuse and Neglect § 6.3 (Tentative Draft 1977).

[24]  Mnookin, *supra* note 23, at 606.

[25]  *See, e.g.*, N.Y. Soc. Serv. Law § 384-b(1)(a)(iii) (1992) (where state assumes guardianship of dependent children, "the state's first obligation is to help the family with services to prevent its break-up or to reunite it if the child has already left home"); Cal. Welf. & Inst. Code § 300(j) (West Supp. 2000) (intent of legislature "that nothing [done by state] disrupt the family unnecessarily").

[26]  *See, e.g.*, Stanley v. Illinois, 405 U.S. 645, 651 (1972) ("the interest of a parent in the companionship, care, custody and management of his or her children come[s] to this Court with a momentum for respect," because the "rights to raise one's children have been deemed 'essential' ").

[27]  *See, e.g.*, Matter of B.K., 429 A.2d 1331 (D.C. 1981).

[28]  *See, e.g.*, *In re* Jeannette S., 156 Cal. Rptr. 262 (Cal. App. 1979).

The foster care system is intended to provide a temporary "normal home" for children unable for one reason or another to reside with their parents or other permanent caretakers.[29] While laudable in theory, foster care is often criticized as being class biased because a high proportion of foster children come from poor families.[30] Moreover, because children experience trauma whenever they are separated from primary caretakers, some critics of foster care argue that such separation should not be legally ordered unless it immediately results in a new permanent custody arrangement with new primary caretakers.[31] Children generally remain in foster care until either they can be returned to their natural parents or adopted.[32]

The relationship between foster parents, child, and child welfare agencies can be complex, particularly where the child has bonded to the foster parents. Generally, upon receiving initial custody of the child, foster parents agree with the child placement agency to return the child to the agency upon its demand.[33] If the foster parents subsequently become attached to the child, they may resist the agency's demands for return of the child, sometimes claiming a constitutionally protected interest in continued custody.[34] Without deciding whether foster parents possess a protected "liberty" interest in the custody of the child, the United States Supreme Court has held that such an interest, if it exists, can be overridden where the agency seeks to return the child to its natural parents and affords the foster parents a trial-type administrative hearing prior to removing the child.[35] Where, however, the agency seeks to remove custody to parties other than the natural parents, the court might deny the agency's attempt to transfer custody from protesting foster parents because of the child's attachment to the foster parents.[36]

---

[29] *See* J. Goldstein, A. Freud & A. Solnit, Beyond the Best Interests of the Child 24 (2d ed. 1979).

[30] Mnookin & Weisberg, *supra* § 1.02, note 8, at 440; M. Wald, *State Intervention on Behalf of "Neglected" Children: A Search for Realistic Standards*, 27 STAN. L. REV. 985, 1021–24 (1975).

[31] *See* Goldstein, Freud & Solnit, *supra* note 29, at 24–26, 97–101. For a critique of Goldstein, Freud & Solnit, see M. Wald, *Thinking About Public Policy Toward Abuse and Neglect of Children: A Review of Before the Best Interests of the Child*, 78 MICH. L. REV. 645, 655–70 (1980).

[32] Mnookin & Weisberg, *supra* note 30, at 461.

[33] Clark, *supra* note 17, at 834.

[34] *See, e.g.*, Smith v. Organization of Foster Families for Equality and Reform, 431 U.S. 816 (1977).

[35] *Id.* In *Smith*, the Court rejected the claim that the state procedures for removing children from foster parents violated the procedural due process rights of the foster parents. Under the procedures at issue in *Smith*, foster parents were provided notice of any removal ten days prior to the time the agency sought to remove the child. If the parents objected to the removal, they were entitled to a "conference" with an agency official at which time they would be informed of the reasons for the proposed removal and afforded an opportunity to provide reasons why the child should not be removed, through legal counsel if they so chose. The agency official would then render a written decision within five days of the conference.

Several lower courts have held that foster parents do not possess constitutionally protected liberty interest in maintaining foster care relationships. *See, e.g.*, McLaughlin v. Pemsley, 654 F. Supp. 1567 (E.D. Pa. 1987); Gibson v. Merced County Dept. of Human Resources, 799 F.2d 582, 586 (9th Cir. 1986).

[36] Clark, *supra* note 17, at 835. On the other hand, if psychological attachment between foster parent and child provides a basis for retaining custody in the foster parents, the underlying purpose of the institution of foster care as a *temporary* caretaking arrangement may be frustrated. *Id.* at 835–36.

## [3]  Termination of Parental Rights

State responses to parental neglect often seek to maintain the parent-child relationship. But when parents egregiously breach their duty of care to their children, the state may seek permanent termination of the parents' ties to their children. Statutory grounds for termination of parental rights typically include abandonment, child abuse, severe neglect, non-support, and an inability to perform parental duties because of physical or mental illness.[37] Statutes and caselaw often require the courts to find that the conditions resulting in the child's inadequate care, support, or protection are irremediable.[38]

Parents may consent to termination of their parental rights.[39] But where the state seeks involuntary termination, the United States Supreme Court has recognized that fundamental constitutional rights of the parents are at stake. Because "the fundamental liberty interest of natural parent[s] in the care, custody, and management of their child does not evaporate simply because they have not been model parents."[40] The Court found that the Due Process Clause requires that the government prove the grounds for termination by "clear and convincing evidence" rather than by the usual, less rigorous, "preponderance of the evidence" standard.[41]

Concerning the issue of right to counsel, the Court has held that there is no requirement that counsel be appointed for indigent parents in every proceeding aimed at terminating parental rights.[42] Rather, trial courts have discretion to make case-by-case decisions regarding whether due process requires appointment of counsel, subject to appellate review.[43] The denial of an absolute right to appointed counsel is perhaps a bit surprising in light of the court's recognition that a natural parent's right to a relationship with her children "is an interest far more precious than any property right."[44]

---

[37] Gregory, Swisher & Scheible, *supra* § 3.02, note 107, at 144–45. While usually not listed as an explicit statutory ground for termination, the lengthy incarceration of a parent often results in termination of the incarcerated parent's rights. *See, e.g., In re* Adam M., 802 A.2d 1218 (N.H. 2002).

[38] For example, Unif. Adoption Act § 19(c), 9 U.L.A. 72 (1988), requires that the court find that the parental neglect or incapacity are "irremediable or will not be remedied by the parent." *See also* Minn. Stat. Ann. § 260C.301(5) (West Supp. 2002). In *People* ex rel. *C.R.*, 577 P.2d 1225, 1228 (Colo. Ct. App. 1976) the court stated:

> In decreeing termination of parental rights, a trial court must find that the conditions which resulted in the earlier determination of dependency will in all probability continue into the future, and that under no reasonable circumstances would the welfare of the children be served by a continuation of the parent-child relationship.

[39] The law governing the validity of voluntary relinquishment of parental rights is extensive. A host of issues are entailed, ranging from problems of determining the degree of formality required to whether consent to terminate parental rights, once given, can be revoked. Moreover, problems surrounding consent by unwed fathers have reached the United States Supreme Court in a series of cases. For a discussion of these and other issues, see Clark, *supra* note 17, at 876–87; Gregory, Swisher & Scheible, *supra* note 37, at 153–57; and Kramer, *supra* note 4, at 277–87.

[40] Santosky v. Kramer, 455 U.S. 745, 753 (1982).

[41] *Id.* at 756–70.

[42] Lassiter v. Department of Social Servs., 452 U.S. 18 (1981).

[43] *Id.*

[44] *Id.* at 27. For a critique of *Lassiter*, see D. Besharov, *Terminating Parental Rights: The Indigent*

When the parent-child relationship has been terminated, either consensually or involuntarily, the child no longer has any legal relationship with her natural parents. The child will either reside in foster care or other nonpermanent arrangements or be adopted and thus enter into a permanent relationship with her adoptive parents.

## [4] Foster Care

When children are removed from the parental home because of abuse and neglect or because the parent has voluntarily relinquished custody, the state may place the child in the foster care system with foster parents who care for the child with compensation from the state. Although foster care is intended to be an interim placement for the child until they are able to return home to their parents or other relatives, or until they are adopted, some children remain in foster care indefinitely. Some children meet with abuse in foster care that is similar to that which precipitated their removal from the parental home, but other children develop deep emotional ties to their foster parents.

Do foster parents have any rights when the state seeks to remove a foster child from the home of the foster parent? In 1977, the Supreme Court heard the claim of a foster parent group that the Due Process Clause requires a hearing before the state can remove a child from a foster home if the child has been in the foster home for a substantial amount of time.[45] The Court discussed the purported interest of the foster parent in the familial relationship with the foster child, and determined in dicta that even if the foster parent had a protected constitutional interest, the state's hearing procedure satisfied the requirements of due process. The Court distinguished the natural, biological family from the foster family, saying that "the State here seeks to interfere, not with a relationship having its origins entirely apart from the State, but rather with a foster family which has its source in state law and contractual arrangements."[46] The Court also noted that recognizing a liberty interest in foster parents would infringe on the pre-existing liberty interests of the natural parents of foster children in voluntary placement.[47] While the Court decided the issue based on its narrow reasoning that the State provided adequate pre-removal procedures, its dicta indicates that it does not favor granting foster parents constitutional rights, a view generally embraced by the lower courts.[48]

Because the underlying premise of foster care is that it is to be an interim placement until the child can be returned to his or her parents, or put up for

---

*Parent's Right to Counsel After* Lassiter v. North Carolina, 15 FAM. L.Q. 205 (1981). On the other hand, the strength of the parental interest played a significant role in *M.L.B. v. S.L.J.*, 65 U.S.L.W. 4035 (1996), in which the Court held unconstitutional a state rule as applied to indigent parents requiring payment of transcript preparation fees as prerequisites to effectuating appeals.

[45] Smith v. Org. of Foster Families for Equality and Reform, 431 U.S. 816 (1977).

[46] *Id.* at 845.

[47] *Id.* at 846.

[48] Procopio v. Johnson, 994 F.2d 325 (7th Cir. 1993); Kyees v. County Department of Public Welfare, 600 F.2d 693 (7th Cir. 1979); Drummond v. Fulton County Dept. of Family and Children's Services, 563 F.2d 1200 (5th Cir. 1977) (en banc), *cert. denied*, 437 U.S. 910 (1978). *But see* Division of Family Services v. Harrison, 741 A.2d 1016 (Del. 1999) (holding parents had standing to pursue guardianship of a foster child after he had been in their care for most of his life); *In re* Jonathan G., 482 S.E.2d 893 (W. Va. App. 1996 (based on statutory grounds, foster parents who had custody of an abused child for over two years were entitled to limited participation in parental termination proceedings).

adoption, some state agencies traditionally adopted specific policies that prohibited foster parents from adopting the children in their care. One asserted reason for this position was the concern that foster parents, because the arrangement is temporary, must remain somewhat detached so that they will be able and willing to facilitate the child's return to the biological parent.[49] More recently, however, some states have passed statutes that allow foster parents to adopt their foster children,[50] and some courts have been more receptive to the idea than in the past.[51]

In addition, Congress enacted the Adoption and Safe Families Act of 1997 (ASFA), which encourages states to expedite adoption for abused and neglected children.[52] ASFA includes provisions to reduce the numbers of foster care children and to alleviate "foster care drift."[53] It provides incentives for increasing the number of children adopted out of foster care and reduces inter-jurisdictional barriers that delay adoptions across state lines. ASFA also sets forth new timelines regulating the amount of time children can remain in foster care before being placed for adoption.[54]

Not surprisingly, considering the turmoil and upheaval in foster children's lives, many foster children experience significant problems in foster care. The results of one study of 749 17-year-olds in foster care showed that over one-half could read only at a seventh-grade level, about one-third had repeated a grade, and almost 20% had been expelled from school.[55] Nearly two-thirds of the boys, and one-half of the girls, had been arrested, convicted of a crime, or sent to a correctional facility.

---

[49] B. B. Woodhouse, *Horton Looks at the ALI Principles*, 4 J.L. & Fam. Stud. 151, 158 (2002).

[50] *See, e.g.*, N.Y. Soc. Services Law § 383(3) (2003) (giving preference to foster parents who have had the child in their care for over 12 months).

[51] *See e.g.*, Matter of M.D.H., 595 S.W.2d 448 (Mo. Ct. App. 1980) (affirming order allowing foster parents to adopt foster child and denying biological grandparent's petition for adoption); Middleton v. Department of Human Services, 183 P.3d 1041, 1049 (Or. Ct. App. 2008) (allowing adoption of child by foster parents, rather than child's great aunt); *In re* Daevon Lamar P., 849 N.Y.S.2d 806 (N.Y. App. Div. 2008) (affirming family court order terminating biological father's parental rights in order to free child for adoption by foster parents).

[52] 42 U.S.C. § 675(5) (2000).

[53] Symposium, *From Anticipation to Evidence: Research on the Adoption and Safe Families Act*, 12 Va. J. Soc. Pol'y & L. 371, 372–73 (2005).

[54] Timelines under previous legislation, the Child Welfare Act, required that every child in foster care receive a dispositional hearing within the first eighteen months in state custody. ASFA changed "dispositional" hearings to "permanency" hearings and requires states to hold these hearings within the child's first twelve months in foster care and at least once every twelve months as long as the child remains in state custody. ASFA requires that every child have a permanent plan within twelve months, and it requires states (with some exceptions) to petition a court for termination of parental rights once a child has resided in state custody for fifteen of the most recent twenty-two months. 42 U.S.C. § 675(5)(E). One important exception to the State's duty to seek permanent placement is where the state has failed to make reasonable efforts to reunite the family, although the state does not need to try to reunite the family first if the safety of the child would be jeopardized by placing the child back with the parents. *Id.*; 42 U.S.C. § 671(a)(15)(D). Whether or not the child's safety would be jeopardized depends on whether the parent's current or previous conduct falls into one of several carefully delineated categories under U.S.C. § 671(a)(15)(D).

[55] J. Blair, *Foster Care Children Are Poorly Educated, 3-StateStudy Charges*, Educ. Wk., Feb. 25, 2004 (citing Midwest Evaluation of Adult Functioning of Former Foster Care Youth — Wave 1 from Chapin Hall Center for Children at the University of Chicago).

Many of those foster children had switched schools five or more times during their foster care.[56] Abuse in foster care is also too often a reality.[57]

Recently, children who have been abused by foster parents while in foster care have brought actions against the state under 42 U.S.C. § 1983, requiring that they "establish that a right protected by the laws or Constitution of the United States was violated and that the violation was committed by a person acting under color of State law."[58] If these same children were injured while living with their biological parents, they would not have a cause of action under the Supreme Court case, *DeShaney v. Winnebago County of Social Services*,[59] which held that a child injured by his father did not have a cause of action against state social service agencies for failing to protect him from his father's violence, even after his step-mother had asked social services to intervene. However, some courts recognize an affirmative state duty of protection to *foster children*.[60] However, such courts sometimes impose a standard of deliberate indifference on these claims, making them difficult to win in practice.[61] Other courts hold that qualified immunity applies to bar tort actions brought by foster children based on a lesser negligence standard.[62]

The problems foster children face do not necessarily end when they reach adulthood. An estimated "20,000 teens leave foster care each year 'because they have reached eighteen years of age and are expected to support themselves.' "[63] Such young people often find themselves suddenly thrown into an adult world without a support network to fall back on when they fall on hard times. One study of 810 young adults leaving foster care found that 2.5 to 4 years after aging out of the system, 51% of the former foster children were unemployed and 25% had been

---

[56] *Id.*

[57] *See* S. Balmer, *From Poverty to Abuse and Back Again: The Failure of Legal and Social Services Communities to Protect Foster Children*, 32 FORDHAM URB. L.J. 935, 935 (2005). Statistics vary greatly regarding the rate of abuse of foster children, but many studies agree that the rate of abuse is much higher for foster children than it is for children raised by their biological parents. *Id.*

[58] M. Kearney, *DeShaney's Legacy in Foster Care and Public School Settings*, 41 WASHBURN L.J. 275, 275 (2002) (citing 42 U.S.C. § 1983 (1996)).

[59] 489 U.S. 189, 191–92 (1989).

[60] *See e.g.*, Nicini v. Morra, 212 F.3d 798, 814–15 (3d Cir. 2000) (allowing the foster child to bring his claim, but finding that the social worker's failure did not descend to the level of "deliberate indifference," and that any negligence claim was barred by qualified immunity); Taylor v. Ledbetter, 818 F2d 791, 797 (11th Cir. 1987), *cert. denied*, Ledbetter v. Taylor, 489 U.S. 1065 (1989) (holding "that a child involuntarily placed in a foster home is in a situation so analogous to a prisoner in a penal institution and a child confined in a mental health facility that the foster child may bring a section 1983 action for violation of fourteenth amendment rights."); Doe v. N. Y. City Dept. of Soc. Serv., 709 F.2d 782 (2d Cir. 1983), *cert. denied*, Catholic Home Bureau v. Doe, 464 U.S. 864 (1983) (finding that agency was deliberately indifferent in failing to supervise a foster father that repeatedly physically and sexually abused his foster daughter).

[61] *Nicini*, 212 F.3d at 812.

[62] *Id.*; Porter v. Williams, 436 F.3d 917, 923 (8th Cir. 2006) (holding that claim against the supervisor of the social worker by natural parents of deceased foster child was barred by official immunity because supervisor's acts were discretionary). *But see* Whisman Through Whisman v. Rinehart, 119 F.3d 1303, 1306 (8th Cir. 1997) (holding that defendants were not entitled to qualified immunity for their failure to investigate, their detaining the child, or their delay in filing court proceedings because these things did not further the state objective).

[63] S. Mangold, *Extending Non-Exclusive Parenting and the Right to Protection for Older Foster Children: Creating Third Options in Permanency Planning*, 48 BUF. L. REV. 835, 861 (2000).

homeless at least one night,[64] while another showed that 35% of the former foster children studied had "spent time in jail or prison."[65]

In order to respond to the problem of foster children "aging out" of the foster care system without necessary life skills and education, Congress passed the Foster Care Independence Act of 1999.[66] The statute provides training for foster children who will leave the system because of age and some additional resources for them after they leave the system.[67]

## § 3.04 ADOPTION

Adoption is the statutory mechanism by which permanent parent-child relationships are created between persons not already so related.[1] Adoptions occur in every jurisdiction through state-licensed child care agencies.[2] In some states, private placements are permitted, independent of any prior authorization by state agencies or state-licensed private agencies, where parents relinquish their children to be adopted either directly to prospective adopters or to non-licensed intermediaries such as physicians, lawyers, relatives, or friends.[3]

Prospective adoptive parents initiate adoption proceedings by filing a petition with the court.[4] In what appears to be an accommodation to the personhood theory of rights, the statutes generally require the child's consent to the proposed adoption if she is of a specified age.[5] Adoption hearings are usually informal and uncontested, with the court determining whether the proposed adoption is in the child's "best interests."[6]

---

[64] *Id.* at 865 (citing Westat, Inc., A National Evaluation of Title IV-E Foster Care Independent Living Programs for Youth: Phase 2, Final Report (1991)).

[65] S. V. Mangold, *supra* note 20 (citing Richard P. Barth, *On Their Own: The Experiences of Youth After Foster Care*, 7 CHILD & ADOLESCENT SOC. WORK, No. 5, 424 (1990)).

[66] Pub. L. No. 106-169, 113 Stat. 1822 (codified at 42 U.S.C. § 677 (1999)). This act replaced the older Independent Living Initiative of 1986, Pub. L. No. 99-272, tit. Xii, § 12307(a), 100 Stat. 294 (codified at 42 U.S.C. § 677 (1997).

[67] 42 U.S.C. § 477(a)(1) (1999).

[1] Wadlington, *supra* § 3.02, note 11, at 826. In some jurisdictions, natural parents are permitted to adopt their own children in certain circumstances. *See, e.g.*, Bridges v. Nicely, 497 A.2d 142 (Md. 1985) (natural father adopts his biological child born out of wedlock for purposes of legitimation); Adoption of Tammy, 619 N.E.2d 315 (Mass. 1993) (child adopted by her mother and mother's female companion where child conceived through artificial insemination of mother by companion's cousin).

[2] Gregory, Swisher & Scheible, *supra* § 3.02, note 107, at 150.

[3] Independent adoptions are sometimes referred to as "gray market" adoptions because they fall into a gray area of the law, somewhere between highly regulated agency adoptions and universally illegal black market adoptions where children are bought and sold for a fee. *Id.*; Wadlington, *supra* note 1, at 827. In an attempt to discourage the involvement of third persons who act as paid intermediaries in placing children with adoptive parents, some states have enacted legislation to discourage or bar private (non-agency) placements. *See, e.g.*, Mass. Gen. Laws Ann. ch. 210, § 11A (West 1998).

[4] Kramer, *supra* § 3.02, note 11, at 265.

[5] *Id.* at 266–67.

[6] *Id.* at 267.

Children may be adopted by their relatives.[7] Statutes in some states direct that children be matched if possible with adoptive parents of the same racial or ethnic background as the child.[8] Similarly, some statutes require religious matching "where practicable."[9] Courts in some states have upheld statutes specifically prohibiting gay or lesbian persons from adopting,[10] but adoptions by such persons are not necessarily precluded in other states.[11] Moreover, while some courts hold that a party petitioning to adopt need not be married, others hold that two unmarried adults cannot jointly adopt a child.[12]

Because adoption is viewed as a "new beginning," statutes usually adopt the policy of severing all past ties for the good of the child, the adoptive parents, and the biological parents.[13] As a consequence, adoption records are generally "sealed" so that adopted children, even when reaching adulthood, are denied access to the records when seeking information that identifies or otherwise concerns their biological parents.[14] By the same token, biological parents are routinely denied access to adoption records to avoid their reentry into the life of the child and her adoptive parents.[15] While most statutes permit courts to unseal adoption records only upon strict findings of "good cause,"[16] some states permit more liberal access, particularly when the party seeking access alleges a medical interest in obtaining information contained in the records.[17]

## § 3.05 INHERITANCE

Under traditional intestacy laws, children of married parents were entitled to inherit from both parents pursuant to statutory provisions proportioning the parent's estate for each child.[1] Under English common law, illegitimate children were denied inheritance rights from either parent.[2]

---

[7] *See, e.g., In re* Adoption of Tachick, 210 N.W.2d 865 (Wis. 1973) (child adopted by grandparents). Some statutes embrace preferences in favor of adoption by relatives. *See, e.g.,* Cal. Family Code § 8708(a) (West 1994).

[8] *See, e.g.,* Minn. Stat. Ann. § 259.57, subd. 2 (West 1998 & Supp. 2002).

[9] *See, e.g.,* N.Y. Fam. Ct. Act. § 116 (McKinney 1998). An earlier version of this statute was upheld against First Amendment attack in *Dickens v. Ernesto,* 281 N.E.2d 153 (N.Y. 1972).

[10] *See, e.g., In re* Opinion of the Justices, 530 A.2d 21 (N.H. 1987).

[11] *See* Kramer, *supra* note 4, at 268.

[12] *Id.* at 269.

[13] *Id.* at 314.

[14] Adopted children are routinely denied information about their biological parents in order to protect privacy interests of the latter, who often consent to their child's adoption on the condition that the facts surrounding their consent be kept secret. *Id.*

[15] By sealing the records, adoptive parents can expect to raise the child free from interference or involvement by the biological parents. Furthermore, sealing the records permits the court to conduct a full investigation into the lives of both the biological parents and the prospective adoptive parents without causing concerns about any possible disclosure of embarrassing or intimate facts. *Id.*

[16] *Id.* An adopted child's mere curiosity or desire to know her biological roots unusually does not constitute a sufficient level of "good cause" to justify opening the records. *See, e.g., In re* Roger B., 418 N.E.2d 751 (Ill. 1981) (rejecting adoptee's argument that sealing the adoption records violates his constitutional right to know his identiy).

[17] Kramer, *supra* note 4, at 315.

[1] Krause, *supra* § 3.01, note 1, at 259.

[2] Clark, *supra* § 1.02, note 4, at 149.

Historically, the American law permitted illegitimate children to inherit from their mothers, but not from their fathers.[3] Under Supreme Court caselaw, such denials of paternal inheritance are constitutionally permissible only if "substantially related" to such "important state interests" as avoiding spurious claims against the estate and precluding proof of paternity after the father's death.[4] Therefore, where paternity has clearly been established during the life of the father, for example by a court in a paternity suit, it is apparently unconstitutional to deny illegitimate children rights to inherit from their fathers. Many states now provide statutory frameworks through which illegitimate children may be permitted paternal inheritance.[5]

Under most statutes, adopted children inherit from their adoptive parent as if they were their biological children.[6] Most statutes deny adopted children a right to inherit from their natural parents.[7]

On the other hand, stepchildren generally are not entitled to inherit from their stepparents.[8] However, some statutes permit stepchildren to take as heirs of their intestate stepparent if the property would otherwise escheat to the state[9] or if the stepparent had manifested a serious intent to adopt the child.[10]

The child's ability to take from her parent's estate may be restricted, even eliminated altogether, if the parent dies testate. Parents may disinherit their children so long as the intent to do so is clearly expressed in their will.[11]

The parental power to disinherit appears at odds with the general duty of parents to support their children. Some states alleviate the harmful effects of parental disinheritance on minor children by enacting statutes that, among other things, provide a family allowance from the estate during probate administration and set aside certain property as exempt from execution in order to assist the support needs of surviving children.[12] Furthermore, testators are unable to disinherit surviving spouses who will generally take from the estate of their deceased spouse, thus indirectly benefitting disinherited children to whom the surviving spouse owes ongoing duties of support.[13]

---

[3] Horowitz & Davidson, *supra* § 3.02, note 28, at 39.

[4] Lalli v. Lalli, 439 U.S. 259, 275 (1978). The interests noted in the text are arguably important in maintaining an accurate and efficient method of dispensing intestate property.

[5] Kramer, *supra* § 3.02, note 11, at 358–59 (statutes permit inheritance where, *inter alia*, the natural father acknowledges paternity, engages in conduct evidencing his voluntary acceptance of the child as his own, or marries the child's mother.).

[6] Horowitz & Davidson, *supra* note 3, at 34.

[7] *Id.* at 35.

[8] *Id.*

[9] *Id.*

[10] Kramer, *supra* note 5, at 335.

[11] *Id.* at 341.

[12] Mnookin & Weisberg, *supra* § 1.02, note 8, at 303.

[13] *Id.*

## § 3.06 CHILD CUSTODY

Parents possess rights to custody of their minor children that will not be disturbed absent a showing that parental custody is inconsistent with the welfare of the children.[1] To assure the child's welfare, courts became involved in determining or modifying custody arrangements when parents separate or divorce, when a child has been entrusted to the care of a nonparent, or when circumstances arise which require reconsideration of the existing custodial arrangement.[2]

While custody disputes arise in a variety of contexts, two doctrinally distinct categories of cases can be identified. These categories — disputes between natural parents and disputes between natural parents and nonparents — will be considered in turn.

### [A] Disputes Between Natural Parents

With marital breakup now common, courts increasingly face the issue of determining child custody.[3] Where only one parent asserts a custody claim, the court will routinely award custody to that parent so long as doing so is not inconsistent with "the best interests of the child."[4] Similarly, if the court finds only one of the two parents to be a fit parent, that parent will receive custody. Where, however, neither parent is unfit and both assert custody claims, the court faces a perplexing problem.

Leaving the recent phenomenon of joint custody aside for the moment, a judicial award of custody to a parent means that the parent will live with the child and possess rights to make decisions regarding the care, control, education, and religion of the child.[5] The non-custodial parent is routinely awarded visitation rights and sometimes permitted physical custody of the child for periods of time during the year.[6]

At common law, fathers were primarily responsible for child custody, support, and maintenance and therefore were considered the sole guardians of their children.[7] This paternal preference no longer exists, however, with mothers now enjoying equal or superior claims to custody of their children.[8]

In determining custody awards, courts apply the "best interests of the child" criterion.[9] This flexible standard permits broad judicial discretion to take into account a variety of factors including the child's preferences, the child's health and social behavior, the moral fitness of the respective parents and their mental and emotional stability and physical health, the quality of existing relationships

---

[1] *See supra* § 3.01, note 2 and accompanying text.

[2] Wadlington, Whitebread & Davis, *supra* § 3.02, note 34, at 649.

[3] Clark, *supra* § 1.02, note 4, at 786.

[4] Agreements between divorcing parents as to custody of their children are generally enforced by courts unless clearly inconsistent with the welfare of the children. *Id.* at 807.

[5] *Id.* at 790.

[6] *Id.* at 811–13.

[7] Custody rights of fathers could be deprived at common law only upon proof of danger to the child or corruption of the father. *Id.* at 799.

[8] *See infra* notes 11–19 and accompanying text.

[9] Clark, *supra* note 3, at 797.

between the child and the respective parents, and the parents' relative capacity to satisfy the physical and emotional needs of the child.[10] Determinations of the child's "best interests" tend to be *ad hoc*, although some courts rely on certain presumptions in reaching their decisions.

## [1]  The Tender Years Presumption

In the nineteenth century, the courts rejected the common law paternal preference rule. In its place they began applying the "tender years presumption," a doctrine premised on the view that as between two otherwise fit parents contesting custody of their young children, the mother is better suited than the father to care for the children.[11] By the early twentieth century, the tender years doctrine was well-established throughout the nation.[12]

Recently, the doctrine has come under attack. Some courts see presumptive rules of any kind as inconsistent with the "best interests of the child" standard.[13] Other courts find a maternal preference to be based on outmoded gender stereotypes and thus unconstitutional under the Equal Protection Clause.[14] Furthermore, some legislatures expressly forbid the use of presumptions of any kind in custody determinations.[15] On the other hand, some courts have upheld the tender years presumption against equal protection attack[16] and the doctrine continues to be applied in a few jurisdictions.[17]

Regardless of the applicability of the tender years doctrine, courts continue to award custody to mothers in a majority of cases.[18] This may reflect the fact that

---

[10] Kramer, *supra* § 3.02, note 11, at 30. Some statutes attempt to specify factors to be considered in determining "the best interest of the child." *See, e.g.*, Uniform Marriage and Divorce Act § 402 (1998).

The court shall determine custody in accordance with the best interest of the child. The court shall consider all relevant factors including:

    (1) the wishes of the child's parent or parents as to his custody;

    (2) the wishes of the child as to his custodian;

    (3) the interaction and interrelationship of the child with his parent or parents, his siblings, and any other person who may significantly affect the child's best interest;

    (4) the child's adjustment to his home, school, community; and

    (5) the mental and physical health of all individuals involved.

The court shall not consider conduct of a proposed custodian that does not affect his relationship to the child.

[11] Kramer, *supra* note 10, at 31. The presumption takes several forms. Sometimes it is rebuttable, operating to award custody to the mother unless the father can show that the mother is unfit to have custody. At other times, the presumption operates in conjunction with the best interests rule and serves as one factor in favor of the mother to be weighted in conjunction with all other relevant considerations. Finally, the presumption sometimes operates as a "tie breaker" in favor of the mother, all other things considered. *Id.* at 35–36.

[12] The rule was embraced by the courts and also sometimes by legislative enactment. *Id.* at 31–35.

[13] *See, e.g.*, Johnson v. Johnson, 564 P.2d 71 (Alaska 1977), *cert. denied*, 434 U.S. 1048 (1978).

[14] *See, e.g., Ex parte* Devine, 398 So. 2d 686 (Ala. 1981).

[15] *See, e.g.*, Neb. Rev. Stat. § 42-364(3) (Reissue 1998) ("in determining custody arrangements . . . no presumption shall exist that either parent is more fit or suitable than the other").

[16] *See, e.g.*, Gordon v. Gordon, 577 P.2d 1271 (Okla. 1978), *cert. denied*, 439 U.S. 863 (1978).

[17] Clark, *supra* note 3, at 799.

[18] *Id.* at 800.

mothers tend to be the primary caretakers and courts find that decisive in awarding custody.[19]

## [2]  The Primary Caretaker Presumption

Some courts explicitly employ a presumption in favor of the "primary caretaker," the parent who has shouldered the majority of responsibility for the day-to-day care of the child. One court defined the primary caretaker as follows:

> In establishing which natural or adoptive parent is the primary care-taker, the trial court shall determine which parent has taken primary responsibility for *inter alia*, the performance of the following caring and nurturing duties of a parent: (1) preparing and planning of meals; (2) bathing, grooming, and dressing; (3) purchasing, cleaning, and care of clothes; (4) medical care, including nursing and trips to physicians; (5) arranging for social interaction among peers after school, *i.e.*, transporting to friends' houses, or for example, to girl or boy scout meetings; (6) arranging alternative care, *i.e.* babysitting, day-care, etc.; (7) putting child to bed at night, attending to child in the middle of the night, waking child in the morning; (8) disciplining, *i.e.* teaching general manner and toilet training; (9) educating, *i.e.* religious, cultural, social, etc.; and (10) teaching elementary skills, *i.e.* reading, writing and arithmetic.[20]

Once the court designates a primary caretaker who is an otherwise fit parent, that person automatically gets custody under some cases.[21] Some courts permit the preferences of the child to rebut the presumption in favor of the primary caretaker.[22] Other courts merely weigh the presumption as one among many factors in determining custody.[23]

Particularly in its irrebuttable form, the primary caretaker presumption is outcome-determinative and thus injects into custody determinations a modicum of predictability otherwise lacking in the largely *ad hoc* decision-making process that occurs when courts apply the best interest of the child standard with no presumptions. Unpredictability of outcome in custody cases is believed to contribute to unhealthy out-of-court bargaining between spouses who, for example, make bad faith claims for custody in order to induce their spouses to reduce demands for child support, alimony, or property division.[24]

In addition to enhancing the predictability of custody determinations, the primary caretaker presumption tends to maintain intimate parent-child bonds. Assuming that the child is more closely attached to the primary caretaker than to

---

[19]  *Id.*

[20]  Garska v. McCoy, 278 S.E.2d 357, 363 (W. Va. 1981).

[21]  *Id.*

[22]  Rose v. Rose, 340 S.E.2d 176 (W. Va. 1985).

[23]  *See, e.g.*, Brooks v. Brooks, 466 A.2d 152 (Pa. Super. Ct. 1983).

[24]  *See* Garska v. McCoy, 278 S.E.2d 357, 360–61 (W. Va. 1981). One court stated the problem this way:

> Since the legislature has concluded that private ordering by divorcing couples is preferable to judicial ordering, we must insure that each spouse is adequately protected during out-of-court bargaining. Uncertainty of outcome is very destructive to the position of the primary caretaker parent because he or she will be willing to sacrifice everything else in order to avoid the terrible prospect of losing the child in the unpredictable prospect of litigation.

*Id.* at 362.

the other parent, by applying the presumption, the stability of these *status quo* bonds is maintained.[25] On the other hand, courts routinely determine the primary caretaker by merely tallying-up which parent does the larger quantity of tasks associated with the child's day-to-day care without attending to the quality of the parenting. As a result, the child may not necessarily be bonded particularly closely with the primary caretaker nor more closely with the primary caretaker than with the other parent.[26]

## [3]   Race, Religion, and Sexual Orientation of Parents

Until the late twentieth century, courts routinely considered race as a determinative factor in custody cases when parents of different races divorced, generally awarding custody to the minority parent on the theory that society considers the child to be a member of that race.[27] This practice is no longer permissible, however, in light of United States Supreme Court case law interpreting the Equal Protection Clause as forbidding the use of racial considerations in custody cases.[28]

The extent to which courts can or should take religious consideration into account is less clear. While under the Establishment Clause courts cannot favor any particular religion,[29] neither can they deny either parent's exercise of religion when deciding custody cases.[30] Some courts appear to see religious practices of parents as essentially irrelevant, even where they arguably negatively impact the welfare of the child.[31] Other courts expressly consider religious matters when

---

[25]   Clark, *supra* note 3, at 801.

[26]   *See* D. Chambers, *Rethinking the Substantive Rules for Custody Disputes in Divorce*, 83 MICH. L. REV. 477, 527–38 (1984).

[27]   Friedman, *supra* § 3.02, note 14, at 158.

[28]   Palmore v. Sidoti, 466 U.S. 429 (1984). *Palmore* involved two Caucasian parents who divorced. The mother was awarded custody of a three-year old daughter. Several months later the father sought to modify the custody order based on "changed circumstances," namely the mother's cohabitation with a black man whom she eventually married. The father argued that the child would be socially stigmatized if she remained with the mother. The trial court modified the custody award, seeing the mother's interracial relationship as potentially damaging to the child. The Supreme Court reversed, declaring:

> The question . . . is whether the reality of private biases and the possible injury they might inflict are permissible considerations for removal of an infant child from the custody of its natural mother. We have little difficulty concluding that they are not. The Constitution cannot control such prejudices, but neither can it tolerate them. Private biases may be outside the reach of the law, but the law cannot, directly or indirectly, give them effect. "Public officials sworn to uphold the Constitution may not avoid a constitutional duty by bowing to the hypothetical effects of private racial prejudice that they assume to be both widely and deeply held." Palmer v. Thompson, 403 U.S. 217, 260–61 (1971). . . . The effects of racial prejudice, however real, cannot justify a racial classification removing an infant child from the custody of its natural mother found to be an appropriate person to have such custody.

466 U.S. at 433.

[29]   *See, e.g.*, Bonjour v. Bonjour, 592 P.2d 1233 (Alaska 1979) (trial court offended the Establishment Clause by awarding custody to parent simply because court considered her more religious than the other parent).

[30]   *See, e.g.*, Johnson v. Johnson, 564 P.2d 71 (Alaska 1977), *cert. denied*, 434 U.S. 1048 (1978) (mother's free exercise rights violated when trial court considered the potential negative effect on her children of mother's religious views against celebrating holidays and birthdays, joining such organizations as the Brownies, and attending college).

[31]   *Id.*

determining which parent should receive custody. Thus, some courts factor into their decisions such things as a parent's religious beliefs against using particular medical procedures fearing that such beliefs risk potential harm to the child.[32] Sometimes courts identify a parent's radical religious views as themselves inherently inconsistent with the psychological well-being of the child.[33] On the other hand, courts may award custody to the parent deemed better able to meet the religious needs of a "mature child" who has articulated a preference for a particular form of religious life.[34]

The courts have adopted a variety of positions in custody cases raising the issue of parental sexual orientation. Although in the past, few homosexual parents were successful in obtaining custody of their children,[35] the situation has recently changed. While some courts continue to hold that homosexuality is *per se* evidence of parental unfitness,[36] the majority view now requires proof that the parent's homosexuality has an adverse impact on the child.[37] Some courts adopt a rebuttable presumption of adverse impact, placing the burden of showing the absence of an adverse impact on the homosexual parent.[38]

## [4]  The Child's Preference

In some jurisdictions, statutes either require the court to honor the child's preference as to her custodian or permit the court to consider such preferences when granting custody, provided the child has reached a specified age or the child is sufficiently mature to make a decision as to custody.[39] In the absence of direct statutory guidance, the courts have discretion to give the child's preferences whatever input they see fit.[40]

---

[32] *See, e.g., In re* Marriage of Short, 698 P.2d 1310 (Colo. 1985) (evidence of a party's religious belief or practice, here Jehovah Witness views forbidding blood transfusions, is relevant in custody cases if shown that such belief or practice is reasonably likely to cause present or future harm to physical or mental development of child).

[33] *See, e.g.,* Burnham v. Burnham, 304 N.W.2d 58 (Neb. 1981) (permissible to consider possible adverse impact on child of mother's beliefs as member of Tridentine Church that child is illegitimate, that child will be cut out of mother's life if the child disobeys rules of the Church, and that a "master plot" exists between Jews and Communists to "gain control of the world"). For criticism of *Burnham,* see R.C. Mangrum, *Exclusive Reliance on Best Interests May be Unconstitutional: Religion as a Factor in Child Custody Cases,* 15 CREIGHTON L. REV. 25 (1981).

[34] *See supra* note 29; *see also* T. v. H., 245 A.2d 221 (N.J. Super. Ct. Ch. Div. 1968) (where parental separation agreement specifies that children will be raised in Jewish faith, court awarded custody of children to father on ground that their upbringing in that religion could better occur in New Jersey where father lived rather than in Idaho where mother resided).

[35] Mnookin & Weisberg, *supra* § 1.02, note 8, at 827.

[36] *Id.*

[37] *Id.*

[38] *Id.*

[39] *Id.*

[40] *See* Friedman, *supra* note 27, at 161.

## [5]  Joint Custody

In the latter quarter of the twentieth century, joint custody awards have become widespread.[41] Under joint custody situations, legal custody is at all times shared equally by both parents even though one may possess a more extensive right to physical custody than the other.[42] In some jurisdictions, joint custody is preferred,[43] in others it is merely optional,[44] and in still others it is permitted but disfavored except in rare cases.[45]

Proponents of joint custody see it benefitting both parents and children by preserving the child's contacts with both parents and avoiding the trauma associated with her loss of contact with either.[46] Moreover, parents in joint custody arrangements may feel loss hostility towards each other than if a traditional sole custody order had been imposed.[47]

On the other hand, critics argue that joint custody may result in less stability for the child if she experiences extensive contact with the noncustodial parent.[48] In addition, joint custody may exacerbate long-standing inter-parental hostilities creating distress and anxiety in the child.[49] Finally, parents who are not primary caretakers might make bad faith claims for joint custody in order to induce the primary caretaker to agree to reductions in the amounts she claims for maintenance or child support.[50]

Whatever its merits, joint custody is disfavored if the parents are unwilling to work together in promoting the benefits of the arrangement.[51] Lack of parental cooperation is often a factor leading to divorce, and often persists thereafter inhibiting the effectiveness of joint custody.[52]

## [6]  Visitation Rights

In making custody awards, courts routinely grant visitation rights to noncustodial parents where consistent with "the best interests of the child."[53] Generally, the same factors are used to determine the child's best interest for both custody and visitation issues.[54]

---

[41]  Horowitz & Davison, *supra* § 3.02, note 28, at 239.

[42]  *Id.*

[43]  Clark, *supra* note 3, at 815.

[44]  *Id.*

[45]  *See, e.g.*, Neb. Rev. Stat. § 42-364(5) (Reissue 1998) ("the court may place the custody of a minor child [in] joint custody"); Wilson v. Wilson, 399 N.W.2d 802, 803 (Neb. 1987) ("joint custody is not favored and must be reserved for only the rarest of cases").

[46]  Clark, *supra* note 3, at 816.

[47]  *Id.*

[48]  *Id.*

[49]  *Id.* at 817.

[50]  *Id.; see* K. Bartlett & C. Stack, *Joint Custody, Feminism and the Dependency Dilemma*, 2 Berkeley Women's L.J. 9, 19–20 (1986).

[51]  *See, e.g., In re* Marriage of Weidner, 338 N.W.2d 351 (Iowa 1983).

[52]  Mnookin & Weisberg, *supra* note 35, at 858.

[53]  Horowitz & Davidson, *supra* note 41, at 252.

[54]  Clark, *supra* note 3, at 812.

Recently, nearly all jurisdictions have allowed for grandparent visitation in one form or another.[55] Some statutes limit such visitation to situations where the parent is deceased, while others extend the right to cases of divorce, annulment, or separation.[56]

The United States Supreme Court has held that grandparents do not enjoy a constitutional right to visit their grandchildren when such visitation is objected to by the children's parents.[57] The Court reaffirmed the fundamental right of parents to make decisions concerning the care, custody, and control of their children. In explaining how the application of the state nonparental visitation statute granting grandparent visitation rights offended parental rights, the Court observed:

> The Washington nonparental visitation statute is breathtakingly broad. According to the statute's text, "*any person* may petition the court for visitation rights *at any time*," and the court may grant such visitation rights whenever "visitation may serve *the best interest of the child*." That language effectively permits any third party seeking visitation to subject any decision by a parent concerning visitation of the parent's children to state-court review.

> Once the visitation petition has been filed in court and the matter is placed before a judge, a parent's decision that visitation would not be in the child's best interest is accorded no deference. [The statute] contains no requirement that a court accord the parent's decision any presumption of validity or any weight whatsoever. Instead, the Washington statute places the best-interest determination solely in the hands of the judge. Should the judge disagree with the parent's estimation of the child's best interests, the judge's view necessarily prevails. Thus, in practical effect, in the State of Washington a court can disregard and overturn *any* decision by a fit custodial parent concerning visitation whenever a third party affected by the decision files a visitation petition, based solely on the judge's determination of the child's best interests.[58]

Similar to grandparents, stepparents sometimes are allowed visitation rights.[59] Some courts authorize visitation to anyone standing *in loco parentis* to the child[60] although this rarely extends beyond stepparentage situations.[61]

While court ordered visitation clearly recognizes the rights of noncustodial parents to have a relationship with their children, visitation is also thought beneficial for the child by promoting contacts with both parents.[62] Some leading commentators vehemently disagree with this latter point and oppose judicial

---

[55] Krause, *supra* § 3.01, note 1, at 322.

[56] *Id.* at 322–23.

[57] Troxel v. Granville, 530 U.S. 57 (2000).

[58] *Id.* at 67.

[59] Wadlington, *supra* § 3.02, note 11, at 721–23.

[60] *Id.* at 721–22.

[61] *See, e.g.*, Alison D. v. Virginia M., 572 N.E.2d 27 (N.Y. 1991) (court denied visitation to woman who had lived with child and her mother during child's early years — child referred to both women as "Mommy").

[62] Clark, *supra* note 3, at 811–12.

visitation orders as potentially disruptive to the stability of the child's relationship with the custodial parent and thus inconsistent with the child's best interest.[63]

## [B] Disputes Between Parents and Non-Parents

Sometimes custody disputes arise between a natural parent or parents and a non-parent.[64] Aside from cases where the natural parent is unfit,[65] the courts usually apply a heavy preference in favor of the natural parent on the theory that the parent possesses a constitutional right to custody of the child.[66] Many courts automatically award custody to the natural parent without making a specific finding that such disposition is in "the best interest of the child."[67] In some jurisdictions, courts are directed to award custody to the parent unless it is shown that such a decision would be detrimental to the child.[68]

Other courts pay somewhat less deference to parental rights. For example, some apply the best interests of the child test with a rebuttable presumption that those interests will be better served by granting custody to the natural parent.[69]

When applying the best interests of the child standard, courts sometimes afford a preference to "psychological parents,"[70] persons with whom the child has

---

[63] *See* Goldstein, Freud & Solnit, *supra* § 3.03, note 29, at 38 (noncustodial parent should have no visitation rights; any visitation should be within the discretion of the custodial parent).

[64] These disputes arise in a variety of contexts, for example, as a consequence of divorce; in proceedings determining guardianship, dependency, or neglect; and actions preceding adoption. Clark, *supra* note 3, at 820.

[65] "Unfitness" entails serious parental inadequacy including neglect, abandonment, child abuse, inability to care for the child, or a showing that the child will suffer serious physical or emotional harm if permitted to reside with the parent. *Id.* at 823.

[66] *Id.* at 821–24; *see also* Stanley v. Illinois, 405 U.S. 645 (1972) (statute making children of unwed parents automatic wards of the state upon death of the mother held unconstitutional as denial of father's right to custody, at least where father had assumed parental responsibilities prior to the mother's death); Bennett v. Jeffreys, 356 N.E.2d 277, 281 (N.Y. 1976) ("parent has a 'right' to rear her child, and child has a 'right' to be reared by its [sic] parent"); Custody of Minor, 452 N.E.2d 483, 489 (Mass. 1983) ("parents have a natural right to custody of their children").

[67] Clark, *supra* note 3, at 801.

[68] *See, e.g.*, Cal. Fam. Code § 3040(a) (1994 & Supp. 2002).

Custody should be granted in the following order of preference according to the best interest of the child as provided in Sections 3011 and 3020:

(1) To both parents jointly pursuant to Chapter 4 (commencing with Section 3080) or to either parent. In making an order granting custody to either parent, the court shall consider, among other factors, which parent is more likely to allow the child frequent and continuing contact with the noncustodial parent, consistent with Section 3011 and 3020, and shall not prefer a parent as custodian because of that parent's sex. The court, in its discretion, may require the parents to submit to the court a plan for the implementation of the custody order.

(2) If to neither parent, to the person or persons in whose home the child has been living in a wholesome and stable environment.

(3) To any other person or persons deemed by the court to be suitable and able to provide adequate and proper care and guidance for the child.

---

[69] *See, e.g.*, Rowles v. Rowles, 668 A.2d 126 (Pa. 1995) (parent-child relationship should be accorded "special weight" and "deference" and should not be disturbed absent a showing of harm or other circumstances that clearly indicate an award of custody to a non-parent is appropriate).

[70] "A psychological parent is one who, on a continuing, day-to-day basis, through interaction,

established a parent-child bond. Thus, one court found that while ordinarily natural parents automatically prevail in custody disputes with non-parents, the fact that the child had resided all eight years of her life with the non-parent constituted an "extraordinary circumstance" requiring application of the best interest test.[71] Under that test, the court eventually found that the non-parent was the child's psychological parent and awarded custody to her, in part at least, because "to remove the child from th[e] relationship [with the non-parent] would endanger the development of the child."[72]

## [C] Jurisdictional Issues

Historically, courts liberally assumed jurisdiction to impose original custody orders or to modify existing ones. Courts possessed jurisdiction over custody matters if, *inter alia*, the child in question was domiciled or merely present in the court's state.[73] Moreover, since the United States Supreme Court has never held that the Full Faith and Credit Clause of the Constitution applies to custody decrees of sister states, state courts felt little constraint in modifying decrees of sister sates and awarding custody to a different person.[74] As a consequence of these jurisdictional doctrines, non-custodial parents often "snatched" children from custodians and took the children to other states in order to gain favorable custody orders from the courts of the latter state.[75]

In order to discourage child-snatching and to afford greater stability to custody arrangements, Congress enacted the Parental Kidnapping Prevention Act (PKPA).[76] The states adopted a similar statutory model, the Uniform Child Custody Jurisdiction Act (UCCJA).[77] Both the PKPA and UCCJA eliminate jurisdiction based on mere presence and grant jurisdiction, *inter alia*, to the child's "homestate"[78] or to a state in which the child and at least one parent have a

---

companionship, interplay, and mutuality, fulfills the child's psychological needs for a parent, as well as the child's physical needs." Goldstein, Freud & Solnit, *supra* note 61, at 98. Another commentator describes a "psychological parent" as "a person or group of persons who provide [infants and young children] consistent expressions of affection, confirmation of self-worth, and stimulation or curiosity and growth." Richards, *supra* § 1.01, note 1, at 21. For an example of a court's recognition of psychological parenthood as an influential factor in its decision, see *Daley v. Gunville*, 348 N.W.2d 441, 445 (N.D. 1984) ("establishment of a psychological parent relationship . . . furnishes justification for the award of custody to a party other than the natural parent" if "such an award would be in the child's best interests").

[71] Bennett v. Jeffreys, 356 N.E.2d 277 (N.Y. 1976).

[72] Bennett v. Marrow, 399 N.Y.S.2d 697, 699–700 (N.Y. App. Div. 1977).

[73] B. Bodenheimer & J. Neeley-Kvarme, *Jurisdiction Over Child Custody and Adoption After Shaffer and Kulko*, U.C. Davis L. Rev. 229, 245 (1979).

[74] People *ex rel.* Halvey v. Halvey, 330 U.S. 610 (1947); Comment, Ford v. Ford *: Full Faith and Credit To Child Custody Decrees?*, 73 Yale L.J. 134 (1963).

[75] Child-snatching became increasingly common in the 1950s and 1960s. Bodenheimer & Neeley-Kvarme, *supra* note 73, at 245–46.

[76] Parental Kidnapping Prevention Act of 1980, 28 U.S.C. § 1738A (West 1994) (hereinafter PKPA).

[77] Uniform Child Custody Jurisdiction Act, 9 U.L.A. 115 (1988 & Supp. 1995) (hereinafter UCCJA). The UCCJA was adopted, with minor modifications, in all fifty states. Krause, *supra* note 55, at 329.

[78] Both the UCCJA and the PKPA define "homestate" in essence as

the state in which the child immediately preceding the time involved lived with his parents, a parent, or a person acting as a parent, for at least 6 consecutive months, and in the case of a child less than 6 months old the state in which the child lived from birth with any of the

"significant connection."[79] Both statutory models place severe restrictions on the ability of courts to modify orders issued by a court in a sister state.[80]

The UCCJA has been replaced in most states by its successor, the Uniform Child Custody Jurisdiction and Enforcement Act (UCCJEA).[81] The UCCJEA was

---

persons mentioned. Periods of temporary absence of any of the named persons are counted as part of the 6-month or other period.

UCCJA, *supra* note 77, § 2(5). *Cf.* PKPA, *supra* note 76, §§ 1738A(b)(4), (c)(2)(A).

[79] *Compare* UCCJA, *supra* note 77, § 3(a)(2), *with* PKPA, *supra* note 76, § 1738A (c)(2)(B). The federal statute grants jurisdiction under the "significant connection" provision only if no other state would have "homestate" jurisdiction. On the other hand, the UCCJA posits either the "homestate" or the "significant connection" provision as sufficient ground for jurisdiction. Some courts have held that the federal statute preempts the UCCJA on this point. *See, e.g.,* Shute v. Shute, 607 A.2d 890 (Vt. 1992).

The United States Supreme Court has determined that the PKPA does not create federal court jurisdiction to resolve custody disputes between two or more states. In Thompson v. Thompson, 484 U.S. 174, 175 (1988) the Court held:

> The PKPA does not provide an implied cause of action in federal court to determine which of two conflicting state custody decisions is valid. The context in which the PKPA was enacted — the existence of jurisdictional deadlocks among the States in custody cases and a nationwide problem of interstate parental kidnapping — suggests that Congress' principal aim was to extend the requirements of the Full Faith and Credit Clause to custody determinations and not to create an entirely new cause of action. The language and placement of the Act reinforce this conclusion, in that the Act is an addendum to, and is therefore clearly intended to have the same operative effect as, the federal full faith and credit statute, the Act's heading is "Full faith and credit given to child custody determinations," and, unlike statutes that explicitly confer a right on a specified class of persons, the Act is addressed to States and to state courts. [T]he PKPA's legislative history provides an unusually clear indication that Congress did not intend the federal courts to play the enforcement role.

[80] UCCJA, *supra* note 77, § 14 provides:

[Modification of Custody Decree of Another State.]

(a) If a court of another state has made a custody decree, a court of this State shall not modify that decree unless (1) it appears to the court of this State that the court which rendered the decree does not now have jurisdiction under jurisdictional prerequisites substantially in accordance with this Act or has declined to assume jurisdiction to modify the decree and (2) the court of this State has jurisdiction.

See the analogous provision in the PKPA, *supra* note 76, § 1738A(f).

Consider also UCCJA, *supra* note 77, § 8 which provides:

[Jurisdiction Declined by Reason of Conduct.]

(a) If the petitioner for an initial decree has wrongfully taken the child from another state or has engaged in similar reprehensible conduct the court may decline to exercise jurisdiction if this is just and proper under the circumstances.

(b) Unless required in the interest of the child, the court shall not exercise its jurisdiction to modify a custody decree of another state if the petitioner, without consent of the person entitled to custody, has improperly removed the child from the physical custody of the person entitled to custody or has improperly retained the child after a visit or other temporary relinquishment of physical custody. If the petitioner has violated any other provision of a custody decree of another state the court may decline to exercise its jurisdiction if this is just and proper under the circumstances.

---

[81] Unif. Child Custody Jurisdiction and Enforcement Act, 9(1A) U.L.A. 657 (1997), *available at* http://www.law.upenn.edu/bll/archives/ulc/fnact99/1990s/uccjea97.pdf. As of 2008, the UCCJEA had

created to (1) clarify points of law interpreted inconsistently by the various states under the UCCJA, (2) fix problems of application created by the intersection of the UCCJA with federal statutes such as the PKPA, and (3) implement procedures for enforcing interstate child custody and visitation decisions.[82] The UCCJEA incorporated the PKPA's home state preference, and at least one court has said that the "best interests of the child" analysis is not an appropriate alternative to "home state" analysis where a home state exists.[83]

Parental kidnapping also occurs on an international basis, and for those cases the Hague Convention on Civil Aspects of International Child Abduction and its implementing legislation, the International Child Abduction Remedies Act (ICARA), apply.[84] Like the UCCJA and UCCJEA, the Hague Convention and ICARA address the procedures for choosing which court will decide the substantive custody issues.[85] They generally require that the wrongfully taken child be returned to the country from which he or she was removed, but provide exceptions for situations wherein the child would be in danger of physical or psychological harm.[86]

## [D] Theoretical Implications

Child custody law almost exclusively assumes a protectionist attitude towards children. The personhood theory of rights appears, if at all, only in those cases and statutes that afford the mature child a right to decide which parent will be her custodian.[87]

---

been adopted in all states except Vermont, New Hampshire, Missouri, and Massachusetts. National Conference of Commissioners on State Laws, A Few Facts About the Uniform Child Custody Jurisdiction and Enforcement Act, http://www.nccusl.org/Update/uniformact_factsheets/uniformacts-fs-uccjea.asp (last visited June 19, 2008). The UCCJEA has also been adopted in the District of Columbia. D.C. Code §§ 16-4601.1 to -4604.2 (LexisNexis 2001); V.I. Code Ann. tit. 16, §§ 115–140 (LexisNexis 2008).

[82] Unif. Child Custody Jurisdiction and Enforcement Act, *supra* note 81, prefatory note.

[83] 1 D. Kramer, Legal Rights of Children § 5:17 (rev. 2d ed. 2005 & Supp. 2007) (citing Welch-Doden v. Roberts, 42 P.3d 1166 (Ariz. Ct. App. 2002)).

[84] 42 U.S.C. §§ 11601–11610 (1988); Hague Convention on Civil Aspects of International Child Abduction, S. Treaty Doc. No. 99-11, 99th Cong., 1st Sess. 9 (1980) (hereinafter "Convention"); *see also* M. Ventrell & D. Duquette, Child Welfare Law and Practice 242–44 (2005) (discussing these laws in depth).

[85] Ventrell & Duquette, *supra* note 83, at 242.

[86] *Id.* at 243. "Removal or retention of a child is wrongful under the Hague Convention if a parent has taken the child out of the country in violation of the other parent's custody rights." Kramer, *supra* note 83, at § 5:23.

[87] *See supra* notes 35–40 and accompanying text.

# Chapter 4
# CHILD ABUSE

## § 4.01  OVERVIEW

As mentioned earlier, parents historically have been afforded broad authority to discipline their children "in a reasonable manner."[1] Under the common law, parents are permitted to inflict corporal punishment so long as it does not become "excessive."[2] Moreover, the common law extends the right to use reasonable force in disciplining children to non-parents who stand *in loco parentis*.[3] While excessive corporal punishment or other manifestations of child mistreatment constitute crimes at common law and are clearly outside the scope of any constitutionally protected parental right,[4] until recently prosecutions of child abusers were few and reserved for cases of blatant and clearly outrageous misconduct.[5]

Because child abuse usually occurs outside the public eye with victims often incapable of reporting its occurrence, the incidence and extent of the problem has always been difficult to document.[6] Lately, however, alarming evidence has surfaced suggesting extensive mistreatment of children manifesting itself in a variety of shocking forms of physical, psychological, and sexual abuse.[7]

In the mid 1950's, the medical profession identified the "battered child syndrome," a diagnostic vehicle for distinguishing accidental injuries common to

---

[1] *Supra* § 3.01, note 7 and accompanying text.

[2] *See, e.g.*, Interest of Aaronson, 382 N.E.2d 853 (Ill. App. Ct. 1978) (paddling one's own child permissible in absence of clear evidence the paddling was "vicious" or done for other than disciplinary reasons); *In re* Edward C., 178 Cal. Rptr. 694 (Cal. App. 1981) (repeated beatings of eight-year-old girl by her father, using a leather strap, in order to discipline her according to "God's will" held impermissible).

[3] *See, e.g.*, Clasan v. Pruhs, 95 N.W. 640 (Neb. 1903) (one caring for child); Gorman v. State, 42 Tex. 221 (1875) (stepfather); State v. Alford, 68 N.C. 322 (1873) (paramour of mother). *But see* Rodriguez v. Johnson, 504 N.Y.S.2d 379 (1986) (slap of child by school bus matron constituted "physical abuse" that the court held to be "immoral, unethical, and seriously harmful" to the child).

At common law, a child's teacher stood *in loco parentis, see, e.g., In re* Donaldson, 75 Cal. Rptr. 220 (Cal. Ct. App. 1969), and was therefore permitted to impose reasonable, but not excessive, force to discipline the student. 1 W. Blackstone, Commentaries *134, *453, 3 W. Blackstone, Commentaries *120. While courts generally no longer see teachers as standing *in loco parentis, see, e.g.,* New Jersey v. T.L.O., 469 U.S. 325, 336 (1985), teachers nevertheless continue to be permitted to use "reasonable" force to control, train, and educate the student. Restatement (Second) of Torts § 147(2) (1965). Model Penal Code § 3.08(1), (2) (1985) specifically justifies parents, guardians, and teachers in using force against minors in their charge in order to "promote the welfare of the minor" or "maintain reasonable discipline" so long as the force is "not designed to cause or create a substantial risk of causing death, serious bodily harm, disfigurement, extreme pain, or mental distress or gross degradation."

Some states have legislatively outlawed corporal punishment. *See, e.g.*, Mass. Gen. Laws. Ann. ch. 71, § 37G (West 1996); N.J. Stat. Ann. § 18A:6-1 (West 1999).

[4] Kramer, *supra* § 3.03, note 15, at 6–7, 10.

[5] M. Paulsen, G. Parker & L. Adelman, *Child Abuse Reporting Laws — Some Legislative History*, 34 Geo. Wash. L. Rev. 482, 483 (1966); Kramer, *supra* note 3, at 6–7.

[6] Comment, *Evidentiary Problems in Criminal Child Abuse Prosecutions*, 63 Geo. L.J. 257, 259–61 (1974). Even where child abuse victims are old enough to recount their abuse, they are often pressured by the abuser to keep quiet. *Id.*

[7] Kramer, *supra* note 4, at 5–6.

children from injuries inflicted by adult human agents.[8] With this development, policy makers became aware of the widespread problem of child abuse.[9] In response, legislatures nationwide enacted criminal statutes specifically aimed at curbing this insidious evil.[10] Moreover, regarding evidentiary issues, courts and legislatures have generated a body of law sensitized to the problem of child abuse.[11]

## § 4.02  CHILD ABUSE LEGISLATION

### [A]  Defining Child Abuse

Most states have enacted statutes specifically prohibiting abuse of children.[1] A number of these statutes attempt to define the term "child abuse," sometimes limiting the definition to situations resulting in physical harm to the child, thus excluding cases of psychological injury. For example, Georgia defines child abuse as "[p]hysical injury or death inflicted upon a child by a parent or caretaker thereof by other than accidental means; provided, however, physical forms of discipline may be used as long as there is no physical injury to the child."[2] In addition to specifying physical injury, the statutes routinely include adult sexual interaction with a child under their definitions of child abuse.[3] In California, for example, child abuse includes not only physical injuries non-accidently caused by human agents[4] but also, *inter alia*, "sexual abuse" and "sexual exploitation"[5] of a child.

---

[8] The "battered child syndrome" is a term used to characterize a clinical condition in young children who have received serious and often recurrent physical injuries, generally at the hands of a parent or primary caretaker. *See* C. Kempe, F. Silverman, P. Steelel, W. Droegemuller, & H. Silver, *The Battered Child Syndrome*, 181 JAMA 17 (1962). For a history of the medical profession's role in identifying the syndrome, see A. McCoid, *The Battered Child and Other Assaults Upon the Family*, 50 MINN. L. REV. 1 (1965). For further discussion of the battered child syndrome, see *infra* § 4.03, notes 3–12 and accompanying text.

[9] While it is difficult to accurately measure the extent of child abuse in American society, the evidence suggests that at least one million children are abused and mistreated yearly. *See* Davis & Schwartz, *supra* § 3.02, note 51, at 169–73.

[10] *See* Paulsen, Parker & Adelman, *supra* note 5, at 482–83.

[11] *See infra* § 4.03.

[1] Friedman, *supra* § 3.02, note 14, at 134.

[2] Ga. Code Ann. § 19-15-1(3)(A) (1999). "Sexual abuse" or "sexual exploitation" of a minor also constitute child abuse; *see id.* at § (C), (D) (1999).

[3] *See, e.g., infra* notes 4–5.

[4] Cal. Penal Code § 11165.6 (West 2000 & Supp. 2001) (" 'child abuse' means a physical injury inflicted by other than accidental means on a child by another person").

[5] *Id.* The California statute defines "sexual abuse" and "sexual exploitation" as follows:

As used in this article, "sexual abuse" means sexual assault or sexual exploitation as defined by the following:

(a) "Sexual assault" means conduct in violation of one or more of the following sections: Section 261 (rape), subdivision (d) of Section 261.5 (statutory rape), 264.1 (rape in concert), 285 (incest), 286 (sodomy), subdivision (a) or (b) or Section 288 (lewd or lascivious acts upon a child under 14 years of age), 288a (oral copulation), 289 (penetration of a genital or anal opening by a foreign object), or 647a (child molestation).

. . .

(c) "Sexual exploitation" refers to any of the following:

(1) Conduct involving matter depicting a minor engaged in obscene acts in violation of Section 311.2 (preparing, selling, or distributing obscene matter) or subdivision (a) of

Section 311.4 (employment of minor to perform obscene acts).

(2) Any person who knowingly promotes, aids, or assists, employs, uses, persuades, induces, or coerces a child, or any person responsible for a child's welfare, who knowingly permits or encourages a child to engage in, or assist others to engage in, prostitution or a live performance involving obscene sexual conduct, or to either pose or model alone or with others for purposes of preparing a film, photograph, negative, slide, drawing, painting, or other pictorial depiction, involving obscene sexual conduct. For the purpose of this section, "person responsible for a child's welfare" means a parent, guardian, foster parent, or a licensed administrator or employee of a public or private residential home, residential school, or other residential institution.

(3) Any person who depicts a child in, or who knowingly develops, duplicates, prints, or exchanges, any film, photograph, video tape, negative, or slide in which a child is engaged in an act of obscene sexual conduct, except for those activities by law enforcement and prosecution agencies and other persons described in subdivisions (c) and (e) of Section 311.3.

*Id.* § 11165.1. The California statute also includes the following as manifestations of "child abuse":

Willful cruelty or unjustifiable punishment of a child.

As used in this article, "willful cruelty or unjustifiable punishment of a child" means a situation where any person willfully causes or permits any child to suffer, or inflicts thereon, unjustifiable physical pain or mental suffering, or having the care or custody of any child, willfully causes or permits the person or health of the child to be placed in a situation such that his or her person or health is endangered.

*Id.* § 11165.3.

Unlawful corporal punishment or injury.

As used in this article, "unlawful corporal punishment or injury" means a situation where any person willfully inflicts upon any child any cruel or inhuman corporal punishment or injury resulting in a traumatic condition. It does not include an amount of force that is reasonable and necessary for a person employed by or engaged in a public school to quell a disturbance threatening physical injury to person or damage to property, for purposes of self-defense, or to obtain possession of weapons or other dangerous objects within the control of the pupil. . . .

*Id.* 11165.4.

Neglect; severe neglect; general neglect.

As used in this article, "neglect" means the negligent treatment or the maltreatment of a child by a person responsible for the child's welfare under circumstances indicating harm or threatened harm to the child's health or welfare. The term includes both acts and omissions on the part of the responsible person.

. . . .

*Id.* § 11165.2.

Abuse or neglect in out-of-home care.

As used in this article, the term 'abuse or neglect in out-of-home care' includes physical injury inflicted upon a child by another person by other than accidental means, sexual abuse as defined in Section 11165.1, neglect as defined in Section 11165.2, unlawful corporal punishment or injury as defined in Section 11165.4, or the willful cruelty or unjustifiable punishment of a child, as defined in Section 11165.3, where the person responsible for the child's welfare is a licensee, administrator, or employee of any facility licensed to care for children, or an administrator or employee of a public or private school or other institution or agency. 'Abuse or neglect in out-of-home care' does not include an injury caused by reasonable and necessary force used by a peace officer acting within the course and scope of his or her employment as a peace officer.

In addition to focusing on physical injury and sexual exploitation, many statutes also define child abuse in terms of conduct that causes psychological harm to the child. For example, Florida defines child abuse as "any willful act or threatened act that results in any physical, mental, or sexual injury or harm that causes or is likely to cause the child's physical, mental, or emotional health to be significantly impaired."[6] The Wyoming statutes elaborate on psychological harm as a manifestation of child abuse:

> 'Abuse' means inflicting or causing physical or mental injury, harm or imminent danger to the physical or mental health or welfare of a child other than by accidental means, including abandonment, excessive or unreasonable corporal punishment, malnutrition or substantial risk thereof by reason of intentional or unintentional neglect, and the commission or allowing the commission of a sexual offense against a child as defined by law:
>
> (A) 'Mental injury' means an injury to the psychological capacity or emotional stability of a child as evidenced by an observable or substantial impairment in his ability to function within a normal range of performance and behavior with due regard to his culture. . . .[7]

Similar to situations of neglect,[8] the presence of child abuse may trigger a variety of state responses. Often the state will take custody of the abused child and move to terminate the parental rights of the abusive parents if the situation is sufficiently serious.[9] Moreover, child abuse is a crime that may subject the abuser to punishment through the criminal justice system.

As a criminal matter, proof of child abuse generally requires showing that the abuser culpably committed the offense.[10] As with most other crimes, purposely, knowingly, or recklessly committing the proscribed acts constitutes sufficient criminal intent to render the offender guilty of child abuse.[11] Some statutes extend liability further to persons who negligently cause a child to be abused,[12] sometimes punishing negligent abuse less severely than abuse intentionally or knowingly inflicted.[13] At least one court seemingly has taken the highly controversial position

---

*Id.* § 11165.5.

[6] Fla. Stat. Ann § 39.01(2) (West 2000); *see also* Cal. Penal Code § 11165.3 (West 2000).

[7] Wyo. Stat. § 14-3-202(a)(ii) (2001).

[8] *See supra* § 3.03[B][2], [3].

[9] *Id.*

[10] Kramer, *supra* § 3.03, note 15, at 13.

[11] *See* M. Gardner, *The Mens Rea Enigma: Observations on the Role of Motive in the Criminal Law Past and Present,* 1993 UTAH L. REV. 635, 667–85; State v. O'Brien, 508 N.E.2d 144 (Ohio 1987) ("recklessness" is the minimal culpability essential for the crime of child abuse).

[12] *See, e.g.,* Neb. Rev. Stat. § 28-710(3) (Reissue 1995):

> "Abuse . . . shall mean knowingly, intentionally, or negligently causing or permitting a minor child to be: [p]laced in a situation that endangers his or her life or physical or mental health; cruelly . . . punished; . . . sexually abused; or sexually exploited. . . ."

[13] *See, e.g.,* Tex. Penal Code Ann. § 22.04(e), (g) (West 1994) ('intentionally or knowingly" injuring a child is a "felony of the first degree" while "negligently" doing so constitutes a "state jail felony").

that child abuse is a strict liability crime requiring no showing that the abuser acted culpably.[14]

A substantial number of cases address the situation where parents are charged with child abuse for failing to protect their children from abuse directly inflicted by the parent's lover.[15] Where the parent is aware of the abuse, she is generally held liable, even where she offers the common excuses that she tolerated the abuse because she feared losing her lover or being abused herself if she intervened.[16] If the parent is unaware of the abuse, she may nevertheless be guilty under statutes embracing negligence as a basis for liability. In any case, the person directly abusing the child is of course himself also guilty.

## [1] Constitutional Attacks

While a number of child abuse statutes have been attacked on vagueness grounds, the courts have generally upheld their constitutionality.[17] In a Maryland case,[18] for example, the defendant appealed his conviction for a disciplinary beating of the fifteen-year-old daughter of his live-in companion. The defendant struck the daughter fifteen to twenty times with a belt on her back, legs, arms, and neck. He was convicted under a child abuse statute prohibiting "physical injury or injuries sustained by a child as a result of cruel or inhuman treatment or as a result of malicious acts" by parents or caretakers.[19] In rejecting defendant's argument that the terms "cruel or inhuman treatment" and "malicious acts" were unconstitutionally vague, the court stated:

> Webster's Third New International Dictionary defines the word "cruel" as "disposed to inflict pain [especially] in a wanton, insensate, or vindictive manner: pleased by hurting others: sadistic." The word "inhuman," a variant of "inhumane," is defined by the same authority as "lacking the qualities of mercy, pity, kindness, or tenderness: cruel, barbarous, savage . . . ." Black's Law Dictionary (4th ed. 1968) defines the term "cruelty" as "the intentional and malicious infliction of physical suffering upon living creatures, particularly human beings; . . . applied to the latter, the wanton and unnecessary infliction of pain upon the body.' Clearly, then, the standard "cruel or inhumane" has a settled and commonly understood meaning.
>
> . . . Long before the advent of contemporary child abuse legislation, it was a well-recognized precept of Anglo-American jurisprudence that the

---

[14] *See* State v. Lucero, 647 P.2d 406, 408–9 (N.M. 1982) (court rejected mother's duress defense to the charge that she permitted her paramour to abuse her child on ground that child abuse is a "strict liability" crime even though statute defines the offense in terms of "knowingly, intentionally, or negligently" endangering a child). For criticism of *Lucero*, see Gardner, *supra* note 11, at 738–41. *See also* Santillanes v. State, 849 P.2d 358 (N.M. 1993) ("criminal negligence" rather than "civil negligence" is the proper ground for culpability under the New Mexico child abuse statute). *Santillanes* thus appears to reject the *Lucero* court's view that child abuse is a "strict liability" crime in New Mexico.

[15] Kramer, *supra* note 10, at 15.

[16] *Id.* See also *State v. Lucero*, 647 P.2d 406 (N.M. 1982), where a mother was held guilty of child abuse for failing to protect her child from beatings at the hands of the mother's live-in companion whom the mother feared would also beat her if she intervened to protect her child.

[17] Davis & Schwartz, *supra* § 3.02, note 51, at 168.

[18] Bowers v. State, 389 A.2d 341 (Md. 1978).

[19] *Id.* at 344.

parent of a minor child or one standing *in loco parentis* was justified in using a reasonable amount of force upon a child for the purpose of safeguarding or promoting the child's welfare. So long as the chastisement was moderate and reasonable, in light of the age, condition and disposition of the child, and other surrounding circumstances, the parent or custodian would not incur criminal liability for assault and battery or a similar offense.

> . . . .

> . . . [T]he terminology employed in [the instant statute] appears to be nothing but a codification of the common law principles concerning the limits of permissible parental chastisement. Since the contours of the common law privilege have been subject for centuries to definition and refinement through careful and constant judicial decisionmaking, terms like "cruel or inhumane" and "malicious" have acquired a relatively widely accepted connotation in the law. The use of such phraseology in the child abuse statute would, therefore, not render the law constitutionally infirm. . . .[20]

On the other hand, at least one court has invalidated child abuse legislation as unconstitutionally vague. In a Kansas case[21] the court struck down a statute prohibiting "willfully . . . [c]ausing or permitting a child under eighteen (18) years to suffer unjustifiable physical pain or mental distress. . . ."[22] Because the case involved physical spanking,[23] the court focused its attention on the vagueness of the "unjustifiable physical pain" language. The court stated:

> How does one decide whether or not a spanking is due a child and, if so, should it be administered with the hands, a fly swatter, or a belt? Is one slap, two slaps, or five slaps too many? Are two hard slaps a violation of the statute but five very light slaps not? Do red marks lasting only one hour relieve one from prosecution? Some persons do not believe in any form of corporal punishment and to them any such treatment would be unjustified. On the other hand others may believe any correction, however severe, which produces temporary pain only, and no lasting injury or disfigurement, is justified. The statute could conceivably cover anything from a minor spanking or slapping to severe beating depending upon the personal beliefs of the individual.[24]

## [2]  Policy Implications

As the discussion immediately above illustrates, the line between permissible parental discipline and illicit child abuse is sometimes difficult to draw, particularly where statutes employ imprecise definitions of illegal abuse. Broad definitions are sometimes defended on the basis that child protective workers and courts require

---

[20]  *Id.* at 347–49. For other cases upholding child abuse statutes attacked as unconstitutionally vague, see *State v. Sinica*, 372 N.W.2d 445 (Neb. 1985) ("cruelly punished" not vague), and *People v. Jennings*, 641 P.2d 276 (Colo. 1982) ("cruelly punished" not vague).

[21]  State v. Meinert, 594 P.2d 232 (Kan. 1979).

[22]  *Id.* at 233, 235.

[23]  The defendant spanked a three-year-old whom she was baby-sitting because the child urinated on the floor. The child's parents claimed that red marks were still visible on the child's buttocks four hours after the spanking took place. *Id.* at 232.

[24]  *Id.* at 234–35.

flexibility to exercise discretion in determining, on a case-by-case basis, whether particular situations constitute "child abuse."[25] On the other hand, some see broad and imprecise definitions as encouraging arbitrariness and injustice.[26] The potential for misuse of discretion by state authorities is especially acute where statutes permit state intervention for emotional, as well as physical abuse.[27] With these problems in mind, some statutory models do not include emotional harm within their definitions of child abuse and limit state intervention to cases of physical, indeed "serious," injury.[28]

In addition to the risks of arbitrary state action, broad definitions of child abuse raise other sensitive issues. States adopting broad definitions make policy decisions inviting, perhaps mandating, extensive state intervention into the lives of families in an attempt to regulate family behavior.[29] While such an approach is surely understandable given the extent of the child maltreatment problem, coercive intervention carries inherent costs. Families being investigated are subjected to considerable trauma, the child being investigated may be removed from the home and subjected to questioning and court appearances, and other children in the family may become frightened and upset.[30] Moreover, even when eventually exonerated, allegedly "abusive" parents may be unfairly and indelibly stigmatized,[31] perhaps eventually resulting in a self-fulfilling prophecy.[32]

How child abuse is defined thus raises a host of delicate issues. Protecting children is a necessary aspect of state power. Undue exercise of that power, however, risks infringing on sensitive areas of family privacy.

## [B] Duty to Report

In addition to providing definitions of child abuse, the statutes in all states impose duties upon certain persons or entities to report any abuse that they know of, suspect, or have reason to believe is occurring.[33] The statutes typically require that reports be made to specified child protection agencies which must maintain central registries of abusers.[34] Moreover, the statutes abrogate certain privileged communications[35] and preclude tort actions against persons who in good faith make false accusations of abuse.[36]

---

[25] D. Besharov, *"Doing Something" About Child Abuse: The Need to Narrow the Grounds for State Intervention*, 8 HARV. J.L. & PUB. POL'Y 545, 568 (1985).

[26] *Id.* at 569. Definitional problems have proven to be especially controversial in cases where mothers harm their children by illegal drug use during pregnancy. While most courts deny the applicability of child abuse statutes in such situations, at least one appellate court has held a statute applicable. *See supra* § 3.02, note 80 and accompanying text.

[27] Davis & Schwartz, *supra* note 17, at 169.

[28] See, *e.g.*, Institute of Judicial Admin. & American Bar Ass'n. Juvenile Justice Standards Project, Standards Relating to Abuse and Neglect § 2.1(A) (Tentative Draft 1977), which limits state intervention to physical harm causing or risking "disfigurement, impairment of bodily functioning, or other serious physical injury."

[29] Davis & Schwartz, *supra* note 17, at 169.

[30] Institute of Judicial Admin. & American Bar Ass'n, *supra* note 28, § 2.1 commentary.

[31] Besharov, *supra* note 25, at 557–58.

[32] *Id.* at 567.

[33] Kramer, *supra* note 10, at 58–59.

[34] *Id.* at 59.

[35] For purposes of their reporting statutes, most states have specifically abrogated the privileges of

Statutorily obligated reporters who fail to report known or suspected abuse are themselves subject to criminal liability, although such failure is seldom prosecuted.[37] Breach of the duty to report may also result in loss of employment or other non-criminal consequences for persons who deal with children on an on-going basis.[38]

## [1]  Persons Obligated to Report

The first generation of statutes, initiated in the 1960s, applied reporting obligations only to physicians who came in contact with abused children.[39] Legislators saw the medical profession, with its new-found ability to diagnose battered child syndrome, as uniquely privy to an awareness of the incidence of child abuse.[40] After the initial wave of legislation, the categories of persons obligated to report have been expanded in all jurisdictions to include other persons who routinely have contact with children such as mental health professionals, nurses, dentists, teachers and other school personnel, social workers, law enforcement officials and day care providers.[41] Approximately half the state statutes now extend the duty to report to *any* person.[42]

In jurisdictions imposing reporting duties on everyone, attorneys may be obligated to report child abuse,[43] even where evidence thereof is obtained from client disclosures otherwise covered by the attorney-client privilege, if the attorney believes the client will continue the practice of child abuse in the future.[44] In such circumstances, attorneys may be permitted to report abuse without violating the

---

doctors, social workers, clergymen, psychiatrists, and spouses to remain silent. *Id.* at 59, 63. At least three states abrogate the attorney-client privilege. P. Mosteller, *Child Abuse Reporting Laws and Attorney-Client Confidences: The Reality and the Specter of Lawyer as Informant*, 42 DUKE L.J. 203, 218–19 (1992). Moreover, the United States Supreme Court has held that a parent may not invoke the Fifth Amendment privilege against self-incrimination to resist a court order to produce a child abused at the hands of the parent. Baltimore Dept. of Social Serv. v. Bouknight, 493 U.S. 549 (1990).

[36] Kramer, *supra* note 10, at 66. Some jurisdictions grant tort immunity even where the reporter of abuse makes a knowingly false accusation. *See, e.g.*, Hartley v. Hartley, 537 N.E.2d 706 (Ohio Ct. App. 1988) (former wife who filed false charges of sexual abuse of her child against the wife's former husband found to be "absolutely immune" from tort liability in an action brought by the former husband — court found immunity extends to anyone making reports "whether in good faith or not").

[37] Kramer, *supra* note 10, at 65, 67 (failure to report is a misdemeanor in every state punishable by imprisonment, a fine, or both).

[38] *See, e.g.*, Pesce v. Morton High Sch. Dist. No. 201, 651 F. Supp. 152 (N.D. Ill. 1986), *aff'd*, 830 F.2d 789 (7th Cir. 1987) (school psychologist suspended without pay for failing to report an incidence of abuse of a student by a teacher after the student informed the psychologist of alleged abuse).

[39] Mosteller, *supra* note 35, at 212.

[40] Kramer, *supra* note 10, at 60.

[41] *Id.* at 61–62.

[42] *Id.* at 62.

[43] Mosteller, *supra* note 35, at 208, 217 (twenty-two states have mandatory reporting applicable specifically or generally to lawyers: four state statutes specifically include lawyers as persons obligated to report while the remaining jurisdictions place the reporting duty on "any person," arguably including lawyers).

[44] *Id.* at 209. The reporting statutes of some states can be read to go so far as abrogating the attorney-client privilege altogether, thus raising questions about the extent to which the privilege is grounded in constitutional law. *Id.*

attorney-client privilege even if the statute does not specifically mandate reporting by attorneys.[45]

Similarly, mental health professionals do not offend the psychiatrist-patient privilege by reporting abusive clients thought likely to continue the abuse.[46] While many states require clergy to report instances of abuse, revealing confidences transmitted during religious rituals would violate many clerics' religious tenets, thus raising constitutional questions under the Free Exercise Clause of the First Amendment.[47]

## [2] Civil Liability for Failure to Report or Investigate

While failing to report child abuse constitutes a crime, it is less clear whether the reporting statutes, silent on their face as to civil liability, afford a basis for tort liability for injuries resulting from the failure of obligated persons to make reports. In a California case,[48] the court held that a doctor may be civilly liable for damages incurred through his failure to properly treat his patient's battered child syndrome and through his failure to report the abuse to the authorities. The court held that if the doctor was aware that the child had been abused and failed to report the abuse, he might be liable for subsequent injuries resulting from the child being returned to her abusive parent. In such circumstances, given the recurring tendencies of child abuse, the court saw the subsequent injuries as foreseeable and perhaps thus proximately caused by the doctor even though the intervening acts of the abusive parent were the direct cause of the child's injuries.

Other courts, probably reflecting the majority view,[49] hold that in adopting statutes that criminally punish failure to report, legislatures do not intend to create private tort actions premised on failures to report.[50] Moreover, the United States Supreme Court has held that state social service agencies do not violate the federal civil rights of children when the agency fails to respond to reports of abuse and thus fails to protect children from subsequent harm.[51] Similarly, most jurisdictions

---

[45] Because it constitutes a crime likely to be repeated, information regarding child abuse may be subject to disclosure under an exception to the confidentiality rules that permits or requires attorneys to reveal their clients' intentions to commit future crimes. *Id.*

[46] *See* Tarasoff v. Regents of Univ. of Cal., 551 P.2d 334 (Cal. 1976) (notwithstanding the psychiatrist-patient privilege, mental health professional liable in tort for failing to warn a potential victim of the client's intent to injure the victim).

[47] Traditionally, the list of personnel required to report child abuse has included doctors, childcare workers, teachers, but not clergy. In light of revelations regarding child abuse by clergy in the Catholic Church, some states, such as Massachusetts, have revised child abuse statutes to include all clergy. The Massachusetts statute, while requiring that clergy report reasonable suspicions of abuse, does exempt information "solely gained in a confession or similarly confidential communication in other religious faith." Mass. Gen. Laws Ann. Ch. 119, § 51A (West 2002). This issue is explored in the following: L. Smith, *Lifting the Veil of Secrecy: Mandatory Child Abuse Reporting Statutes May Encourage the Catholic Church to Report Priests Who Molest Children*, 18 L. & Psychol. Rev. 409 (1994); R. O'Brien & M. Flannery, *The Pending Gauntlet to Free Exercise: Mandating That Clergy Report Child Abuse*, 25 Loy. L.A. L. Rev. 1 (1991).

[48] Landeros v. Flood, 551 P.2d 389 (Cal. 1976).

[49] Kramer, *supra* note 10, at 65.

[50] *See, e.g.,* Fischer v. Metcalf, 543 So. 2d 785 (Fla. Dist. Ct. App. 1989) (psychiatrist not tortiously liable for failing to report his alleged knowledge or suspicions that his patient was physically and mentally abusing his children).

[51] DeShaney v. Winnebago County Dept. of Social Serv., 489 U.S. 189 (1989).

deny a cause of action under state law when a state agency investigates a claim of abuse, but decides to leave the child with the parents in an attempt to implement a case plan to teach the parents techniques to avoid abusing the child, even if the decision results in the child's death.[52] On the other hand, some jurisdictions hold state agencies liable under state law for their failure to adequately investigate known complaints of abuse and to afford protection from its subsequent recurrence.[53]

## [3] Policy Implications

Child abuse reporting statutes constitute an exception to the general rule of Anglo-American jurisprudence that imposes no duty upon the citizenry to report crime nor to come to the aid of another.[54] The statutes thus break with the traditional approach of legally permitting one to "mind her own business"[55] which instead entrusts personal moral compunctions to motivate reporting crime and aiding others in need.[56]

With the advent of statutes imposing a duty to report, along with massive public awareness campaigns, reported incidence of abuse has increased markedly.[57] When such reports identify actual cases of serious abuse, the reporting incentives afford invaluable aid to vulnerable children. On the other hand, to the extent child abuse reports are unfounded, the consequences are often devastating for those falsely accused of abuse.[58]

---

[52] Kramer, *supra* note 10, at 77.

[53] *Id.* at 76.

[54] Comment, *Reporting Child Abuse: When Moral Obligations Fail*, 15 Pac. L.J. 189, 191–92 (1983). Failing to come to the aid of another is culpable only where one has a "legal duty" to act, imposed by special statute, status relationship, contract, or by conduct that excludes the possibility of others providing aid. *See* Jones v. United States, 308 F.2d 307 (D.C. Cir. 1962).

[55] *See, e.g.*, H. McNiece & J. Thornton, *Affirmative Duties in Tort*, 58 Yale L.J. 1272, 1288 (1949) (the "rugged individualism" of the common law views people as independent and self-reliant and sees more serious restraints on personal liberty flowing from legal requirements to act than by ones that limit action).

[56] At least two states have broken with the general rule of the common law and imposed a duty to aid others exposed to grave harm whenever the rescuer can do so without danger or peril to herself. *See* Vt. Stat. Ann. tit. 12, § 519 (1973); Minn. Stat. Ann. § 604A.01 (West 2000).

[57] *See* Besharov, *supra*, note 25, at 545.

[58] *See supra* notes 29–32 and accompanying text. Even where reports of abuse may be technically accurate, accused abusers may experience negative consequences disproportionate to their degree of culpability. See, *e.g.*, Valmonte v. Bane, 18 F.3d 992 (2d Cir. 1994), where a mother became entangled in the legal system when she slapped her eleven-year-old daughter on the side of her face with an open hand because the daughter had been caught stealing. An unidentified employee at the daughter's school made a complaint to the child abuse hotline. As a consequence, child abuse investigators concluded that the mother had engaged in "excessive corporal punishment." While the court ultimately dismissed the child abuse proceedings against the mother on the condition that she receive counseling, the mother's name was included in the "Central Register of Child Abuse" (created as part of the child abuse legislative scheme to keep a record of known child abusers). Under the statute, employers in the child care field are required to consult the Department of Social Services to determine whether potential employees are among those listed on the Register. If the potential employee's name is so listed, the Department of Social Services informs the employer that the potential employee has a record on file, but does not inform the employer of the nature of the record. If the potential employee is in the Register, the employer can hire the individual only if the employer "maintains a written record . . .of the specific reasons why such person was determined to be appropriate" for working with children. The *Valmonte* court held that the

In addition to the threat of criminal and sometimes civil sanctions, persons obligated to report child abuse are routinely offered further incentives to report through grants of immunity from civil liability for erroneous reports. Some jurisdictions offer absolute immunity while others require that the report be based on "reasonable cause" or "good faith."[59] Whether to grant immunity at all, and if so to what extent, involves a difficult policy decision balancing the need for reporting against the harms entailed in erroneous, perhaps negligent or even malicious, reporting.[60]

Other questions regarding the wisdom of reporting statutes may be raised. Where statutes impose duties upon medical, legal, and social welfare professionals, parents might be disinclined to avail their children of needed services provided by such professionals where the parents have either abused the children or fear that the professional will believe that they have abused the children.[61] On the other hand, when parents do seek the aid of family service professionals for their abused children, the professional may be reluctant to report the abuse in order to avoid becoming involved as adversaries in criminal proceedings against their patients/clients.[62]

## § 4.03 THE JUDICIAL PROCESS

The prosecution of child abuse cases raises a variety of unique procedural issues. Many of the issues arise through an attempt to protect the child victim from being traumatized by the judicial process while at the same time assuring that the defendant's constitutional rights are safeguarded. Moreover, because child abuse routinely occurs in the privacy of the home, the crime is often proved solely on the

---

state Registry system implicated a "liberty" interest in the mother/abuser and remanded the case to the lower court to consider the constitutionality of procedures to expunge names from the Registry.

For further examination of the issue raised in *Valmonte*, see Note, *The Constitutionality of Employer-Accessible Child Abuse Registries: Due Process Implications of Governmental Occupational Blacklisting*, 92 Mich. L. Rev. 139 (1993). For a general discussion on child abuse "registries" which exist in nearly every state, see Kramer, *supra* note 10, at 77–79.

[59] Mnookin & Weisberg, *supra* § 1.02, note 8, at 357.

[60] Absolute immunity would seemingly preclude sanctioning any false report, even ones maliciously made. *See supra* note 36. Some jurisdictions have provided for possible civil or criminal liability for some false reporting. *See, e.g.,* Cal. Penal Code § 11172(a) (West Supp. 2001):

> No mandated reporter shall be civilly or criminally liable for any report required or authorized by this article. Any other person reporting a known or suspected instance of child abuse or neglect shall not incur civil or criminal liability as a result of any report authorized by this article unless it can be proven that a false report was made and the person knew that the report was false or was made with reckless disregard of the truth or falsity of the report, and any person who makes a report of child abuse or neglect known to be false or with reckless disregard of the truth or falsity of the report is liable for any damages caused. No person required to make a report pursuant to this article, nor any person taking photographs at his or her direction, shall incur any civil or criminal liability for taking photographs of a suspected victim of child abuse or neglect, or causing photographs to be taken of a suspected victim of child abuse or neglect, without parental consent, or for disseminating the photographs with the reports required by this article. However, this section shall not be construed to grant immunity from this liability with respect to any other use of the photographs.

[61] Mnookin & Weisberg, *supra* note 59, at 352.

[62] V. De Francis, Child Abuse Legislation in the 1970's 3–4 (1970); M. Paulsen, *The Legal Framework for Child Protection*, 66 Colum. L. Rev. 679, 710 (1966).

basis of circumstantial evidence enriched by expert testimony, as well as through a variety of presumptions and relaxation of some ordinary rules of evidence. The following sections discuss these points.

## [A]  Expert Testimony

Expert testimony is often essential in proving child abuse. Witnesses to the abuse are frequently either nonexistent or family members of the abuser who are intimidated into noncooperation.[1] Even the child victim, when mature enough and physically able to testify, is often influenced to give a false account consistent with that alleged by the abuser.[2] To help fill this evidentiary void, the courts have permitted liberal use of expert testimony.

### [1]  Battered Child Syndrome

Expert testimony by medical professionals on the battered child syndrome (BCS) is often the mechanism that links outward manifestations of injury to child abuse, usually inflicted by a parent or caretaker. The syndrome is a recognized medical diagnosis that a child has sustained certain kinds of injuries by nonaccidental means.[3] Moreover, the expert is sometimes permitted to testify not only that the child's injuries were inflicted by a human agent, but by one in close constant contact with the child.[4]

Expert testimony that a child fits the BCS is crucial in refuting the claims often raised by the defendant that the child's injuries were incurred accidently. Thus, in one case,[5] a father claimed that his infant daughter's scald wounds resulted from hot water accidently splashing against her body. The father was convicted of intentionally scalding the child, however, after a medical expert testified that the burned and unburned skin of the child was divided by a distinct line thus establishing that the child had been immersed in boiling water rather than accidentally burned by splashing water. In another case,[6] a father's claims that his son had choked to death on some cereal were refuted by medical evidence showing no signs of drowning, but evidence of death by abdominal hemorrhage from a ruptured liver along with bruises on the child's body that were not "the typical bruising pattern that is normally sustained by children in (their) normal day-to-day life."[7]

Utilizing expert testimony as to cause of death or injury is relatively non-controversial, but testimony by the expert as to who caused the death or injury raises questions about whether the expert has exceeded the realm of her expertise and invaded the province of the jury. Thus, in a North Carolina case,[8] a doctor who performed an autopsy on a child victim he had diagnosed as a battered child,

---

[1] *See* Comment, *supra* § 4.01, note 6, at 260.

[2] *Id.* at 259–60.

[3] Kramer, *supra* § 3.03, note 15, at 100.

[4] See, *e.g.*, State v. Wilkerson, 247 S.E.2d 905 (N.C. 1978), discussed *infra* notes 6–10 and the accompanying text.

[5] Sipress v. State, 562 N.E.2d 758 (Ind. Ct. App. 1990).

[6] State v. Wilkerson, 247 S.E.2d 905 (N.C. 1978).

[7] *Id.* at 908.

[8] *Supra* note 4.

testified at the murder trial of the child's father, and explained his diagnosis to the jury as follows:

> These [BCS children] are children who suffer multiple injuries inflicted by others. . . . [The injuries] are seen in children who have been perhaps over-zealously disciplined or have in other ways upset . . . their guardians or their caretakers or usually some adult who is in [physical] relation to the child. . . . The syndrome usually occurs in a disciplinary situation involving the child and some guardian or custodian, a parent, a relative, a babysitter. . . .[9]

The defendant contended that such testimony was inadmissible because it constituted the doctor's conclusion as to the ultimate fact of defendant's guilt (the defendant was apparently the sole person in physical contact with his son on the evening of the child's death) and thus invaded the jury's province. In rejecting the defendant's argument and permitting the evidence, the court found the testimony to be within the doctor's realm of expertise[10] and did not usurp the role of the jury because the doctor did not specifically name any person or class of persons as causing the child's death.

A California court, in upholding the admissibility of similar medical testimony, explained the role of the expert as follows:

> A finding, as in this case, of the "battered child syndrome" is not an opinion by the doctor as to whether any particular person has done anything, but, as this doctor indicated, "it would take thousands of children to have the severity and number and degree of injuries that this child had over the span of time that we had" by accidental, means. In other words, the "battered child syndrome" simply indicates that a child found with the type of injuries outlined above has not suffered those injuries by accidental means. This conclusion is based upon an extensive study of the subject by medical science. The additional finding that the injuries were probably occasioned by someone who is ostensibly caring for the child is simply a conclusion based upon logic and reason. Only someone regularly "caring" for the child has the continuing opportunity to inflict these types of injuries; an isolated contact with a vicious stranger would not result in this pattern of successive injuries stretching through several months.[11]

The United States Supreme Court has rejected the argument that introduction of evidence of the victim's prior injuries violates a defendant's due process rights.[12]

## [2]  Other "Syndrome" Evidence

In addition to evidence of BCS, courts permit expert testimony on a variety of other syndromes evidencing mistreatment or abuse of children. Medical testimony of "maternal deprivation syndrome" (an infant's "failure to thrive" as evidenced by

---

[9] *Id.* at 909.

[10] *Id.* at 911. The court described the test for determining whether expert testimony is within the realm of her expertise as follows: "whether the 'opinion required expert skill or knowledge in the medical or pathologic field about which a person of ordinary experience would not be capable of satisfactory conclusions, unaided by expert information from one learned in the medical profession.' " *Id.*

[11] People v. Jackson, 95 Cal. Rptr. 919, 921 (Cal. Ct. App. 1971).

[12] Estelle v. McGuire, 502 U.S. 62 (1991). For a general discussion of the admissibility of expert testimony on BCS, see M. Roberts, Annotation, *Admissibility of Expert Medical Testimony on Battered Child Syndrome*, 98 A.L.R.3d 306 (1980).

a marked retardation or cessation of growth during the first three years of life) is often introduced in prosecutions associated with inappropriate mothering.[13] Some courts permit experts to testify on the "sexually abused child syndrome," used to explain why child victims often retract previous statements of sexual abuse against their parents.[14] Thus far, courts have rejected evidence of "fetal alcohol

---

[13] Kramer, *supra* note 3, at 101.

[14] *See, e.g.*, Steward v. State, 652 N.E.2d 490 (Ind. 1995) (holding admissible expert testimony on child sexual abuse syndrome to explain why, *inter alia*, child recanted prior allegation of abuse, such testimony not admissible, however, on issue of proving that child abuse occurred); State v. Middleton, 657 P.2d 1215 (Or. 1983) (court permitted expert testimony that victim fits the profile of child rape victims who typically retract rape accusations against family members; expert testimony labeled in concurring opinion as "familial child sexual abuse syndrome"). *Id.* at 1221 (Roberts, J., concurring). *But see* Newkirk v. Commonwealth, 937 S.W.2d 690 (Ky. 1997) (rejecting child sexual abuse syndrome evidence even for purposes of rebuttal where prosecution sought to rehabilitate child victim witness who had recanted out of court accusations against defendant prior to testifying against him at trial); Lantrip v. Commonwealth, 713 S.W.2d 816 (Ky. 1986) (expert testimony of "sexual abuse accommodation syndrome," "elements" of which are "secrecy, helplessness, entrapment, accommodation, delay in disclosure, and retraction," held to be inadmissible where no evidence was offered that syndrome had attained scientific acceptance); People v. Wells, 12 Cal. Rptr. 3d 762, 773 (Cal. Dist. Ct. App. 2004) (holding that evidence that a victim's behavior is consistent with that of "child sexual abuse accommodation syndrome" may not be used to show that a victim was sexually abused).

In *State v. Myers*, 359 N.W.2d 604, 608–10 (Minn. 1984), the court upheld the admission of a psychological expert (Dr. Bell) who testified to the uniqueness of incest, defined as "sexual abuse by any person occupying a caring-parenting role with respect to the child victim" whether or not there is a legal or blood relationship between them:

> [I]ncest . . . ordinarily goes on for a long period of time; unlike most crimes, it is unusual for it to occur only on a single occasion. Over defendant's objection Dr. Bell was permitted to describe characteristics or traits typically observed in sexually abused children. Dr. Bell testified that she observed these general characteristics in sexually abused children: fear — the child is afraid to tell of the abuse because she fears she will be blamed or punished, she fears the possible breakup of the family, she fears she won't be believed; confusion, particularly in young children — the child feels this is not right, but the adult perpetrator, a person in authority, tells the child it is right; a poor relationship between mother and daughter — the child does not trust the mother, is afraid of what she will do with the information, and does not look to her mother for support.

> Dr. Bell also stated that she looked for these more specific individual characteristics: fear of men, nightmares that have an assaultive content, sexual knowledge unusual in a child of the patient's age, and that the child looks and acts older than she is. Dr. Bell then identified those characteristics commonly exhibited by sexually abused children which she had observed in the complainant.

> Finally, Dr. Bell explained that it is extremely rare for children to fabricate tales of sexual abuse and stated that in her opinion the complainant knew the difference between the truth and falsehood and was truthful in her allegations.

> . . .

> The second segment of Dr. Bell's testimony consists of her description of characteristics or emotional conditions she observed in the complainant. [Defendant] contends that this part of Dr. Bell's testimony was inadmissible because it was unreliable. He contends that the conditions described by Dr. Bell are highly subjective and not necessarily the result of sexual molestation. That Dr. Bell's observations of the complainant's psychological and emotional condition are not physically demonstrable does not justify the conclusion that they were of no help to the jury. The cause of many physical and emotional ailments and even the existence of those conditions which are identified chiefly by subjective complaints cannot be demonstrated to an absolute certainty; they are, nevertheless, the subject of expert testimony. Moreover, the prosecution did not attempt to prove causation through Dr. Bell's testimony but only to demonstrate that the child's emotional condition was not inconsistent with the profile of a sexually abused child.

syndrome," caused by a mother's ingestion of alcohol during pregnancy, as itself sufficient to constitute child abuse[15] although some jurisdictions permit the evidence to trigger actions to remove the child from the mother's custody, especially where she continues to drink after the child is born.[16]

## [a]  Munchausen Syndrome by Proxy

One of the more fascinating contexts of expert testimony in child abuse cases involves the "Munchausen Syndrome."[17] A vivid example is provided by a California case[18] in which a mother was convicted of murdering one of her adopted daughters and of willfully endangering the life of another. The defendant-mother was a well-educated person who gave much of her time to volunteer work, including significant labor devoted to combating the evils of child abuse. As a seemingly dutiful wife and loving parent, she took her recently adopted infant daughter to the hospital for what would be the first of a series of visits. The child was treated for an ear infection and released. The mother returned to the hospital several times with the child who increasingly displayed symptoms of vomiting and diarrhea. Specialists conducted extensive tests which revealed only that the child's body contained mysteriously high levels of sodium, even after doctors began monitoring her food intake. The child eventually died in the hospital of complications caused by extreme levels of sodium in the blood.

One year to the day after the child's death, the mother brought to the hospital a second child whom she had recently adopted. This child also displayed symptoms of vomiting and diarrhea. The child was hospitalized and found to possess abnormally high levels of sodium in her body. Realizing that the second child was genetically unrelated to the deceased child, the physician in charge began to suspect that the child was being poisoned. After reading a medical journal article discussing "Munchausen syndrome by proxy," a phenomenon in which persons, often mothers, cause others, sometimes their own children, to be ill in order to draw attention and sympathy to themselves, the doctor hypothesized that the mother had murdered the first child and poisoned the second. The mother had spent endless hours at various hospitals with her children, helping with their care by, among other things, preparing and administering their formula. The doctor's suspicions were heightened when she tested the formula of the second child and found it to contain dangerously high levels of sodium.

---

For criticism of current use of expert testimony in child abuse cases, see D. McCord, *Expert Psychological Testimony in Child Abuse Prosecutions: A Foray Into the Admissibility of Psychological Evidence*, 77 J. Crim. L. & Criminology 1 (1986); R. Roe, *Expert Testimony in Child Sexual Abuse Cases*, 40 U. Miami L. Rev. 97 (1985).

[15]  Kramer, *supra* note 3, at 101. While not constituting child abuse, some states treat evidence of fetal alcohol syndrome as *prima facie* evidence of neglect. *See, e.g.*, Ill. Ann. Stat. ch. 705 para. 405/2-18(2)(c) (Smith-Hurd 1999). Similarly, a majority of courts have refused to find child abuse where children are born addicted to cocaine or other controlled substances caused by their mother's use of such drugs during pregnancy. *See, e.g.*, State v. Gray, 584 N.E.2d 710 (Ohio 1992); People v. Hardy, 469 N.W.2d 50 (Mich. Ct. App. 1991); Reyes v. Superior Court, 141 Cal. Rptr. 912 (Cal. Ct. App. 1977). *But see* Whitner v. State, 492 S.E.2d 777 (S.C. 1997) (holding mother guilty of child abuse for illegal drug use during her pregnancy).

[16]  Kramer, *supra* note 3, at 51.

[17]  *See infra* note 19 and accompanying text.

[18]  People v. Phillips, 175 Cal. Rptr. 703 (Cal. Ct. App. 1981). The facts of *Phillips* are taken from Gardner, *supra* § 4.02, note 11, at 728–30.

Acting on this evidence from the doctor, the state charged the mother with second-degree murder of the first child and willfully endangering the life of the second. At trial, over the mother's objection, the state was permitted to introduce evidence suggesting she poisoned her children in order to obtain sympathy for herself, a classic manifestation of "Munchausen's syndrome by proxy" (MSBP) as described by the state's psychiatric expert, who personally had never examined the defendant.[19] The mother testified in her defense, denying ever administering any sodium compound to either of her children. She also presented an array of witnesses who praised her general character and her specific love for her children. Defense psychiatrists testified that the defendant was mentally healthy and manifested none of the "distortions of thinking" associated with MSBP.[20]

The mother was convicted of "willfully mingling a harmful substance with food . . . with intent that the same shall be taken by [a] human being to his injury,"[21] a felony offense utilized by the state as its predicate for felony murder. The jury convicted the mother of murder and she appealed, contesting, among other things, the state's use of evidence of motive as provided by the psychiatric expert. The appellate court upheld the conviction and found the expert testimony proper. The court observed:

> While a prosecutor ordinarily need not prove motive as an element of a crime . . . the absence of apparent motive may make proof of the essential elements less persuasive. . . . Clearly that was the principal problem confronting the prosecutor here. In the absence of a motivational hypothesis, and in light of other information which the jury had concerning her personality and character, the conduct ascribed to appellant was incongruous and apparently inexplicable. As both parties recognize, [the] testimony [of the state's psychiatric expert] was designed to fill that gap. The evidence was relevant, and therefore admissible.[22]

The appellate court apparently took the position that the state's evidence of motive was relevant to show both that the defendant performed the *actus reus* of mingling poison with food and that she did so with the requisite *mens rea* elements of "willfulness" and "intent." The court appreciated that evidence of motive posed "some risk" of prejudice to the defendant.[23] Indeed, without it, the jury would have

---

[19] Dr. Blinder, testifying for the state, theorized: "[A] mother who repeatedly and surreptitiously administered a cathartic sodium compound to her adopted children, under circumstances identical to those presented by this case, displayed symptoms consistent with Munchausen's syndrome by proxy." People v. Phillips, 175 Cal. Rptr. at 708–9. Dr. Blinder further testified that the syndrome

> is one in which an individual either directly or through the vehicle of a child feigns, simulates, or actually fabricates a physical illness. . . . Typically, the illness is a dramatic one. And 'by proxy' simply means instead of the person making themselves [sic] ill, they go through the psychodynamic process in another. It's usually the mother. . . . She's outwardly devoted to the child and invariably, the child is very small, less than two years of age. . . . The mothers who perpetrate a child abuse or Munchausen's form of child abuse typically will transfer their own unmet parental needs . . . onto pediatricians, nurses, spouses, maybe even the community and get from these people through their child's illness the attention and sympathy then never got from their own parents.

*Id.* at 709.

[20] *Id.* at 709.

[21] *Id.* at 712.

[22] *Id.*

[23] *Id.* at 714. Indeed, the appellate court saw the risks of prejudice and confusion created by the

been presented with the appearance of a grieving mother inexplicably charged with poisoning her children on the basis of tenuous circumstantial evidence. With the evidence, however, the state painted a vastly different picture of the defendant, presenting a convincing case that she intentionally poisoned the children to satisfy her own selfish desires.

Some courts have denied the admissibility of expert testimony of MSBP in cases similar to the California case discussed above,[24] perhaps on the theory that the testimony constitutes improper use of character evidence.[25] While MSBP accounts for only a small fraction of reported child abuse cases,[26] some experts claim that the syndrome nevertheless manifests itself at an alarming rate, particularly in cases that are mistakenly diagnosed as "sudden infant death syndrome" (crib death).[27]

## [b]   Battering Parent Syndrome

The courts have been less receptive to the use of expert testimony regarding "battering parent syndrome" (BPS), a profile of traits and personal histories thought to be associated with the typical child abuser.[28] The profile, derived from past cases of known child abusers, identifies certain characteristics commonly found in battering parents: that they were themselves abused as children; that they possess low self-esteem and expect their children to make up for their self-perceived deficits; and that they are short-tempered, act impulsively, and overreact to insignificant events.[29] Prosecutors often seek to introduce expert testimony of BPS and to establish that the accused fits the profile, thus affording evidence of his or her guilt in the instant case.

The courts routinely deny the admissibility of prosecution-proffered BPS evidence,[30] finding it to be improper use of character evidence[31] unduly prejudicial to the accused. One court articulated the following objections to BPS evidence: (1)

---

evidence as so substantial that it might have held the evidence inadmissible had it been in the trial court's position. *Id.* However, because admission of the evidence represented no abuse of trial court discretion, the appellate court felt bound to uphold its action. *Id.*

[24] *See, e.g.,* Commonwealth v. Robinson, 565 N.E.2d 1229, 1237–38 (Mass. App. Ct. 1991) (discussing trial court's exclusion of state's expert evidence of MSBP where mother charged with causing her hospitalized child's death by poisoning her with massive doses of salt).

[25] *See* Gardner, *supra* note 18, at 730–32; *infra* notes 31–32 and accompanying text.

[26] Experts estimate that MSBP accounts for fewer than 1,000 of the more than 2.5 million cases of child abuse reported each year. B. Kantrowitz & K. Springen, *Parental Indiscretion*, Newsweek, Apr. 22, 1991, at 64.

[27] A. Toufexis, *When Is Crib Death a Cover for Murder?*, Time, Apr. 11, 1994, at 63–64.

[28] Kramer, *supra* note 3, at 103.

[29] *Id.*

[30] *See, e.g.,* Sloan v. State, 522 A.2d 1364 (Md. Ct. Spec. App. 1987), *cert. denied,* 528 A.2d 1287 (Md. 1987); Sanders v. State, 303 S.E.2d 13 (Ga. 1983). However courts permit the defendant to admit BPS evidence in order to show that another person was the abuser. *See, e.g.,* State v. Conlogne, 474 A.2d 167 (Me. 1984); *see* G. Sarno, Annotation, *Admissibility at Criminal Prosecution of Expert Testimony on Battering Parent Syndrome*, 43 A.L.R.4th 1203 (1986).

[31] As a codification of common law doctrine, Rule 404(a) of the Federal Rules of Evidence provides: "Evidence of a person's character or a trait of character is not admissible for the purpose of proving action in conformity therewith on a particular occasion." Fed. R. Evid. 404(a). *See also* 1 J. Strong et al., McCormick on Evidence §§ 186–88, at 786–93 (4th ed. 1992). An exception to the rule states that "unless and until the accused gives evidence of his good character, the prosecution may not introduce evidence of (or otherwise seek to establish) his bad character." *Id.* § 190, at 797.

the possibility of the jury convicting the defendant in order to punish him for being an undesirable person; (2) the danger that the jury might overvalue character evidence in assessing guilt for the crime charged; and (3) the unfairness of requiring the accused to be prepared not only to defend against immediate charges, but also to explain his personality.[32] Some courts have suggested, however, that BPS evidence may be admissible in the future if its scientific accuracy and predictive value is more firmly established.[33]

### [3] Policy Implications

As the above discussion illustrates, expert testimony is extensively utilized on behalf of children as a means of bringing to light the insidious evil of child abuse. To the extent the expert offers information firmly established within her discipline, she provides an invaluable service, particularly where her testimony does not unduly prejudice the rights of the accused abuser. However, the line between acceptable expert opinion and undue prejudice to the defendant is sometimes difficult to draw and perhaps arbitrarily drawn in some cases. It is difficult to explain why, for example, prosecution-proffered evidence of BPS is inadmissible character evidence while at least some courts permit the prosecution to use evidence of MSBP. It is difficult for courts to decide whether to err on the side of innocent children or presumptively innocent defendants.

## [B] Children's Testimony

The testimony of children, either as a victim or a witness of another's abuse, is often admitted in child abuse prosecutions. While such testimony is often crucial in proving the defendant guilty, its utilization raises distinct problems, primarily: whether the individual child whose testimony is sought is competent to participate as a witness in legal proceedings; and, if so, whether special protections should be employed to reduce the risks of traumatizing the child through the experience of testifying.

### [1] Competency to Testify

Until well into the twentieth century, English common law held that children under seven years of age were excluded as competent witnesses on the theory that they lacked appreciation of the difference between right and wrong.[34] In the United States, the courts generally reject age requirements and permit even very young children to testify so long as the court is satisfied that they appreciate the difference between truth and falsehood.[35] Some state statutes specify a particular age (usually ten) under which children may not testify if they appear unable to

---

[32] State v. Loebach, 310 N.W.2d 58, 63 (Minn. 1981).

[33] *See, e.g., id.* at 64.

[34] Note, *An Overview of the Competency of Child Testimony*, 13 N. Ky. L. Rev. 181, 182–83 (1986); J. Oseid, *Defendant's Rights in Child Witness Competency Hearings: Establishing Constitutional Procedures for Sexual Abuse Cases*, 69 Minn. L. Rev. 1377, 1381 (1985). At common law, a rebuttable presumption of incompetency to testify applied to children ages seven to fourteen. Kramer, *supra* § 3.02, note 11, at 548.

[35] *See* Note, *supra* note 34, at 184; State v. Skipper, 387 So. 2d 592 (La. 1980) (court finds children, ages 5 and 7, competent to testify because they knew the "difference between telling the truth and not telling the truth" and also because they knew "why they were in court"). The standard applied by most courts in determining competency to testify is whether the child can intelligently relate the facts,

understand the facts about which they are to testify or to relate a truthful account of their occurrence.[36] Most jurisdictions, however, reject specific age standards and, if they address the issue at all, assess competency on a case-by-case basis.[37] Indeed, many jurisdictions follow the federal approach[38] which presumes the competency of all witnesses, including children, except perhaps in extremely rare situations.[39] Some states go so far as to require the courts to hear the testimony of child abuse victims without qualification.[40]

Courts generally require child witnesses to testify under oath.[41] While the courts often do not specify the form of the oath, it must be administered in a form sufficient to "quicken the conscience" of the witness.[42] Where children are unable to meet the oath requirement, some courts nevertheless permit unsworn testimony where the child possesses sufficient truth-telling capacity.[43]

Some states require corroboration of child witness testimony, thus precluding conviction of abusers solely on the testimony of the victim.[44] In some jurisdictions, the child's complaint affirms her testimony, thus providing corroboration.[45]

Because children are expected to be unfamiliar with anatomical terms, attorneys routinely use anatomically correct dolls to elicit testimony from children unfamiliar with appropriate physiological terminology.[46] Moreover, most jurisdictions relax

---

distinguish between truth and falsehood, and understand the importance of an oath or the consequences of lying. *See* Oseid, *supra* note 34, at 1381–82.

The competency issue addressed here is not unique to the area of criminal child abuse. The issue also arises when children testify in civil actions. *See* M. Cross, Annotation *Competency of Young Child as Witness in Civil Case*, 81 A.L.R. 2d 386 (1962).

[36] *See* Note, *supra* note 34, at 184–85; *see, e.g.*, Ariz. Rev. Stat. Ann. § 12-2202(2) (1994) (children under ten years of age shall not be witnesses if they "appear incapable of receiving just impressions of the facts respecting which they are to testify, or of relating them truly").

[37] *See supra* note 35.

[38] Kramer, *supra* note 34, at 548–49.

[39] Federal Rule of Evidence 601 provides in part: "Every person is competent to be a witness except as otherwise provided by these rules. . . ." Rule 601 arguably does not preclude a judge from excluding child witnesses if the child's testimony could not reasonably be taken to make a significant fact more or less probable under rules defining relevancy of evidence. 32B Am. Jur. 2d *Federal Rules of Evidence* § 322 (1982).

[40] *See, e.g.*, Ala. Code § 15-25-3(c) (1995) (child victim of abuse "shall be considered a competent witness and shall be allowed to testify without prior qualification"); Utah Code Ann. § 76-5-410 (1995) (child victim of sexual abuse under the age of ten "is a competent witness and shall be allowed to testify without prior qualification").

[41] Kramer, *supra* note 34, at 555.

[42] Note, *Are Children Competent Witnesses? A Psychological Perspective*, 63 Wash. U. L.Q. 815, 817 (1985). While child witnesses are generally required to testify under oath, the courts have been reluctant to find perjury law applicable to young children who testify untruthfully. *See, e.g.*, Hughes v. Detroit, 31 N.W. 603 (Mich. 1913) (six-year-old not criminally responsible for perjury); Gehl v. Bachmann-Bechtel, 141 N.Y.S. 133 (1913) (court opines that nine-year-old is not subject to perjury law); *see* Annotation, *Competency of Child as Witness as Affected by Fact That His Prosecution for Perjury is Prohibited*, 159 A.L.R. 1102 (1945).

[43] Note, *supra* note 42, at 817.

[44] *See, e.g.*, N.Y. Fam. Ct. Act § 1046 (1998) (allegations by child of abuse or neglect admissible but if not corroborated then not "sufficient to make a fact-finding of abuse or neglect").

[45] *See, e.g.*, Isbell v. People, 405 P.2d 744 (Colo. 1965).

[46] *See* Mnookin & Weisberg, *supra* § 1.02, note 8, at 426.

the usual rules against the use of leading questions when lawyers conduct direct examination of child witnesses.[47]

The trend towards more liberal use of child testimony assumes that children are no less competent than adults when acting as witnesses and that the reliability of their testimony can be adequately scrutinized through the normal process of cross-examination. As with other child competency issues,[48] empirical research in the child witness area leads some to see children as generally competent and others to be more skeptical.[49]

## [2] The Traumatic Effects of Testifying

It is widely believed that child witnesses testifying in abuse cases, particularly where the abuse is sexual in nature, may suffer trauma if exposed to the ordinary adversarial atmosphere of the courtroom.[50] While empirical support for this belief is questionable,[51] many states have enacted special procedures aimed at reducing the perceived traumatic effect.[52] Several of these procedures raise constitutional questions that have reached the courts.

## [a] Face to Face Confrontation?

In *Coy v. Iowa*,[53] the United States Supreme Court held unconstitutional under the Confrontation Clause of the Sixth Amendment[54] a state statutory procedure that authorized courts to place a screen in the courtroom between the child victim witness and the accused sex offender. The screen, aimed at reducing testimony trauma to the witness, was employed in such a manner that the accused could dimly perceive the witness as she testified but entirely prevented the witness from seeing the accused. The Court found that the screen denied the defendant his right

---

[47] Kramer, *supra* note 34, at 576.

[48] See, *e.g.*, *supra* § 1.02, notes 21–27 discussing social science issues regarding the competency of adolescents.

[49] For a review of social science research on the reliability of children as witnesses, see Note, *supra* note 42, at 819–29. For a study suggesting that liberal use of children's testimony is well-founded and often as "competent" as that provided by adults, based on categories of memory, cognitive development, moral development, and suggestibility, see G. Melton, *Children's Competency to Testify*, 5 L. & HUM. BEHAV. 73 (1981). For studies suggesting that children are substantially more vulnerable to suggestion than adults and often unable to separate fantasy or suggestion from reality, see T. Feher, *The Alleged Molestation Victim, the Rules of Evidence and the Constitution: Should Children Really Be Seen and Not Heard?*, 14 AM. J. CRIM. L. 227, 230–33 (1987); J. Christiansen, *The Testimony of Child Witnesses: Fact, Fantasy and the Influence of Pretrial Interviews*, 62 WASH. L. REV. 705, 708–711 (1987).

[50] Among other things, child witnesses may experience severe psychological stress in reliving the witnessed event through their testimony, may fear that their testimony will result in abuse that is even more severe, and may perceive their act of testifying against the abuser, often a parent, as an act of ultimate disloyalty. *See generally* J. Parker, *The Rights of Child Witnesses: Is the Court a Protector or Perpetrator?*, 17 NEW ENG. L. REV. 643 (1982). More than thirty states have passed legislation aimed, in part at least, at reducing the trauma to child witnesses testifying in abuse cases. *See* Kramer, *supra* note 3, at 106–113.

[51] *See* J. Montoya, *On Truth and Shielding in Child Abuse Trials*, 43 HASTINGS L.J. 1259, 1280–91 (1992).

[52] *Supra* note 50.

[53] 487 U.S. 1014 (1988).

[54] The Sixth Amendment of the United States Constitution provides that "[i]n all criminal prosecutions, the accused shall enjoy to right . . . to be confronted with the witnesses against him. . . ."

to a "face-to-face meeting with witnesses appearing before the trier of fact," a component of the Confrontation Clause similar in dignity to the right of cross-examination.[55] While the Court recognized that facing the accused while testifying might be traumatic to many sexual assault victims, the defendant's Sixth Amendment rights outweighed the state's attempts to protect the sensitivities of the witnesses.

> The state can hardly gainsay the profound effect upon a witness of standing in the presence of the person the witness accuses, since that is the very phenomenon it relies upon to establish the potential "trauma" that allegedly justified the extraordinary procedure in the present case. That face-to-face presence may, unfortunately, upset the truthful rape victim or abused child; but by the same token it may confound and undo the false accuser, or reveal the child coached by a malevolent adult. It is a truism that constitutional protections have costs.[56]

The Court found that the Iowa statute, which permitted the use of the screen in any case where a child witness testified, effectively created a legislative "presumption of trauma."[57] While such an overly broad presumption could not be upheld, the Court recognized that the right to face-to-face confrontation is not absolute. The Court specifically left open the question whether a procedure such as that employed in *Coy* might be constitutional if shown to be necessary to avoid trauma to a particular child witness.[58]

The Court soon answered the question it left open in *Coy*. In *Maryland v. Craig*,[59] the Court considered a state statutory procedure permitting a child witness to testify against her alleged abuser outside the defendant's presence, by one-way closed circuit television viewed by the defendant and the jury who remained in the courtroom. Under the statute, use of the procedure was authorized only when the trial court determined that testimony in the defendant's presence would "result in the child suffering serious emotional distress such that the child [could] not reasonably communicate."[60] In making its decision to deny face-to-face confrontation, the trial court in *Craig* relied on expert testimony predicting that the particular child witness would experience trauma and anxiety if required to testify in the presence of the defendant.[61] The Supreme Court upheld the the trial court decision and rejected the defendant's argument that the closed circuit procedure violated her confrontation rights. The Court held that while face-to-face confrontation was "highly preferred," it could be denied if such denial is "necessary to further an important public policy" so long as the "reliability of the testimony is

---

[55] 487 U.S. at 1016–17. In an earlier case, *Kentucky v. Stincer*, 482 U.S. 730 (1987), the Court upheld the constitutionality of excluding a defendant from a pre-trial hearing to determine the child's competency as a witness. The Court found that although the defendant was absent, his confrontation rights were not denied because his attorney was present at the hearing and the defendant could later cross-examine the child at trial.

[56] 487 U.S. at 1020.

[57] *Id.* at 1021.

[58] *Id.*

[59] 497 U.S. 836 (1990).

[60] *Id.* at 840–41.

[61] The victim, a six-year-old girl, had allegedly been sexually abused by the owner and operator of a kindergarten day-care center. The expert testimony suggested that the victim and other children allegedly abused by the defendant would likely "stop talking and . . . withdraw and curl up" and "become highly agitated" if made to testify in the defendant's presence. *Id.* at 842.

otherwise assured."[62] The Court found that the interest in avoiding serious trauma to the particular witness, when based upon an individualized judgment that the witness would be so affected if required to testify in the presence of the defendant,[63] qualified as an "important public policy."[64] Moreover, the reliability of the closed circuit testimony was assured because the witness testified under oath, was subject to cross-examination, and her demeanor while testifying was observed by the jury.[65]

In addition to the trauma-reducing procedures employed in *Coy* and *Craig*, states have utilized such devices as receiving the child's testimony *in camera* or in the courtroom with only counsel present; videotaping the child's statement outside the defendant's presence with concurrent broadcasting to the courtroom where counsel may ask questions; and taking testimony with the defendant present but behind a one-way mirror and thus not visible to the witness.[66] The constitutionality of any such deviations from face-to-face confrontation must, of course, be assessed in light of the principles set forth in *Coy* and *Craig*.[67]

## [b] Hearsay Exceptions

The child witness protection measures discussed in the previous section allow taking the child's "live" testimony under circumstances where the defendant can observe and cross-examine the witness. Courts in child abuse cases often face a different problem: whether to permit the use at trial of the child victim's prior out-of-court statements regarding the defendant's alleged abuse. Although such statements constitute hearsay and would thus generally be inadmissible,[68] courts commonly admit such hearsay statements, either under statutes creating specific exceptions to the hearsay rule for child victim statements, or under judicial

---

[62] *Id.* at 845–50.

[63] The Court emphasized that any exception to face-to-face confrontation must be based on "case specific" fact findings that particular witnesses would experience substantial trauma, more than mere nervousness or excitement for example, if required to testify in the defendant's presence. *Id.* at 855–56.

[64] The Court relied on the fact that a "significant majority of States" have enacted statutes to protect child witnesses from trauma as evidence of the importance of the policy issue promoted by the Maryland statute. *Id.* at 853.

[65] *Id.* at 845–46.

[66] Kramer, *supra* note 3, at 113.

[67] Even after *Craig*, some state courts have found testimony outside the presence of the defendant to violate rights to confrontation under their state constitutions. *See, e.g.*, People v. Fitzpatrick, 633 N.W.2d (Ill. 1994) (one-way closed circuit television); Brady v. State, 575 N.E.2d 981 (Ind. 1991) (videotaped testimony). For a sample of the voluminous literature exploring the constitutionality of child witness protection statutes see, *e.g.*, Note, *The Testimony of Child Victims in Sex Abuse Prosecutions: Two Legislative Innovations*, 98 HARV. L. REV. 806 (1985); Note, *The Use of Videotaped Testimony of Victims in Cases Involving Child Sexual Abuse: A Constitutional Dilemma*, 14 HOFSTRA L. REV. 261 (1985); Comment, *Use of Videotaping to Avoid Traumatization of Child Sexual Abuse Victim-Witnesses*, 21 LAND & WATER L. REV. 565 (1986); M. Wixom, *Videotaping the Testimony of an Abused Child: Necessary Protection for the Child or Unwarranted Compromise of the Defendant's Constitutional Rights?*, 1986 UTAH L. REV. 461; M. Small & I. Schwartz, *Commentary: Policy Implications for Children's Law in the Aftermath of* Maryland v. Craig, 1 SETON HALL CONST. L.J. 109 (1990).

[68] Hearsay is defined in Federal Rule of Evidence 801 as follows: " 'Hearsay' is a statement other than one made by the declarant while testifying at the trial or hearing, offered in evidence to prove the truth of the matter asserted." For a discussion of the history of and rationale for excluding hearsay evidence, see 2 J. Strong et al., McCormick on Evidence 90–96 (4th ed. 1992).

application of traditional exceptions to the hearsay rule covering all declarants.[69] Permitting the use of hearsay is controversial because the defendant is denied face-to-face confrontation as well as the opportunity to cross-examine the witness.

A number of states have enacted legislation exempting child victim statements from the general rule against the use of hearsay. Typically such statutes provide that the out-of-court statement of a child victim of a sexual offense is admissible in a criminal proceeding if the court finds, in a hearing outside the presence of the jury, that the time, content, and circumstances of the statement provide sufficient indicia of reliability, the child is "unavailable" to testify at trial, and there is corroborative evidence of the act.[70]

The reliability of the statement can be established through a variety of mechanisms including the testimony of the child's therapist or her parent.[71] In establishing reliability, courts rely on a variety of factors including: the child's general character and physical condition; the nature and duration of the sexual act; the relationship between the child and the accused; whether the statements were made spontaneously; whether more than one person heard the statements; whether the child was distraught or calm when making the statement; and whether the child might have a motive to lie.[72] Furthermore, the statutes often provide safeguards for testing the reliability of the hearsay statements by authorizing out-of-court reliability hearings and requiring psychiatric evaluations of the child's testimony and reactions while making such statements.[73]

The requirement that the child witness be "unavailable" to testify can be satisfied in several ways. Sufficient evidence of unavailability can be supplied by expert testimony that the child's emotional or physical health would be impaired if forced to testify,[74] or by a judicial finding that the child is incompetent to testify.[75]

Some statutes specify "cut off dates" that limit the use of hearsay statements to those made by child victims under a certain age.[76] Under some provisions, the hearsay exception applies only to the victim's first statement about the offense, following its commission, made to an adult.[77]

Another legislative innovation enacted in several states permits the use of child victim hearsay by authorizing the videotaping of the child's testimony outside the courtroom in an environment thought to be more comfortable to the child than the intimidating atmosphere of the courtroom.[78] The videotape is then presented at trial, thus sparing the child repeated appearances in court and reducing the

---

[69] *See infra* notes 70–86 and accompanying text.

[70] *See* Comment, *Accommodating Child Abuse Victims: Special Hearsay Exceptions in Sexual Offense Prosecutions*, 16 Ohio N.U. L. Rev. 663, 672–73 (1989). If the child testifies at trial, the out-of-court statement is often admissible without additional corroboration. *Id.* at 672, 681. For ways in which corroboration is established, see *id.* at 686.

[71] *See, e.g.,* People v. Haynie, 826 P.2d 371, 376 (Colo. Ct. App. 1991).

[72] Kramer, *supra* note 3, at 107.

[73] *Id.* at 108.

[74] People v. Haynie, 826 P.2d 371, 376 (Colo. Ct. App. 1991).

[75] Ind. Code Ann. § 35-37-4-6 (d)(2)(B)(iii) (Burns 1998). *But see* State v. Ryan, 691 P.2d 197, 202–3 (Wash. 1984) (incompetency to testify does not establish "unavailability" to testify).

[76] Kramer, *supra* note 34, at 564.

[77] *Id.*

[78] Harvard Note, *supra* note 67.

potential trauma to the child.[79] The statutes generally require that the defendant be present and allowed to cross-examine the child at the videotaping session, although some statutes dispense with such requirements if the child later testifies at trial.[80] Even where cross-examination rights are afforded, the videotaped testimony is technically hearsay[81] The statutes, however, generally do not require a showing of "unavailability" as a prerequisite either to taping the testimony in the first place or to admitting it subsequently at trial.[82]

The lower courts have generally upheld the constitutionality of statutes permitting the use of hearsay statements of child victims.[83] A few courts, however, have struck down such statutes as infringing on the rule-making powers of the courts[84] in violation of separation of powers.

In states without specific statutes, the courts have often liberally applied traditional common law exceptions to the hearsay rule in order to admit the out-of-court statements of child victims. Specifically, the courts have relied on the following exceptions to the hearsay rule: excited utterances, spontaneous declarations, statements made for purposes of medical diagnosis and treatment, statements of present pain and suffering, and statements showing a particular state of mind.[85] On the other hand, a few courts have decided against expansive use of hearsay exceptions in child abuse cases.[86]

In *Idaho v. Wright*,[87] the United States Supreme Court addressed the constitutionality of using hearsay statements of child victims in child abuse trials. The Court found that the defendant's confrontation rights were violated when the trial court permitted the prosecution to introduce the statements of a 2½ year-old victim made to a pediatrician who in turn testified at trial. The doctor testified, among other things, that the child responded affirmatively to the doctor's question, "Does daddy [the defendant] touch you with his pee-pee?"[88] Although the defendant objected to the admissibility of the doctor's testimony as hearsay, the

---

[79] *Id.* at 807–8.

[80] *Id.* at 814. At least one court has invalidated a videotape provision not allowing for cross-examination of the child by the defendant as violative of defendant's confrontation rights. *See* People v. Bastien, 541 N.E.2d 670 (Ill. 1989).

[81] Note, *supra* note 78, at 822; *see supra* note 68.

[82] Note, *supra* note 78, at 823. *But see* Cal. Penal Code § 1346(d) (West 1982) (videotape admissible at trial if the court finds that further testimony would cause this victim "emotional trauma so that the victim is medically unavailable or otherwise unavailable within . . . Section 240 of the Evidence Code"); Neb. Rev. Stat. § 29-1926 (1995) (videotaping permitted only upon a showing of "compelling need").

[83] Kramer, *supra* note 3, at 107, 115. State v. Krick, 643 A.2d 331 (Del. Super. Ct. 1993) (statutory hearsay exception for statements of child victims upheld against Confrontation Clause attack); State v. Naucke, 829 S.W.2d 445 (Mo. 1992), *cert. denied*, 506 U.S. 960 (1992) (statute permitting *in camera* videotaping of child victim testimony upheld against Confrontation Clause attack).

[84] *See, e.g.*, State v. Robinson, 735 P.2d 801 (Ariz. 1987); State v. Zimmerman, 829 P.2d 861 (Idaho 1992). For a thorough constitutional assessment of statutory exceptions to the hearsay rule in the context of child abuse, see R. Mosteller, *Remaking Confrontation Clause and Hearsay Doctrine Under the Challenge of Child Sexual Abuse Prosecutions*, 1993 U. Ill. L. Rev. 691.

[85] Kramer, *supra* note 3, at 110.

[86] *See, e.g.*, People v. Zurak, 571 N.Y.S.2d 577, 579 (N.Y. App. Div. 1991), *cert. denied*, 504 U.S. 941 (1992) (court refused to recognize special hearsay exception for statements of child victims, seeing such exceptions in other jurisdictions as resting on statutory liberalizations of evidentiary rules).

[87] 497 U.S. 805 (1990).

[88] *Id.* at 810. The doctor also testified that the child did not describe the kind of touching that took

trial court admitted it under the state's residual hearsay exception after finding the child incompetent to testify herself because of her inability to communicate with the jury.[89]

In finding that the trial court erroneously admitted the testimony, the *Wright* Court noted that the Confrontation Clause generally precludes the use of evidence admissible under an exception to the hearsay rule unless the declarant is "unavailable" to testify at trial and the reliability of the hearsay statement is reliable either because it falls within a "firmly rooted" hearsay exception or its reliability is established by "a showing of particularized guarantees of trustworthiness."[90] While the Court assumed that the child was "unavailable" because of her incapacity to testify,[91] it found that the testimony lacked sufficient "indicia of reliability" because it neither fell within a firmly rooted hearsay exception nor was shown to be trustworthy under the circumstances of the particular case.

The *Wright* Court rejected an argument made by the state that certain corroborating evidence was itself sufficient to show a "particularized guarantee of trustworthiness."[92] Instead, the Court found that standard could be met only by an evaluation of the "circumstances . . . that surround the making of the statement and that render the declarant particularly worthy of belief."[93] At the same time, the Court rejected the defendant's argument that because the child was incompetent to testify at trial, her hearsay statements were *per se* unreliable.[94] Instead, the Court listed the following factors (not meant to be exclusive or to supply a "mechanical test") as relevant in determining the reliability of particular child hearsay statements: the spontaneity of the statement; the reputation and mental state of the declarant; the use of terminology unexpected of children of similar age; and the lack of motive to fabricate.[95] Finally, the Court offered a

---

place but did say that "daddy does do this with me but he does it a lot more with my sister than with me." *Id.* at 811.

[89] Idaho's residual hearsay exception provided:

> Rule 803. Hearsay exceptions: availability of declarant immaterial.— The following are not excluded by the hearsay rule, even though the declarant is available as a witness.
>
> . . . .
>
> (24) Other exceptions. A statement not specifically covered by any of the foregoing exceptions but having equivalent circumstantial guarantees of trustworthiness, if the court determines that (A) the statement is offered as evidence of a material fact; (B) the statement is more probative on the point for which it is offered than any other evidence which the proponent can procure through reasonable efforts; and (C) the general purposes of these rules and the interests of justice will best be served by admission of the statement into evidence.

497 U.S. at 811–12.

[90] *Id.* at 814–15 (citing Ohio v. Roberts, 448 U.S. 56, 65–66 (1980), *abrogated by* Crawford v. Washington, 541 U.S. 36 (2004)).

[91] "For purposes of deciding this case, we assume without deciding that, to the extent the unavailability requirement applies in this case, the [2½-year-old child] was an unavailable witness within the meaning of the Confrontation Clause." 497 U.S. at 816.

[92] *Id.* at 819.

[93] *Id.* at 820.

[94] *Id.* at 824–25.

[95] *Id.* at 821–22.

general principle to guide determinations of reliability: "if the declarant's truthfulness is so clear from the surrounding circumstances that the test of cross-examination would be of marginal utility, then the hearsay rule does not bar admission of the statement at trial."[96]

Shortly after *Wright*, the Court again considered the admissibility of child victim hearsay statements in a sexual abuse case. In *White* v. *Illinois*,[97] the Court refined the position expressed in *Wright* by holding that hearsay evidence could be admitted at trial under "firmly rooted" exceptions without first establishing that the child declarant was unavailable to testify. The *White* Court rejected the defendant's Confrontation Clause objections and upheld the trial court's action in admitting into evidence the testimony of the four-year-old victim's babysitter who testified that she was awakened by the child's screams in the early morning hours. The babysitter further testified that when she went to the child's room to investigate, she saw the defendant leave the child's room and exit the house. The babysitter then testified that she immediately asked the child what had happened and the child responded that the defendant choked her, threatened to whip her if she screamed, and "touched her in the wrong places."[98] The babysitter testified that when she asked the child where the defendant had touched her, the child pointed to her vaginal area.

Moreover, the *White* Court also upheld the admissibility of testimony of the child's mother who testified that the child had told the mother, shortly after making her statements to the babysitter, that the defendant had "put his mouth on her front part."[99] Similarly, the Court upheld the trial court's action in permitting the testimony of medical professionals who testified that in the process of questioning the child during a medical examination conducted approximately four hours after the time the defendant was seen leaving the house, the child provided an account essentially the same as that offered to the babysitter and the mother.

The *White* Court saw no constitutional defect in the fact that the child did not testify at trial and the trial court made no finding that she was unavailable to testify.[100] Indeed, the Court found that requiring a showing of unavailability as a prerequisite for hearsay admissibility would add little to the "trial's truth-determinative process" and would "likely impose substantial additional burdens on the fact-finding process."[101] Moreover, the Court agreed that the trial court properly applied both the "spontaneous declaration" exception in admitting the testimony of the babysitter and the mother and the "medical examination" exception in admitting the testimony of the medical personnel.[102] The Court saw

---

[96] *Id.* at 820.

[97] 502 U.S. at 346 (1992).

[98] *Id.* at 349.

[99] *Id.*

[100] The State attempted twice to call the child as a witness, but she experienced "emotional difficulty on being brought to the courtroom," and in both instances left without testifying. The defense did not seek to call the child as a witness, and "the [trial] court neither made, nor was asked to make, a finding that the child was unavailable to testify." *Id.* at 350.

In finding that a showing of unavailability was unnecessary, the Court distinguished earlier cases that suggested that a showing of unavailability was a necessary condition for the admissibility of any hearsay statement. "[U]navailability analysis is a necessary part of Confrontation Clause inquiry only when the challenged out-of-court statements were made in the course of a prior judicial proceeding." *Id.* at 354.

[101] *Id.* at 354–55.

[102] The trial court had specifically appealed to the spontaneous declaration and medical treatment

these "firmly rooted" exceptions to the hearsay rule as grounded in contexts that themselves provided "substantial guarantees of trustworthiness."[103]

As illustrated by *Wright* and *White*, out-of-court statements made by child victims are sometimes utilized in cases involving child sexual abuse. Although not involving a child witness, the United States Supreme Court decision in *Crawford v. Washington*[104] has impacted the Confrontation Clause analysis in child testimony cases.[105] The Court held, with regard to out-of-court "testimonial" statements covered by an established hearsay exception,[106] that in order to satisfy the Sixth Amendment Confrontation Clause, the witness must be unavailable and the defendant must have had prior opportunity to cross-examine the witness. Although it declined to formulate a definition of "testimonial" in *Crawford*, in a later case, the Supreme Court provided the following test:

> [S]tatements are nontestimonial when made in the course of police interrogation under circumstances objectively indicating that the primary purpose of interrogation is to enable police assistance to meet an ongoing emergency. They are testimonial when the circumstances objectively indicate that there is no such ongoing emergency, and that the primary purpose of the interrogation is to establish or prove past events potentially relevant to later criminal prosecution.[107]

The Supreme Court recognized that *Crawford* called into question its holding in *White*, "which involved, *inter alia*, statements of a child victim to an investigating police officer admitted as spontaneous declarations."[108] Rather than explicitly overruling *White*, however, the *Crawford* Court distinguished the case on the narrow ground that the *White* Court did not at the time have before it the question of "whether certain of the statements, because they were testimonial, had to be excluded *even if* the witness was unavailable."[109]

At a minimum, *Crawford* makes the admissibility of child testimony, where the child is unavailable, questionable.[110] One commentator has noted that *Crawford* has cast doubt over the admissibility of out-of-court statements made by children to a

---

exceptions to the hearsay rule as the basis for admitting the testimony of the respective witnesses. *Id.* at 350–51.

[103] We note . . . that the evidentiary rationale for permitting hearsay testimony regarding spontaneous declarations and statements made in the course of receiving medical care is that such out-of-court declarations are made in contests that provide substantial guarantees of their trustworthiness. But those same factors that contribute to the statements' reliability cannot be recaptured even by later in-court testimony. A statement that has been offered in a moment of excitement — without the opportunity to reflect on the consequences of one's exclamation — may justifiably carry more weight with a trier of fact than a similar statement offered in the relative calm of the courtroom. Similarly, a statement made in the course of procuring medical services, where the declarant knows that a false statement may cause misdiagnosis or mistreatment, carries special guarantees of credibility that a trier of fact may not think replicated by courtroom testimony. *Id.* at 355–56.

[104] 541 U.S. 36 (2004).

[105] R. Mosteller, Crawford's *Impact on Hearsay Statements in Domestic Violence and Child Sexual Abuse Cases*, 71 BROOK L. REV. 411, 412 (2005); S. Davis et al., Children in the Legal System 616 (3d ed. 2004).

[106] In *Crawford*, the relevant exception was the statement against penal interest exception.

[107] *Davis v. Washington*, 547 U.S. 813, 813–14 (2006).

[108] *Crawford*, 541 U.S. at 58, n. 8.

[109] *Id.*

[110] Tom Lininger, *Prosecuting Batterers After* Crawford, 91 VA. L. REV. 747, 748 (2005).

counselor or police officer, and courts are divided over the issue.[111] However, out-of-court statements made by the child to the child's friends, parents, or doctor (in other words, individuals not interviewing the child in an official capacity) are more likely to be found non-testimonial, and the admission of the same, therefore, is less likely to violate the Confrontation Clause.[112]

## [3]  Policy Implications

With its decisions in *Craig* and *White*, the Supreme Court has permitted states broad powers to enact special protective procedures for child victim witnesses, some of which negatively impact the interests of the defendant. The empirical premises of the cases assume that while child victims are not inherently less reliable than adults in providing accurate information, they are often uniquely traumatized if required to testify in judicial proceedings in the presence of their accused abusers. Whether the validity of these assumptions has been sufficiently established[113] to justify compromising the defendant's ability to face and cross-examine witnesses against him is a question that should be taken seriously by courts and policy makers, particularly in light of documented cases of children making false accusations of abuse.[114]

---

[111]  Davis, *supra* note 105, at 617.

[112]  *See* People v. Vigil, 127 P.3d 916, (Colo. 2006) (holding that a seven-year-old boy's out-of-court statements to his father, to his father's friend, and to his doctor were non-testimonial and that their later admissions in court were not a violation of the Confrontation Clause); Herrera-Vega v. State, 888 So. 2d 66, 68 (Fla. Dist. Ct. App.2004) (holding that three-year-old child's spontaneous comment to her mother regarding sexual contact with defendant was non-testimonial); State v. Vaught, 682 N.W.2d 284 (Neb. 2004) (holding that child's statement to doctor was non-testimonial).

[113]  See *supra* notes 49 and 51 for consideration of the empirical validity of the assumptions underlying child victim witness protections. *See also* M. Graham, *Indicia of Reliability and Fact to Face Confrontation: Emerging Issues in Child Sexual Abuse Prosecutions*, 40 U. MIAMI L. REV. 19 (1985); K. MacFarlane, *Diagnostic Evaluations and the Use of Videotapes in Child Sexual Abuse Cases*, 40 U. MIAMI L. REV. 135 (1985); L. Berliner, *The Child Witness: The Progress and Emerging Limitations*, 40 U. MIAMI L. REV. 167 (1985); G. Goodman & V. Helgeson, *Child Sexual Assault: Children's Memory and the Law*, 40 U. MIAMI L. REV. 181 (1985).

[114]  In his dissenting opinion in *Craig*, Justice Scalia noted:

> The "special" reasons that exist for suspending one of the usual guarantees of reliability in the case of children's testimony are perhaps matched by "special" reasons for being particularly insistent upon it in the case of children's testimony. Some studies show that children are substantially more vulnerable to suggestion than adults, and often unable to separate recollected fantasy (or suggestion) from reality. . . .
>
> The injustice their erroneous testimony can produce is evidenced by the tragic Scott County investigations of 1983–84, which disrupted the lives of many (as far as we know) innocent people in the small town of Jordan, Minnesota. At one stage those investigations were pursuing allegations by at least eight children of multiple murders, but the prosecutions actually initiated charged only sexual abuse. Specifically, 24 adults were charged with molesting 37 children. In the course of the investigations, 25 children were placed in foster homes. Of the 24 indicted defendants, one pleaded guilty, two were acquitted at trial, and the charges against the remaining 21 were voluntarily dismissed. . . . There is no doubt that some sexual abuse took place in Jordan; but there is no reason to believe it was as widespread as charged. A report by the Minnesota attorney general's office, . . . concluded that there was an "absence of credible testimony and [a] lack of significant corroboration" to support reinstitution of sex-abuse charges and "no credible evidence of murders.". . .The report describes an investigation full of well-intentioned techniques employed by the prosecution team, police, child protection workers, and foster parents, that distorted and in some cases even coerced the children's recollection. Children were interrogated repeatedly, in some cases as many as 50 times; answers were suggested by telling the children what other witnesses had

On the issue of face-to-face confrontation, *Craig* balances the respective interests of the state and the accused by requiring case-specific showings of necessity as a prerequisite to allowing testimony outside the presence of the defendant. As a practical matter, however, the case could result in wholesale denials of face-to-face confrontation. *Craig* encourages trial courts to rely on predictive evidence supplied by experts in identifying potential trauma to particular child victims without providing guidance as to how much weight such evidence should be afforded and under what evidentiary standard it should be assessed.[115] It is possible that some experts may, in virtually every case, see child victim testimony in the defendant's presence as risking serious trauma. If so, judicial reliance on such expertise, although given in connection with a specific case, would be tantamount to a reliance on a presumption of trauma similar to that rejected by the Court in *Coy*.[116]

Unlike the Court's position in *Craig*, *White* does not require a showing of necessity before admitting into evidence statements prejudicial to the defendant which are given not only outside his presence but also by parties not subject to cross-examination at trial. In rejecting the requirement of unavailability to testify as a prerequisite to admitting hearsay deemed reliable through a firmly rooted exception, the Court found that the demands of the Confrontation Clause were satisfied. *White* thus focused sole attention on the issue of reliability of evidence regardless of the child declarant's availability to testify at trial or the need to protect the child from trauma.

*White* entrusts the trial courts to assess vigilantly the reliability of hearsay before admitting it into evidence. Ironically, however, the case could in certain circumstances result in encouraging judicial laxity in scrutinizing the reliability of hearsay evidence nominally fitting within a "firmly rooted" exception to the hearsay rule.[117] To pose just one possible problem, suppose, as in *Wright*, a doctor

---

said; and children (even some who did not at first complain of abuse) were separated from their parents for months. The report describes the consequences as follows:

> As children continued to be interviewed the list of accused citizens grew. In a number of cases, it was only after weeks or months of questioning that children would "admit" their parents abused them.
>
> . . . .
>
> In some instances, over a period of time, the allegations of sexual abuse turned to stories of mutilations, and eventually homicide.

The value of the confrontation right in guarding against a child's distorted or coerced recollections is dramatically evident with respect to one of the misguided investigative techniques the report cited: some children were told by their foster parents that reunion with their real parents would be hastened by "admission" of their parents' abuse.

Is it difficult to imagine how unconvincing such a testimonial admission might be to a jury that witnessed the child's delight at seeing his parents in the courtroom? Or how devastating it might be if, pursuant to a psychiatric evaluation that "trauma would impair the child's ability to communicate" in front of his parents, the child were permitted to tell his story to the jury on closed-circuit television?

497 U.S. 868–69 (Scalia, J., dissenting).

[115] *See* Mnookin & Weisberg, *supra* note 46, at 419.

[116] *See supra* notes 57–58 and accompanying text.

[117] Some commentators question whether the traditional hearsay exceptions assure reliable evidence. *See, e.g.*, S. Goldman, *Not So "Firmly Rooted": Exceptions to the Confrontation Clause*, 66 N.C.

asks leading questions regarding a possible abuser[118] while examining a suspected child victim. If, as *White* arguably permits, the courts automatically admit such evidence under the medical examination exception, they risk introducing highly prejudicial evidence of questionable reliability given the views of some that children are uniquely subject to suggestibility, particularly when asked leading questions.[119]

These considerations suggest that care should be exercised in employing safeguards for child victim witnesses. Their interests are worthy of zealous protection so long as the legitimate interests of the alleged abuser are also respected.

## [C]   Other Evidentiary Issues

Several other evidentiary issues are especially pertinent to child abuse prosecutions. Two such matters deserve brief attention: the role of traditional privileges in the law of child abuse and the question of whether prior acts of abuse by an abuser are admissible in proving new allegations of abuse.

### [1]   Testimonial Privileges

Similar to the approach taken in the context of reporting statutes,[120] in many jurisdictions certain traditional testimonial privileges are not applicable in the context of child abuse prosecution. Because child abuse routinely occurs in private and may be unprovable without the testimony of eyewitness family members, many courts and legislatures have altered traditional privileges protecting family members from testifying against one another.[121] Many jurisdictions have specifically abrogated the husband-wife privilege in child abuse prosecutions[122] and a growing number of states have denied the applicability of privileges in the contexts of physician-patient, psychotherapist-patient, and priest-penitent.[123]

### [2]   Admissibility of Prior Acts of Abuse

The courts are divided on the issue of whether prior acts of abuse should be admissible as character evidence. Some courts hold such evidence inadmissible,[124] while others permit it to be used to prove who caused the harm and the existence of criminal intent.[125]

---

L. Rev. 1 (1987); *see also*, Note, *A Comprehensive Approach to Child Hearsay Statements in Sex Abuse Cases*, 83 Colum. L. Rev. 1745, 1753–63 (1983).

[118] *See supra* note 88 and accompanying text.

[119] *See, e.g.*, Note, *Determining Reliability Factors in Child Hearsay Statements:* Wright *and Its Progeny Confront the Psychological Research*, 79 Iowa L. Rev. 1149, 1172–74 (1994).

[120] *Supra* § 4.02, note 35.

[121] Kramer, *supra* note 3, at 116.

[122] Wadlington, Whitebread & Davis, *supra* § 3.02, note 34, at 805–6.

[123] Kramer, *supra* note 3, at 116–17.

[124] *See, e.g.*, Harvey v. State, 604 P.2d 586 (Alaska 1979).

[125] *See, e.g.*, Grabill v. State, 621 P.2d 802 (Wyo. 1980).

## § 4.04   CRIMINAL OR CIVIL ALTERNATIVES?

As has been emphasized in this Chapter, child abuse is a criminal offense in every jurisdiction. As noted in Chapter 3, child abuse may also provide the basis for a variety of civil responses under neglect and termination of parental rights provisions.[1] Whether to pursue the matter in criminal court (with heightened burden of proof requirements and dispositional options limited to punitive sanctions) or as a civil matter (with less exacting proof standards and an array of dispositional alternatives) is often a difficult decision for state officials charged with protecting the interests of children.[2]

Some argue that civil alternatives are preferable to the "slow and cumbersome" process of the criminal law.[3] Moreover, if the state initially seeks resolution through the criminal courts, the rigorous proof requirements therein may result in acquittals of abusive parents or caretakers who may then feel that their conduct has been officially justified and vindicated. If so, and unless civil actions are subsequently brought, the victims of such abuse may be exposed to increased risks at the hands of their acquitted abusers.[4]

On the other hand, the threat of criminal action may be the only means of deterring some would-be abusers or inducing parental cooperation in programs to rehabilitate the family.[5] Apart from such utilitarian interests, some child abuse is so despicable that the demands of justice arguably require the invocation of the punitive sanction.

Such considerations suggest that recourse to the criminal process should not be the inevitable response to cases of child abuse, even where the evidence assures convicting the abuser. Those entrusted with discretion to act on behalf of abused children sometimes act wisely in seeking civil remedies rather than punitive sanctions.

---

[1] *See supra* § 3.03.

[2] *See* Kramer, *supra* § 3.03, note 15, at 82–86.

[3] *Id.* at 83.

[4] *Id.*

[5] *Id.*

# Chapter 5
# PRIVATE LAW ISSUES OUTSIDE THE FAMILY

## § 5.01  OVERVIEW

Chapter 3 considered juvenile law issues arising within the family. This chapter attends to a variety of private law matters affecting young people in their interactions with parties outside the family relationship. The discussion will suggest that in these situations the law essentially reflects a protectionist posture towards young people, even though in some legal contexts noted herein minors are treated no differently than adults.

## § 5.02  LITIGATION ISSUES

### [A]  Parties

Under common law, unemancipated minors can sue only through their guardians or "next friends"[1] and can be sued only when their guardians are joined as defendants.[2] Minors who are parties to actions pending before a court become wards of the court. Gaining this status triggers a judicial obligation to assure that the interests of such parties are protected.[3]

Although the traditional common law rules have been somewhat relaxed by today's courts, it is still true that litigation is conducted by an adult guardian on behalf of the minor. As a general rule, a next friend (or guardian ad litem)[4] is required for juvenile parties only where they are without parents or general guardians.[5] Normally, the parent or guardian is duty bound to pursue and defend legal actions on behalf of the child.[6] Some courts hold that even where the minor plaintiff has a guardian, the minor may sue by next friend unless the guardian objects, or regardless of such objections, if the suit is necessary for the minor's

---

[1] A "next friend" is any adult willing to undertake the case on a minor's behalf. Clark, *supra* § 1.02, note 4, at 313. *See infra* note 8.

[2] *Id.*

[3] 42 Am. Jur. 2d *Infants* § 152 (1969).

[4] Traditionally, a "next friend" represented minor plaintiffs while a "guardian ad litem" represented minor defendants. *Id.* § 157. The distinction is also sometimes made that the guardian ad litem is appointed by the court while the next friend need not secure judicial appointment. While these distinctions retain validity in some jurisdictions, in others the terms are used interchangeably. Perhaps more often, the term "guardian ad litem" is used to describe the child's representative whether acting for plaintiffs or defendants or appointed by the court or not. *Id.* Most states now model their rules after the federal rules. Kramer, *supra* § 3.02, note 11, at 531–32. Federal Rule of Civil Procedure 17(c) provides:

> Whenever an infant . . . has a representative, such as a general guardian, committee, conservator, or other like fiduciary, the representative may sue or defend on behalf of the infant. . . . An infant . . . who does not have a duly appointed representative may sue by a next friend or by a guardian ad litem. The court shall appoint a guardian ad litem for an infant . . . not otherwise represented in the action or shall make such other orders as it deems proper for the protection of the infant. . . .

[5] Kramer, *supra* note 4, at 531–32.

[6] *Infants, supra* note 3, § 158.

benefit.[7] In some jurisdictions, courts must appoint persons to act as next friend, while in others, judicial appointment is unnecessary so long as the authority or qualification of the person acting as next friend is not challenged.[8] The court may remove the next friend and appoint someone else if it appears that the interests or actions of the next friend are not consistent with the interests of the minor.[9] The adult representative, whether a general guardian or a next friend, determines the propriety of maintaining the suit and decides the course of the litigation even though the minor is the real party plaintiff[10] and the suit is usually brought in the minor's name.[11]

In actions brought against minors, courts are duty bound to appoint guardians ad litem if the minor is not represented by a general guardian.[12] Courts usually appoint the child's nearest relation to act as guardian ad litem.[13] A guardian ad litem is an officer of the court and is obligated to act in good faith and to diligently defend the minor's interests.[14] Sometimes, but not always, guardians ad litem are attorneys.[15]

Whether plaintiffs or defendants, children are permitted to testify in legal proceedings so long as they meet competency requirements.[16] Moreover, apart from statutes of limitation issues discussed immediately hereafter, minors are subject to and bound by the same rules of procedure as are adult litigants.[17]

## [B]  Statutes of Limitations

Because children rely on adults to pursue legal claims on their behalf, most states have legislatively provided that statutes of limitation applicable to a child's claim do not begin to run until the child reaches the age of majority.[18] Some states

---

[7] *Id.*

[8] *Id.* § 160. Any competent adult person is qualified to serve as a minor's next friend so long as she is a resident of the state wherein the litigation is proceeding and does not have interests that conflict with those of the minor. *Id.* § 159.

[9] *Id.* § 159.

[10] *Id.* § 161.

[11] 43 C.J.S. *Infants* § 221 (1978); Clark, *supra* note 1. The next friend, for example, may negotiate for a settlement of the litigation, but such settlement is not binding upon the minor in the absence of judicial approval. *Infants, supra* note 3, § 185.

[12] *Infants, supra* note 3, § 173. Courts also appoint guardians ad litem whenever a child's general guardians are involved in litigation that creates conflicts of interest between the general guardians and the child. Kramer, *supra* note 4, at 534–35.

[13] *Infants, supra* note 3, § 174.

[14] *Id.* § 179.

[15] *Id.* § 174. Where, however, a statute provides that a minor litigant should be represented by an attorney, courts need not appoint a guardian ad litem, even in the absence of a general guardian, so long as the child is represented by an attorney. *Id.* § 173. When not themselves attorneys, guardians ad litem may employ or select counsel to assist in representing the minor. *Id.* § 179.

[16] *See supra* § 4.03[B][1].

[17] *Infants, supra* note 3, § 151. For a thorough consideration of the issue of minors as parties to litigation, see *id.* §§ 150–224. *Infants, supra* note 11, §§ 215–270.

[18] Kramer, *supra* note 4, at 521–23. Va. Code Ann. § 8.01-229 (Michie 2000) provides a typical provision:

A. Disabilities which toll the statute of limitations. — Except as otherwise specifically provided in . . . other provisions of this Code,

have general provisions governing all claims,[19] while others differentiate between certain types of claims.[20] In particular, legislatures in several states have enacted special rules for medical malpractice actions that reduce the period of time for which the statute of limitations will be tolled for child plaintiffs.[21]

## § 5.03   CONTRACTS

Under what has come to be known as the "infancy doctrine," contracts entered into by minors are voidable by the minor[1] unless the contract was for "necessaries" or unless the minor ratifies the contract after reaching majority.[2] This common law doctrine is aimed at protecting minors "from foolishly squandering their wealth through improvident contracts with crafty adults who would take advantage of them in the market place."[3]

While the common law infancy doctrine is still widely applicable, some jurisdictions have begun to adopt a less protectionist attitude towards contracting minors, particularly adolescents, in light of the modern reality that young people routinely,

---

1. If a person entitled to bring any action is at the time the cause of action accrues an infant, except if such infant has been emancipated . . . such person may bring it within the prescribed limitation period after such disability is removed; or

2. After a cause of action accrues,

    a. If an infant becomes entitled to bring such action, the time during which he is within the age of minority shall not be counted as any part of the period within which the action must be brought except as to any such period during which the infant has been judicially declared emancipated.

[19] *Id. See also, e.g.*, Mich. Comp. Laws Ann. § 600.5851 (West 2000) (one year to bring action after majority).

[20] Kramer, *supra* note 4, at 520.

[21] See, *e.g.*, N.Y. C.P.L.R. § 208 (McKinney 1990) which provides:

    If a person entitled to commence an action is under a disability because of infancy or insanity at the time the cause of action accrues, and the time otherwise limited for commencing the action is three years or more and expires no later than three years after the disability ceases, or the person under the disability dies, the time within which the action must be commenced shall be extended to three years after the disability ceases or the person under the disability dies, whichever event first occurs; if the time otherwise limited is less than three years, the time shall be extended by the period of disability. The time within which the action must be commenced shall not be extended by this provision beyond ten years after the cause of action accrues, except, in any action other than for medical, dental or podiatric malpractice, where the person was under a disability due to infancy. This section shall not apply to an action to recover a penalty or forfeiture, or against a sheriff or other officer for an escape.

*See also* Haw. Rev. Stat. § 657-7.3 (1993). *See* Kramer, *supra* note 4, at 524–25. For a discussion of the constitutionality of statutes of limitations in paternity actions, see *infra* § 6.06[B][2], notes 105–11 and the accompanying text.

[1] Under early cases, contracts by infants (persons under age twenty-one) were void rather than voidable. J. Calamari & J. Perillo, Contracts 306 (3d ed. 1987). To say that the contract is "voidable" is to say that there is a contract if no further action is taken at the instance of the minor but that the effects of the contract can be avoided if appropriate steps are taken on the minor's behalf. E.A. Farnsworth, Contracts 230 (2d ed. 1990).

[2] Calamari & Perillo, *supra* note 1, at 306–8, 310–17, 319–22; Kramer, *supra* § 3.02, note 11, at 501–3.

[3] Halbman v. Lemke, 298 N.W.2d 562, 567 (Wis. 1980).

and perhaps competently, engage in a variety of commercial transactions.[4] As a consequence, legislatures have begun to enact legislation limiting the power of minors to disaffirm their obligations under certain kinds of contracts.[5]

## [A] The Common Law Infancy Doctrine

Except for necessaries, contracts between minors and competent adults[6] are voidable at the election of the minor even if the adult is ignorant of the other party's status as a minor.[7] The minor has the option of either enforcing the contract of disaffirming it during her minority or within a reasonable time after reaching the age of majority.[8] The minor's failure to disaffirm may result in ratification after she reaches majority.[9]

In shaping the scope of the infancy doctrine, the courts have considered several recurring issues. Particularly, the courts have struggled with the following problems: defining the necessaries exception; deciding the extent to which disaffirming minors must make restitution for consideration received; assessing the consequences of misrepresentations of age by contracting minors; determining when ratification occurs; and ascertaining the effect of emancipation on contractual capacity. These issues will be briefly considered in turn.

### [1] The Necessaries Exception

While generally not contractually liable, minors are bound for the reasonable value of necessaries[10] on the theory that "unless an infant can get credit for necessaries he may starve."[11] Liability is generally understood to be quasi-contractual rather than contractual.[12] Thus, a minor may disaffirm an executory contract for necessaries and, where the contract is executed, the minor is liable for the reasonable value of the necessaries furnished rather than the contract price.[13]

Because parents or guardians are responsible for providing necessary support for their children,[14] unemancipated minors are not liable for necessaries unless their parents or guardians are unwilling or unable to supply their needs.[15]

---

[4] Clark, *supra* § 1.02, note 4, at 316–17.

[5] *See infra* notes 67–71 and accompanying text.

[6] A contract between two minors is voidable at the option of either. Hurwitz v. Barr, 193 A.2d 360 (D.C. 1963) (sale of motor scooter).

[7] Kramer, *supra* note 2, at 503. Minors may avoid their contracts even when fully executed. Calamari & Perillo, *supra* note 1, at 307. If the minor seeks to enforce her contract, an adult party to the contract cannot avoid the contract on the basis of the other's infancy. *Id.*

[8] *See supra* note 2.

[9] *Id.*

[10] Farnsworth, *supra* note 1, at 235.

[11] Turner v. Gaither, 83 N.C. 357, 361 (1880).

[12] Calamari & Perillo, *supra* note 1, at 319.

[13] *Id.*

[14] *See supra* § 3.02.

[15] Calamari & Perillo, *supra* note 1, at 321–22. For a rare case that appears to hold both the child and his parents liable for a contract for necessary medical services even though the child was living at home with his parents who were not shown to be unwilling or unable to provide for the medical care themselves, see *Scott County School District 1 v. Asher*, 324 N.E.2d 496 (Ind. 1975). In *Asher*, the court reasoned that since either the minor or his parents were liable for the reasonable value of the child's

Moreover, in order to be liable, the minor must have contracted with the creditor supplying the necessary goods and services.[16] Therefore, the minor is not liable for necessaries contracted for by her parent or guardian.[17]

In determining what constitutes a "necessary," the courts often designate as a matter of law general categories that qualify.[18] Thus, the term clearly includes needed shelter, food, clothing, and essential medical and legal services.[19] The courts have divided on whether an automobile is a necessary.[20] A basic public education is generally considered a necessary, as is an education in a trade under some cases. However, the courts generally hold that a college education is not a necessary.[21] A contract for a loan obtained to pay for necessaries is treated as a contract for necessaries.[22]

Whether a particular article or service falls within an accepted general category of necessaries is a question of fact determined under the circumstances in light of the minor's status, social and financial position, standard of living, and the ability and willingness of a parent or guardian to supply the article or service.[23] One court summarized the issue as follows:

> The word "necessaries" as used in the law is a relative term, except when applied to such things as are obviously requisite for the maintenance of existence, and depends on the social position and situation in life of the infant as well as upon his own fortune and that of his parents.[24]

---

medical care, either the parents or the minor could be compensated in a tort action for those costs incurred through the negligence of the defendant.

[16] Calamari & Perillo, *supra* note 1, at 322; Farnsworth, *supra* note 1, at 236–37.

[17] *Id.*

[18] Farnsworth, *supra* note 1, at 235.

[19] *Id.* at 235–36, Calamari & Perillo, *supra* note 1, at 320. Even when falling within a recognized general category, the minor must be in actual need of the item contracted for in order for it to constitute a necessary. Thus, a contract for shelter may qualify as a necessary only if the minor has no other place to live. *See* Webster Street Partnership v. Sheridan, 368 N.W.2d 439 (Neb. 1985) (holding that an apartment was not a necessary for two minors attempting to void a lease where the minors voluntarily left their family homes with the understanding that they could return home whenever they desired).

The courts have determined that legal services provided to enforce or defend tort claims or criminal or juvenile court prosecutions constitute necessaries. Calamari & Perillo, *supra* note 1, at 320. Some courts have reached a contrary conclusion if the lawyer is retained to protect a minor's property rights. *Id.*

[20] Generally the courts have held that automobiles are not a necessary. *See, e.g.*, Star Chevrolet Co. v. Green, 473 So. 2d 157 (Miss. 1985); Harris v. Raughton, 73 So. 2d 921 (Ala. Ct. App. 1954). A few courts have found to the contrary under the facts of the particular case. *See, e.g.*, Rose v. Sheehan Buick, Inc., 204 So. 2d 903 (Fla. Dist. Ct. App. 1967). *See generally* J. Bryant, Annotation, *Automobile Or Motorcycle As Necessary For Infant*, 56 A.L.R.3d 1335 (1974).

[21] Calamari & Perillo, *supra* note 1, at 320–21; Farnsworth, *supra* note 1, at 236.

[22] Calamari & Perillo, *supra* note 1, at 321. Often the courts theorize that the lender is subrogated to the rights of the person who furnished the necessaries. *See, e.g.*, Price v. Sanders, 60 Ind. 310 (1878). If the funds are advanced for the purpose of purchasing necessaries but are squandered for other purposes, some courts still hold the minor liable. *See, e.g.*, Norwood Nat'l Bank v. Allston, 149 S.E. 593 (S.C. 1929).

[23] *See, e.g.*, Rivera v. Reading Hous. Auth., 819 F. Supp. 1323, 1332 (E.D. Pa. 1993); *see* Kramer, *supra* note 2, at 505.

[24] International Text-Book Co. v. Connelly, 99 N.E. 722, 725 (N.Y. 1912).

Thus, what might be a "luxury" for some minors may be a "necessary" for others.[25]

## [2] Avoidance and Restitution

Where minors disaffirm contracts for non-necessaries and have received some or all of the other party's performance, the courts often must determine the extent to which the minor is accountable for the benefit conferred. The traditional view is that the disaffirming minor is required to return any goods received subject to the contract but is not accountable for any depreciation in the value of the goods even if the minor permitted or negligently caused the goods to lose value.[26] In a Wisconsin case,[27] the court permitted a minor plaintiff to recover the amount he had paid toward the purchase price of an automobile that, while in his possession, the minor had permitted to be damaged thus causing it to depreciate substantially in value.[28] The adult seller argued that he should recover the car itself and the amount of depreciation to the vehicle from the time it left his possession up to the time the minor disaffirmed. The court, however, permitted him to recover only the car in its depreciated state. Indeed, the court noted that the "minor's right to disaffirm is not contingent upon the return of the property . . . as disaffirmance is permitted even where such return cannot be made."[29] In the context of service contracts, the courts traditionally allow minors to recover whatever consideration they have conferred incident to the transaction without requiring anything in return.[30]

Not all courts follow the traditional rule just described. A few courts follow the so-called "New Hampshire view" that permits minors to disaffirm but holds them accountable in full for benefits received, whether necessaries or not.[31] More often,

---

[25] One commentator suggests, for example, that a contract for a home computer may obligate the minor because the computer may be a necessary for proper education when used for educational purposes. On the other hand, the computer would likely not be viewed as a necessary if used for recreation. Kramer, *supra* note 2, at 506.

[26] Calamari & Perillo, *supra* note 1, at 315; Farnsworth, *supra* note 1, at 234. One court stated the matter this way:

> An infant may repudiate or disaffirm his contract . . . but in doing so he is obliged to restore to the other contracting party the fruits of the contract *within his possession* at the time, that is, he must surrender and return the consideration received by him and thus far at least place the parties in *status quo, if the consideration is still in his hands*. . . . If during infancy he has wasted or squandered the consideration, or has otherwise made away with it so that he is unable to restore it, he may nevertheless repudiate the contract without making a tender.

Nelson v. Browning, 391 S.W.2d 873, 877 (Mo. 1965).

[27] Halbman v. Lemke, 298 N.W.2d 562 (Wis. 1980).

[28] After receiving possession of the car, the minor took the car to a garage to be repaired but did not pay the repair bill. As a consequence, the mechanic obtained a lien for the repair costs and removed the car's engine and transmission in satisfaction of the lien. The mechanic then towed the car to the residence of the minor's father where the car was subsequently vandalized, rendering it unsalvageable. *Id.*

[29] Halbman v. Lemke, 298 N.W.2d 562, 564 (Wis. 1980). If the minor had exchanged or sold the property and still possessed the property or money received in exchange, he would be liable for restitution as if the exchanged property or money were the original consideration. Calamari & Perillo, *supra* note 1, at 315.

[30] Farnsworth, *supra* note 1, at 234.

[31] *Id.*; Calamari & Perillo, *supra* note 1, at 323.

courts draw a distinction between cases where 1) the minor, as plaintiff, seeks recovery of money paid and 2) cases where the minor, as defendant, merely raises minority as a defense. In the former, a substantial number of courts require full restitution in the event of avoidance. In the latter cases, courts deny restitution (except, of course, for whatever consideration is still in the minor's hands) when the minor is sued for the contract price.[32]

This distinction, reflecting Chancellor Kent's observation that "the privilege of infancy is to be used as a shield and not as a sword,"[33] is explainable in terms of the risks foreseeable to the parties. Sellers who extend credit to minors often recognize legal and practical risks of nonpayment. In sales for cash, on the other hand, sellers may be genuinely surprised if minors with whom they have contracted could recover the cash paid without also returning the goods in their original condition (or their value if the goods themselves are not returnable).[34]

In cases where the minor sues to recover cash paid for services performed, for example, an airline flight taken by a minor who pays cash for the ticket, many courts deny the minor recovery of the cash paid.[35] These same courts might hold, however, that the minor is not obligated for the price of the flight if she takes the trip and promises to pay for it later.[36]

## [3] Misrepresentation of Age

In situations where minors falsely represent that they are above the age of majority and induce another party to contract with them in reliance on the misrepresentation, most courts hold that the minor may nevertheless disaffirm.[37] Some courts treat the misrepresentation as irrelevant, thus permitting the disaffirming minor a full recovery of the consideration he has already paid in return for whatever consideration still in the minor's possession.[38] Other courts permit disaffirmance but require the minor to restore the adult to the *status quo ante*.[39] A few courts, on the other hand, hold that because of the misrepresentation the minor is estopped from raising the issue of age, thus rendering the minor liable on the contract.[40]

---

[32] Calamari & Perillo, *supra* note 1, at 315–16; Farnsworth, *supra* note 1, at 237.

[33] 2 J. Kent, Commentaries on American Law 240 (3d ed. 1836); *see* Pettit v. Liston, 191 P. 660, 661 (Or. 1920) (quoting Kent and holding that minor plaintiff who disaffirmed a contract for a motorcycle could recover the amount paid, but must return the motorcycle and compensate the seller for damage the motorcycle incurred while in the minor's hands).

[34] Calamari & Perillo, *supra* note 1, at 316.

[35] *Id.*; Farnsworth, *supra* note 1, at 237.

[36] *Id.*

[37] Calamari & Perillo, *supra* note 1, at 318.

[38] *See, e.g.*, Gillis v. Witley's Discount Auto Sales, Inc., 319 S.E.2d 661 (N.C. Ct. App. 1984) (minor who misrepresented his age permitted to disaffirm contract for automobile and recover the entire consideration he had paid from his savings account in return only for the consideration in his possession, even after the automobile had been involved in two accidents); Fisher v. Taylor Motor Co., 107 S.E.2d 94 (N.C. 1959) (minor who misrepresented his age permitted to disaffirm contract for sale of automobile for $750 and recover in full his consideration paid upon return of the automobile valued at only $50 at the time of disaffirmance).

[39] Calamari & Perillo, *supra* note 1, at 318.

[40] Farnsworth, *supra* note 1, at 238; Kramer, *supra* note 2, at 512–13.

Regarding tort liability for misrepresentations of age, the courts again split. Some courts hold that no tort action lies because the claim sounds essentially in contract. These courts deny relief because to do otherwise would be to enforce the contract against the minor.[41] Other courts see the tort claim as independent of the contract and grant relief,[42] effectively requiring the minor to make full restitution for the value of the goods or services provided by the party who has acted in reliance on the misrepresentation.[43]

## [4]  Ratification

As a matter of general contract law, a power of avoidance is surrendered if the contract is ratified.[44] In the case of minors, ratification cannot occur prior to the attainment of majority because the act of ratification would itself be voidable.[45]

Ratification may occur in three ways: failure to make a timely disaffirmance; express ratification; or conduct manifesting an intent to ratify.[46] No consideration is required to effectuate a valid ratification.[47]

## [a]  Failure to Make a Timely Disaffirmance

The courts permit minors to disaffirm their contracts at any time during their minority[48] or within a reasonable time after reaching majority.[49] Generally, determinations of "reasonable time" depend on the circumstances of the case. One court put the matter this way:

> Affirmance is not merely a matter of intent. It may be determined by the actions of a minor who accepts the benefits of a contract after reaching the age of majority, or who is silent or acquiesces in the contract for a considerable length of time. What act constitutes ratification or disaffirmance is ordinarily a question of law to be determined by the trial court. . . . We agree that what constitutes a reasonable time for affirmance or disaffirmance is ordinarily a question of fact to be determined by the facts in a particular case.[50]

Many courts allow a more extensive period for disaffirmance for executory contracts, sometimes until the statute of limitations has run, while restricting the period in cases where the minor has received benefits under the contract.[51]

---

[41]  Calamari & Perillo, *supra* note 1, at 318.

[42]  *Id.*; Kramer, *supra* note 2, at 512.

[43]  Farnsworth, *supra* note 1, at 237.

[44]  Calamari & Perillo, *supra* note 1, at 310; Farnsworth, *supra* note 1, at 232.

[45]  *Id.*

[46]  Calamari & Perillo, *supra* note 1, at 311.

[47]  *Id.*; Farnsworth, *supra* note 1, at 232.

[48]  Calamari & Perillo, *supra* note 1, at 310. Some cases limit disaffirmance of contracts for conveyances of real property to periods after the minor has reached majority. *Id.*

[49]  *Id.* at 310–11.

[50]  Jones v. Dressel, 623 P.2d 370, 374 (Colo. 1981) (minor held to have ratified contract for skydiving services by using services after reaching age of majority).

[51]  Calamari & Perillo, *supra* note 1, at 311.

## [b]  Express Ratification

Ratification may be written or oral but must manifest an intent to be contractually bound.[52] In cases where the contract is fully executed, a mere acknowledgment or other words consistent with an intention to stand on the transaction will constitute ratification.[53]

## [c]  Conduct

While mere failure by the minor to disaffirm within a reasonable time after reaching the age of majority may constitute ratification of the contract, certain overt conduct carries the same effect. Any manifestation to be bound by the original transaction is sufficient to constitute a ratification.[54] Retention and use of property or services received pursuant to the contract for more than a reasonable time after reaching the age of majority constitutes ratification.[55]

## [5]  Emancipation and Contract Capacity

The consequences of emancipation were discussed earlier in connection with parental support duties.[56] Attention here is directed to the ramifications of emancipation on the issue of contractual capacity of the emancipated minor.

The general rule is that emancipation does not remove the disabilities of minority,[57] and thus does not end the young person's right to disaffirm contracts.[58] Some cases hold to the contrary, particularly where emancipation occurs by marriage.[59]

While the cases generally hold that emancipation does not in itself render the minor competent to contract, some courts find the emancipation factor relevant when determining whether a particular contract is for necessaries. Thus, for example, a lease may not be a contract for a necessary where the minor is unemancipated and able to receive lodging from his parents.[60] On the other hand, where parents owe no support duties to a minor because of emancipation, the courts are more likely to view the emancipated minor's contract for housing as enforceable under the necessaries exception.[61] Therefore, the scope of the concept

---

[52] *Id.* at 312.

[53] *Id.* at 313.

[54] Farnsworth, *supra* note 1, at 232. Note, however, that some cases hold that partial payment by the minor after reaching majority is not, without more, a ratification. *See, e.g.,* Int'l Accountants Soc'y v. Santana, 117 So. 768 (La. 1928).

[55] Calamari & Perillo, *supra* note 1, at 313.

[56] *See supra* § 3.02[B][1].

[57] Institute of Judicial Admin. & American Bar Ass'n, Juvenile Justice Standards, Rights of Minors 22 (1980).

[58] Calamari & Perillo, *supra* note 1, at 306; *see, e.g.,* Schoenung v. Gallet, 238 N.W. 852 (Wis. 1931) (emancipated minor permitted to disaffirm contract for automobile that was found not to be a necessary).

[59] *See, e.g., In re* Greer, 184 So. 2d 104 (La. Ct. App. 1966) (thirteen-year-old emancipated by marriage denied right to nullify an agreement to settle a legal claim acquired as result of accidental death of the minor's husband). Some commentators have described this as a "distinctly minority view." Calamari & Perillo, *supra* note 1, at 306 n.5.

[60] Webster St. Partnership v. Sheridan, 368 N.W.2d 439 (Neb. 1985), discussed at *supra* note 19.

[61] *See, e.g.,* Merrick v. Stephens 337 S.W.2d 713 (Mo. Ct. App. 1960) (contract for purchase of home held to be for a necessary where a soon-to-be married emancipated minor, who had misrepresented his

of necessaries is enlarged by emancipation, particularly when it occurs by marriage.[62]

## [6] Non-Necessary Medical Expenses

As discussed in an earlier section of this book,[63] a few courts have held that mature minors may give valid consent for their medical treatment in non-emergency situations. Such consent authorizes what would otherwise be a tortious battery upon the patient.[64] Although the issue appears not to have arisen, cases recognizing the competency of minors to consent to non-necessary medical treatment would seem to imply that such minors would be bound for the costs of the treatment,[65] either on a contract or quasi-contract theory.

## [B] Statutory Innovations

Modern statutes have altered some aspects of the common law rules. Lowering the age of majority from twenty-one to eighteen has obviously broadened the contractual capacity of large numbers of young people. Moreover, many states have enacted statutes that further enhance the freedom of contract in certain circumstances for persons under the age of majority.

Some states statutorily preclude emancipated minors from disavowing their contracts. Some such statutes are limited to classes of minors emancipated by marriage[66] while others apply to all emancipated minors as defined by the statute.[67]

---

age, sought to recover payments made on the mortgage).

[62] Farnsworth, *supra* note 1, at 235; *see, e.g.,* Doubert v. Mosley, 487 P.2d 353 (Okla. 1971) (expenses to repair automobile were necessaries for married 19-year-old).

[63] *See supra* § 3.02[A][3][d].

[64] Wadlington, *supra* § 1.02, note 18, at 115.

[65] *Id.* at 124.

[66] See, *e.g.,* Kan. Stat. Ann § 38-101 (2000), which provides:

Period of Minority. The period of minority extends in all persons to the age of eighteen (18) years, except that every person sixteen (16) years of age or over who is or has been married shall be considered of the age of majority in all matters relating to contracts, property rights, liabilities and the capacity to sue and be sued.

[67] For example, in California, minors may petition the court for a declaration of emancipation. If the court is satisfied that the minor is at least 14 years of age, is living separately from his parents or guardian with their consent, and is financially supporting himself, the court may, after notifying the parents or guardian, issue a declaration of emancipation if "emancipation would not be contrary to the minor's best interest." *See* Cal. Fam. Code §§ 7120, 7121, 7122 (West 1994). The statutes further provide that "emancipated minors shall be considered as being an adult for . . . purposes . . . [of] [t]he minor's capacity to . . . [e]nter into a binding contract or give a delegation of power." *Id.* § 7050.

For a discussion of other statutory procedures for emancipation in other states, some of which perhaps remove disabilities of minority for purposes of contracting, see Katz et al., *supra* § 3.02, note 92, at 232–34.

Several states have enacted statutes dealing with the contracts of minors who are professional athletes or entertainers.[68] Statutes also routinely hold minors to their contracts with bankers[69] and with lenders providing them educational loans.[70]

Commentators have suggested that the *ad hoc* nature of these statutory deviations from established common law doctrine justifies a systematic reexamination of the power of children to make binding contracts.[71] One such "reexamination" has been conducted by the drafters of the Juvenile Justice Standards who would hold "mature" or emancipated minors financially liable when they consent to medical care.[72] In addition, the drafters propose the following provision defining contractual liability of minors:

Minors' contracts.

The validity of contracts of minors, other than those governed by other standards of this volume, should be governed by the following principles:

---

[68] *See, e.g.,* Cal. Fam. Code §§ 6750, 6751 (West 1994) (contract by minor for artistic, creative, or sports services cannot be disaffirmed by minor if court has approved the contract); N.Y. Arts & Cult. Aff. Law § 35.03 (McKinney 1984) (after judicial approval of contract made by a minor who is an artist or athlete, the minor is precluded from disaffirming).

[69] *See, e.g.,* Colo. Rev. Stat. § 11–105–104 (2007) (bank may operate a deposit account for a minor "with the same effect upon its liability as if the minor were of full age" unless guardian directs otherwise); Mo. Ann. Stat. § 362.465 (Vernon 1997) (deposits made by minor held for exclusive right and benefit of minor).

[70] *See, e.g.,* Wis. Stat. Ann. § 39.32(4) (West 2002) (minority not a defense to collection of student loan made to minors); Uniform Minor Student Capacity to Borrow Act § 2, 9B U.L.A. 4 (1987) (minors over age 16 entitled to contract for educational loans).

[71] *See, e.g.,* Clark, *supra* note 4, at 317. *See also infra* notes 74–75 and accompanying text.

[72] Institute of Judicial Admin. & American Bar Ass'n, *supra* note 57, at 60–68 provides the following:

§ 4.3 Financial Liability

. . .

B. A minor who consents to his or her own medical treatment under Standards 4.6–4.9 should be financially liable for payment for such services and should not disaffirm the financial obligation on account of minority.

. . .

§ 4.4 Emancipated minor.

A. An emancipated minor who is living separate and apart from his or her parent and who is managing his or her own financial affairs may consent to medical treatment on the same terms and conditions as an adult. Accordingly, parental consent should not be required, nor should there be subsequent notification of the parent, or financial liability.

1. If a physician treats a minor who is not actually emancipated, it should be a defense to a suit basing liability on lack of parental consent, that he or she relied in good faith on the minor's representations of emancipation.

. . .

§ 4.6 Mature minor.

A. A minor of [sixteen] or older who has sufficient capacity to understand the nature and consequences of a proposed medical treatment for his or her benefit may consent to that treatment on the same terms and conditions as an adult.

Standard 4.7 allows minors of any age to consent to medical services to treat chemical dependency and Standard 4.8 does the same in the context of venereal disease, contraception, and pregnancy. *Id.* at 70–72.

A. The contract of a minor who is at least twelve years of age should be valid and enforceable by and against the minor, as long as such a contract of an adult would be valid and enforceable, if:

1. the minor's parent or duly constituted guardian consented in writing to the contract; or

2. the minor represented to the other party that he or she was at least eighteen years of age and a reasonable person under the circumstances would have believed the representation; or

3. the minor was a purchaser and is unable to return the goods to the seller in substantially the condition they were in when purchased because the minor lost or caused them to be damaged, the minor consumed them, or the minor gave them away.

B. The contract of a minor who has not reached the age of twelve should be void.

C. Release of a tort claim by a minor should be valid, if an adult's release would be valid under the same circumstances:

1. if the minor is at least twelve years of age, if the release is approved by the minor, the minor's parent, and, if suit is pending, by the court; or

2. if the minor has not reached the age of twelve, if the release is approved by the minor's parent, and, if suit is pending, by the court.[73]

## [C] Policy Implications

The infancy doctrine of contract law developed as a means for protecting supposedly vulnerable children from their own bad judgment and exploitation by adults. Strict adherence to this doctrine has been questioned, however, in the context of modern society where children routinely have access to money and engage in a variety of commercial activities.[74] Whether the doctrine has outlived its usefulness and become a vehicle for the unfair treatment of adults who contract with minors in good faith is a question for serious consideration by policy makers.[75]

The various judicial responses assessing the responsibilities of minors upon disaffirmance illustrate the difficulty of reconciling the interests of both minors and their adult contracting parties. One commentator describes this area of the law as "a patchwork of rules, lack[ing] any single consistent principle."[76] One court stated that "the law regarding rights and responsibilities of the parties relative to the

---

[73] *Id.* at 111.

[74] *See, e.g.,* L. DiMatteo, *Deconstructing the Myth of the "Infancy Doctrine": From Incapacity to Accountability*, 21 Ohio N.U. L. Rev. 481 (1995); R. Edge, *Voidability of Minors' Contracts: A Feudal Doctrine in a Modern Economy*, 1 Ga. L. Rev. 205 (1967); I. Mehler, *Infant Contractual Responsibility: A Time for Reappraisal and Realistic Adjustment?*, 11 Kan. L. Rev. 361 (1963); W. Navin, Jr., *The Contracts of Minors Viewed from the Perspective of Fair Exchange*, 50 N.C. L. Rev. 517 (1972); *see also supra*, note 4.

[75] *See, e.g., supra* note 74.

As long as young men and women, under twenty-one years of age, having the semblance and appearance of adults, are forced to make a living and enter into business transactions, how are the persons dealing with them to be protected if the infant's word cannot be taken or recognized at law? Are business men to deal with young people at their peril?

Sternlieb v. Normandie Nat'l Sec. Corp., 188 N.E. 726, 728 (N.Y. 1934).

[76] Note, *Restitution in Minors' Contracts in California*, 19 Hastings L.J. 1199 (1968).

consideration exchanged on a disaffirmed contract [is] characterized by confusion, inconsistency, and a general lack of uniformity as jurisdictions attempt to reach a fair application of the infancy doctrine in today's marketplace."[77] The piecemeal legislative responses described in Section [B] above further exemplify the absence of a systematically coherent theory of children and the law of contract.

The difficulty of reconciling the interests of both minors and adults in an era where the two classes increasingly enter into contractual relationships with one another provides only partial explanation for the unsettled nature of law. The unevenness of the law in this area is also a function of a fundamental uncertainty about the extent to which traditional protectionist principles should give way to recognition of personhood rights and corresponding responsibilities for at least some minors. Some courts cling tenaciously to the infancy doctrine, shielding minors from contractual consequences, even when they are emancipated,[78] induce transactions by misrepresenting their age,[79] or waste the other party's consideration.[80] Other courts may view some minors as sufficiently mature to be contractually liable for non-necessary medical treatment.[81] It is not clear why courts taking such a position should limit the enforceability of the contracts of mature minors to the context of medical treatment.[82] If, for example, minors are competent and mature enough to drive automobiles, courts or legislators might someday find them sufficiently competent and mature to be bound by their contracts when they purchase the automobiles they drive.

## § 5.04  TORTS

As suggested by the discussion of misrepresentation of age cases under contract law,[1] the courts have historically been more likely to hold minors liable for their torts than for their contracts. Unlike the contract context, where exploitation of juveniles by adults is a distinct possibility, tort actions against minors aim to compensate injured plaintiffs[2] who generally pose no risk of exploiting or taking advantage of the minor defendant. To effectuate these compensatory purposes, children of virtually all ages are potentially liable in most jurisdictions for their tortious conduct. Sometimes, however, more lenient standards are applied to minors than would be applied to adults. Thus, apart from a few jurisdictions that follow the criminal law infancy defense and impose tort immunity for children under seven,[3] minority in itself is generally no defense to a tort action against a minor.

---

[77] Halbman v. Lemke, 298 N.W.2d 562, 565 (Wis. 1980).

[78] *See supra* notes 58–59 and accompanying text.

[79] *See supra* notes 37–38 and accompanying text.

[80] *See supra* notes 26–30 and accompanying text.

[81] *See supra* notes 64–66 and accompanying text.

[82] For an argument that competent minors should be contractually bound because persons "should be encouraged to keep their promises," see DiMatteo, *supra* note 74, at 516.

[1] *See supra* § 5.03[A][3].

[2] Kramer, *supra* § 3.02, note 11, at 454.

[3] Prosser & Keeton, *supra* § 3.03, note 1, at 1071 n.6; *see* DeLuca v. Bowden, 329 N.E.2d 109 (Ohio 1975) (minors under seven years of age held immune from liability for alleged battery or negligence when they hit plaintiff in eye with BB fired from BB gun).

## [A]  Intentional Torts

Children are liable for their intentional torts so long as they are sufficiently mature to formulate the requisite intent.[4] For some torts, such as trespass, where the required intent is merely to do the act which constitutes the trespass,[5] very young children may be held liable. Thus, for example, courts have upheld the liability of a six-year-old for breaking and entering the plaintiff's premises and destroying his shrubbery[6] and of a seven-year-old for setting fire to the plaintiff's house.[7] Similarly, most courts hold minors liable for battery if they merely intend to cause the bodily contact that results in harm whether or not they intended the harm.[8] On the other hand, at least one court has held that to be liable for battery a minor must not only intend to cause bodily contact but also intend to cause harm, at least in the sense of "appreciat[ing] the wrongfulness of his act."[9]

By their nature, some intentional torts require fairly sophisticated and morally culpable states of mind that may be beyond the ability of very young children to formulate. For example, in certain actions for defamation requiring malicious action,[10] very young children may be unable to form the requisite intent because of their limited experience or intelligence.[11]

## [1]  Punitive Damages

The prevailing view permits liability on the basis of intentional action without necessarily establishing that the defendant culpably anticipated the consequences of his actions. This view reflects a liberal policy in favor of compensating injured parties, taking the position that where "property has been damaged or other loss occasioned by a wrongful act, it is just that the loss should fall upon the estate of the wrongdoer rather than on the guiltless person."[12] The situation is different, however, when plaintiffs seek punitive damages from juvenile defendants.

In cases where minors commit intentional torts with "malicious intent," punitive damages may be imposed to punish the defendant and deter him and others from similar conduct in the future.[13] Minors "old enough to be capable of knowing the

---

[4] Prosser & Keeton, *supra* note 3, at 1071.

[5] *See, e.g.*, Gymnastics USA v. McDougal, 758 P.2d 881 (Or. Ct. App. 1988) (where ten-year-old placed non-explosive firework in hole in plaintiff's building, minor trespassed as a matter of law and was liable for damage to the building as a result of a fire caused by the firework).

[6] Huchting v. Engel, 17 Wis. 230 (1863).

[7] Brown v. Dellinger, 355 S.W.2d 742 (Tex. Civ. App. 1962) (seven and eight-year-olds held liable for damage to house resulting from fire started in charcoal burner in garage).

[8] Prosser & Keeton, *supra* note 3, at 1071; *see, e.g.*, Baily v. C.S., 12 S.W.3d 159 (Tex. Civ. App. 2000) (a four-year-old is capable of battery); Ellis v. D'Angelo, 253 P.2d 675 (Cal. Dist. Ct. App. 1953) (plaintiff states a cause of action for battery when she alleges that four-year-old defendant injured her by intentionally pushing her to the floor even if the push occurred in play and was not intended to inflict substantial injury).

[9] Horton v. Reaves, 526 P.2d 304, 307 (Colo. 1974) (three and four-year-old children entered the infant plaintiff's home, picked up plaintiff and dropped her on the floor, crushing her skull; to be held liable for battery, the defendants must "intend harmful contact").

[10] *See* Prosser & Keeton, *supra* note 3, at 833–34.

[11] *Id.* at 1071; Kramer, *supra* note 2, at 455.

[12] *Infants, supra* § 5.02, note 3, § 90.

[13] Prosser & Keeton, *supra* note 3, at 9-10; Anello v. Savignac, 342 N.W.2d 440, 442–43 (Wis. Ct. App.

wrongfulness of [their] acts" may be liable for punitive damages.[14] Some authority exists, at least in *dicta*, supporting the view that the criminal law infancy defense defines the category of juvenile defendants who are the proper subjects for punitive damages.[15] Thus, under this view, children under seven are immune from punitive damages, while those seven to fourteen are subject to a rebuttable presumption of immunity, and those over fourteen are treated as adults.[16] Other courts apparently proceed on a case-by-case basis in determining whether particular defendants, even ones under seven years of age, act "maliciously" and thus qualify for punitive damages.[17]

## [2] Parental Liability Statutes

The longstanding common law rules holding minors liable for their torts also mean that minors alone are liable.[18] Thus, unless parents are themselves negligent in the supervision of their children or in some sense authorize their children's harmful acts, parents are not responsible for their children's tortious wrongdoing.[19]

In recent years, however, many states have enacted statutes holding parents vicariously liable for certain damage caused by their children.[20] The statutes typically provide a monetary ceiling on the amount that can be imposed against the parent.[21] Some statutes limit liability to particular acts of vandalism[22] while others

---

1983) (punitive damages properly imposed against high school student who battered plaintiff teacher with his fists); Harkness v. Smith, 478 N.Y.S.2d 239, 241–42 (N.Y. App. Div. 1984) (punitive damages properly imposed against fourteen-year-old paperboy who burglarized plaintiff's home).

[14] Harkness v. Smith, 478 N.Y.S.2d 239, 242 (N.Y. App. Div. 1984).

[15] *See, e.g.*, Munden v. Harris, 134 S.W. 1076, 1080 (Mo. Ct. App. 1911) (five-year-old plaintiff seeking damages from adult defendant for libel and invasion of privacy); Huchting v. Engel, 17 Wis. 237, 239–40 (1863) (court upheld compensatory damages against six-year-old for trespass but noted that had the youngster been criminally charged or had punitive damages been sought, "undoubtedly his extreme youth and consequent want of discretion would [have been] a good answer").

[16] Munden v. Harris, 134 S.W. 1076, 1080 (Mo. Ct. App. 1911).

[17] See *Walker v. Kelley*, 314 A.2d 785 (Conn. Cir. Ct. 1973), where the court rejected the argument that a five-year-old is *per se* incapable of causing injury "deliberately, willfully, and maliciously" under a statute holding parents liable for such conduct of their children. The court stated that whether the five-year-old acted with the requisite intent was a question of fact and upheld the lower court's conclusion that the child had not in fact acted "deliberately, willfully, and maliciously." *Id.* at 786.

[18] Prosser & Keeton, *supra* note 3, at 913. Unlike the common law, civil law countries have long held parents vicariously liable for the conduct of their children. K. Takayanagi, *Liability Without Fault in the Modern Civil and Common Law*, 16 ILL. L. REV. 163, 291 (1921). A current Louisiana statute reflects the civil law tradition:

> The father and the mother and, after the decease of either, the surviving parent, are responsible for the damage occasioned by their minor or unemancipated children, residing with them, or placed by them under the care of other persons, reserving to them recourse against those person.

> The same responsibility attaches to the tutors of minors.

La. Civ. Code Ann. art. 2318 (West 1996).

[19] Prosser & Keeton, *supra* note 3, at 914–15.

[20] *Id.* at 913; Gregory, Swisher & Scheible, *supra* § 3.02, note 107, at 167.

[21] *See, e.g.*, Mass. Gen. Laws Ann. ch. 231, § 85G (West 2000):

> Parents of an unemancipated child under the age of eighteen and over the age of seven

hold parents liable for any damage to persons or property intentionally caused by their children.[23]

## [B]  Negligence

In negligence actions brought against children or when child plaintiffs are alleged to be contributorily negligent,[24] the fact finder measures the child's conduct in terms of that of a "reasonable person of like age, intelligence, and experience under like circumstances."[25] This standard departs significantly from the more objective "reasonable person" test applied in assessing the negligence of adults.[26] The variable standard applicable to children recognizes that children lack the maturity and experience of adults and sometimes act impulsively.[27] The standard also permits more accurate assessments of subjective fault than the adult standard because it, unlike the adult standard, assesses the capacity of the particular child to appreciate risks and formulate judgments.[28]

---

years shall be liable in a civil action for any willful act committed by said child which results in injury or death to another person or damage to the property of another, which shall include any damages resulting from a larceny or attempted larceny of property as set forth in section thirty A of chapter two hundred and sixty-six, damage to cemetery property or damage to any state, county or municipal property or damage as set forth in sections one hundred and twenty-six A and one hundred and twenty-six B of chapter two hundred and sixty-six. This section shall not apply to a parent who, as a result of any decree of any court of competent jurisdiction, does not have custody of such child at the time of the commission of the tort. Recovery under this section shall be limited to the amount of proved loss or damage but in no event shall it exceed five thousand dollars.

*See also* Neb. Rev. Stat. § 43-801 (Reissue 1998):

The parents shall be jointly and severally liable for the willful and intentional infliction of personal injury to any person or destruction of real and personal property occasioned by their minor or unemancipated children residing with them, or placed by them under the care of other person; Provided, that in the event of personal injuries willfully and intentionally inflicted by such child or children, damages shall be recoverable only to the extent of hospital and medical expenses incurred but not to exceed the sum of one thousand dollars for each occurrence.

[22]  *See, e.g.,* N.J. Stat. Ann. § 18A:37-3 (West 1999):

The parents or guardian of any minor who shall injure any public or nonpublic school property shall be liable for damages for the amount of injury to be collected by the board of education of the district or the owner of the premises in any court of competent jurisdiction, together with costs of suit.

[23]  *See supra* note 21.

[24]  While some authority exists for the view that child defendants should be held to stricter negligence standards than child plaintiffs, most courts and commentators apply the same standards to the child litigant whether the child is a plaintiff or a defendant. O. Gray, *The Standard of Care for Children Revisited*, 45 Mo. L. Rev. 597, 597 n.1 (1980).

[25]  Restatement (Second) of Torts § 283 (1977).

[26]  Prosser & Keeton, *supra* note 3, at 173–79.

[27]  *See, e.g.,* Hall v. Hall, 397 S.E.2d 829, 831 (Va. 1990).

[28]  Prosser & Keeton, *supra* note 3, at 176–77, 179. The standard is not entirely subjective, however, because the child may be found negligent, even as a matter of law, if his conduct is unreasonable in light of his estimated capacity. *Id.* at 180.

Some courts have applied the age categories of the criminal law infancy defense in determining the capacity of a minor to act negligently.[29] Under this view, children under age seven are immune from negligence liability while those between seven and fourteen are subject to a rebuttable presumption of incapacity to act negligently.[30] Children above age fourteen are presumed capable of negligent conduct.[31]

A majority of states specify that children under four years of age are incapable of negligent conduct while others set the limit at age five or six.[32] A minority of jurisdictions provide no age limits as cutoffs for possible negligence liability.[33]

Many courts have developed special rules in cases where children engage in activities normally associated with adults such as driving automobiles or flying planes. In such situations, the courts in about half the states hold the child to the adult standard of care without any accommodations due to age.[34]

## [C]  Policy Implications

Assessments of tort liability of juveniles require balancing the interests of injured parties against those of young people whose responsibility for their conduct is, sometimes at least, questionable. As the above discussion makes clear, the balance is routinely struck in favor of compensating parties injured by the intentional torts of minors. On the other hand, for claims requiring findings of malice or some other morally culpable state of mind, the courts more strictly assess the issue of the minor's fault and are less prone to permit damage recoveries, punitive or otherwise. The law of negligence rests somewhere between these approaches, routinely immunizing very young children but permitting recovery against all others found to have acted unreasonably under a standard permitting a fairly extensive assessment of subjective fault.

## § 5.05  PROPERTY

Children may acquire and own both personal and real property.[1] They may also convey their property.[2] However, because of the contractual disabilities of minors,[3] property acquisitions and conveyances are customarily conducted by guardians who manage the minor ward's estate under the guidance of the court.[4] Property conveyances involving the minor alone are voidable and, in the case of personal property, may be disaffirmed by the minor during minority or within a reasonable

---

[29] Approximately a dozen states have adopted this approach. *See* Gray, *supra* note 24, at 598–99.

[30] *Id.*

[31] *Id.*

[32] *Id.* at 598.

[33] *Id. But see* Kramer, *supra* note 2, at 458 (suggesting the "prevailing view" to be that no "arbitrary limits" as to minimum age should be set).

[34] Gray, *supra* note 24, at 604–19; Prosser & Keeton, *supra* note 3, at 181–82.

[1] Clark, *supra* § 1.02, note 4, at 310; Kramer, *supra* § 3.02, note 11, at 394–95.

[2] Clark, *supra* note 1.

[3] *See supra* § 5.03.

[4] *Supra* note 1.

time after reaching majority.[5] Conveyances of real property executed by minors can generally be disaffirmed only after reaching majority.[6]

As a means of avoiding the expense and inconvenience of guardianships,[7] management of the property of minors is increasingly being effectuated through the Uniform Transfers to Minors Act[8] adopted in most states.[9] The Act provides for the transfer of all kinds of property to minors.[10] The Act permits transfers or gifts to be made to minors with provisions entrusting a designated custodian to the management of the property during the period of minority.[11] The custodian, usually a parent or parents of the minor recipient, is afforded discretion to administer the property for the benefit of the minor, but not in a manner that satisfies any existing support obligations owed the minor by the custodian.[12]

While children may own property, parents possess property rights in items they furnish to their children for purposes of support unless the property has been given to the child as a legally recognized gift.[13] Thus, parents are routinely permitted to recover for damage to their children's clothing, books, or other items of personal property caused by the tortious acts of third parties.[14]

Under common law rules, still applicable in most states today, parents are entitled to the services and earnings of their unemancipated minor children as a corollary of the parents' support obligation.[15] Thus, parents may recover for the loss of their child's services caused by the acts of a third person.[16] As discussed in § 5.07 *infra*, the employment of children is regulated by a variety of state and federal legislation.

## § 5.06  MAKING A WILL

At common law, children over the age of fourteen were capable of disposing of their personal estates by will.[1] The law thus followed the criminal law rule that fourteen-year-olds are fully responsible persons for purposes of punishment.[2]

---

[5] *See, e.g., supra* § 5.03, notes 27–29 and accompanying text.

[6] Calamari & Perillo, *supra* § 5.03, note 1, at 310.

[7] Among other things, guardianships frequently require the posting of bonds, and are often viewed as expensive and inefficient. Kramer, *supra* note 1, at 395.

[8] 8B U.L.A. 497 (1993).

[9] Kramer, *supra* note 1, at 448–49 (UTMA adopted in 40 states and the District of Columbia).

[10] *Id.* at 418.

[11] *Id.* at 419.

[12] *Id.*

[13] *See generally* Annotation, *Parents' Rights with Respect to Clothing, Books, Toys, and the Like Purchased for, or Furnished to, Child,* 61 A.L.R.2d 1270 (1958) (child has title to property given by parent only when parent makes a fully executed *inter vivos* gift to child).

[14] *See, e.g.,* Junius v. Food Transp., Inc., 258 F. Supp. 508 (M.D. Pa. 1966) (parent, not child, has cause of action against third party who causes loss or destruction of child's clothing); Mathies v. Kittrell, 354 P.2d 413 (Okla. 1960) (things given to child by parent by way of necessary support remain property of parent when third party destroys such property).

[15] Clark, *supra* note 1, at 314; Kramer, *supra* note 1, at 422–23.

[16] Clark, *supra* note 1, at 314.

[1] Deane v. Littlefield, 18 Mass. (1 Pick.) 239 (1822).

[2] W. LaFave & A. Scott, Criminal Law 399 (2d ed. 1986).

Early statutes sometimes distinguished between real and personal property, applying the common law rule for testators devising personalty, but raising the age to twenty-one for valid testamentary dispositions of real property.[3] Today, state laws generally provide that only persons over the age of eighteen can dispose of property by will.[4]

## § 5.07   EMPLOYMENT

Legislatures at both the state and federal levels have enacted laws restricting the ability of young people to work for pay in an effort to prevent the exploitation of children, encourage their education, and protect them from workplace hazards.[1] The statutes attempt to accommodate the long-standing recognition that work is beneficial to a child's upbringing with the realization that too much, or certain kinds of, work may not be in a child's best interest.[2] Regulations governing the employment of children emerged in the late nineteenth century during a period of industrial growth where the unhealthiest factory work was often relegated to child workers.[3] At the same time that legislators addressed the problem of child labor, pressure was increasing to enact compulsory education laws. The eventual passage of compulsory education laws impacted the problem of minors in the workplace by effectively reducing the availability of child labor.[4] Apart from humanitarian concerns for the welfare of young people, some economists and labor leaders urged regulating child labor as a means of avoiding depressed wages for adult workers.[5]

### [A]   State Legislation

Child labor reform began initially at the state level.[6] The earliest legislation required employers to provide an education for their child workers.[7] Statutes eventually dictated minimum age standards and regulated the number of daily and weekly hours the child could work.

Today, all states have laws setting the minimum age at which a child can be employed, generally at age fourteen for safe work outside school hours, and age sixteen for work in industrial plants or for work during school hours.[8] Many states allow exceptions to the general minimum age for casual employment and for jobs associated with young people such as newspaper delivery and golf caddying.[9] Moreover, many states, typically ones with large populations, have enacted statutes setting minimum ages, usually at ten or twelve, and requiring special

---

[3] *See, e.g.*, Deane v. Littlefield, 18 Mass. (1 Pick.) 239 (1822).

[4] Clark, *supra* § 1.02, note 4, at 311; Wadlington, Whitebread & Davis, *supra* § 3.02, note 34, at 31.

[1] Mnookin & Weisberg, *supra* § 1.02, note 8, at 916–17.

[2] *Id.* at 919.

[3] *See* A. Giampetro-Meyer & T. Brown, *Protecting Society from Teenage Greed: A Proposal for Revising the Ages, Hours and Nature of Child Labor in America*, 25 Akron L. Rev. 547, 550–51 (1992); Note, *Child Labor Laws — Time to Grow Up*, 59 Minn. L. Rev. 575, 576 (1976).

[4] Mnookin & Weisberg, *supra* note 1, at 918.

[5] *Id.*

[6] *Id.*

[7] *Id.*

[8] Giampetro-Meyer & Brown, *supra* note 3, at 557–58; Note, *supra* note 3, at 584, 604–8.

[9] Note, *supra* note 3, at 585.

permits for minors engaging in so-called street trades such as peddling or boot-blacking.[10]

Nearly all states require children between six and sixteen to attend school full-time.[11] Minimum age for work corresponds in most states with the compulsory school attendance age.[12] Some states provide exemptions for young people employed as apprentices or students enrolled in vocational training programs.[13]

Most state labor laws limit the number of hours a minor may work, generally permitting no more than eight hours a day and forty hours a week for children under sixteen.[14] Some states have adopted even more restrictive rules prohibiting juveniles who are attending school from working more than three or four hours on school days or limiting to ten the combined hours of school and work.[15] All states also prescribe certain hours at night during which children cannot work, but some states prohibit night work only during the academic year.[16]

All states restrict employment in certain hazardous occupations.[17] Some statutes merely prohibit "dangerous" work generally[18] while others list specific occupations thought to be unduly hazardous for young people.[19] Whether or not

---

[10]  *Id.*; P. McGovern, *Children's Rights and Child Labor: Advocacy on Behalf of the Child Worker*, 28 S.D. L. REV. 293, 298 (1983).

[11]  Note, *supra* note 3, at 586.

[12]  *Id.*

[13]  *Id.*

[14]  *Id.* at 588; Giampetro-Meyer & Brown, *supra* note 3, at 558–61.

[15]  *Id.*

[16]  Note, *supra* note 3, at 588–89, 604–8; Giampetro-Meyer & Brown, *supra* note 3, at 561.

[17]  Note, *supra* note 3, at 589.

[18]  See, *e.g.*, Neb. Rev. Stat. § 48-313 (Reissue 1998) which provides:

> No child under the age of sixteen years shall be employed in any work which by reason of the nature of the work or place of performance is dangerous to life or limb or in which his or her health may be injured or his or her morals may be depraved. No parent, guardian, or other person, who has under his or her control any child, shall cause or permit such child to work or be employed in violation of this section.

[19]  See, *e.g.*, Cal. Lab. Code §§ 1292–93 (West 1989) and §§ 1293.1–1294 (West Supp. 2002):

> § 1292. Tasks prohibited to minors under 16
>
> No minor under the age of sixteen years shall be employed or permitted to work in any capacity in:
>
> (a) Adjusting any belt to any machinery.
>
> (b) Sewing or lacing machine belts in any workshop [sic]
>
> (c) Oiling, wiping, or cleaning machinery, or assisting therein.

> § 1293. Tasks prohibited to minors under 16
>
> No minor under the age of sixteen years shall be employed, or permitted, to work in any capacity in operating or assisting in operating any of the following machines:
>
> (a) Circular or band saws; wood shapers; wood-jointers; planers; sandpaper or wood-polishing machinery; wood turning or boring machinery.
>
> (b) Picker machines or machines used in picking wool, cotton, hair, or other material; carding machines; leather-burnishing machines; laundry machinery.

legislatures specify prohibited jobs, most states have authorized special commissions to declare which occupations are hazardous for minors.[20]

When a young person works illegally, a variety of sanctions may be imposed. Some statutes direct sanctions against parents who permit their children to work in violation of state child labor laws.[21] More often, sanctions — in the form or civil

---

(c) Printing-presses of all kinds; boring or drill presses; stamping machines used in sheet-metal and tinware, in paper and leather manufacturing, or in washer and nut factories; metal or paper-cutting machines; paper-lace machines.

(d) Corner-staying machines in paper-box factories; corrugating rolls, such as are used in corrugated paper, roofing or washboard factories.

(e) Dough brakes or cracker machinery of any description.

(f) Wire or iron straightening or drawing machinery; rolling-mill machinery; power punches or shears; washing, grinding or mixing machinery; calendar rolls in paper and rubber manufacturing; steamboilers; in proximity to any hazardous or unguarded belts, machinery or gearing.


§ 1293.1. Tasks prohibited to minors under 12

(a) Except as provided in subdivision (c) of Section 1394, no minor under the age of 12 years may be employed or permitted to work, or accompany or be permitted to accompany an employed parent or guardian, in an agricultural zone of danger. As used in this section, "agriculture zone of danger" means any or all of the following:

(1) On or about moving equipment.

(2) In or about unprotected chemicals.

(3) In or about any unprotected water hazard.


. . .


§ 1294. Places of employment prohibited to minors under 16

No minor under the age of 16 years shall be employed or permitted to work in any capacity:

(a) Upon any railroad, whether steam, electric, or hydraulic.

(b) Upon any vessel or boat engaged in navigation or commerce within the jurisdiction of this state.

(c) In, about, or in connection with any processes in which dangerous or poisonous acids are used, in the manufacture or packing of paints, colors, white or red lead, or in soldering.

(d) In occupations causing dust in injurious quantities, in the manufacture or use of dangerous or poisonous dyes, in the manufacture or preparation of compositions with dangerous or poisonous gases, or in the manufacture or use of compositions of lye in which the quantity thereof is injurious to health.

(e) On scaffolding, in heavy work in the building trades, in any tunnel or excavation, or in, about or in connection with any mine, coal breaker, coke oven or quarry.

(f) In assorting, manufacturing or packing tobacco.

(g) Operating any automobile, motorcar, or truck.

(h) In any occupation dangerous to the life or limb, or injurious to the health or morals of the minor.

---

[20] Note, *supra* note 3, at 589–90.

[21] *See, e.g.*, Cal. Lab. Code § 1303 (West Supp. 2002) (parents of minor who violates child labor provisions subject to up to $5000 fine or six months in jail or both).

fines and sometimes criminal penalties — are directed against employers.[22] Moreover, caselaw holds employers strictly liable for injuries suffered by minors whom they illegally hire.[23] Apparently, no state imposes sanctions against minors who accept employment in violations of the labor laws, even if they do so knowingly or misrepresent their age to their employer.[24]

## [B]  Federal Legislation

Early in the twentieth century, child labor reform shifted from the state to the federal level.[25] While many states had enacted child labor legislation, some of the existing laws were deemed inadequate and many states were without any regulation.[26] This situation created considerable economic pressure as manufacturers threatened to move their plants from states with strict regulation to ones with fewer restrictions.[27] Such threats effectively ended the reform movement at the state level[28] as states with restrictive child labor laws were forced to compete for the benefits of industry against states where child labor produced goods of equal quality at a lower cost.[29] These conditions led reformers to seek national regulation.[30]

After two early attempts at federal regulation were declared unconstitutional,[31] Congress in 1938 passed the Fair Labor Standards Act (FLSA) regulating "oppressive child labor," complemented by Department of Labor regulations.[32]

---

[22] *Id.* (employer subject to criminal penalties); Mnookin & Weisberg, *supra* note 1, at 924–25. For an example of a civil fine provision, common in many states, see Cal. Lab. Code §§ 1287–88 (West 1989 & Supp. 2002).

[23] *See, e.g.,* Vincent v. Riggi & Sons, Inc., 285 N.E.2d 689 (N.Y. 1972) (building contractor-defendant liable, notwithstanding any possible contributory negligence of thirteen-year-old plaintiff, for injuries suffered by plaintiff while mowing a lawn after defendant hired him to mow the lawn of a new house built by defendant). The employer is not liable, however, if, after exercising due diligence, he is led to believe that the minor he hires is above the statutory age. *Id.* at 694 (dicta).

[24] Mnookin & Weisberg, *supra* note 1, at 926.

[25] *Id.* at 919.

[26] *Id.*

[27] *Id.*; Note, *supra* note 3, at 577.

[28] Comment, *Child Labor Legislation — Its Past, Present, and Future*, 7 Fordham L. Rev. 217, 220 (1933).

[29] Mnookin & Weisberg, *supra* note 1, at 919; Note, *supra* note 3, at 577.

[30] *Id.*

[31] Hammer v. Dagenhart, 247 U.S. 251 (1918) (striking down the Keating-Owen bill of 1916 as exceeding scope of congressional authority over commerce and unduly involving federal authority in purely local matters); *overruled by* U.S. v. Darby, 312 U.S. 100, 117 (1941); The Child Labor Tax Case, 259 U.S. 20 (1922) (striking down the Child Labor Tax Act of 1918 on grounds that statute's tax on products of child labor constituted a penalty on conduct within area of state regulation thus exceeding federal taxing power).

[32] Mnookin & Weisberg, *supra* note 1, at 920. The current wording of the act defines "oppressive child labor" as follows:

> "Oppressive child labor" means a condition of employment under which (1) any employee under the age of sixteen years is employed by an employer (other than a parent or a person standing in place of a parent employing his own child or a child in his custody under the age of sixteen years in an occupation other than manufacturing or mining or an occupation found by the Secretary of Labor to be particularly hazardous for the employment of children between the ages of sixteen and eighteen years or detrimental to their health or well-being in

The constitutionality of the Act was upheld[33] and, with several subsequent amendments, it remains an important attempt at protecting children from workplace hazards.[34]

The FLSA applies to employees who "engage in commerce" or produce "goods for commerce" that cross state lines.[35] The Act also applies to public employees and enterprises that meet certain commercial and dollar volume standards.[36]

The FLSA sets a minimum age of sixteen for most nonagricultural employment.[37] For occupations declared hazardous by the Secretary of Labor, eighteen is the minimum age.[38] There are seventeen occupations, including such jobs as coal-mining and logging, currently on the list of hazardous occupations.[39]

---

any occupation, or (2) any employee between the ages of sixteen and eighteen years is employed by an employer in any occupation which the Secretary of Labor shall find and by order declare to be particularly hazardous for the employment of children between such ages or detrimental to their health or well-being. . . . The Secretary of Labor shall provide by regulation or by order that the employment of employees between the ages of fourteen and sixteen years in occupations other than manufacturing and mining shall not be deemed to constitute oppressive child labor if and to the extent that the Secretary of Labor determines that such employment is confined to periods which will not interfere with their schooling and to conditions which will not interfere with their health and well-being.

29 U.S.C.A. § 203(l) (West 1998). For a general discussion of the FLSA, see A. Schwartz, Annotation, *Validity, Construction, Application and Effect of Child Labor Provisions of Fair Labor Standards Act (29 U.S.C.S. § 212 and Related Sections)*, 21 A.L.R. Fed. 391 (1974).

[33] United States v. Darby, 312 U.S. 100 (1940) (overruling Hammer v. Dagenhart, 247 U.S. 251 (1918)).

[34] *See* M. Rothstein et al., Employment Law 195, 214–16 (1994). The FLSA specifically preserves state laws but supersedes them in areas of overlap. Note, *supra* note 3, at 590.

[35] *See* Rothstein, *supra* note 34, at 197–201.

[36] *Id.*

[37] *See supra* note 32, *infra* note 45 and accompanying text.

[38] *See supra* note 32.

[39] Child Labor Regulations, 29 C.F.R. § 570.120 (1996), prohibits the following occupations:
No. 1.   Occupations in or about plants manufacturing explosives or articles containing explosive components.
No. 2.   Occupations of motor-vehicle driver and helper.
No. 3.   Coal-mine occupations.
No. 4.   Logging occupations and occupations in the operation of any sawmill, lath mill, shingle mill, or cooperage-stock mill.
No. 5.   Occupations involved in the operation of power-driven woodworking machines.
No. 6.   Occupations involving exposure to radioactive substances.
No. 7.   Occupations involved in the operation of power-driven hoisting apparatus.
No. 8.   Occupations involved in the operation of power-driven metal forming, punching, and shearing machines.
No. 9.   Occupations in connection with mining, other than coal.
No. 10.  Occupations in or about slaughtering and meat packing establishments and rendering plants.
No. 11.  Occupations involved in the operation of bakery machines.
No. 12.  Occupations involved in the operations of paper products machines.
No. 13.  Occupations involved in the manufacture of brick, tile, and kindred products.
No. 14.  Occupations involved in the operation of circular saws, bandsaws, and guillotine shears.
No. 15.  Occupations in wrecking, demolition, and shipbreaking operations.
No. 16.  Occupations in roofing operations.

. The Secretary of Labor has authorized the employment of fourteen and fifteen-year-olds in certain specified sales and office jobs as well as work in retail, food service, and gasoline service establishments so long as work conditions do not interfere with the welfare of the minor.[40] The regulations also limit work hours and proscribe work during school hours.[41]

The act specifically exempts from its prohibitions employment in agriculture, entertainment, newspaper delivery, evergreen wreath making, and employment by a parent in nonhazardous occupations so long as the work is performed outside of school hours.[42] The agriculture exception permits minors fourteen and older to work in nonhazardous farm jobs outside school hours while allowing twelve and thirteen-year-olds to work in agriculture outside of school hours only with parental consent.[43]

The FLSA authorizes injunctive actions against the commercial distribution of goods produced in violation of the statute.[44] The Act also provides for civil fines, injunctions, and criminal prosecution for willful violation as possible sanctions against violators of the child labor provisions.[45] Similar to the state child labor provisions, the federal law apparently does not direct sanctions against minor employees who work in violation of the FLSA.[46] However, unlike the position taken by at least some state child labor laws,[47] there is no private cause of action against employers for injuries to minors employed in violation of the FLSA.[48]

## [C]   Policy Implications

Child labor laws have existed for nearly a century with little critical evaluation or modification.[49] Recently, however, critics have begun to question the wisdom of retaining child labor legislation in its present form. Some commentators see the existing law as unduly restrictive of children's autonomy,[50] while others fault it for denying children economic opportunity and experience valuable to their social development.[51] Moreover, some argue that conditions in the workplace have changed since the inception of the protective legislation making its continued

---

No. 17.   Occupations in excavation operations.

[40] *Id.* § 570.119.

[41] *Id.*

[42] *See supra* note 32; 29 U.S.C.A. § 213(c), (d) (West 1965 & Supp. 1996).

[43] 29 U.S.C.A. § 213(c) (West Supp. 1996).

[44] 29 U.S.C.A. § 212(b) (West 1965).

[45] 29 U.S.C.A. § 216 (West 1965 & Supp. 1996). A provision of the statute authorizing private actions for damages against nonconsenting states in state courts has been held unconstitutional by the Supreme Court in *Alden v. Maine*, 527 U.S. 706 (1999).

[46] *See supra* note 23 and accompanying text.

[47] Mnookin & Weisberg, *supra* note 1, at 926.

[48] *See, e.g.,* Breitwieser v. KMS Indus. Inc., 467 F.2d 1391 (5th Cir. 1972), *cert. denied*, 410 U.S. 969 (1973).

[49] Wadlington, Whitebread & Davis, *supra* § 3.02, note 34, at 27 n.1; Institute of Judicial Admin. & American Bar Ass'n, *supra* § 5.03, note 57, at 89.

[50] N. Klapmuts, *Children's Rights, The Legal Rights of Minors in Conflict with Law or Social Custom*, 4 CRIME & DELINQ. . LITERATURE 449, 452 (1968).

[51] Mnookin & Weisberg, *supra* note 1, at 926. For social science data supporting the idea that employment has positive benefits for teenagers, see Giampetro-Meyer & Brown, *supra* note 3, at 565 (working students show increased self discipline, self confidence, and responsibility).

application, at least in its present form, unnecessary.[52] Perhaps more importantly, some critics question whether the child labor regulations themselves create harmful social effects by contributing to idleness which may in turn lead minors to engage in deviant behavior.[53] Such concerns might suggest eliminating all age-based restrictions, thus allowing children the same work opportunities as adults.[54]

Less extreme alternatives might include a model maintaining current age-based restrictions, but permitting broad exemptions whenever parents consent to the employment of their children or whenever children must work to support their families.[55] The drafters of the Juvenile Justice Standards propose a model that dispenses with most age-graded restrictions or occupational restrictions for children above age twelve, except those defining hazardous activity, so long as the child possesses a work permit and does not work during school hours.[56] The Standards permit children under twelve to work in certain nonhazardous jobs with parental consent.[57] The Standards place no restrictions on the employment of minors over the age of sixteen.[58]

On the other hand, some commentators favor more restrictive child labor laws, arguing that providing more work opportunities for young people is not necessarily a good idea.[59] Some social science data supports the conclusion that students who work extensive hours may suffer because of their employment.[60] Moreover, studies show that working youth tend to spend their income on luxury items rather than saving or investing their money for their future.[61]

These various considerations obviously suggest that policy makers face difficult choices in deciding how, or even whether, to regulate the employment of young people. Such choices are sufficiently difficult that they will likely occupy the time of courts and legislatures at both the state and federal levels for some time.

---

[52] Note, *supra* note 3, at 592; *see also* S. Willborn, S. Schwab, & J. Burton, Employment Law 473 (1993); Institute of Judicial Admin. & American Bar Ass'n, *supra* note 49, at 91–92.

[53] Note, *supra* note 3, at 579–80; Willborn, Schwab & Burton, *supra* note 52, at 473; Mnookin & Weisberg, *supra* note 1, at 942–46 (discussing problems of youth unemployment and passage of federal "subminimum wage" for minors, 29 U.S.C.A. § 206 (West 1998)).

[54] For consideration of this idea, see Mnookin & Weisberg, *supra* note 1, at 937–39.

[55] *Id.* at 939–41.

[56] Institute of Judicial Admin. & American Bar Ass'n, *supra* note 49, at 87–88.

[57] *Id.* at 87 (minors below twelve years of age permitted to work for their parents or for third parties in domestic service, casual labor, or as a performer so long as work does not occur during school hours).

[58] *Id.* at 87–88, 95.

[59] *See, e.g.*, Giampetro-Meyer & Brown, *supra* note 3, at 568 (legislation should place "far more significant restrictions on the ages and hours teenagers may work" in "fast food restaurants and retail stores").

[60] *Id.* at 563–64 (students working more than 15–20 hours per week are more likely to do worse in school, use drugs and alcohol, experience decreased closeness to parents, and develop cynical attitudes about work than their peers working less than 15–20 hours per week).

[61] *Id.* at 565.

# Chapter 6
# CONSTITUTIONAL RIGHTS

## § 6.01  OVERVIEW

The idea that children possess constitutional rights that can be asserted against the state or even their parents is a relatively new concept.[1] While some cases early in the twentieth century vaguely discussed the notion that families, and perhaps children, possessed constitutionally protected interests,[2] the United States Supreme Court did not meaningfully begin defining the status of juveniles under the Constitution until a series of cases beginning in the latter half of the century.[3] In these cases, the Court has generated an extensive body of caselaw under a host of doctrinal provisions.

Even minimal familiarity with this caselaw reveals that the Court has encountered difficulty in defining a consistent and coherent theory of children's rights. The Court's problem is confounded by the fact that it must determine the constitutional merits of children's claims made against the state in contexts raising sensitive and sometimes conflicting interests of the children's parents. Thus, the Court is often required to accommodate three sets of interests: the child's, the state's, and the parent's.

Recognizing the difficulty of its task, the Court has disclaimed any effort to systematically "consider the impact of [constitutional protections] upon the totality of the relationship of the minor and the State."[4] Instead, the Court has proceeded *ad hoc* in deciding a variety of cases. Some cases appear to adopt a protectionist posture that suggests that children do not enjoy constitutionally protected autonomy and may be subjected to paternalistic rules and procedures that if imposed against adults would violate their constitutional rights.[5] In other cases, however, the Court appears to view children as full-fledged constitutional persons, entitled to the same protections as adults.[6] These apparent inconsistencies have led one leading commentator to describe the fruits of the Court's labors as a "monumentally confusing" body of constitutional law, at least so far as adolescents are concerned.[7]

Because the Court appears not to have adopted a single view of the nature of children's rights, the cases cannot easily be organized around a single conceptual principle. Rather than attempting that approach, or an approach that discusses the cases chronologically, this book proceeds by first noting the Court's earliest cases — appearing during the first quarter of the twentieth century before the Bill of

---

[1] Wadlington, Whitebread & Davis, *supra* § 3.02, note 34, at 1, 47.

[2] *See infra* § 6.02.

[3] *See supra* note 1.

[4] L. Harris, L. Teitelbaum & C. Weisbrod, Family Law 873 (1996) (quoting Ginsburg v. New York, 390 U.S. 629, 636 (1968)).

[5] *See, e.g.*, Bethel Sch. Dist. No. 403 v. Fraser, 478 U.S. 675 (1986) (high school student disciplined for giving a speech judged by school authorities to be offensive), discussed in detail *infra* § 6.03[B][1], notes 50–57 and accompanying text; *see also supra* § 2.01, notes 1–6 and accompanying text.

[6] *See, e.g.*, Planned Parenthood v. Danforth, 428 U.S. 52 (1976) (minor pregnant woman entitled to make abortion decision without parental consent), discussed in detail *infra* § 6.06[A][1][a], notes 2–9 and accompanying text; *see also supra* § 2.01, notes 1–6 and accompanying text.

[7] Zimring, *supra* § 1.02, note 11, at 7.

Rights provisions were applicable to the States[8] — and then by considering the cases as they fall under the various amendments to the Constitution, considered in numerical order.

## § 6.02  THE EARLY CASES: *MEYER* AND *PIERCE*

In *Meyer v. Nebraska,*[1] the United States Supreme Court considered the constitutionality of a state statute that required all educators to teach their courses in English and forbade them from teaching modern foreign languages in any public or private school until the eighth grade or later.[2] While acknowledging that the state possessed broad powers to compel education and regulate its quality,[3] the Court, nevertheless, reversed the conviction of Meyer, who had been found guilty under the statute for teaching German to a ten-year-old, and found that the statute constituted an unreasonable infringement of Meyer's liberty under the Due Process Clause of the Fourteenth Amendment.[4]

The Court did not limit its discussion to the narrow issue of the impact of the statute on teachers. Instead, the Court posited a sweeping definition of constitutionally protected "liberty" that included the interests of parents and children as well as teachers:

> While this court has not attempted to define with exactness the liberty thus guaranteed, the term has received much consideration and some of the included things have been definitely stated. Without doubt, it denotes not merely freedom from bodily restraint but also the right of the individual to contract, to engage in any of the common occupations of life, to acquire useful knowledge, to marry, establish a home and bring up children, to worship God according to the dictates of his own conscience, and generally to enjoy those privileges long recognized at common law as essential to the orderly pursuit of happiness by free men.[5]

The Court found that the statute not only improperly interfered with the "calling of modern language teachers" but also with "the opportunities of pupils to acquire knowledge, and with the power of parents to control the education of their own."[6]

---

[8] Prior to 1934, the Bill of Rights provisions of the Constitution were applicable to the federal government only. J. Nowak & R. Rotunda, Constitutional Law 368–370 (6th ed. 2000). Since that time, virtually all of the Bill of Rights have been incorporated into the Fourteenth Amendment and made applicable to the states. *Id.* at 385–87.

[1] 262 U.S. 390 (1923).

[2] The Nebraska Supreme Court had earlier described the purposes of the statute as a vehicle "to rear and educate [Nebraska] children in the language of their native land" and to prevent emigrant children from being brought up speaking their parents' "mother tongue" rather than English. *Id.* at 397–98.

[3] The Court noted that Nebraska and nearly all other states had compulsory school attendance laws to promote education, "a matter of supreme importance that should be diligently promoted." *Id.* at 400. The Court went on to observe that "the state may do much, go very far . . . in order to improve the quality of its citizens . . . mentally." *Id.* at 401.

[4] The Fourteenth Amendment to the United States Constitution provides in part: "No state . . . shall deprive any person of life, liberty, or property without due process of law." The *Meyer* Court found that "the statute as applied is arbitrary and without reasonable relation to any end within the competency of the state." 262 U.S. at 403. For a description of the purpose of the Nebraska statute struck down in *Meyer*, see *supra* note 2.

[5] 262 U.S. at 399.

[6] *Id.* at 401.

Two years later, in *Pierce v. Society of Sisters*,[7] the Court assessed the constitutionality of a statute that required parents to send their children, between the ages of eight and sixteen, to public schools.[8] Enforcement of the statute was contested by private parochial and military school educators who argued that the statute denied them rights to practice their profession. In addition, it was argued that the statute denied parents the right to send their children to schools offering religious and other alternatives to public education, and denied children the right to influence the parents' choice of a school.[9] Again, the Court found the statute unconstitutional under the Fourteenth Amendment Due Process Clause as an "unreasonabl[e] interfer[ence] with the liberty of parents . . . to direct the upbringing and education of [their] children" and as a threat to the property rights of the private educators to engage in their business activities.[10]

The Court spoke obliquely of children's rights when it found that the statute was not reasonably related to promoting a legitimate state interest: "The fundamental theory of liberty upon which all governments in this Union repose excludes any general power of the state to standardize its children by forcing them to accept instruction from public teachers only."[11] The Court also paid deference to the authority of parents: "The child is not the mere creature of the state; those who nurture him and direct his destiny have the right, coupled with the high duty, to recognize and prepare him for additional obligations."[12]

## § 6.03 THE FIRST AMENDMENT[1]

### [A] The Religion Clauses

### [1] The Establishment Clause and the Public Schools

The United States Supreme Court has decided several cases under the Establishment Clause of the First Amendment that bear upon the rights of school children. Several of those matters will be discussed here. As noted in Chapter 3,

---

[7] 268 U.S. 510 (1925).

[8] The Court identified the "manifest purpose" of the statute as a means of compelling attendance at public schools by "normal children" until they have completed at least the eighth grade. *Id.* at 531. The Court recognized that the state may legitimately regulate educational quality of all the schools within the state, presumably including private schools.

Commentators have identified less benign purposes for the Oregon statute, noting that it reflected anti-Catholic sentiments and had been enacted after a referendum campaign sponsored by the Ku Klux Klan and the Scottish Rite Masons who sought to "Americanize" Oregon schools. Mnookin & Weisberg, *supra* § 1.02, note 8, at 65.

[9] 268 U.S. at 532.

[10] *Id.* at 534–36. The Court noted that the private schools in the instant case were engaged in a "useful and meritorious" undertaking and that nothing in the record indicated that they had failed to discharge their obligations to patrons, students, or the state. *Id.* at 534.

[11] *Id.* at 535.

[12] *Id.*

[1] The First Amendment to the United States constitution provides:

Congress shall make no law respecting an establishment of religion, or prohibiting the free exercise thereof; or abridging the freedom of speech, or of the press, or the right of the people peaceably to assemble, and to petition the Government for a redress of grievances.

the Court has struck down as violative of the Establishment Clause statutes forbidding teachers from teaching organic evolution.[2] That matter will not be further elaborated on.

## [a] School Prayer

The Court has addressed the question of prayer in the public schools in a series of cases beginning with *Engel v. Vitale*,[3] which found the voluntary recitation of an official prayer by public school children at the beginning of each school day to violate the Establishment Clause.[4] Shortly after *Engel*, the Court decided *School District of Abington v. Schempp*[5] where it again invalidated a voluntary school prayer, this time pursuant to a school district rule providing for the reading of the Lord's Prayer and other Bible verses as part of the opening exercises of each school day. In finding the rule to constitute an unconstitutional promotion of religion, the Court commented on the place of religion in public education:

> It is insisted that unless these religious exercises are permitted a "religion of secularism" is established in the schools. We agree of course that the State may not establish a "religion of secularism" in the sense of affirmatively opposing or showing hostility to religion, thus "preferring those who believe in no religion over those who do believe." . . . We do not agree, however, that this decision in any sense has that effect. In addition, it might well be said that one's education is not complete without a study of comparative religion or the history of religion and its relationship to the advancement of civilization. It certainly may be said that the Bible is worthy of study for its literary and historic qualities. Nothing we have said here indicates that such study of the Bible or of religion, when presented objectively as part of a secular program of education, may not be effected consistently with the First Amendment. But the exercises here do not fall into those categories. They are religious exercises, required by the States in violation of the command of the First Amendment that the Government maintain strict neutrality, neither aiding nor opposing religion.[6]

Following the lead of *Engel* and *Schempp*, the Court subsequently invalidated a state statute authorizing a period of silence during class so that students may engage in "meditation or voluntary prayer."[7]

Finally, in *Lee v. Weisman*,[8] the Court found that nonsectarian prayers offered by members of the clergy at public school graduation ceremonies violate the

---

All of the provisions of the First Amendment have been held applicable to the states. Nowak & Rotunda, *supra* § 6.01, note 8, at 397–98.

[2] *Supra* § 3.02, note 37.

[3] 370 U.S. 421 (1962).

[4] The district Board of Education had directed the school district's principals to require the following prayer to be said aloud by each class in the presence of a teacher at the beginning of each school day: "Almighty God, we acknowledge our dependence upon Thee, and beg Thy blessings upon us, our parents, our teachers and our Country." Under the Board of Education directive, school officials were precluded from compelling any student to join in the prayer over his or her parents' objection. *Id.* at 422–23.

[5] 374 U.S. 203 (1963).

[6] *Id.* at 225. See also *Stone v. Graham*, 449 U.S. 39 (1980), where the Court invalidated a statute requiring the posting of the Ten Commandments on the wall of each public classroom.

[7] Wallace v. Jaffree, 472 U.S. 38 (1985).

[8] 505 U.S. 577 (1992).

Establishment Clause. The *Weisman* Court based its decision on "heightened concerns with protecting freedom of conscience from subtle coercive pressures in the elementary and secondary schools."[9] The Court added:

> [P]rayer exercises carry a particular [and pronounced risk] of indirect coercion. . . . What to most believers may seem nothing more than a reasonable request that the nonbeliever respect their religious practices, in a school context may appear to the nonbeliever or dissenter to be an attempt to employ the machinery of the State to enforce a religious orthodoxy.
>
> We need not look beyond the circumstances of this case to see the phenomenon at work. The undeniable fact is that the school district's supervision and control of a high school graduation ceremony places public pressure, as well as peer pressure, on attending students to stand as a group or, at least, maintain respectful silence during the invocation and benediction. This pressure, though subtle and indirect, can be as real as any overt compulsion. . . . [F]or the dissenter of high school age, who has a reasonable perception that she is being forced by the State to pray in a manner her conscience will not allow, the injury is no less real. There can be no doubt that for many, if not most, of the students at the graduation, the act of standing or remaining silent was an expression of participation in the . . . prayer. That was the very point of the religious exercise. It is of little comfort to a dissenter, then, to be told that for her the act of standing or remaining in silence signifies mere respect, rather than participation. What matters is that, given our social conventions, a reasonable dissenter in this milieu could believe that the group exercise signified her own participation or approval of it.
>
> Finding no violation under these circumstances would place objectors in the dilemma of participating, with all that implies, or protesting. We do not address whether that choice is acceptable if the affected citizens are mature adults, but we think the State may not, consistent with the Establishment Clause, place primary and secondary school children in this position. Research in psychology supports the common assumption that adolescents are often susceptible to pressure from their peers towards conformity, and that the influence is strongest in matters of social convention. . . .[10]

Relying on *Weisman*, the Supreme Court struck down a school district policy authorizing students to decide whether invocations should be given at school-sponsored football games and, if so, to decide which students should offer the invocations.[11] In finding inappropriate school sponsorship of religion, the Court observed:

> Even if we regard every high school student's decision to attend a home football game as purely voluntary, we are nevertheless persuaded that the

---

[9] *Id.* at 592. The Court found the prayer to have coercive effects on students even though they were technically not required to attend the graduation ceremonies. The Court noted that given the nature of graduation ceremonies and their importance in students' lives, students were "not free to absent [themselves] from the graduation exercise in any real sense of the term 'voluntary.'" *Id.* at 594–95.

[10] *Id.* at 592–93. Following *Lee*, the Third Circuit has held that student-initiated prayers at public high school graduations violate the Establishment Clause. ACLU of New Jersey v. Black Horse Pike, 84 F.3d 1471 (3d Cir. 1996) (en banc). *But see* Adler v. Duval County Sch. Bd., 851 F. Supp. 446 (M.D. Fla. 1994) (permitting students to write and deliver graduation prayer without faculty review).

[11] Santa Fe Independent Sch. Dist. v. Doe, 530 U.S. 290 (2000).

delivery of a pregame prayer has the improper effect of coercing those present to participate in an act of religious worship. For "the government may no more use social pressure to enforce orthodoxy than it may use more direct means." . . . The constitutional command will not permit the District "to exact religious conformity from a student as the price" of joining her classmates at a varsity football game. . . . [N]othing in the Constitution as interpreted by this Court prohibits any public school student from voluntarily praying at any time before, during, or after the school day. But the religious liberty protected by the Constitution is abridged when the State affirmatively sponsors the particular religious practice of prayer.[12]

## [b]  Accommodating Student Religious Belief

The school prayer cases make it clear that the State may not make religious practice an official part of its educational program. On the other hand, the Supreme Court has held that under certain conditions students may use public school facilities to study or practice religion. While the Court has held that religious exercises cannot be conducted on a public school campus during school hours,[13] students may be permitted under the Establishment Clause to use school facilities for religious purposes, for example, to conduct the affairs of a "Christian club." Such activities may take place only during periods of time when school is not in session and no faculty member or other school official may actively participate.[14]

## [2]  The Free Exercise Clause

In an early case, *Prince v. Massachusetts*,[15] the United States Supreme Court first addressed a child's claim that the State had infringed on her rights to practice her religion. In *Prince*, the Court affirmed the conviction of a woman who had assented to her nine-year-old niece's request to take the niece with her to sell magazines one evening on a public street. This conduct was prohibited under state child labor laws.[16] The woman, who was the child's guardian, argued that application of the statute against her violated her free exercise rights and those of her niece. She based this claim on the fact that the magazines they attempted to sell were religious tracts and she and her niece were both ordained Jehovah's

---

[12]  *Id.* at 312–13.

[13]  Illinois *ex rel.* McCollum v. Board of Educ., 333 U.S. 203 (1948). On the other hand, the Court has upheld a program that permitted students to leave campus during a specified period each day for off-campus religious instruction. Zorach v. Clauson, 343 U.S. 306 (1952).

[14]  Board of Educ. of Westside Community Sch. v. Mergens, 496 U.S. 226 (1990) (Equal Access Act requires permitting students to form "noncurriculum related" Christian club to meet after school in school facilities); *see also* Zobrest v. Catalina Foothills Sch. Dist., 509 U.S. 1 (1993) (providing services of interpreter under Individuals with Disabilities Act to student attending Catholic high school did not violate Establishment Clause). For a discussion of lower court cases, see generally Annotation, *Use of Public School Premises for Religious Purposes During Non-School Time*, 79 A.L.R.2d 1148 (1961). For a discussion of the complex issue of state financial aid to religiously affiliated schools under the Establishment Clause, see Nowak & Rotunda, *supra* note 1, at 1235–51, 1254–66.

[15]  321 U.S. 158 (1944).

[16]  The relevant statutes prohibited boys under 12 and girls under 18 from selling "newspapers, magazines, [or] periodicals . . .in any street or public place" and prohibited others from furnishing minors such items to sell. *Id.* at 160–61. The statutes also punished "parents, guardians, or custodians" who permitted their children to engage in prohibited selling activity. *Id.* at 161. For a general discussion of child labor laws, see *supra* § 5.07.

Witness ministers with religious obligations to proselytize through distributing the magazines.[17] The Court rejected the free exercise claims and upheld the statute as a legitimate means of protecting the safety and welfare of children under both the state's police and *parens patriae* powers.[18]

The *Prince* Court recognized the "rights of children to exercise their religion, and of parents to train and encourage their children in the practice of religious belief" but found those interests outweighed by the public interest embodied in the child labor statutes.[19] Notwithstanding its allusion to free exercise rights, the Court described children as incapable of making decisions for themselves and in need of protection by the state:

> Th[is] case reduces itself . . . to the question whether the presence of the child's guardian puts a limit to the state's power. That fact may lessen the likelihood that some evils the legislation seeks to avert will occur. But it cannot forestall all of them. The zealous though lawful exercise of the right to engage in propagandizing the community, whether in religious, political or other matters, may and at times does create situations difficult enough for adults to cope with and wholly inappropriate for children, especially of tender years, to face. Other harmful possibilities could be stated, of emotional excitement and psychological or physical injury. Parents may be free to become martyrs themselves. But it does not follow they are free, in identical circumstances, to make martyrs of their children before they have reached the age of full and legal discretion when they can make that choice for themselves. . . . We think that with reference to the public proclaiming of religion, upon the streets and in other similar public places, the power of the state to control the conduct of children reaches beyond the scope of its authority over adults, as is true in the case of other freedoms, and the rightful boundary of its power has not been crossed in this case.[20]

While *Prince* afforded narrow protection for religious liberty, the Court later took a broader constitutional view in *Wisconsin v. Yoder.*[21] In *Yoder*, the Court upheld a claim raised by Amish parents that a state statute requiring them and all other parents to send their children to school until age sixteen violated the rights both of the parents and the children to freely practice their religion.[22] The Amish parents had sent their children, ages fourteen and fifteen, to school through the eighth grade but refused to send them to high school. The parents believed that to do so would expose the children to influences inconsistent with the communal traditions of the Amish faith, thus endangering their own salvation and that of the

---

[17] The Court identified two "claimed liberties" in *Prince*: one, "the parent's [right] to bring up the child . . . and teach [her] the tenets and practices of their faith" and two, the "child's [freedom] to observe [those tenets]" and to "preach the gospel by public distribution of the [religious literature] in conformity with . . . scripture." 321 U.S. at 164.

[18] The Court cited the state's *parens patriae* power to "guard the general interest in youth's well being" as well as its authority under the police power to address "the evils" attending "the crippling effects of child employment . . . especially in public places." *Id.* at 166, 168–69.

[19] *Id.* at 165.

[20] *Id.* at 169–70.

[21] 406 U.S. 205 (1972).

[22] While the Amish parents were the parties against whom the statute was directed, the parents argued that not only their religious rights, but also those of their children were infringed by enforcement of the statute. *Id.* at 215.

children. In recognizing the merits of the parents' claim, the Court noted the unique importance of communal living to the Amish, observing that for them salvation requires life in a church community separate and apart from modern society and worldly influences.[23] The Court thus found that the statute interfered with the practice of a legitimate religious belief and could not be sustained unless supported by a state interest of the "highest order" to override the [religious] interest.[24] While compulsory education laws promote important state interests,[25] the Court found that requiring the Amish children to attend school for an additional year or two would not serve those interests. The children were already sufficiently educated to read, write, and do basic mathematics and would receive useful vocational training by working full-time in their religious commune.[26]

The *Yoder* Court distinguished *Prince*, arguing that *Prince* was "narrow in scope" and raised issues of possible physical and psychological harm to children not

---

[23] *Id.* at 210. The Court suggested that perhaps only the Amish could present a claim sufficiently strong to justify exemption from the compulsory education statute. *Id.* at 235–36.

[24] *Id.* at 214–15. The Court subjected the Wisconsin statute to a higher level of scrutiny than the usual "rational basis" test. The Court noted the presence of both a free exercise and a parental rights claim as justification for elevating its scrutiny of the statute.

> [T]he Court's holding in *Pierce* [*see supra* § 6.02] stands as a charter of the rights of parents to direct religious upbringing of their children. And, when the interests of parenthood are combined with a free exercise claim of the nature revealed by this record, more than merely a "reasonable relation to some purpose within the competency of the State" is required to sustain the validity of the State's requirement under the First Amendment.

*Id.* at 233. For a discussion of "levels of scrutiny" applied by courts in assessing the constitutionality of legislation, see J. Barron & C. Dienes, Constitutional Law 160, 167, 228 (3d ed 1995). To briefly note, under the "rational basis" test, a law is constitutional if it is rationally related to a permissible governmental interest, while under the "strict scrutiny" test a law is unconstitutional unless "necessary" to promote a "compelling governmental interest." The rational basis test is applicable to most socioeconomic legislation, but strict scrutiny applies when legislation burdens the exercise of "fundamental personal rights" or discriminates against "suspect classes" of people. Under "intermediate scrutiny," a law is unconstitutional unless it is "substantially related" to an "important governmental objective." For a discussion of "intermediate scrutiny," see the discussion of legislative distinctions pertaining to illegitimate children, *infra* § 6.06[B][2]. *See also* Nowak & Rotunda, *supra* note 1, at 390, 601–3, 758–72.

[25] The Court noted two such interests: to prepare citizens to participate effectively in the political process and to prepare individuals to be self-reliant and self-sufficient participants in society. 406 U.S. at 221.

[26] The Court summarized the basis for its decision in *Yoder* as follows:

> Aided by a history of three centuries as an identifiable religious sect and a long history as a successful and self-sufficient segment of American society, the Amish in this case have convincingly demonstrated the sincerity of their religious beliefs, the interrelationship of belief with their mode of life, the vital role that belief and daily conduct play in the continued survival of Old Order Amish communities and their religious organization, and the hazards presented by the State's enforcement of a statute generally valid as to others. Beyond this, they have carried the even more difficult burden of demonstrating the adequacy of their alternative mode of continuing informal vocational education in terms of precisely those overall interests that the state advances in support of its program of compulsory high school education. In light of this convincing showing, one that probably few other religious groups or sects could make, and weighing the minimal difference between what the State would require and what the Amish already accept, it was incumbent on the State to show with more particularity how its admittedly strong interest in compulsory education would be adversely affected by granting an exemption to the Amish.

*Id.* at 235–36.

present in *Yoder*.[27] Thus, the state's *parens patriae* interest in *Prince* was supposedly stronger. Moreover, the *Yoder* Court maintained that the state's infringement on religion in *Prince* was less substantial than would occur if Wisconsin had enforced its compulsory education law against the Amish.[28]

The Court offered some views on *Yoder*'s implications for children's rights:

> [O]ur holding today in no degree depends on the assertion of the religious interest of the child as contrasted with that of the parents. It is the parents who are subject to prosecution here for failing to cause their children to attend school, and it is their right of free exercise, not that of their children, that must determine Wisconsin's power to impose criminal penalties on the parent. . . . The children are not parties to this litigation. The State has at no point tried this case on the theory that respondents were preventing their children from attending school against their expressed desires. . . .

> Our holding in no way determines the proper resolution of possible competing interests of parents, children, and the State in an appropriate state court proceeding in which the power of the State is asserted on the theory that Amish parents are preventing their minor children from attending high school despite their expressed desires to the contrary. Recognition of the claim of the State in such a proceeding would, of course, call into question traditional concepts of parental control over the religious upbringing and education of their minor children recognized in this Court's past decisions. It is clear that such an intrusion by a State into family decisions in the area of religious training would give rise to grave questions of religious freedom comparable to those raised here and those presented in *Pierce*. . . .[29]

Following the *dicta* of the *Yoder* Court, the lower courts have granted parents broad power to make religious choices for their children.[30] As discussed in Chapter 3, parents are generally permitted to withhold particular forms of medical treatment from their children where the parents object to the treatment on religious grounds and the treatment is not immediately necessary to preserve the child's life.[31] In the area of education, some state legislatures have enacted statutes specifically exempting certain religious communities from the state compulsory education law.[32] Moreover, most states permit parents who wish to expose their

---

[27] *Id.* at 229–30.

[28] As stated by the Court,

> [I]t seems clear that if the State is empowered as *parens patriae*, to "save" a child from himself or his Amish parents by requiring an additional two years of compulsory formal high school education, the State will in large measure influence, if not determine, the religious future of the child. Even more markedly than in *Prince*, therefore, this case involves the fundamental interest of parents, as contrasted with that of the State, to guide the religious future and education of their children.

*Id.* at 232.

[29] *Id.* at 232. For a discussion of *Pierce*, see *supra* § 6.02, notes 7–12 and accompanying text.

[30] For a discussion of deference to parental free exercise rights in adoption, foster care, and child custody cases, see Dwyer, *supra* § 3.01, note 9, at 1389–90 n.62.

[31] *Supra* § 3.02[A][3][a].

[32] *See, e.g.,* Iowa Code Ann. § 299.24 (West 1996) (permission to educate children at home even where education does not comply with requirements imposed on other "home schoolers" [*see id.* § 299.1] if the

children to religious values to educate their children at home so long as the parents meet certain state-imposed conditions on home schooling.[33] Where parents have attacked state regulations of home schooling as violations of the parent's free exercise rights to give their children a religious education, the courts have upheld the regulations as a means for promoting the state's compelling interest in educating its citizens.[34]

## [B] Free Speech

### [1] In School

In an early decision, *West Virginia State Board of Education v. Barnette*,[35] the United States Supreme Court held that the free speech rights of school students were violated by a board of education rule requiring students to salute the flag while reciting the Pledge of Allegiance. Although the rule was attacked by Jehovah's Witnesses as an infringement of their free exercise rights, the Court instead found that mandatory participation in the flag ceremony required students to "declare a belief" in violation of the Free Speech Clause.[36] Thus, students who opposed saluting the flag for whatever reason could not be required to do so. The Court did not specifically identify whose rights — students, their parents, or both — were at stake in *Barnette*, although it did express a fear that the flag salute requirement might "strangle the free minds" of students:

> Boards of Education . . . have, of course, important, delicate, and highly discretionary functions, but none that they may not perform within the limits of the Bill of Rights. That they are educating the young for citizenship is reason for scrupulous protection of Constitutional freedoms of

---

religious community's tenets "differ substantially from the objectives, goals, and philosophy of education embodied in" a list of required subjects for private schools). While *Yoder* requires exemptions from compulsory education laws for certain religious groups, the Court has found that the Establishment Clause is violated if a state creates a special school district to accommodate the interests of a religious community. *See* Board of Educ. v. Grumet, 512 U.S. 687 (1994) (creation of school district within Hasidic Jewish community so as to permit developmentally disabled children to attend school within the religious community violates the Establishment Clause).

[33] The regulations on home schooling vary greatly from state to state. Some states provide virtually no regulation while others impose strict requirements, sometimes specifying qualifications of home teachers, requiring standardized testing of students and regular consultation with certified teachers, and mandating school board approval of home education decisions and programs. Harris, Teitelbaum & Weisbrod, *supra* § 6.01, note 4, at 935.

[34] *See, e.g.*, Blackwelder v. Safnauer, 689 F. Supp. 106 (N.D.N.Y. 1988), *appeal dismissed*, 866 F.2d 548 (2d Cir. 1989); Duro v. District Attorney, 712 F.2d 96 (7th Cir. 1983), *cert. denied*, 465 U.S. 1006 (1984). For an argument that *Yoder* does not support a constitutional right to engage in home schooling, see I. Lupu, *Home Education, Religious Liberty and Separation of Powers*, 67 B.U. L. Rev. 971, 974–76 (1987) (state interest in adequately socializing and educating students not necessarily satisfied through home schooling whereas such interest was satisfied in *Yoder* when Amish parents sent their children to school through the eighth grade and subsequently provided them with communal vocational education).

[35] 319 U.S. 624 (1943).

[36] *Id.* at 631. The Court saw the flag salute ceremony as "requir[ing] the individual to communicate by word and sign his [adherence to government as presently organized] and his acceptance of the political ideas" symbolized by the flag. *Id.* at 633. For a recent case holding that public schools may lead the Pledge of Allegiance daily so long as students choosing not to participate are not forced to do so, see *Sherman v. Community Consolidated School District 21 of Wheeling Township*, 980 F.2d 437 (7th Cir. 1992), *cert. denied*, 508 U.S. 950 (1993).

the individual, if we are not to strangle the free mind at its source and teach youth to discount important principles of our government as mere platitudes.[37]

Twenty-six years after *Barnette*, the Court decided *Tinker v. Des Moines Independent Community School District*,[38] a case where several junior and senior high students claimed free speech rights to make political protests at school. The case arose after a group of adults and students held a meeting at which they decided to publicize their objections to the Vietnam War by wearing black armbands. Three of the students attending the meeting, fifteen-year-old John Tinker, his thirteen-year-old sister, Mary Beth, and another sixteen-year-old, Eckhardt, had, along with their parents, previously engaged in anti-war protests. The students and their parents decided that the students would wear the armbands to school. When school authorities discovered this plan, fearing disruption of the educational process if it were carried out, they adopted a policy to suspend from school any student wearing an armband and refusing to remove it. The Tinker children and Eckhardt wore their armbands to school and were suspended. The students contested their suspension, arguing that their wearing of the armbands was protected under the Free Speech Clause.

The Supreme Court agreed with the students, seeing the conduct of the students under the circumstances as tantamount to "pure speech."[39] The Court found no evidence that the conduct of the students had any disruptive effect.[40] Noting that students do not "shed their constitutional rights to freedom of speech or expression at the schoolhouse gate," the Court found that the school authorities' fears of disruption were unfounded and that their actions were based on no more than an "urgent wish to avoid controversy."[41] The Court discussed the status of children under the Constitution as follows:

> In our system, state-operated schools may not be enclaves of totalitarianism. School officials do not possess absolute authority over their students. Students in school as well as out of school are "persons" under our Constitution. They are possessed of fundamental rights which the State must respect, just as they themselves must respect their obligations to the State. In our system, students may not be regarded as close-circuit recipients of only that which the State chooses to communicate. They may not be confined to the expression of those sentiments that are officially approved. In the absence of a specific showing of constitutionally valid reasons to regulate their speech, students are entitled to freedom of expression of their views.[42]

---

[37] 319 U.S. at 637.

[38] 393 U.S. 503 (1969).

[39] *Id.* at 505.

[40] The Court found "no indication" that the work of the school or of any class was disrupted even though a few students made "hostile remarks" outside the classroom to the children wearing the armbands. *Id.* at 508, 514.

[41] *Id.* at 506, 510.

[42] *Id.* at 511. The Court added:

> The principal use to which the schools are dedicated is to accommodate students during prescribed hours for the purpose of certain types of activities. Among those activities is personal intercommunication among the students. This is not only an inevitable part of the process of attending school; it is also an important part of the educational process. A student's rights, therefore, do not embrace merely the classroom hours. When he is in the cafeteria, or

The lower courts have generally held, in light of *Tinker*, that students possess free speech rights that can be restrained only where their exercise would materially disrupt the work and discipline of the school.[43] Schools may, however, impose reasonable regulations with respect to the time, place, and manner in which students conduct their speech-related activities.[44] Applying these principles, the lower courts have, for example, permitted school officials to prohibit students from loitering in certain areas of the school.[45]

The courts are severely split, however, on whether schools can regulate student dress and personal appearance. A bare majority of courts hold that school rules absolutely banning a student from wearing long hair are unconstitutional.[46] For the majority of courts, long hair can be banned only where it constitutes a health or safety hazard that cannot be avoided by any alternative other than cutting the hair.[47]

The courts have granted greater deference to school dress codes, particularly where the schools have articulated the purpose of prohibiting displays of gang affiliation. Some courts have upheld school "anti-gang" policies prohibiting male students from wearing earrings.[48] Other courts have upheld school rules prohibiting students from wearing clothing identified with street gangs.[49] Many schools concerned with growing disruption and violence due to gang membership regulate student apparel, prohibiting such things as baggy clothing,[50] baseball caps,

---

on the playing field, or on the campus during the authorized hours, he may express his opinions, even on controversial subjects like the conflict in Vietnam, if he does so without "materially and substantially interfer[ing]" with the requirements of appropriate discipline in the operation of the school" and without colliding with the rights of others. . . . But conduct by the student, in class or out of it, which for any reason — whether it stems from time, place, or type of behavior — materially disrupts classwork or involves substantial disorder or invasion of the rights of others is, of course, not immunized by the constitutional guarantee of freedom of speech.

*Id.* at 512–13.

[43] Kramer, *supra* § 3.03, note 15, at 510.

[44] *Id.*

[45] *See, e.g.*, Wiemerslage v. Maine Township High Sch. Dist. 207, 824 F. Supp. 136 (N.D. Ill. 1993).

[46] Kramer, *supra* note 43, at 519.

[47] *Id.*; *see also* 68 Am. Jur. 2d *Schools* §§ 267–68 (1993).

[48] *See, e.g.*, Olesen v. Board of Educ. of Sch. Dist. No. 228, 676 F. Supp. 820 (N.D. Ill. 1987).

[49] *See , e.g.*, Jeglin v. San Jacinto Unified Sch. Dist., 827 F. Supp. 1459 (C.D. Cal. 1993) (dress code constitutional when applied to high school students but not to elementary and middle school students where evidence of gang activity was negligible in the elementary and middle schools but substantial in the high schools).

In 1994, California enacted legislation allowing school districts to require all students to wear a uniform. Cal. Educ. Code § 35183 (West Supp. 2002). The statute is aimed at curbing gang activity in schools, limiting disruptions in education, providing a safer and healthier environment for students, improving grades, and decreasing absences, misconduct, class tension, and economic pressure on students. Note, *A Nation of Robots? The Unconstitutionality of Public School Uniform Codes*, 28 J. MARSHALL L. REV 645, 656 (1995). Several California school districts have implemented rules requiring student uniforms. Comment, *Undressing the First Amendment in Public Schools: Do Uniform Dress Codes Violate Student's First Amendment Rights*, 28 LOY. L.A. L. REV. 1415, 1421 (1995). Utah has also enacted legislation permitting school districts with parental approval to require that public school students dress uniformly. *See* Utah Code Ann. § 53A-15-1103 (West 2007).

[50] *See, e.g.*, Bivens v. Albuquerque Pub. Sch., 899 F. Supp. 556 (D.N.M. 1995) (wearing saggy pants is not speech for the purposes of First Amendment rights).

bandannas, jewelry, headbands, overalls with one strap up and one strap hanging down, gang-related insignias, gloves, shoelaces, clothing that is all red or blue, sexually obscene and explicit clothing or paraphernalia, clothing than contains pictures that promote violence, drugs, tobacco or alcohol, or clothing such as trench coats that can easily conceal weapons.[51]

Finally, the lower courts are split on whether it is constitutionally permissible for school officials to require that written materials be submitted to them for approval prior to being distributed in school.[52] The Supreme Court expanded the protections recognized in *Tinker* in *Board of Education, Island Trees Free School District v. Pico*[53] which held that school officials violated the First Amendment rights of high school and junior high school students by removing certain books from school libraries after parents objected to the books as containing immoral material. Justice Brennan, joined by Justices Marshall and Stevens wrote the opinion for the Court in which he identified a violation of a student "right to receive ideas" as the source of the constitutional evil.[54] Justice Brennan emphasized, however, that the Court's action affected only the *removal* of books from schools and did not in "any way affect the discretion of a local school board to choose books to *add* to the libraries of their schools"[55] Although the existence of a student "right to receive ideas" commanded only a plurality of the *Pico* Court, lower courts often cite *Pico* as recognizing the right.[56]

While *Tinker* and *Pico* appear to give students broad free speech protections,[57] the Court's subsequent opinion in *Bethel School District No. 403 v. Fraser*[58] is another matter. In *Fraser*, a high school student was suspended from school for giving a speech at a school assembly deemed by school authorities to be "obscene and profane" under a school disciplinary rule.[59] Prior to giving the speech, the student had been advised by two teachers that the speech was "inappropriate" and should not be given. Nevertheless, the student delivered the speech, given for the purpose of nominating a fellow student for student elective office, in which the speaker made constant references to the candidate in terms of "an elaborate graphic, and explicit sexual metaphor."[60] The student audience responded to the

---

[51] Comment, *Undressing the First Amendment in Public Schools*, *supra* note 49, at 1416; Note, *Restricting Gang Clothing in Public Schools: Does a Dress Code Violate a Student's Right of Free Expression?*, 64 S. Cal. L. Rev. 1321, 1323–24, 1328 (1991); *see also* R. Miller, Annotation, *Validity of Regulation by Public School Authorities as to Clothes or Personal Appearance of Pupils*, 58 A.L.R. 5th 1 (1998).

[52] Kramer, *supra* note 43, at 516.

[53] 457 U.S. 853 (1982).

[54] *Id.* at 867–68.

[55] *Id.* at 871–72.

[56] See, *e.g.*, the following cases citing *Pico* for the proposition that students enjoy a right to receive ideas: *United States v. Miami Univ.*, 91 F. Supp. 2d 1132 (S.D. Ohio 2000); *Schuloff v. Fields*, 960 F. Supp. 66 (E.D.N.Y 1997); *Student Press Law Center v. Alexander*, 778 F. Supp. 1227 (D.C.D.C. 1991).

[57] In *Tinker's* aftermath students have brought hundreds of cases challenging the actions of public school authorities concerning dances, demonstrations, discipline, student elections, hair length, library books, school plays, and other matters. *See* Note, Tinker *Revisited:* Fraser v. Bethel School District *and Regulation of Speech in Public School*, 1985 Duke L.J. 1164, 1167–68.

[58] 478 U.S. 675 (1986).

[59] The rule prohibited "[c]onduct which materially and substantially interferes with the education process . . . including the use of obscene, profane language or gestures." *Id.* at 678.

[60] *Id.* at 677. For example, the speech referred to the candidate as "a man who is firm, . . . firm in

speech with a mixture of hooting, gesturing, bewilderment and embarrassment. The day after the speech, the assistant principal suspended the student who subsequently contended that the suspension violated his free speech rights under *Tinker*.

The Supreme Court rejected the student's argument, distinguishing *Tinker* as a case, unlike *Fraser*, involving political speech. Moreover, unlike *Tinker*, the Court found that the speech in *Fraser* intruded upon the interests of other students. In addition, the *Fraser* Court acknowledged the role of educators to act *in loco parentis* in teaching "the habits and manners of civility" as values important for the healthy development of their students.[61] The Court elaborated:

> These fundamental values of 'habits and manners of civility' essential to a democratic society must, of course, include tolerance of divergent political and religious views, even when the views expressed may be unpopular. But these 'fundamental values' must also take into account consideration of the sensibilities of others, and, in the case of a school, the sensibilities of fellow students. The undoubted freedom to advocate unpopular and controversial views in schools and classrooms must be balanced against the society's countervailing interest in teaching students the boundaries of socially appropriate behavior. Even the most heated political discourse in a democratic society requires consideration for the personal sensibilities of the other participants and audiences.[62]

Finally, the Court suggested that even if the nominating speech in *Fraser* could somehow be characterized as a political statement, it would nevertheless be unprotected when given by a student in a school setting. The Court noted that while adults possess "wide freedom" to engage in offensive speech making what the speaker considers a political point, "it does not follow . . . that . . . the same latitude must be permitted to [school] children" to engage in similar speech.[63] "The constitutional rights of students in public school are not automatically coextensive with the rights of adults in other settings."[64] Schools must teach students like "the confused boy" in *Fraser* the "shared values of a civilized social order" as well as protect the sensitivities of other students from exposure to "vulgar and offensive language."[65]

Shortly after *Fraser*, the Court decided *Hazelwood School District v. Kuhlmeier*[66] which examined the extent to which school officials could exercise editorial control over the contents of a high school newspaper published as part of the school's journalism curriculum. The newspaper was written and edited by students in the journalism class and then submitted to the school principal for review prior to publication. After the principal ordered two stories to be deleted from publication because he deemed them inappropriate and offensive,[67] student

---

his pants, . . . who takes his point and pounds it in, [who] drives hard, pushing and pushing until [he goes to the climax]. . . . *Id.* at 687 (Brennan, J., concurring).

[61] *Id.* at 681.

[62] *Id.*

[63] *Id.* at 682.

[64] *Id.*

[65] *Id.* at 683–84.

[66] 484 U.S. 260 (1988).

[67] One of the stories detailed three fellow students' experiences with pregnancy. Although the story used false names, the principal was concerned that the pregnant students might nevertheless be

staff members of the paper brought an action claiming their free speech rights had been violated by the principal's action. After concluding that the student newspaper was intimately linked to the educational curriculum and thus not a "public forum," the Court held that the principal had acted properly in "reasonably regulating" the contents of the paper.[68]

The Court again distinguished *Tinker*, a case raising the issue of "whether the First Amendment requires a school *to tolerate* particular student speech," from *Kuhlmeier* which raised the question of "whether the First Amendment requires a school affirmatively *to promote* particular student speech."[69] While *Tinker* involved educators' ability to silence a student's personal expression occurring incidentally on school premises, *Kuhlmeir* concerned educators' authority over school-sponsored activity that students, parents, and members of the public might reasonably perceive to bear "the imprimatur of the school."[70] Because educators possess greater authority to control the latter form of student expression, the school may, as in *Fraser*, "disassociate itself" from student speech that infringes on the rights of others, does not meet academic standards, or is inconsistent with the moral values the school wishes to inculcate.[71] Therefore, "educators do not offend the First Amendment by exercising editorial control over the style and content of student speech in school-sponsored expressive activities so long as their actions are reasonably related to legitimate pedagogical concerns."[72]

The Supreme Court took the occasion to further distinguish *Tinker* in *Morse v. Fredrick*,[73] a case posing the question whether school authorities can, consistent with the First Amendment, restrict student speech at a school event when that speech can reasonably be viewed as promoting illegal drug use. *Morse* dealt with a situation where a high school student sued the school's principal for suspending him from school for ten days for waving a banner with the inscription "Bong Hits 4 Jesus" written on it after the principal confiscated the banner during an off-campus school-sponsored event. In upholding the principal's actions and rejecting the student's First Amendment claims, the Court appealed to the "special characteristics of the school environment"[74] in performing "custodial and tutelary" respon-

---

identified, thus causing them embarrassment and emotional distress. Moreover, the principal believed the article's references to sexual activity and birth control were inappropriate for some of the younger students at the school. *Id.* at 263.

The other story discussed the impact of divorce on students at the school. The principal was concerned that parents disparagingly referred to in the story should either be given an opportunity to respond to the accusations in the story or consent to its publication. *Id.*

[68] *Id.* at 270.

[69] *Id.* at 270–71 (emphasis added).

[70] *Id.* at 271.

[71] *Id.*

[72] *Id.* at 273. For two thoughtful and contrasting assessments of the Supreme Court's student speech cases, see B. Hafen, *Developing Student Expression Through Institutional Authority: Public Schools as Mediating Structures*, 48 Ohio St. L.J. 663 (1987); S. Wilborn, *Teaching the New Three Rs—Repression, Rights, and Respect: A Primer of Student Speech Activities*, 37 B.C. L. Rev. 119 (1995).

Some states have statutorily extended greater rights to student expression than recognized in *Kuhlmeier. See, e.g.*, Mass. Gen Laws Ann. Ch. 71, § 82 (1996); Pyle v. South Hadley Sch. Comm., 861 F. Supp. 157 (D. Mass. 1994) (statute applies same standard for school-tolerated and school-sponsored speech).

[73] 127 S. Ct. 2618 (2007).

[74] *Id.* at 2626 (quoting *Tinker*, 393 U.S. 503, 506 (1969)).

sibilities for children[75] as grounds for permitting the banner's confiscation and the student's suspension as a means of deterring drug use in the school. The Court noted:

> School principals have a difficult job, and a vitally important one. When Frederick suddenly and unexpectedly unfurled his banner, Morse had to decide to act—or not act—on the spot. It was reasonable for her to conclude that the banner promoted illegal drug use—in violation of established school policy—and that failing to act would send a powerful message to the students in her charge, including Frederick, about how serious the school was about the dangers of illegal drug use. The First Amendment does not require schools to tolerate at school events student expression that contributes to those dangers.[76]

## [2] Outside School

While the bulk of its attention focuses on juvenile freedom of speech in the school context, the Supreme Court has spoken, at least obliquely, to issues arising outside school. In *Ginsberg v. New York*,[77] the Court considered the facial validity of a state statute prohibiting the sale of obscene materials to minors under age seventeen and embracing a broader definition of obscenity than that applicable to adults.[78] After selling two "girlie" magazines[79] to a sixteen-year-old, Ginsberg was

---

[75] 127 S. Ct. at 2628 (quoting Veronica School Dist., 47J v. Acton, 515 U.S. 646, 656 (1995)).

[76] 127 S. Ct. at 2629.

[77] 390 U.S. 629 (1968).

[78] *Id.* at 631–34. The statute defined juvenile obscenity and prohibited its distribution as follows:

§ 484-h. Exposing minors to harmful materials

1. Definitions. As used in this section:

(a) "Minor" means any person under the age of seventeen years.

(b) "Nudity" means the showing of the human male or female genitals, pubic area or buttocks with less than a full opaque covering, or the showing of the female breast with less than a fully opaque covering of any portion thereof below the top of the nipple, or the depiction of covered male genitals in a discernible turgid state.

(c) "Sexual conduct" means acts of masturbation, homosexuality, sexual intercourse, or physical contact with a person's clothed or unclothed genitals, pubic area, buttocks or, if such person be a female, breast.

(d) "Sexual excitement" means the condition of human male or female genitals when in a state of sexual stimulation or arousal.

(e) "Sado-masochistic abuse" means flagellation or torture by or upon a person clad in undergarments, a mask or bizarre costume, or the condition of being fettered, bound or otherwise physically restrained on the part of one so clothed.

(f) "Harmful to minors" means that quality of any description or representation, in whatever form, of nudity, sexual conduct, sexual excitement, or sadomasochistic abuse, when it:

(i) predominantly appeals to the prurient, shameful or morbid interest of minors, and

(ii) is patently offensive to prevailing standards in the adult community as a whole with respect to what is suitable material for minors, and

(iii) is utterly without redeeming social importance for minors.

2. It shall be unlawful for any person knowingly to sell or loan for monetary consideration to a minor:

convicted under the statute[80] and argued on appeal that because the material he sold was not obscene for adults, and therefore protected speech, the state could not remove the material from First Amendment protection by defining it as obscene on the basis of its appeal to minors. Ginsberg did not contest whether the magazines were obscene under the statute,[81] but argued instead that "the scope of the constitutional freedom of expression secured to a citizen to read or see material concerned with sex cannot be made to depend on whether the citizen is an adult or a minor."[82]

The Court agreed that the magazines were not obscene for adults, but nevertheless upheld the statute, finding that it did not invade the "constitutionally protected freedoms" of minors under age seventeen.[83] Citing *Prince*, the Court reaffirmed that the power of the state to control the conduct of children reaches beyond the scope of its authority over adults.[84] The *Ginsberg* Court identified two interests justifying the legislation: a parental right to rear children free from the influence of sex-related materials they deemed harmful, and an independent state interest in protecting the welfare of its youth.[85] Although recognizing that the issue was extremely controversial, the Court found that the state may "rationally conclude" that exposure to the materials proscribed by the statute is harmful to the well-being of young people.[86] Therefore, the statute was constitutional because the Court found insufficient evidence that defining the obscenity of material on the basis of its appeal to minors "has no rational relation to the objective of safeguarding such minors from harm."[87]

With the advent of the ubiquitous exposure of the Internet, Congress has attempted to protect minors from harmful effects of Internet communications. In

---

> (a) any picture, photograph, drawing, sculpture, motion picture film, or similar visual representation or image of a person or portion of the human body which depicts nudity, sexual conduct or sadomasochistic abuse and which is harmful to minors, or
>
> (b) any book, pamphlet, magazine, printed matter however reproduced, or sound recording which contains any matter enumerated in paragraph (a) of subdivision two hereof, or explicit and detailed verbal descriptions or narrative accounts of sexual excitement, sexual conduct or sado-masochistic abuse and which, taken as a whole is harmful to minors. . . .

*Id.* at 645–47.

[79] *Id.* at 634.

[80] The magazine contained nude pictures of female buttocks and breasts. *Id.* at 632. *See supra* note 68.

[81] 390 U.S. at 631 n.1.

[82] *Id.* at 636. The Court had held in earlier cases that obscenity is not protected speech under the First Amendment. Roth v. United States, 354 U.S. 476, 485 (1957).

[83] 390 U.S. at 634, 638.

[84] *Id.* at 638.

[85] *Id.* at 639–40.

[86] New York made a legislative finding that the material defined as obscene for juveniles under its statute is "a basic factor in impairing the ethical and moral development of our youth and a clear and present danger for the people of the state." *Id.* at 641. The Court found it "very doubtful" that this finding expressed "an accepted scientific fact" but nevertheless held that it was not "irrational" for the state to adopt this view in light of the fact that empirical studies did not disprove a causal link between obscenity and harm to healthy child development. *Id.* at 641–43.

[87] *Id.* at 643.

the Community Decency Act of 1996, Congress proscribed use of a computer to, *inter alia*, transmit any "obscene or indecent" communication known by the sender to be sent to anyone under the age of eighteen.[88] In addition, the statute prohibited using a computer to transmit to a minor a communication that depicted or described sexual or excretory functions that are patently offensive to contemporary community standards or to transmit the communication is such a way that it would be accessible to anyone under 18 years old.[89] The United States Supreme Court struck these provisions down in *Reno v. American Civil Liberties Union*,[90] determining that they lacked the precision required of statutes that regulate the content of speech. The Court held that the provisions were overbroad (because there was no feasible way for adults to engage in constitutionally protected indecent speech) and vague (because the failure to define terms like "indecent" and "patently offensive" left speakers uncertain as to what the terms meant).

Congress responded by passing the Child Online Protection Act (COPA) which makes it a crime knowingly to make "any communication for commercial purposes that is available to any minor and that includes any material that is harmful to minors."[91] The statute defines "harmful to minors" in terms of established obscenity standards, prohibiting material that "the average person, applying contemporary community standards, would find, taking the material as a whole and with respect to minors, is designed to appeal to or is designed to pander to, the prurient interest."[92] The United States Supreme Court upheld the COPA provisions against First Amendment attack in *Ashcroft v. American Civil Liberties Union*.[93]

The constitutional status of COPA has, however, become uncertain. On remand from the *Ashcroft* case, the Third Circuit affirmed an injunction issued by the district court against the statute.[94] Then in *Ashcroft v. American Civil Liberties Union*,[95] the Supreme Court upheld the injunction and the appellate decision, reasoning that COPA did not utilize the least restrictive means possible to achieve its goal of restricting juvenile access to Internet pornography and remanded the case for further consideration. On remand, the district court found the statute unconstitutional on vagueness and overbreadth grounds.[96]

Apart from *Ginsberg* and the Internet cases, the Supreme Court has said little regarding the scope of juvenile free speech rights outside the school context.[97]

---

[88] Telecommunications Act of 1996, 47 U.S.C. § 223(a)(1)(A) (Supp. 1996).

[89] *Id.* at § 223(a)(1)(B).

[90] 521 U.S. 844 (1997).

[91] 47 U.S.C. § 231(a)(1) (1998).

[92] *Id.* at § 231(e)(6)(A).

[93] 535 U.S. 564 (2002). The narrow question before the Court was whether COPA was unconstitutionally overbroad because it defined obscenity based on community standards. The plaintiffs argued that it would restrict organizations and their members from placing sexually explicit material on the web which would have been permissible in some communities. The Court rejected the argument that it was overbroad based on the "community standards" language but said in dicta that it might be overbroad for other reasons if those reasons had been before it. *Id.* at 583–585.

[94] American Civil Liberties Union v. Ashcroft, 322 F.3d 240 (3d Cir. 2003).

[95] 542 U.S. 656 (2004).

[96] American Civil Liberties Union v. Gonzales, 478 F. Supp. 2d 775, 777–78 (E.D. Pa. 2007).

[97] In *Denver Area Educational Telecommunications Consortium, Inc. v. Federal Communications*

While never directly ruling on the matter, the Court has on at least two occasions refused to review challenges to juvenile curfew ordinances upheld by lower courts after juveniles and their parents attacked the statutes as violative of rights of free speech and association.[98] The lower courts are split on the constitutionality of juvenile curfew measures, which are routinely enacted in hopes of reducing juvenile crime and protecting children by keeping them off the streets during the late night and early morning hours. Some courts uphold curfew provisions as permissible under the First Amendment, particularly where exceptions are allowed for juveniles who are accompanied by their parents or guardians, traveling to or from work, or engaged in other permissible activities.[99] Other courts, however, have invalidated juvenile curfew rules under the First Amendment.[100] Aside from the particular context of statutes and ordinances imposing curfews,[101] the courts have generally upheld other juvenile status offense provisions even though, as discussed in Part Three of this text, they are broadly worded and often attacked as unconstitutionally vague or violative of free speech rights under the First Amendment.[102]

## § 6.04   THE FOURTH AMENDMENT[1]

The United States Supreme Court has decided three cases, *New Jersey v. T.L.O.*,[2] *Vernonia School District 47J v. Acton*,[3] and *Board of Educ. Indep. Sch. Dist. 92 v. Earls*[4] defining the rights of school children under the Fourth

---

*Commission*, 518 U.S. 727 (1996), a majority of the Supreme Court upheld against First Amendment attack federal statutory provisions aimed at protecting children which permitted cable operators to prohibit material on leased channels which "the operator reasonably believes describes or depicts sexual or excretory activities or organs in a patently offensive manner."

A different majority, however, struck down a separate provision requiring operators to segregate patently offensive programming, place it on a single channel, and block the channel from viewer access unless the viewer provides advance, written requests. The Court held that the provision was not appropriately tailored to achieve the state's objective to protect children from exposure to patently offensive material. The Court noted that "children spend more time watching television and view more channels than do their parents, whether their household subscribes to cable or receives television over the air." *Id.* at 744–45.

Yet another majority found unconstitutional a third provision which permitted cable operators to allow or prohibit programming on public access channels that the operator reasonably believes depicts sexual activities or organs in a patently offensive manner. The Court found that the government failed to meet its burden of showing that the regulation is necessary to protect children or that it is appropriately tailored to secure that end. The Court reasoned, in part, that there was no showing that there was a nationwide pattern of indecent or obscene programs on public access channels to necessitate such regulations. Further, the Court expressed fear that cable operators would opt to prohibit "borderline" material that may not, in fact, be patently offensive.

[98] *See, e.g.*, Qutb v. Strauss, 11 F.3d 488 (5th Cir. 1993), *cert. denied*, 511 U.S. 1127 (1994); Bykofsky v. Middleton, 401 F. Supp. 1242 (M.D. Pa. 1975), *aff'd*, 535 F.2d 1245 (3d Cir. 1976), *cert. denied*, 429 U.S. 964 (1976).

[99] *See, e.g.*, Qutb v. Bartlett, 11 F.3d 488 (5th Cir. 1993); People v. Chambers, 360 N.E.2d 55 (Ill. 1976).

[100] *See, e.g.*, Waters v. Barry, 711 F. Supp. 1125 (D.D.C. 1989) (also violates due process and equal protection).

[101] For a general discussion of juvenile curfew regulations, see D. Veilleux, Annotation, *Validity, Construction, and Effect of Juvenile Curfew Regulations*, 83 A.L.R.4th 1056 (1991).

[102] *See infra* § 8.04[C][2].

[1] The Fourth Amendment to the United States Constitution provides:

The right of the people to be secure in their persons, houses, papers, and effects, against

Amendment. The cases involved searches of school children by school officials and established different standards for school searches than those applicable outside of school where law enforcement officers are generally involved. This section examines the application of the Fourth Amendment in the schools and leaves law enforcement searches to be addressed in the context of the juvenile justice system in Part Three.[5]

*New Jersey v. T.L.O.* marked the Court's first examination of the Fourth Amendment consequences of searches by school officials of students and their property.[6] T.L.O. was a fourteen-year-old high school freshman. A teacher at the school observed T.L.O. and another girl smoking cigarettes in a school lavatory in violation of a school rule prohibiting smoking in certain designated areas, including the lavatory.

The teacher took the two girls to the principal's office where they met with Assistant Vice Principal Theodore Choplick. In response to Choplick's questioning, T.L.O.'s companion admitted violating the rule, but T.L.O. denied that she had been smoking in the lavatory and claimed that she did not smoke at all. After asking her to accompany him into his private office, Choplick demanded to see T.L.O.'s purse, which he opened, discovering a pack of cigarettes. Choplick removed the cigarettes and accused T.L.O. of lying. In removing the cigarettes, Choplick noticed that the purse also contained cigarette rolling papers which he associated with marijuana use. Suspecting that it might contain further evidence of illegal drug use, Choplick searched the purse extensively and discovered a small amount of marijuana, a pipe, a number of empty plastic bags, a substantial number of one dollar bills, an index card that appeared to be a list of students who owed T.L.O. money, and two letters which Choplick read thoroughly. The letters, which were located with the index cards in a separate, zippered compartment of the purse, implicated T.L.O. in marijuana dealing.

Choplick turned the evidence over to the police, and juvenile authorities brought a delinquency action against T.L.O. who unsuccessfully sought to suppress the evidence as the inadmissible fruits of an illegal search and seizure. T.L.O. was adjudicated a delinquent, appealed, and eventually took her case to the Supreme Court.

The Court rejected arguments made by the State that the Fourth Amendment was limited to searches by law enforcement personnel, and was thus inapplicable to searches by school officials.[7] Similarly, the Court disagreed with the State's

---

unreasonable searches and seizures, shall not be violated, and no Warrants shall issue, but upon probable cause, supported by Oath or affirmation, and particularly describing the place to be searched, and the persons or things to be seized.

[2] 469 U.S. 325 (1985).

[3] 515 U.S. 646 (1995).

[4] 536 U.S. 822 (2002).

[5] *See infra* § 9.02[A].

[6] The author has considered the case in detail elsewhere. *See* M. Gardner, *Student Privacy in the Wake of* T.L.O.: *An Appeal for an Individualized Suspicion Requirement for Valid Searches and Seizures in the Schools*, 22 GA. L. REV. 897 (1988). Some of the discussion that follows here draws from that earlier work.

[7] 469 U.S. at 335. The Court cited a variety of cases holding the Fourth Amendment applicable to governmental intrusions by non-police officers including *Camara v. Municipal Court*, 387 U.S. 523

contention that school officials stand *in loco parentis* and are thus private actors not subject to the Fourth Amendment.[8] The Court also rejected the argument that school searches were governed by its holding that the Fourth Amendment is inapplicable to searches of prison inmates' cells given the especially strong state interests in maintaining institutional discipline that outweigh any inmate privacy interest.[9] While prisoners lack the "legitimate expectations of privacy" essential to trigger Fourth Amendment protection[10] when their cells are searched in the name of maintaining order and safety within the prison, students "stand in wholly different circumstances" from prisoners even though school searches are also characteristically conducted to maintain order and safety.[11] Although state officials subject both prisoners and school children to intense supervision, students, unlike prisoners, possess "legitimate privacy expectations" in items of personal property found within the area of such supervision, and are thus protected under the Fourth Amendment.[12] Quoting *Barnette*, the Court reiterated "[t]hat [boards of education]

---

(1967) (building inspectors); *Marshall v. Barlow's, Inc.*, 436 U.S. 307, 312–13 (1978) (OSHA inspectors); and *Michigan v. Tyler*, 436 U.S. 499, 506 (1978) (firemen). The Court noted that the arbitrary invasion of individual privacy and security by governmental officials, whatever their capacity, is the principal evil addressed by the Fourth Amendment.

[8] *Id.* at 336. After initially granting certiorari in *T.L.O.* to consider the appropriateness of the exclusionary rule as a remedy for illegal school searches, 464 U.S. 991 (1983), the Court ordered reargument on the issue of what limits, if any, the Fourth Amendment places on school officials. 469 U.S. 325, 332 (1985). Upon reargument, the State of New Jersey contended, *inter alia*, that because of minimal student privacy expectations, the Fourth Amendment did not apply to the search of the student in the case at hand. *See* Supplemental Brief for Petitioner upon Reargument at 23–24, New Jersey v. T.L.O., 469 U.S. 325 (1985) (No. 83-712). Prior to *T.L.O.*, several lower courts denied the applicability of the Fourth Amendment to searches and seizures of students by school officials. Some cases held that school officials were "private citizens," and thus not within the scope of the Fourth Amendment which applies only to governmental action. *See, e.g., In re* Donaldson, 75 Cal. Rptr. 220 (Cal. Ct. App. 1969) (holding vice principal of high school was not a "governmental official"), rejected by *In re* William G. 709 P.2d 1287 (Cal. 1985). Others held that school officials stand *in loco parentis*, and thus serve a non-governmental function when they search students. *See, e.g.*, Mercer v. State, 450 S.W.2d 715 (Tex. Civ. App. 1970) (principal ordering student to empty his pockets was not acting as arm of government), abrogated by Shoemaker v. State, 971 S.W. 2d 178 (Tex. Ct. App. 1998).

The *T.L.O.* Court characterized the notion that educators assume parental roles as a view "in tension with [the] contemporary reality" of compulsory education. *Id.* School officials are state actors who act in furtherance of publicly mandated educational policies rather than private parties receiving delegations of parental authority. 469 U.S. at 336. For a discussion and criticism of the *in loco parentis* cases, *see* Buss, *The Fourth Amendment and Searches of Students in Public Schools*, 59 Iowa L. Rev. 739, 765–68 (1974).

Although the *T.L.O.* Court refused to see educators as standing *in loco parentis* for purposes of search and seizure law, the Supreme Court has, subsequent to *T.L.O.*, characterized school authorities as acting *in loco parentis* for purposes of protecting students from exposure to sexually explicit, indecent, or lewd speech. *See* Bethel Sch. Dist. No. 403 v. Fraser, 478 U.S. 675, 683–85 (1986), discussed *supra* § 6.03, note 53 and accompanying text.

[9] 469 U.S. at 338–39 (rejecting an analogy to Hudson v. Palmer, 468 U.S. 517 (1984)).

[10] The scope of the Fourth Amendment has been defined at least since the time of Katz v. United States, 389 U.S. 347 (1967) (listening device attached to phone booth violated petitioner's justifiably relied-upon privacy), in terms of whether the person alleging an illegal governmental search or seizure possessed sufficient "expectations of privacy" to trigger Fourth Amendment protection. *See* M. Gardner, *Sniffing for Drugs in the Classroom — Perspectives on Fourth Amendment* Scope, 74 Nw. U. L. Rev. 803, 831–33 (1980).

[11] 469 U.S. at 338–40 (citing Ingraham v. Wright, 430 U.S. 651, 669 (1977)).

[12] *Id.* Apart from noting that prisoners and school children are separated by the harsh facts of

are educating the young for citizenship is reason for scrupulous protection of Constitutional freedoms of the individual, if we are not to strangle the free mind at its source and teach youth to discount important principles of our government as mere platitudes."[13]

Directing its attention to the issue of the applicable Fourth Amendment standard, the *T.L.O.* Court held that the determination of 'reasonableness" under the Fourth Amendment "depends on the context within which a search takes place," which in turn requires "balancing the need to search against the invasion which the search entails."[14] On one side of the balance is the individual interest in "legitimate expectations of privacy and personal security; on the other, the government's need for effective methods to deal with breaches of public order," and to assure safety and discipline within the educational environment.[15] Determining the reasonableness of any search involves a two-fold inquiry: "whether the action was justified at its inception and whether the search as actually conducted was reasonably related in scope to the circumstances which justified the interference in the first place."[16] The Court noted that searches of students by school officials will generally be "justified at their inception" when there are reasonable grounds for suspecting that the search will turn up evidence that the student has violated or is violating either the law or the rules of the school.[17] Such searches "will be permissible in their scope when the measures adopted are reasonably related to the objectives of the search and not excessively intrusive in light of the age and sex of the student and the nature of the infraction."[18]

The *T.L.O.* Court recognized that the search of a student's person or of a closed purse or other container carried on her person constitutes a "severe violation of legitimate expectations of privacy."[19] Against that privacy interest the Court balanced "the substantial interest of teachers and administrators in maintaining discipline in the classroom and on school grounds."[20] The Court noted the "major social problem" created by a recent influx of drug use and violent crime in the schools as well as the "value of preserving the informality of the student-teacher relationship" as factors requiring "a certain degree of flexibility in school disciplinary procedures."[21] Therefore, the Court dispensed with the requirement of obtaining a warrant prior to conducting school searches and seizures. Moreover, the Court relied on several previous cases that upheld Fourth Amendment intrusions where "probable cause" was lacking in holding that the traditional standard need not be met as a condition for valid Fourth Amendment intrusions by school officials as long as the "reasonable grounds" standard is satisfied.[22] "By focusing attention

---

criminal conviction and incarceration, *Id.* at 338 (quoting *Ingraham*, 430 U.S. at 669), the *T.L.O.* Court did not attempt to explain why students possess privacy protection while prisoners do not.

[13] *Id.* at 334. For a discussion of *Barnette*, see *supra* § 6.03[B][1], notes 35–37 and the accompanying text.

[14] 469 U.S. at 337 (quoting Camara v. Municipal Court, 387 U.S. 523, 536–37 (1967)).

[15] *Id.* at 337, 339.

[16] *Id.* at 341 (quoting Terry v. Ohio, 392 U.S. 1, 20 (1968)).

[17] *Id.* at 341–42.

[18] *Id.* at 342.

[19] *Id.* at 327–28, 338.

[20] *Id.* at 339.

[21] *Id.* at 339–40.

[22] *Id.* at 340–43 (citing the following as authority for dispensing with the general requirement of

on the question of reasonableness," the Court hoped to "spare teachers and school administrators the necessity of schooling themselves in the niceties of probable cause" while permitting them "to regulate [student] conduct according to the dictates of reason and common sense."[23]

Applying its standard to the facts, the *T.L.O.* Court upheld the actions of Principal Choplick. The Court justified the initial search for cigarettes, which Choplick suspected would be in the purse based on the teacher's report that T.L.O. had been smoking in the lavatory, as a reasonable attempt to provide an evidentiary basis to support the alleged offense. Moreover, the Court felt the presence of cigarettes in her purse discredited T.L.O.'s claims that she neither smoked in the lavatory nor smoked at all. Having justified the initial intrusion, the Court found that Choplick reasonably conducted the subsequent intrusions. The discovery of the rolling papers gave rise to a "reasonable suspicion" that T.L.O. was carrying marijuana in addition to cigarettes. The discovery of the pipe, bags, marijuana, and money justified opening the zippered compartment and reading the index cards and the letters.

In *Vernonia School District 47J v. Acton*,[24] the Court addressed an issue left open by *T.L.O.* when it considered whether the reasonable suspicion standard applicable for school searches entailed an individualized suspicion requirement.[25] In upholding a school district rule requiring random drug testing of student athletes,[26]

---

"probable cause" as necessary for valid searches and seizures: *Terry v. Ohio*, 392 U.S. 1, 2–3 (1968) (search without probable cause for arrest warranted where officer believes his safety or that of others is endangered); *United States v. Brignoni-Ponce*, 422 U.S. 873, 881 (1975) (cars containing suspected aliens may be stopped briefly at the border); *Delaware v. Prouse*, 440 U.S. 648, 654–55 (1979) (reasonable suspicion that a car is not registered is sufficient to warrant detaining it); *United States v. Martinez-Fuerte*, 428 U.S. 543, 543 (1976) (border stops permissible even without individualized suspicion); and *Camara v. Municipal Court*, 387 U.S. 523, 534–39 (1967) (probable cause unnecessary to secure a warrant to search a dwelling for housing code violations)).

[23] 469 U.S. at 343. The Court specifically left open issues relating to whether students possess Fourth Amendment interests in their lockers, desks, or other school property; whether a different standard from that applied in *T.L.O.* is required when school officials, in conjunction with law enforcement agents, search students; and whether the exclusionary rule applies to illegal searches and seizures within the schools. *Id.* at 327–28, 333 n.3, 337–38 n.5, 341 n.7. Moreover, the Court did not decide the question of whether "individualized suspicion" is an essential element of the reasonableness standard, but noted that while "some quantum of individualized suspicion is usually a prerequisite to a constitutional search or seizure, the Fourth Amendment imposes no irreducible requirement of such suspicion." *Id.* at 342 n.8. Because the facts of *T.L.O.* manifested individualized suspicion, the Court, of course, could not generate a holding regarding searches lacking such suspicion. The Court hinted, however, at how it might resolve the issue in the future, pointing out that

[e]xceptions to the requirements of individualized suspicion are generally appropriate only where the privacy interests implicated by a search are minimal and where "other safeguards" are available "to assure that the individual's reasonable expectation of privacy is not 'subject to the discretion of the official in the field.'"

*Id.* (citing Delaware v. Prouse, 440 U.S. 648, 654–55 (1979)).

[24] 515 U.S. 646 (1995). For an in-depth analysis of *Acton*, see M. Rosenberg, *Public School Drug Testing: The Impact of* Acton, 33 AM. CRIM. L. REV. 349 (1996).

[25] *See supra* note 23.

[26] The drug testing rule, applicable to all student athletes, required them and their parents to sign a form consenting to an initial drug test and agreeing to submit to further tests if their names were drawn from a pool of names during a weekly drawing. The tests required the student to provide a urine sample, given in an empty locker room in the company of an adult monitor of the same sex. Male students

the Court rejected the argument that school searches and seizures were *per se* unreasonable unless based on suspicion of each particular student prior to being searched.

The school district believed that student athletes were the leaders of a drug culture that was manifesting itself through disciplinary problems in its schools. After attempting other alternatives,[27] the school district implemented a policy requiring all students wishing to play interscholastic sports to sign, along with their parents, a form consenting to a mandatory drug test at the beginning of the sports season and random tests thereafter.[28] James Acton, a seventh-grader, signed up to play football. Acton and his parents refused to sign the consent form and as a result Acton was denied participation in football. The Actons filed suit contesting enforcement of the drug testing program as violative of the Fourth Amendment.

Acknowledging that the drug testing program constituted a governmental "search," the *Acton* Court reiterated *T.L.O.*'s finding that the "special needs" of schools to control discipline justify dispensing with the normal Fourth Amendment probable cause standard. The Court also rejected the argument that individualized suspicion of wrongdoing was a necessary precondition for valid school searches and seizures. Instead, the reasonableness of the drug policy was determined by "balancing its intrusion on the individual's . . . interests against its promotion of legitimate governmental interests."[29]

In assessing the nature of the privacy interest of the student intruded upon by the drug policy, the Court commented:

> [A]t common law, and still today, unemancipated minors lack some of the most fundamental rights of self-determination — including even the right of liberty in its narrow sense, *i.e.*, the right to come and go at will. They are subject, even as to their physical freedom, to the control of their parents or guardians.[30]

Moreover, the Court noted that the State's power over school children is "custodial and tutelary," thus permitting a degree of "supervision and control that could not be exercised over free adults.[31] Quoting *Fraser*, the Court pointed out that "for many purposes 'school authorities act *in loco parentis'*."[32] The Court went on to say: Fourth Amendment rights, no less than First and Fourteenth Amendment rights, are different in public schools than elsewhere; the "reasonableness" inquiry cannot disregard the schools' custodial and tutelary responsibility for children. For

---

provided the sample by turning their back to the monitor and, while fully clothed, urinating in a container. Female students provided samples in an enclosed bathroom stall while the monitor listened outside. The samples were sent to a laboratory and tested for amphetamines, cocaine, and marijuana. Positive test results, 99.94% accurate, were relayed to school officials who implemented a second test and notified the student's parents if the second test returned positive. The student was then given the option of participating in a drug treatment program or being suspended from athletic participation. A second offense resulted in automatic dismissal from athletics while a third offense meant dismissal from athletics for the next two athletic seasons. 515 U.S. at 650–51.

[27] Initially, the school district offered special classes, speakers, and presentations designed to deter drug use. The district also brought in a drug-sniffing dog to detect the presence of drugs. *Id.* at 649.

[28] *See supra* note 26.

[29] 515 U.S. at 652–53.

[30] *Id.* at 654.

[31] *Id.* at 655.

[32] *Id.* (quoting Bethel Sch. Dist. No. 403 v. Fraser, 478 U.S. 675, 684 (1986)); *see supra* § 6.03, notes 59–60 and accompanying text.

their own good and that of their classmates, public school children are routinely required to submit to various physical examinations, and to be vaccinated against various diseases. . . . Particularly with regard to medical examinations and procedures, therefore, "students within the school environment have a lesser expectation of privacy than members of the population generally."[33] Finally, the Court observed that athletes, who dress together, shower together, consent to medical examinations, and to obedience to team rules in order to play sports, possess less legitimate privacy expectation than other students.[34]

While the Court saw student privacy only marginally invaded by the drug testing policy, it found that the policy itself enhanced a sufficiently important governmental interest — deterring student drug use — to justify the "relative unobtrusiveness of the search"[35] in a context of "decreased expectation of privacy."[36] Continued enforcement of the drug policy was thus "reasonable" and permissible under the Fourth Amendment. The Court cautioned, however, that it might more severely scrutinize suspicionless drug testing programs occurring outside the school setting.[37]

Following *Acton*, the Supreme Court again addressed the issue of suspicionless drug testing of school students in *Board of Educ. Ind. Sch. Dist. 92 v. Earls*.[38] In *Earls*, the Court considered the Fourth Amendment acceptability of a school district policy requiring students to consent to urinalysis testing as a condition for participating in any extracurricular school activity.[39] In light of evidence of drug problems in the district's schools, the Court again found that "special needs" inhere in the public school context permitting school searches without the traditional Fourth Amendment requirement of individualized suspicion. As in *Acton*, the Court found a limited privacy interest in students given the school's responsibilities as "guardian and tutor" of the children in its charge.[40] In response to arguments that there was little reason to suspect a pervasive drug problem in the district's schools, the Court stated:

> [In previous cases] this Court has not required a particularized or pervasive drug problem before allowing the government to conduct suspicionless drug testing. . . .
>
> Likewise, the need to prevent and deter the substantial harm of childhood drug use provides the necessary immediacy for a school testing policy. Indeed, it would make little sense to require a school district to wait for a substantial portion of its students to begin using drugs before it was allowed to institute a drug testing program designed to deter drug use.[41]

---

[33] 515 U.S. at 657.

[34] *Id.*

[35] See *supra* note 26 for a description of the procedures employed in conducting the drug searches in *Acton*.

[36] 515 U.S. at 664.

[37] *Id.* 665.

[38] 536 U.S. 822..

[39] The issue arose when a student member of the school show choir and her parents brought a § 1983 action contesting the constitutionality of the policy. Under the policy, as in *Acton*, the test results were not turned over to law enforcement officials. The result of a failed drug test was to deny the student participation in extra-curricular activities.

[40] 536 U.S. at 830 (quoting *Acton*).

[41] *Id.* at 835–36.

Finally, the Court found little problem with the absence of particularized suspicion in the *Earls* situation:

> We . . . reject [the] argument that drug testing must presumptively be based upon an individualized reasonable suspicion of wrongdoing because such a testing regime would be less intrusive. In this context, the Fourth Amendment does not require a finding of individualized suspicion, and we decline to impose such a requirement on schools attempting to prevent and detect drug use by students. Moreover, we question whether testing based on individualized suspicion in fact would be less intrusive. Such a regime would place an additional burden on public school teachers who are already tasked with the difficult job of maintaining order and discipline. A program of individualized suspicion might unfairly target members of unpopular groups. The fear of lawsuits resulting from such targeted searches may chill enforcement of the program, rendering it ineffective in combating drug use.[42]

The lower courts have dealt with an increasing number of cases involving searches of students since the proliferation of weapons and drugs in the schools. The courts have struggled with determining whether a given intrusion is a violation of a student's "reasonable expectation of privacy" so as to constitute a Fourth Amendment "search." For example, some courts find no search when drug-sniffing dogs sniff the air around students in order to detect drugs,[43] while other courts see the sniffs as searches that must be justified under the Fourth Amendment.[44] The courts are similarly divided on the issue of whether students possess protected privacy expectations in their school lockers.[45] When courts do conclude that Fourth Amendment intrusions have occurred, they generally assess the reasonableness of such searches and seizures in an *ad hoc* fashion by applying the sliding scale standard of *T.L.O.*, *Acton*, and *Earls*.[46]

---

[42] *Id.* at 837.

[43] *See, e.g.*, Doe v. Renfrow, 475 F. Supp. 1012 (N.D. Ind. 1979), *aff'd in part*, 631 F.2d 91 (7th Cir. 1980), *cert. denied*, 451 U.S. 1022 (1981).

[44] *See, e.g.*, B.C. v. Plumas Unified School Dist., 192 F.3d 1260 (Cal. 1999) (holding that a dog sniff of high school students constituted a Fourth Amendment search); Horton v. Goose Creek Indep. Sch. Dist., 690 F.2d 470 (5th Cir. 1982), *cert. denied*, 463 U.S. 1207 (1983) (random dog sniff is a "search" because not supported by prior individualized suspicion). Query whether *Acton* and *Earl's* rejection of an individualized suspicion requirement, *see supra* notes 24–26, 28, 38–42 and accompanying text, calls *Horton* into question.

The author has considered the issue of dog-sniffs of students in detail elsewhere. *See* Gardner, *supra* note 10. For a case holding that a student sniffed by a school official did not have a legitimate expectation of privacy in the air surrounding her person, see *Burham v. West*, 681 F. Supp. 1160 (E.D. Va. 1987).

[45] *See, e.g.*, People v. Overton, 229 N.E. 2d 596 (N.Y. 1967) (locker is property of school and may be opened by principal at his discretion); In Interest of Isiah B., 500 N.W.2d 637 (Wis. 1993) (student has no expectation of privacy when school officials open his locker); In Interest of Dumas, 515 A.2d 984 (Pa. Super. Ct. 1986) (high school student has reasonable expectation of privacy in his locker). *See also In re* Gregory M., 627 N.E.2d 500 (N.Y. 1993) (no search where school security officer ran his hands on the outer surface of student's cloth book bag and felt a gun).

[46] See the general discussion of cases in A. Black, Annotation, *Search Conducted by School Official or Teacher as Violation of Fourth Amendment or Equivalent State Constitutional Provision*, 31 A.L.R.5th 229, 317–483 (1995). For a discussion of strip searches of students, see S. Shatz, M. Donovan & J. Hong, *The Strip Search of Children and the Fourth Amendment*, 26 U.S.F. L. REV. 1 (1991). *See also*, M. Gardner, *The Fourth Amendment and the Public Schools: Observations on an Unsettled State of Search and Seizure Law*, 36 CRIM. L. BULL. 373 (2000).

Several issues have yet to be decided by the Supreme Court[47] and continue to trouble the lower courts. While some courts have found the reasonable suspicion standard inadequate and impose the more rigorous probable cause test when school searches are conducted by school security personnel or by school officials in conjunction with law enforcement officials,[48] others permit such searches when supported merely by reasonable suspicion.[49] Moreover, the courts are split on the issue of whether the exclusionary rule must be applied when evidence is obtained as a result of an illegal search or seizure.[50]

## § 6.05    THE EIGHTH AMENDMENT[1]

### [A]    In School: Corporal Punishment

In *Ingraham v. Wright*,[2] the United States Supreme Court considered whether the Eighth Amendment prohibition against cruel and unusual punishment protects students against excessive corporal punishment[3] at the hands of public school officials. The case was brought by two junior high students, one who claimed he was injured by being paddled more than twenty times[4] because he was slow to respond to his teacher's instructions. The second student claimed he was paddled several times for minor infractions and lost the full use of one of his arms for a week as a result of blows to his arms. The Court assumed the credibility of the students' claims,[5] but held that the Cruel and Unusual Punishment Clause was designed to protect those convicted of crime and thus was inapplicable to school punishment, particularly since criminal and tort remedies were already available to redress instances of abusive corporal punishment.[6]

---

[47] *See supra* note 23.

[48] *See, e.g.*, F.P. v. State, 528 So. 2d 1253 (Fla. Dist. Ct. App. 1988).

[49] *See, e.g.*, Martens v. District No. 220, Bd. of Educ., 620 F. Supp. 29 (N.D. Ill. 1985).

[50] *See, e.g., In re* Lisa, 23 Cal. Rptr. 3d 163, 167–68 (Cal. Ct. App. 2004) (exclusionary rule applies in criminal proceedings for evidence illegally obtained from student); State v. Young, 216 S.E.2d 586 (Ga. 1975), *cert. denied*, 423 U.S. 1039 (1975) (dicta, exclusionary rule inapplicable in criminal court for evidence illegally obtained from student); Gordon J. v. Santa Ana Unified Sch. Dist., 208 Cal. Rptr. 657 (Cal. App. Ct. 1984) (exclusionary rule not applicable in school disciplinary proceeding for evidence illegally obtained from student); *In re* William G., 709 P.2d 1287 (Cal. 1985) (exclusionary rule applies in juvenile court proceedings for evidence illegally obtained from student).

[1] The Eighth Amendment to the United States Constitution provides: "Excessive bail shall not be required, nor excessive fines imposed, nor cruel and unusual punishments inflicted."

[2] 430 U.S. 658 (1977).

[3] The Court noted that the Cruel and Unusual Punishment Clause circumscribes "the kinds of punishment" that can be imposed and proscribes punishment "grossly disproportionate to the severity of [the offense]." *Id.* at 667. Without making the matter entirely clear, the Court appeared to see the claim in *Ingraham* as falling under the latter category of disproportionate punishment. Dissenting Justices in *Ingraham* clarified the matter, offering that the issue was not "that spanking in the public schools is in every instance prohibited by the Eighth Amendment," but whether "barbaric, inhumane, or severe" corporal punishment is limited by the Eighth Amendment. *Id.* at 691–92 (White, J., dissenting).

[4] The injuries included a hematoma requiring medical attention and keeping the student out of school for several days. *Id.* at 657.

[5] The Court noted that the lower courts had assumed the testimony of the students to be credible. *Id.* at 658. The Court nowhere questioned the validity of this assumption.

[6] *Id.* at 664–71. The Court did conclude that "the pertinent constitutional question is whether the imposition [of disciplinary corporal punishment] is consonant with the requirements of due process." *Id.*

The *Ingraham* Court noted that the use of corporal punishment as a means of disciplining children dates back to colonial times and, although highly controversial, currently continues to "play a role" in education in most parts of the country.[7] The Court recognized the continued vitality of the common law principle that teachers may impose reasonable, but not excessive, force including corporal punishment, to discipline their students.[8] The Court drew a distinction between prisons — "closed" institutions where the Eighth Amendment may preclude corporal punishment — and schools — "open" institutions conducive to constant community supervision and protection.[9] Therefore, "[t]he schoolchild has little need for the protection of the Eighth Amendment."[10] Finally, the Court left open the question "whether or under what circumstances persons involuntarily confined in . . . juvenile institutions can claim the protection of the Eighth Amendment."[11]

Prior to *Ingraham*, the Supreme Court affirmed in a summary opinion[12] the decision of a lower court[13] that permitted a school to corporally punish a sixth-grader against the express wishes of his mother. The lower court rejected the mother's claims that she had a right under *Meyer* and *Pierce*[14] to determine the appropriate disciplinary methods for her child. The court recognized that a constitutionally protected parental right was at issue, but not a "fundamental" one so as to trigger strict scrutiny[15] of the practice of corporally punishing school children under the circumstances of the case. Instead, the court found that the school was permitted to corporally punish the student as a "rational" means of promoting its legitimate interest in maintaining school discipline.[16]

## [B] Outside School: Capital Punishment

In *Thompson v. Oklahoma*,[17] the Supreme Court held that the Eighth Amendment prohibits the execution of a convicted murderer who committed his crime when he was fifteen-years-old.[18] Applying the "evolving standards of

---

at 671. The due process issue in *Ingraham* is discussed *infra* § 6.06[A][1][c].

[7] 430 U.S. at 660. The Court noted that as of the time of *Ingraham* (1977), of the 23 states that had addressed the issue, 21 had authorized the use of moderate corporal punishment and only two states had statutorily prohibited its use. *Id.* at 662. Since *Ingraham*, the use of corporal punishment in the schools has declined. One article claims that at the time of the *Ingraham* decision, "less than a handful of states" had legislatively prohibited corporal punishment of students, while as of 2007, 28 states and the District of Columbia have banned corporal punishment in public schools. E. Gershoff & S. Bitensky, *The Case Against Corporal Punishment of Children*, 13 Psychol. Pub. Pol'y & L. 231, 246 (2007).

[8] 430 U.S. at 661–62.

[9] *Id.* at 669–70.

[10] *Id.* at 670.

[11] *Id.* at 669 n.37.

[12] 423 U.S. 907 (1975).

[13] Baker v. Owen, 395 F. Supp. 294 (M.D.N.C. 1975).

[14] *See supra* § 6.02.

[15] 395 F. Supp. at 298–99. For a discussion of the distinction between "strict" and "rational basis" scrutiny, see *supra* § 6.03, note 24.

[16] 395 F. Supp. at 300.

[17] 487 U.S. 815 (1988).

[18] Earlier, in *Eddings v. Oklahoma*, 455 U.S. 104 (1982), the Court had held that the Eighth Amendment was violated where the state imposed the death penalty against a 16-year-old murderer without considering his unhappy upbringing and emotional disturbance as possible mitigating factors.

decency" test common to Eighth Amendment jurisprudence,[19] the Court noted that "there are differences which must be accommodated in determining the rights and duties of children as compared to those of adults.[20] Reviewing various legislative enactments in the various states, the Court observed that there is "complete or near unanimity among all 50 states and in the District of Columbia in treating a person under 16 as a minor for several important purposes."[21] The Court concluded that "[a]ll of this legislation is consistent with the experience of mankind, as well as the long history of our law, that the normal 15-year-old is not prepared to assume the full responsibilities of an adult."[22] The Court went on to say:

> Inexperience, less education, and less intelligence make the teenager less able to evaluate the consequences of his or her conduct while at the same time he or she is much more apt to be motivated by mere emotion or peer pressure than is an adult. The reasons why juveniles are not trusted with the privileges and responsibilities of an adult also explain why their irresponsible conduct is not as morally reprehensible as that of an adult.[23] The Court further observed that the retributive and deterrent purposes of the death penalty were "inapplicable" to the execution of a fifteen-year-old "[g]iven the lesser culpability of the juvenile offender, the teenager's capacity for growth, and society's fiduciary obligations to its children."[24]

The Court dismissed the deterrent value of the death penalty for those under sixteen for two reasons:

> The likelihood that the teenage offender has made the kind of cost-benefit analysis that attaches any weight to the possibility of execution is so remote as to be virtually nonexistent. And, even if one posits such a cold-blooded calculation by a 15-year-old, it is fanciful to believe that he would be deterred by the knowledge that a small number of persons his age have been executed during the 20th century.[25]

In light of all these considerations, the Court concluded that "it would offend civilized standards of decency to execute a person who was less than 16 years old at the time of his or her offense."[26]

---

[19] *See* Trop v. Dulles, 356 U.S. 86, 101 (1958) (punishments assessed under Eighth Amendment in terms of the "evolving standards of decency that mark the progress of a maturing society").

[20] 487 U.S. at 821, 823.

[21] The Court noted that the legal distinction between juveniles and adults is reflected in the law of contracts, torts, crimes, and marriage; in voting laws; in the ability to purchase alcohol and tobacco; and in the ability to sit on juries or hold public office. *Id.* at 823. The Court also drew on the fact that all states have developed a separate juvenile justice system as evidence of the fact that minors are different from adults for many legal purposes. *Id.* at 823–24.

[22] *Id.* at 824–25.

[23] *Id.* at 835. The Court further supported this conclusion by noting that of the 18 states that legislatively set a minimum age in their death penalty statutes, all set the age at 16 or older. *Id.* at 829. Moreover, after reviewing empirical evidence, the Court found a general reluctance by juries to impose the death penalty on children under 16. *Id.* at 831–32.

[24] *Id.* at 836–37.

[25] *Id.* at 837–38.

[26] *Id.* at 830.

On the heels of *Thompson*, the Court decided *Stanford v. Kentucky*,[27] which held that imposition of capital punishment on a person who commits murder at sixteen or seventeen years of age does not violate the Eighth Amendment.[28] The Court found that in accordance with the "common law tradition," hundreds of offenders under the ages of seventeen or eighteen had been executed in the United States.[29] In reviewing the various state statutes, the Court found that a majority of the states that authorize capital punishment permit it for crimes committed at age sixteen and above.[30] Even though conceding that juries were reluctant to impose, and prosecutors to seek, the death penalty for offenders under eighteen, the Court found no national consensus against executing sixteen-year-olds.[31] A four justice plurality went on to make some observations about the moral accountability and deterrability of persons under age eighteen:[32]

> [L]aws . . . set[ting] the legal age for engaging in various activities, ranging from driving to drinking alcoholic beverages to voting [are irrelevant]. It is, to begin with, absurd to think that one must be mature enough to drive carefully, to drink responsibility, or to vote intelligently, in order to be mature enough to understand that murdering another human being is profoundly wrong, and to conform one's conduct to that most minimal of civilized standards. But even if the requisite degrees of maturity were comparable, the age statutes in question would still not be relevant. They do not represent a social judgment that all persons under the designated ages are not responsible enough to drive, to drink, or to vote, but at most a judgment that the vast majority are not. These laws set the appropriate ages for the operation of a system that makes its determinations in gross, and that does not conduct individualized maturity tests for each driver, drinker, or voter. The criminal justice system, however, does provide individualized testing. In the realm of capital punishment in particular, "individualized consideration [is] a constitutional requirement," . . . and one of the individualized mitigating factors that sentencers must be permitted to consider is the defendant's age. . . .

> We also reject . . . [the] argument that we should invalidate capital punishment of 16- and 17-year-old offenders on the ground that it fails to serve the legitimate goals of penology. According to petitioners, it fails to deter because juveniles, possessing less developed cognitive skills than adults, are less likely to fear death; and it fails to exact just retribution because juveniles, being less mature and responsible, are also less morally blameworthy. In support of these claims, petitioners and their supporting amici marshal an array of socioscientific evidence concerning the psychological and emotional development of 16- and 17-year-olds.

---

[27] 492 U.S. 361 (1989), *abrogated by* Roper v. Simmons, 543 U.S. 551 (2005).

[28] The Court reviewed the constitutionality of the death sentences of two offenders, one who committed his crime at age 17, the other at age 16. *Id.* at 365–66.

[29] *Id.* at 368.

[30] *Id.* at 371.

[31] *Id.* at 370–71. The Court observed that it is "probable that the very considerations which induce petitioners . . . to believe that death should *never* be imposed on offenders under 18 cause prosecutors and juries to believe that it should *rarely* be imposed." *Id.* at 374.

[32] Justice O'Connor, who joined the other four justices in the judgment in the case, did not join in the plurality opinion's views quoted in the text. *See* 492 U.S. at 382 (O'Connor, J., concurring).

If such evidence could conclusively establish the entire lack of deterrent effect and moral responsibility, resort to the Cruel and Unusual Punishments Clause would be unnecessary, the Equal Protection Clause of the Fourteenth Amendment would invalidate these laws for lack of rational basis. . . . But as the adjective "socioscientific" suggests (and insofar as evaluation of moral responsibility is concerned perhaps the adjective 'ethicoscientific" would be more apt), it is not demonstrable that no 16-year-old is "adequately responsible" or significantly deterred. It is rational, even if mistaken, to think the contrary.[33]

Finally, in *Roper v. Simmons*,[34] the Supreme Court reconsidered the issue decided in *Stanford* and concluded that the "logic of *Thompson* extends to those who are under 18,"[35] thus holding that the age of 18 is the line for which eligibility for the death penalty rests. The Court observed that the "objective indicia" supporting *Stanford* had changed, noting, *inter alia*, that a majority of states now reject the juvenile death penalty, the penalty is infrequently employed even where it remains on the books, and a consistent trend toward abolition of the practice exists in the states.[36]

In pointing out that the death penalty must be limited to the most culpable offenders committing the most serious crimes,[37] the *Roper* Court concluded that three general differences between juveniles under 18 and adults demonstrate that juveniles cannot reliably be classified among the most culpable offenders. First, the Court referred to scientific evidence showing a tendency in youth to engage in impetuous and ill-considered actions and decisions."[38] Second, the Court noted the susceptibility of juveniles to negative influences from peer pressure and other outside influences.[39] The third exculpatory factor relied on by the Court was premised on the fact that young people tend to possess transitory personality traits manifesting character that is not as well-formed as that of adults.[40]

For the *Roper* Court, the diminished culpability of juveniles meant that retributive justifications for the death penalty apply with lesser force to them than to adults. Moreover, the Court found that the same characteristics rendering juveniles less culpable than adults also suggest that they are less deterable. As the Court observed, "the likelihood that the teenage offender has made the kind of

---

[33] *Id.* at 374–78. For commentary on the death penalty for juveniles see, *e.g.*, G. Bassham, *Rethinking the Emerging Jurisprudence of Juvenile Death*, 5 NOTRE DAME J.L. ETHICS & PUB. POL'Y 467 (1991); S. Strater, *The Juvenile Death Penalty: In the Best Interests of the Child?*, 26 LOY. U. CHI. L.J. 147 (1995); Note, *The Constitutionality of Executing Juvenile and Mentally Retarded Offenders*, 31 B.C. L. REV. 901 (1990); Note, *Executing Minors and the Mentally Retarded: The Retribution and Deterrence Rationales*, 43 RUTGERS L. REV. 15 (1990).

[34] 543 U.S. 551 (2005).

[35] *Id.* at 574.

[36] *Id.*

[37] *Id.* at 568.

[38] *Id.* at 569. For a view favoring the result in *Roper* but critical of the "outdated" social science research utilized by the Court, see D. Denno, *The Scientific Shortcomings of Roper v. Simmons*, 3 OHIO ST. J. CRIM. L. 379 (2006).

[39] 543 U.S. at 369.

[40] *Id.*

cost-benefit analysis that attaches any weight to the possibility of execution is so remote as to be virtually non-existent."[41]

## § 6.06   THE FOURTEENTH AMENDMENT[1]

### [A]   Due Process

#### [1]   Substantive Rights

##### [a]   Reproductive Freedom

In *Planned Parenthood v. Danforth*,[2] the United States Supreme Court struck down a state statute that required an unmarried woman under age eighteen to obtain consent of either of her parents prior to having an abortion. The Court rejected arguments that the legislation was permissible under *Prince*[3] and other cases that permitted the state to subject minors to more stringent limitations than are permissible with adults. The Court instead cited other cases, including *Tinker*,[4] establishing that "[c]onstitutional rights do not mature and come into being magically only when one attains the state defined age of majority. Minors, as well as adults, are protected by the Constitution and possess constitutional rights."[5] Thus, female minors possess the right to terminate their pregnancies, a substantive due process right the Court had earlier recognized for adults,[6] at least where the minor is of sufficient maturity to give consent.[7] The Court found that the statutory grant to parents to veto their daughter's decision to have an abortion was not likely to promote the state's interest in safeguarding the family unit nor enhance parental authority or control "where the minor and the nonconsenting parent are so fundamentally in conflict and the very existence of the pregnancy already has fractured the family structure."[8] In assessing the interests of parents, the Court observed that "[a]ny independent interest the parent may have in the

---

[41]  *Id.* at 572 (quoting Thompson v. Oklahoma, 487 U.S. 815, 837 (1988)).

[1]  The Fourteenth Amendment to the United States Constitution provides in relevant part: "[No] State [shall] deprive any person of life, liberty, or property, without due process of law; nor deny to any person within its jurisdiction the equal protection of the laws."

[2]  428 U.S. 52 (1976).

[3]  *See supra* § 6.03[A][2], notes 15–20 and accompanying text.

[4]  *See supra* § 6.03[B][1], notes 38–42 and accompanying text.

[5]  428 U.S. at 74.

[6]  Roe v. Wade, 410 U.S. 113 (1973). The *Roe* Court held that the right to privacy, "whether it be founded in the Fourteenth Amendment's concept of personal liberty . . . as we feel it is, or . . . in the Ninth Amendment's reservation of rights to the people, is broad enough to encompass a woman's decision whether or not to terminate her pregnancy." *Id.* at 153. *See* L. Tribe, American Constitutional Law 1308 n.3 (2d ed. 1988) (*Roe's* privacy right located in the concept of "liberty" protected by the Fourteenth Amendment); Nowak & Rotunda, *supra* § 6.01, note 8, at 812 (abortion decision "now a part of the liberty protected by the Fourteenth Amendment").

[7]  The Court noted that its invalidation of the parental consent statute "does not suggest that every minor, regardless of age or maturity, may give effective consent for termination of her pregnancy." 428 U.S. at 75.

[8]  *Id.*

termination of the minor daughter's pregnancy is no more weighty than the right to privacy of the competent minor mature enough to have become pregnant."[9]

Following shortly after *Danforth*, the Court decided *Carey v. Population Services International*[10] where it struck down a state statute that prohibited distribution of contraceptives to persons under sixteen years of age. The Court found that minors possess protected liberty interests under the Due Process Clause to make personal decisions relating to procreation and contraception[11] that cannot be restricted except when necessary to promote "compelling state interests."[12] A four Justice plurality[13] noted that "the question of the extent of state power to regulate conduct of minors not constitutionally regulable when committed by adults is a vexing one, perhaps not susceptible of precise answer."[14] In any event, the plurality found state interests in discouraging juvenile sexual activity insufficient to support the denial of access to contraceptives, particularly in light of the fact that the same argument would be uncompelling in light of *Danforth&* if made for denying abortions to minors.[15] The plurality expressed considerable doubt whether limiting access to contraceptives would in fact substantially discourage early sexual behavior.[16]

The issue of abortion rights of minors, considered initially in *Danforth*, again reached the Court in *Bellotti v. Baird (Bellotti II)*.[17] There the Court invalidated a statute that permitted unmarried women under eighteen to have abortions only if they obtained the consent of both their parents or, if either or both of the parents refused, satisfied a court that an abortion would be in their best interests. The Court[18] recognized that although children often lack "the experience, perspective, and judgment to recognize and avoid choices that could be detrimental to them,"[19] the "unique nature and consequences of the abortion decision make it inappropriate 'to give a third party an absolute, and possibly arbitrary, veto over the decision of the physician and his patient to terminate the patient's pregnancy, regardless of the reason for withholding the consent.' "[20] The Court therefore concluded that "if the state decides to require a pregnant minor to obtain [parental] consent to an abortion, it must provide an alternative procedure

---

[9] *Id.*

[10] 431 U.S. 678 (1977).

[11] *Id.* at 685.

[12] "[W]here a decision as fundamental as that whether to bear or beget a child is involved, regulations imposing a burden on it may be justified only by compelling state interests, and must be narrowly drawn to express only those interests." *Id.* at 686.

[13] Justices Brennan, Stewart, Marshall, and Blackmun joined this part of the opinion. *Id.* at 691.

[14] *Id.* at 692.

[15] *Id.* at 694.

[16] The Court referred to a body of social science data suggesting denial of access to contraceptives does not deter juvenile sexual activity. *Id.* at 695–96.

[17] 443 U.S. 622 (1979). The Court earlier had ruled that the federal courts should have abstained from considering the *Bellotti* case because a possible state court construction of the statute in issue might avoid a constitutional challenge to the statute. Bellotti v. Baird, 428 U.S. 132 (1976).

[18] A four Justice plurality joined in the opinion from which the language quoted in the text is taken. Four other Justices concurred in the judgment invalidating the statute.

[19] 443 U.S. at 635.

[20] *Id.* at 643 (quoting Planned Parenthood v. Danforth, 428 U.S. 52, 74 (1976)).

whereby authorization for the abortion can be obtained."[21] At such a procedure, the minor is entitled to show either that "she is mature enough and well enough informed to make her abortion decision, in consultation with her physician, independently of her parents' wishes" or that even if she is not able to make this decision independently, "the desired abortion is in her best interests."[22] Thus "every minor must have the opportunity — if she so desires — to go directly to a court without first consulting or notifying her parents."[23] Where, however, a court determines that a minor is "immature," it may include the parents in making its decision whether an abortion is in the minor's best interests.[24]

The Supreme Court further elaborated on the balancing of parent and child rights in the abortion context in H.L. v. Matheson,[25] where it upheld a state statute requiring physicians to notify, if possible, the parents of minors seeking abortions. The case dealt with an unmarried fifteen-year-old who became pregnant and sought an abortion. Her physician would not perform the abortion until the minor's parents were notified pursuant to the statute.[26] The minor challenged the statute on its face, claiming that it could be construed to apply to all unmarried minor girls, including those who are mature and emancipated. The Court did not address that question since the minor attacking the statute lived at home with her parents, was dependent upon them for support, and did not allege or proffer evidence that she was "mature or emancipated."[27] The Court distinguished *Bellotti II* as a case involving a statute that impermissibly allowed a court to substitute its decision for the decisions of mature and competent minors to have abortions without parental consent.[28] While reiterating its holdings in *Planned Parenthood* and *Bellotti II* that parents do not possess absolute veto over their daughter's abortion decision,[29] the *Matheson* Court saw the parental notice provision as a permissible attempt to encourage parental consultation, to accommodate parents' authority to rear their children, and to provide a mechanism for parents to supply medical information to their daughter's physician.[30]

---

[21] *Id.* at 643.

[22] *Id.* at 643–44.

[23] The Court noted that many parents hold "strong views on the subject of abortion" and may attempt to obstruct both their child's attempt to obtain an abortion and her access to the courts. *Id.* at 647.

[24] *Id.* at 648.

[25] 450 U.S. 398 (1981).

[26] The statute required physicians to "[n]otify, if possible, the parents or guardian of the woman upon whom [an] abortion is to be performed, if she is a minor or the husband of the woman, if she is married." Utah Code Ann. § 76-7-304 (1953). Violation of this provision subjected the physician to possible imprisonment for not more than one year or a fine of up to $1,000. 450 U.S. at 401.

[27] 450 U.S. at 405–6.

[28] *Id.* at 408.

[29] *Id.* 408–9.

[30] *Id.* at 409–13. In *City of Akron v. Akron Center for Reproductive Health,* 462 U.S. 416 (1983), *overruled on other grounds by* Planned Parenthood v. Ashcroft, 462 U.S. 476 (1983), the Court invalidated an ordinance forbidding physicians from performing abortions on young women under the age of fifteen without first obtaining the consent of their parents or guardians or a court order permitting the abortion. The Court found that the ordinance made a blanket determination that all minors under age fifteen are too immature to make their own decisions to have abortions and thus created an unconstitutional veto power in the parent or the court under *Planned Parenthood* and *Bellotti II. Id.* at 439–40.

The Court again considered the constitutionality of a parental notification statute in *Hodgson v. Minnesota*[31] which held that a state cannot constitutionally require notification of both parents of a minor prior to her having an abortion without also providing a judicial bypass procedure for mature minors to have abortions without notifying their parents.[32] The Court found fault with two-parent notification requirements because they create the potential for harmful effects on both the minor and the custodial parent in the common situation where the minor's parents are divorced or separated.[33] Even where the minor lives with both parents, the Court found that two-parent notification requirements create a serious risk of violence at the hands of family members.[34] Thus, the "requirement that both parents be notified, whether or not both wish to be notified or have assumed responsibility for the upbringing of the child, does not reasonably further any state interest."[35] On the other hand, the Court concluded that a two-parent notification requirement is constitutional where a judicial bypass procedure is provided.[36] Moreover, a majority of the Court found constitutionally permissible a forty-eight hour waiting period after parental notification as "reasonably further[ing] the legitimate state interest in ensuring that the minor's decision is knowing and intelligent."[37]

The Supreme Court considered the criteria for constitutional bypass procedures in *Ohio v. Akron Center for Reproductive Health*[38] where it upheld a state procedure permitting a minor to avoid parental notification requirements by showing a court that she possessed sufficient maturity to make her own decision without notifying her parent. The Court held that the state could require the minor

---

In *Planned Parenthood v. Ashcroft*, 462 U.S. 476 (1983), the Court upheld a provision requiring a minor to receive the consent of one of her parents to have an abortion or, in the alternative, to obtain the consent of a juvenile court judge. The statute directed the court to give its consent if the minor established that she was competent to make the abortion decision herself if the court determined an abortion to be in the minor's best interests. *Id.* at 479 n.4. *Ashcroft* marked the first time the Court upheld a parental consent requirement. Nowak & Rotunda, *supra* note 6, at 839. The Court reaffirmed the constitutionality of a parental consent provision with a judicial bypass alternative in *Planned Parenthood v. Casey*, 505 U.S. 833, 899 (1992).

[31]  497 U.S. 417 (1990).

[32]  *Id.* at 450–58.

[33]  *Id.* at 450–51.

[34]  *Id.* at 439, 450.

[35]  *Id.* at 450.

[36]  *Id.* at 455–58. This issue was decided by a different majority than that which held unconstitutional two-parent notification requirements without judicial bypass procedures. *See* Nowak & Rotunda, *supra* note 6, at 842. Lower court caselaw has invalidated one-parent notification provisions that do not include judicial bypass options. *See, e.g.*, Planned Parenthood v. Miller, 860 F. Supp. 1409 (D.S.D. 1994), *cert. denied sub nom.*, 517 U.S. 1174 (1996) (statutory judicial bypass available only for abused and neglected minors; statute thus unconstitutional).

[37]  The Court added:

The brief waiting period provides the parent the opportunity to consult with his or her spouse and a family physician, and it permits the parent to inquire into the competency of the doctor performing the abortion, discuss the religious or moral implications of the abortion decision, and provide the daughter needed guidance and counsel in evaluating the impact of the decision on her future.

497 U.S. at 448–49.

[38]  497 U.S. 502 (1990).

to show by "clear and convincing" evidence that she could competently decide to have the abortion or, in lieu of establishing her maturity, that the abortion was in her best interests.[39] The Court concluded that the government "may require a heightened standard of proof when, as here, the bypass procedure contemplates an *ex parte* proceeding at which no one opposes the minor's testimony."[40] The *Akron Center* Court also found that bypass procedures would be upheld so long as the statutory procedure "takes reasonable steps to prevent the public from learning the minor's identity."[41] Moreover, the Court held that the minor's rights were not impaired by a statutory procedure that required the trial court to make a decision in bypass proceedings within five business days after the minor filed her request even though, with an expedited appeal mechanism, the entire bypass procedure could take up to twenty-two days.[42] The Court implied, however, that, depending on the facts in a particular case, the minor might show that her rights were impaired due to the length of the bypass procedures.[43] Finally, *Akron Center* held that the rights of minors were not infringed by requirements of filing forms and the presentation of oral or written testimony in bypass proceedings. The Court reasoned that such procedures permit judges to make accurate decisions regarding the maturity of the minor or her best interests. In a portion of the opinion joined by three other Justices, Justice Kennedy, the author of the Court's *Akron Center* opinion, offered these views regarding the interests at stake in parental notification provisions:

> The [instant statute] does not impose an undue, or otherwise unconstitutional, burden on a minor seeking an abortion. We believe, in addition, that the legislature acted in a rational manner. . . . A free and enlightened society may decide that each of its members should attain a clearer, more tolerant understanding of the profound philosophic choices confronted by a woman who is considering whether to seek an abortion. Her decision will embrace her own destiny and personal dignity, and the origins of the other human life that lie within the embryo. The State is entitled to assume that, for most of its people, the beginnings of that understanding will be within the family, society's most intimate association. It is both rational and fair for the State to conclude that, in most instances, the family will strive to give a lonely or even terrified minor advice that is both compassionate and mature. The statute in issue here is a rational way to further those ends. It would deny all dignity to the family to say that the State cannot take this reasonable step in regulating its health professions to ensure that, in most cases, a young woman will receive guidance and understanding from a parent. . . .[44]

---

[39] *Id.* at 515–16.

[40] *Id.* at 516.

[41] The Court held that confidentiality, but not necessarily anonymity, was required. *Id.* at 512–13.

[42] *Id.* at 513–14.

[43] The Court implicitly left open the possibility that application of rules imposing time delays might, in some cases, violate minors' rights. Because the challenge in the instant case was a facial challenge that the statute was unconstitutional under any circumstances, the Court did not address whether some applications of the statute might be unconstitutional. *Id.* at 514.

[44] *Id.* at 519–20. For commentary on the Court's jurisprudence of abortion rights for minors, see C. Schmidt, *Where Privacy Fails: Equal Protection and the Abortion Rights of Minors*, 68 N.Y.U. L. REV. 597 (1993); Note, *The Judicial Bypass Procedure and Adolescents' Abortion Rights: The Fallacy of the "Maturity" Standard*, 23 HOFSTRA L. REV. 453 (1994).

## [b] Education

In *San Antonio Independent School District v. Rodriguez*,[45] the United States Supreme Court rejected the argument that the Constitution affords a right to education. The case arose as a class action attack on the Texas property tax system of financing public education. The case was brought by poor families who argued that the reliance on property taxes favored more affluent families. While the claim sounded in equal protection, the trial court found that education was a "fundamental" right as partial grounds for its application of the strict scrutiny standard and its finding that the Texas system was unconstitutional.[46] The Supreme Court reversed, denying that education was a fundamental constitutional right. The Court observed:

> Education, of course, is not among the rights afforded explicit protection under our Federal Constitution. Nor do we find any basis for saying it is implicitly so protected. As we have said, the undisputed importance of education will not alone cause this Court to depart from the usual standard for reviewing a State's social and economic legislation. It is appellees' contention, however, that education is distinguishable from other services and benefits provided by the State because it bears a peculiarly close relationship to other rights and liberties accorded protection under the Constitution. Specifically, they insist that education is itself a fundamental personal right because it is essential to the effective exercise of First Amendment freedoms and to intelligent utilization of the right to vote. In asserting a nexus between speech and education, appellees urge that the right to speak is meaningless unless the speaker is capable of articulating his thoughts intelligently and persuasively. The "marketplace of ideas" is an empty forum for those lacking basic communicative tools. Likewise, they argue that the corollary right to receive information becomes little more than a hollow privilege when the recipient has not been taught to read, assimilate, and utilize available knowledge.

> A similar line of reasoning is pursued with respect to the right to vote. Exercise of the franchise, it is contended, cannot be divorced from the educational foundation of the voter. The electoral process, if reality is to conform to the democratic ideal, depends on an informed electorate: a voter cannot cast his ballot intelligently unless his reading skills and thought processes have been adequately developed.

> We need not dispute any of these propositions. The Court has long afforded zealous protection against unjustifiable governmental interference with the individual's rights to speak and to vote. Yet we have never presumed to possess either the ability or the authority to guarantee to the citizenry the most *effective* speech or the most *informed* electoral choice. That these may be desirable goals of a system of freedom of expression and of a representative form of government is not to be doubted. These are indeed goals to be pursued by a people whose thoughts and beliefs are freed from governmental interference. But they are not values to be implemented by judicial intrusion into otherwise legitimate state activities.[47]

---

[45] 411 U.S. 1 (1973).

[46] *Id.* at 16. *See supra* § 6.03, note 24 (explanation of "strict scrutiny").

[47] 411 U.S. at 35–36.

## [c] Corporal Punishment

As discussed above, the United States Supreme Court denied the applicability of the Cruel and Unusual Punishment Clause to corporal punishment of school children.[48] The Court left open, however, whether such punishment, in some circumstances, might offend the due process rights of students.[49]

Some lower courts have recognized a federal cause of action based on substantive due process rights for victims of excessive corporal punishment or other physical force. Some such courts hold that violations of these rights are determined by assessing the severity of injuries received by the student, the proportionality of force applied to the need presented, and whether the force was motivated by malice or sadism in circumstances manifesting inhumane abuse of power shocking to the conscience.[50] Other courts do not require findings of malice, but instead permit inferences of intent, recklessness, or gross negligence where serious injury is inflicted by punishment or other force unnecessarily severe under the circumstances.[51] On the other hand, some courts deny a federal due process cause of action for excessive corporal punishment, following the reasoning of *Ingraham* in the Eighth Amendment context that state civil and criminal laws provide adequate remedies.[52]

## [d] Marriage

Although the United States Supreme Court has recognized marriage as a fundamental right,[53] states routinely prescribe age levels at which young people can legally marry. The lower courts have found that such laws do not violate a fundamental right of young people to marry and have upheld such age restrictions

---

[48] *Supra* § 6.05[A], notes 2–11 and accompanying text.

[49] *See supra* § 6.05, note 6.

[50] *See, e.g.,* Hall v. Tawney, 621 F.2d 607, 611 (4th Cir. 1980) (court remanded for reconsideration of due process claim where seventh grade student was beaten with a rubber paddle so severely that she had to receive emergency medical treatment and was hospitalized for ten days); Webb v. McCullough, 828 F.2d 1151 (6th Cir. 1987) (court remanded for determination of whether student's due process rights were violated where her high school principal allegedly burst through her bathroom door while on a field trip and grabbed her, threw her against the wall, and slapped her).

[51] *See, e.g.,* Garcia v. Miera, 817 F.2d 650, 655 n.7 (10th Cir. 1987), *cert. denied*, 485 U.S. 959 (1988) (court remanded for consideration of due process rights of nine-year-old student who was held upside down by her ankles by a teacher while the school principal hit the student with a split wooden paddle which caused injuries from which she bled through her clothes); Metzger v. Osbeck, 841 F.2d 518, 520 (3d Cir. 1988) (remand to consider student's due process claims where teacher applied choke hold to student causing him to lose consciousness and fall, suffering lip lacerations, a broken nose, fractured teeth, and other injuries requiring hospitalization).

[52] *See, e.g.,* Cunningham v. Beavers, 858 F.2d 269 (5th Cir. 1988), *cert. denied*, 489 U.S. 1067 (1989) (no due process claim where school authorities paddled two kindergarten students with five swats, causing bruises to girls' buttocks, for "snickering" in the hall and classroom); Fee v. Herndon, 900 F.2d 804, 808 (5th Cir. 1990), *cert. denied*, 498 U.S. 908 (1990) (no due process claim where sixth-grade special education student argued that principal beat him so excessively that he was forced to remain in psychiatric rehabilitation for months and incur large treatment costs. The court stated: "injuries sustained incidentally to corporal punishment, irrespective of the severity of these injuries or the sensitivity of the student, do not implicate the Due Process Clause if the forum state affords adequate post-punishment civil or criminal remedies for the student to vindicate legal transgressions").

[53] Zablocki v. Redhail, 434 U.S. 374 (1978) (state restrictions which "directly and substantially" interfere with "fundamental right to marry" are strictly scrutinized).

as reasonable attempts by the state to protect minors from immature decision-making and to prevent unstable marriages.[54]

## [e] Curfews

As discussed above,[55] juvenile curfew provisions have met with a variety of judicial responses. Some courts uphold such measures against due process attack, especially where the statutes provide exceptions.[56] Other courts, however, have struck down curfews as violations of protected liberty under the Due Process Clause.[57]

## [2] Procedural Rights

### [a] School Discipline

In *Goss v. Lopez*,[58] the United States Supreme Court considered whether procedural due process rights were denied to public high school students who, because of acts of misconduct in school,[59] were suspended from school for up to ten days without a hearing. While reaffirming that students possess no constitutional right to an education, the Court found that students do possess constitutionally protected "liberty" and "property" interests in education, flowing from state compulsory education statutes. Thus, the Court held that schools are required to apply fair procedures in suspension actions. Citing *Tinker*, the Court found that although schools possess "very broad" authority to prescribe and enforce standards of conduct, they must nevertheless follow constitutional safeguards. Therefore, in order for school authorities to suspend a student and thus deprive the student of protected property (his interest in educational benefits) and liberty (his interest in his "good name, reputation [and] honor"), the student must be provided "oral or written notice of the charges against him and, if he denies them, an opportunity to present his side of the story."[60] The Court declined to impose more rigorous procedural protections, at least for suspensions of ten days or less:[61]

> We stop short of construing the Due Process Clause to require, countrywide, that hearings in connection with short suspensions must afford the student the opportunity to secure counsel, to confront and

---

[54] *See, e.g.*, Moe v. Dinkens, 533 F. Supp. 623 (S.D.N.Y. 1981), *cert. denied*, 459 U.S. 827 (1982) (state statute requiring parental consent to marry for minors under age 18 constitutional as a mere temporary impediment to exercise of right to marry).

[55] *Supra* § 6.03[B][2], notes 89–92 and accompanying text.

[56] *See, e.g.*, Bykofsky v. Middletown, 401 F. Supp 1242 (M.D. Pa. 1975), *aff'd*, 535 F.2d 1245 (3d Cir. 1976), *cert. denied*, 429 U.S. 964 (1976).

[57] *See, e.g.*, Waters v. Barry, 711 F. Supp. 1125 (D.D.C. 1989) (Fifth Amendment Due Process Clause). For detailed discussion of juvenile curfews, see Veilleux, *supra* § 6.03, note 92.

[58] 419 U.S. 565 (1975).

[59] One student refused an order by the school principal to refrain from disrupting a class; another physically attacked a police officer in the presence of the principal as the officer attempted to remove the disruptive student from the class. *Id.* at 569–70.

[60] *Id.* at 574, 576, 581.

[61] The Court allowed that "longer suspensions or expulsions for the remainder of the school term, or permanently, may require more formal procedures." *Id.* at 584. See, however, *Alex v. Allen*, 409 F. Supp. 379 (W.D. Pa. 1976), where a lower court held that a 30-day disciplinary suspension could be imposed if the school merely satisfied the *Goss* requirements of notice of the charges and opportunity to be heard.

cross-examine witnesses supporting the charge, or to call his own witnesses to verify his version of the incident. Brief disciplinary suspensions are almost countless. To impose in each such case even truncated trial-type procedures might well overwhelm administrative facilities in many places and, by diverting resources, cost more than it would save in educational effectiveness. Moreover, further formalizing the suspension process and escalating its formality and adversary nature may not only make it too costly as a regular disciplinary tool, but also destroy its effectiveness as part of the teaching process.

On the other hand, requiring effective notice and informal hearing permitting the student to give his version of the events will provide a meaningful hedge against erroneous action. At least the disciplinarian will be alerted to the existence of disputes about facts and arguments about cause and effect. He may then determine himself to summon the accuser, permit cross-examination, and allow the student to present his own witnesses. In more difficult cases, he may permit counsel. In any event, his discretion will be more informed and we think the risk of error substantially reduced.[62]

The Court again addressed the issue of student procedural due process rights in *Ingraham v. Wright*,[63] which held that school officials may corporally punish students without affording them prior notice of the charges against them or conducting a hearing prior to inflicting the punishment. The Court recognized that students possess a protected liberty interest in being free from unjustified intrusions on physical security.[64] But, the Court saw state remedies redressing excessive corporal punishment as adequate to protect that interest, even though such remedies are available only after the punishment has been imposed. The Court found little risk that school officials would routinely impose excessive punishment given the available sanctions applicable for after-the-fact violations of students' rights.[65] Moreover, "because paddlings are usually inflicted in response to conduct directly observed by teachers in their presence, the risk that a child will be paddled without cause is typically insignificant."[66] Finally, the Court declined to unduly limit legitimate exercises of discretion by school officials in refusing to impose procedural protections before imposing corporal punishment:

But even if the need for advance procedural safeguards were clear, the question would remain whether the incremental benefit could justify the cost. Acceptance of [a prior notice and hearing requirement] would work a

---

[62] 419 U.S. at 583–84. In *Board of Curators of University of Missouri v. Horowitz*, 435 U.S. 78, 89–90 (1978), the Court suggested that the due process requirements of *Goss* are applicable only to "disciplinary" determinations by educators and not to "academic" evaluations of a student.

[63] 430 U.S. 658 (1977). The Eighth Amendment aspects of *Ingraham* were discussed *supra* § 6.05[A].

[64] 430 U.S. at 673–74. The Court does not recognize all governmental restrictions of physical security as infringements of due process liberty. *See, e.g.*, Reno v. Flores, 507 U.S. 292 1439 (1993) (rejecting the claim by alien children in government custody that they possessed rights to be placed in the custody of a willing-and-able private custodian rather than of a governmental-operated or government selected child care institution where such children had no relatives or guardians in the United States to whom they could be released).

[65] "Teachers and school authorities are unlikely to inflict corporal punishment unnecessarily or excessively when a possible consequence of doing so is the instigation of civil or criminal proceedings against them." 430 U.S. at 678.

[66] *Id.* at 677–78.

transformation in the law governing corporal punishment in Florida and most other States. Given the impracticability of formulating a rule of procedural due process that varies with the severity of the particular imposition, the prior hearing . . . would have to precede *any* paddling, however moderate or trivial.

Such a universal constitutional requirement would significantly burden the use of corporal punishment as a disciplinary measure. Hearings — even informal hearings — require time, personnel, and a diversion of attention from normal school pursuits. School authorities may well choose to abandon corporal punishment rather than incur the burdens of complying with the procedural requirements. Teachers, properly concerned with maintaining authority in the classroom, may well prefer to rely on other disciplinary measures — which they may view as less effective — rather than confront the possible disruption that prior notice and a hearing may entail. Paradoxically, such an alteration of disciplinary policy is most likely to occur in the ordinary case where the contemplated punishment is well within the common-law privilege. . . . Assessment of the need for, and the appropriate means of maintaining, school discipline is committed generally to the discretion of school authorities subject to state law.[67]

The lower courts have routinely supplemented the Goss requirements and imposed more extensive procedural protections in cases of serious charges of student misconduct where sanctions of long-term suspension or expulsion are at stake.[68] Thus, the courts have sometimes required written notice and recognized that students sometimes possess confrontation and counsel rights.[69] In certain circumstances, some courts also require school officials to allow prehearing access to adverse evidence and to advise students of their rights.[70] Furthermore, state statutes often provide extensive procedural frameworks that must be followed in student discipline cases.[71]

## [b] Mental Health Commitments

In *Parham v. J.R.*,[72] the United States Supreme Court ruled on the question of the procedural protections due a child as prerequisites to commitment to a mental hospital. The Court reviewed Georgia procedures which permitted minors to be hospitalized if their parent or guardian so requests and if designated mental health professionals at the hospital agree that hospitalization is appropriate.[73] The Court

---

[67] *Id.* at 680–82.

[68] *See* 1 W. Valente, Education Law Public and Private 555 (1985). For general discussion of school disciplinary law, see 2 J. Rapp, Education Law § 9.05 (1996).

[69] Valente, *supra* note 68, at 558–67.

[70] *Id.* at 566–67.

[71] *Id.* at 567–70. For discussion of school discipline for nonschool conduct, see D. Feld, Annotation, *Right to Discipline Pupil for Conduct Away from School Grounds or Not Immediately Connected With School Activities*, 53 A.L.R.3d 1124 (1973). For commentary on school disciplinary procedures, see L. Teitelbaum, *School Discipline Procedures: Some Empirical Findings and Some Theoretical Questions*, 58 IND. L.J. 547 (1983); M. Mass, *Due Process Rights of Students: Limitations on Goss v. Lopez — A Retreat Out of the Thicket*, 9 J. L. & EDUC. 449 (1980); Note, *Due Process, Due Politics, and Due Respect: Three Models for Legitimate School Governance*, 94 HARV. L. REV. 1106 (1981).

[72] 442 U.S. 584 (1979).

[73] The Georgia statutes provided for discharge at the request of the parent or guardian when, in the

upheld the Georgia procedures, rejecting arguments that due process requires that minors be afforded both notice of the impending action and an adversary-type hearing before a judicial tribunal prior to hospitalization.

The Court recognized that children possess "substantial liberty interest[s] in not being confined unnecessarily" but noted that although commitment to a mental hospital carries a stigma, failure to commit troubled youngsters" needing but not receiving appropriate medical care may well [mean that such persons will] face even greater social ostracism resulting from observable symptoms of an untreated disorder."[74] Against the child's liberty interest the Court balanced the interest of parents in obtaining hospital care for their children. The Court distinguished *Danforth*,[75] a case raising the issue of whether parents could exercise absolute veto power over their child's exercise of constitutional rights, from *Parham*, where parents possessed no absolute veto of their child's liberty interest because the decision to hospitalize required ratification by mental health professionals. The Court assessed the parent-child relationship as follows:

> Simply because the decision of a parent is not agreeable to a child or because it involves risks does not automatically transfer the power to make that decision from the parents to some agency or officer of the state. The same characterizations can be made for a tonsillectomy, appendectomy, or other medical procedure. Most children, even in adolescence, simply are not able to make sound judgments concerning many decisions, including their need for medical care or treatment. Parents can and must make those judgments.[76]

In addition, the Court recognized the state's *parens patriae* interest in helping parents provide care for the mental health of their children. The court concluded that the state's interest would be frustrated if admissions to mental hospitals were "too onerous, too embarrassing, or too contentious."[77]

Further bolstering its decision, the Court found that the Georgia procedures were not likely to yield an undue number of erroneous hospital commitments given that the mental health decision makers act as "neutral factfinders."[78] The Court

---

opinion of hospital authorities, hospitalization of the child is "no longer desirable." *Id.* at 590–91.

[74] *Id.* at 600–1.

[75] *See supra* notes 2–9 and accompanying text.

[76] 442 U.S. at 603.

[77] *Id.* at 605. The Court observed: "It is surely not idle to speculate as to how many parents who believe they are acting in good faith would forego state-provided hospital care if such care is contingent on participation in an adversary proceeding designed to probe their motives and other family matters" in seeking hospital admission. *Id.*

[78] *Id.* at 606–7. The Court discounted the possibility that mental hospitals might, unless rigorous pre-admission procedures were imposed, become "dumping grounds" for troubled youth not genuinely in need of hospitalization:

> It has been suggested that a hearing conducted by someone other than the admitting physician is necessary in order to detect instances where parents are "guilty of railroading their children into asylums" or are using "voluntary commitment procedures in order to sanction behavior of which they disapprov[e].". . . Curiously, it seems to be taken for granted that parents who seek to "dump" their children on the state will inevitably be able to conceal their motives and thus deceive the admitting psychiatrists and the other mental health professionals who make and review the admission decision. It is elementary that one early diagnostic inquiry into the cause of an emotional disturbance of a child is an examination into the environment of the child. It is unlikely, if not inconceivable, that a decision to abandon an emotionally normal, healthy child and thrust him into an institution will be a discrete act

characterized the commitment decision as "essentially medical" and thus better made by "trained specialists" in medical science than by "untrained judge[s]."[79] The Court noted that requiring formal commitment proceedings would also create family disharmony:

> Pitting the parents and child as adversaries often will be at odds with the presumption that parents act in the best interest of their child. It is one thing to require a neutral physician to make a careful review of the parents' decision in order to make sure it is proper from a medical standpoint; it is a wholly different matter to employ an adversary contest to ascertain whether the parent's motivation is consistent with the child's interests. Moreover, it is appropriate to inquire into how such a hearing would contribute to the successful long-range treatment of the patient. Surely, there is a risk that it would exacerbate whatever tensions already exist between the child and the parents.[80]

Finally, the *Parham* Court upheld the Georgia procedures in cases where children are wards of the state despite the absence of concerns of family disharmony or infringements of parental rights if rigorous procedural protections were imposed as prerequisites to hospitalization. The Court trusted that the state as *parens patriae* would act in good faith in protecting the interests of children in state care, concluding that "[t]he absence of an adult who cares deeply for a child has little effect on the reliability of the initial admission decision."[81]

---

> leaving no trail of circumstances. Evidence of such conflicts will emerge either in the interviews or from secondary sources. It is unrealistic to believe that trained psychiatrists, skilled in eliciting responses, sorting medically relevant facts, and sensing motivational nuances will often be deceived about the family situation surrounding a child's emotional disturbance. Surely a lay, or even law-trained, factfinder would be no more skilled in the process than the professional.

*Id.* at 611–12.

[79] *Id.* at 609.

[80] *Id.* at 610. The Court further observed:

> Since the parents can and usually do play a significant role in the treatment while the child is hospitalized and even more so after release, there is a serious risk that an adversary confrontation will adversely affect the ability of the parents to assist the child while in the hospital. Moreover, it will make his subsequent return home more difficult. These unfortunate results are especially critical with an emotionally disturbed child; they seem likely to occur in the context of an adversary hearing in which the parents testify. A confrontation over such intimate family relationships would distress the normal adult parents and the impact on a disturbed child almost certainly would be significantly greater.

*Id.*

[81] *Id.* at 619. The Court remanded the case and instructed the lower courts to consider whether procedures for reviewing minor's need for continuing care should be more rigorous when the minor is a ward of the state than when parents seek hospitalization for their child. *Id.*

For commentary on *Parham*, see A. Watson, *Children, Families, and Courts: Before the Best Interests of the Child and* Parham v. J.R., 66 Va. L. Rev. 653 (1980); F. Mabbutt, *Juveniles, Mental Hospital Commitment and Civil Rights: The Case of* Parham v. J.R., 19 J. Fam. L. 27 (1980); Note, *Institutionalization of Juveniles: What Process is Due?*, 59 Neb. L. Rev. 190 (1980).

## [B] Equal Protection

### [1] Childhood as a Suspect Class?

The United States Supreme Court has held that when legislation distinguishes between persons on a "suspect" basis, the courts should "strictly scrutinize" the legislation and invalidate it unless it is necessary to promote compelling governmental interests.[82] Thus, laws that differentiate between people on the basis of race or national origin are "suspect" and almost unvariably unconstitutional under the Equal Protection Clause.[83]

Although arguments are often made that legislative distinctions based on youth should be treated as "suspect,"[84] the Court has never recognized minority as a suspect trait.[85] Because youth is relevant to a person's ability to perform or contribute to society in many respects, the Court typically does not view with general suspicion laws differentiating between juveniles and adults.[86] Thus, such laws are generally assessed in terms of "rational basis" scrutiny and are upheld so long as they reasonably promote some permissible governmental interest.[87]

### [2] Illegitimacy

While generally applying the rational basis test to laws creating age classifications, the Supreme Court has looked more suspiciously at statutes that discriminate against illegitimate children. Indeed, in such cases the Court has begun to apply a level of scrutiny more rigorous than the rational basis standard but not as exacting as strict scrutiny.[88] Under this so-called "middle-tier" scrutiny the Court will invalidate a statutory classification based on illegitimacy unless it has a "substantial relationship" to an "important" government interest.[89]

Without explicitly applying the middle-tier test, the Court, in *Levy v. Louisiana*,[90] held that a state could not create a right of action in favor of children for wrongful death of their parents but exclude illegitimate children from bringing such actions. The Court found that "[l]egitimacy or illegitimacy of birth has no relation to the nature of the wrong allegedly inflicted on [the parent]," because of

---

[82] *See* Nowak & Rotunda, *supra* § 6.01, note 8, at 639–640.

[83] *Id.* The Court has identified three properties that a trait must possess in order to qualify as "suspect": immutability, stigma, and general irrelevance to ability or merit. Note, *Developments in the Law — The Constitution and the Family*, 93 HARV. L. REV. 1156, 1365 (1980).

[84] For a summary and assessment of such arguments, see Tribe, *supra* note 6, at 1588–93.

[85] Note, *supra* note 83, at 1365–66.

[86] *Id.*

[87] *Id. See, e.g.*, Michael H. and Victoria D. v. Gerald D., 491 U.S. 110 (1989) (statute denying standing to children born in wedlock to rebut presumption of legitimacy is constitutional under rational basis test).

[88] Note, *supra* note 83, at 1365.

[89] Nowak & Rotunda, *supra* note 82, at 640–644. In some children's cases not involving illegitimacy issues, the Court has arguably also applied the middle tier test. See Harris, Tietelbaum & Weisbrod, *supra* § 6.01, note 4, at 893 discussing *Plyler v. Doe*, 457 U.S. 202 (1982), which struck down as violative of equal protection a Texas provision denying undocumented alien children a free public education available to children who are citizens or legally admitted aliens.

[90] 391 U.S. 68 (1968).

the fact that "no action, conduct or demeanor of [illegitimate children] is possibly relevant to the harm . . . done to [their parent]."[91]

In *Weber v. Aetna Casualty and Surety Co.*,[92] the Court invalidated a statutory exclusion of illegitimate children from bringing worker's compensation claims, available to legitimate children, on behalf of their deceased parents. Again, the Court did not expressly invoke middle-tier scrutiny, finding the statute unconstitutional under rational basis analysis.[93] The Court saw the statute as an "illogical and unjust" attempt by the state to deter births out of wedlock.[94] "[I]mposing disabilities on the illegitimate child is contrary to the basic concept . . . that legal burdens should bear some relationship to individual responsibility or wrongdoing. Obviously, no child is responsible for his birth."[95]

On the other hand, in *Mathews v. Lucas*,[96] the Court, again applying rational basis scrutiny,[97] upheld provisions of the Federal Social Security Act[98] that condition the eligibility of certain illegitimate children for a surviving child's insurance benefits upon a showing that the deceased wage earner was the child's parent and, at the time of his death, was living with the child or was contributing to his support. The Court found the requirement reasonably related to the statutory

---

[91] *Id.* at 72. In a companion case to *Levy, Glona v. American Guarantee & Liability Insurance Co.*, 391 U.S. 73 (1968), the Court invalidated another Louisiana law that precluded parents from bringing actions for the wrongful death of their illegitimate children while permitting such actions for deaths of legitimate children.

[92] 406 U.S. 164 (1972). In the same year it decided *Weber*, the Court decided *Stanley v. Illinois*, 405 U.S. 645 (1972). Although *Stanley* is usually understood as a "fathers' rights" case, *see, e.g.*, Harris, Teitelbaum & Weisbrod, *supra* note 89, at 1101; Mnookin & Weisberg, *supra* § 1.02, note 8, at 745–46, the case carries important implications for illegitimate children as well. In *Stanley*, the Court struck down an Illinois provision which denied biological fathers of illegitimate children a hearing prior to the adoption of the children by other persons. The father in *Stanley* had lived intermittently with his illegitimate children for years. Under such circumstances, the Court found the father's due process rights were violated when the state removed custody of the children from the father upon the death of the children's mother without affording the father an opportunity to establish his fitness to retain custody.

For a discussion of cases addressing the rights of unwed fathers in the adoption context, see Nowak & Rotunda, *supra* note 82, at 817–19.

[93] 406 U.S. at 176 (classification in *Weber* justified by "no legitimate state interest"). Earlier, in *Labine v. Vincent*, 401 U.S. 532 (1971), the Court applied rational basis scrutiny and upheld a state statute that denied illegitimate children from sharing in the intestate distribution of their parents' estates. The Court saw the statute as a rational means for the state to promote interests in supervising the distribution of estates without involving itself in onerous problems of proving paternity.

[94] 406 U.S. at 175. See also *New Jersey Welfare Rights Organization v. Cahill*, 411 U.S. 619 (1973), where the Court held that states could not deny welfare benefits to families with illegitimate children while providing them to married couples with natural or adopted children.

[95] 406 U.S. at 175.

[96] 427 U.S. 495 (1976).

[97] "[D]iscrimination between individuals on the basis of their illegitimacy does not command extraordinary protection which our most exacting scrutiny would entail." *Id.* at 506.

[98] Because the case involved a federal statute, the Court did not apply the Equal Protection Clause which is limited to the states, but subjected the statute to equal protection analysis under the Due Process Clause of the Fifth Amendment. In an earlier case interpreting the Social Security Act, *Jimenez v. Weinberger*, 417 U.S. 628 (1974), the Court invalidated a provision of the statute which barred worker disability support to the children of unwed workers where the children were born after the onset of the worker's disability.

goal of distributing benefits to dependent children. Congress was thus free to require unacknowledged illegitimate children to prove their dependency on a case-by-case basis while requiring no such proof from children born in wedlock.

Without explicitly adopting a test more rigorous than the rationality standard, the Court arguably heightened its scrutiny in *Trimble v. Gordon*,[99] a case which struck down an Illinois probate provision which permitted illegitimate children to inherit only from their mothers. The Court found that the blanket denial of paternal inheritance to illegitimate children did not adequately promote the articulated state interests of encouraging marriage and promoting the orderly administration of decedents' estates. Regarding the latter interest, the Court noted that the statute "failed to consider the possibility of a middle ground between the extremes of complete exclusion and case-by-case determination of paternity," suggesting that inheritance rights could be recognized for some illegitimate children of intestate men without jeopardizing the orderly settlement of estates.[100]

In *Lalli v. Lalli*,[101] a plurality of the Court expressly adopted the middle-tier test in upholding a state statute that required illegitimate children to receive judicial orders of filiation declaring paternity during the lives of their fathers in order for children to share in their fathers' intestate estates. Although legitimate children were not similarly required to obtain paternity orders before inheriting, the Court upheld the measure, with the plurality finding that it was "substantially related to important state interests"[102] in assuring the just and orderly disposition of property at death. Requiring a judicial order of paternity during the father's lifetime was a permissible means of addressing the "peculiar problems of proof" that are involved in paternal inheritance by illegitimate children.[103] The Court recognized that the statute excluded some "known" illegitimate children who, despite the absence of an order of filiation obtained during their fathers' lifetimes,

---

[99] 430 U.S. 762 (1977). Although denying that illegitimacy was a "suspect" class requiring strict scrutiny, the Court noted that scrutiny of classifications based on illegitimacy is "not a toothless one." *Id.* at 767. Moreover, Justice Rehnquist in dissent criticized the *Trimble* majority for invoking a more rigorous scrutiny than rational basis. *Id.* at 781–82 (Rehnquist, J., dissenting).

[100] *Id.* at 770–71. The Court noted, for example, that proof of paternity is not invariably an issue in cases of illegitimate children inheriting from intestate fathers given that court actions during the life of the father sometimes make paternity clear. *Id.* at 772.

The Court also addressed the argument that the Illinois statute reflects what most people would do if they wrote a will, *i.e.*, to exclude their illegitimate children.

> The issue . . . becomes [one of] where the burden of inertia in writing a will is to fall. At least when the disadvantaged group has been a frequent target of discrimination, as illegitimates have, we doubt that a State constitutionally may place the burden on that group by invoking the theory of "presumed intent."

*Id.* at 775 n.16.

[101] 439 U.S. 259 (1978).

[102] Four dissenting Justices thought the statute "was not substantially related to the legitimate interests that the state purports to promote." 439 U.S. at 279 (Brennan, J., concurring). If the dissent's "legitimate state interest" standard equates to the plurality's "important state interest" test, a majority of the Court in *Lalli* embraced the middle-tier standard although dividing on its application to the facts of the case.

[103] The Court noted that establishing maternity, inside or outside marriage, is seldom difficult. "In most cases the child remains with the mother and for a time is necessarily reared by her." 439 U.S. at 268. Proof of paternity is a different matter as unwed fathers are often not part of a formal family unit and even the mother sometimes may not know who fathered her child. *Id.* at 268–69.

could present other convincing proof of paternity and could thus inherit without jeopardizing the orderly settlement of their intestate fathers' estates. The Court noted that for such illegitimate children the statute appeared to operate "unfairly" but noted:

> [F]ew statutory classifications are entirely free from the criticism that they sometimes produce inequitable results. Our inquiry under the Equal Protection Clause does not focus on the abstract "fairness" of a state law, but on whether the statute's relation to the state interests it is intended to promote is so tenuous that it lacks the rationality contemplated by the Fourteenth Amendment.[104]

The Court further addressed procedural issues involving paternity actions in *Mills v. Habluetzel*[105] and *Pickett v. Brown*.[106] In *Mills*, the Court struck down a provision requiring that paternity actions for the purpose of establishing support obligations be brought before the child was one year old.[107] In *Pickett*, the Court struck down a two-year limitation requirement except for "acknowledged" children or for children likely to become a "public charge." The *Mills* and *Pickett* Courts found that the respective statutes of limitation afforded inadequate opportunity for illegitimate children to assert support claims on their behalf and were not substantially related to the articulated state interests of preventing the litigation of stale or fraudulent claims.

Finally, in *Clark v. Jeter*,[108] the Court unanimously adopted the middle-tier approach in holding that a six-year statute of limitation period, beginning with the birth of an illegitimate child, for paternity actions for support brought by the child was invalid because illegitimate children were treated less favorably than legitimate children who could sue their parents for support at any time. The Court found that the disparate treatment of illegitimate children was not "substantially related to an important state interest" such as avoiding stale or fraudulent claims from being litigated.[109] The *Clark* Court reinterated a concern articulated in its earlier paternity cases: the period for obtaining support must be sufficiently long in duration to present a "reasonable opportunity" for those with an interest in illegitimate children to assert claims on their behalf.[110] In light of this concern, the Court explained why the six-year period was unreasonable:

> [S]ix years does not necessarily provide a claim on behalf of an illegitimate child. "The unwillingness of the mother to file a paternity action on behalf of her child, which could stem from her relationship with the natural father or . . . from the emotional strain of having an illegitimate child, or even from the desire to avoid community and family disapproval, may continue years after the child is born. The problem may be exacer-

---

[104]  *Id.* at 273.

[105]  456 U.S. 91 (1982).

[106]  462 U.S. 1 (1983).

[107]  The Court again rejected arguments that imposing disabilities on illegitimate children promoted continuation of the institution of marriage. The Court reiterated the view that burdens should bear some relationship to individual responsibility or wrongdoing absent for the illegitimate children who are negatively impacted by the statutes. 456 U.S. at 99–101 n.8.

[108]  486 U.S. 456 (1988).

[109]  *Id.* at 461. The Court noted that "scientific advances in blood testing had alleviated some problems of proof in paternity actions." *Id.* at 463.

[110]  *Id.* at 462.

bated if, as often happens, the mother herself is a minor." . . . Not all of these difficulties are likely to abate in six years. A mother might realize only belatedly a "loss of income attributable to the need to care for the child." . . . Furthermore, financial difficulties are likely to increase as the child matures and incurs expenses for clothing, school, and medical care. . . . Thus it is questionable whether a State acts reasonably when it requires most paternity and support actions to be brought within six years of an illegitimate child's birth.[111]

## § 6.07  SUMMARY

The previous sections illustrate that the Supreme Court has proceeded in an *ad hoc* manner and has yet to develop a consistent theory of rights for children.[1] Such cases as *Tinker*,[2] *Danforth*,[3] *Carey*,[4] and *Bellotti II*[5] appear to give minors full personhood status. Some commentators, however, argue that *Tinker* is really a case protecting family rights, given the strong parental encouragement of the children in the case to make the political point espoused by the parents;[6] others see the reproductive rights cases as examples of protectionist rights, allowing young people rights in order to protect them from the harmful consequences of their sexual choices.[7] On the other hand, such cases as *Prince*,[8] *Fraser*,[9] *Kuhlmeier*,[10] *Ginsberg*[11] and *Parham*[12] are clear protectionist cases. The Fourth Amendment cases, *T.L.O.*, *Acton*, and *Earls*,[13] recognize that students possess privacy rights, perhaps as a nod in the direction of their personhood,[14] yet the Court arguably leaves students with toothless privacy protection by allowing broad discretion to school authorities to search upon "reasonable," but not necessarily particularized, suspi-

---

[111] *Id.* at 463–64. For a discussion of statutes of limitations in paternity cases, see L. Russ, Annotation, *Statutes Limiting Time for Commencement of Action to Establish Paternity of Illegitimate Child as Violating Child's Constitutional Rights*, 16 A.L.R.4th 926 (1982); Comment, *Not Enough Time?: The Constitutionality of Short Statutes of Limitations for Civil Child Sexual Abuse Litigation*, 50 Ohio St. L.J. 753 (1989). For other discussion of illegitimate children and equal protection, see Note, *Is Discrimination Against Illegitimate Children Worthy of Stricter Scrutiny Under the Constitution? — The Relationship Between State Intestate Succession Statutes and the Social Security Act in Claims for Child Benefits*, 33 J. Fam. L. 79 (1995).

[1] *See* J. Coons, R. Mnookin & S. Sugarman, *Puzzling Over Children's Rights*, 1991 B.Y.U. L. Rev. 307.

[2] *Supra* § 6.03, notes 38–42 and accompanying text.

[3] *Supra* § 6.06, notes 2–9 and accompanying text.

[4] *Supra* § 6.06, notes 10–16 and accompanying text.

[5] *Supra* § 6.06, notes 17–24 and accompanying text.

[6] *See, e.g.*, J. Garvey, *Child, Parent, State, and the Due Process Clause: An Essay on the Supreme Court's Recent Work*, 51 S. Cal. L. Rev. 769, 784–85 (1978); Hafen, *supra* § 1.01, note 4, at 646.

[7] Zimring, *supra* § 1.02, note 11, at 63–63.

[8] *Supra* § 6.03, notes 15–20 and accompanying text.

[9] *Supra* § 6.03, notes 56–63 and accompanying text.

[10] *Supra* § 6.03, notes 64–70 and accompanying text.

[11] *Supra* § 6.03, notes 71–81 and accompanying text.

[12] *Supra* § 6.06, notes 72–81 and accompanying text.

[13] *Supra* § 6.04, notes 42 and accompanying text.

[14] Gardner, *supra* § 6.04, note 6, at 898–906.

cion.[15] The death penalty cases present further anomalies. A sixteen-year-old, who in the words of the *Parham* Court "simply [is] not able to make sound judgments"[16] for purposes of medical treatment, is nevertheless possessed of sufficient "judgment" and moral accountability to be punished for his crimes to the fullest extent the law allows. Yet, while sixteen-year-olds may be full-fledged persons for purposes of imposing capital punishment,[17] no fifteen-year-old can be held to account for his actions by paying the ultimate penalty.[18]

Clearly the Court's attempts to balance the interests of children's autonomy, parental control, and state authority ebb and flow over time and from context to context.[19] The uncertainty and lack of a consistent, coherent theory of rights reflects the problem introduced in Chapter 2 and which runs throughout this book: When, if ever, are children entitled to respect as autonomous persons and when are they entitled to protection, even from their own choices? That the Court has not given a clear answer to this question is not surprising given the ambivalent position adopted by many thoughtful commentators: Young people should be given autonomy rights in certain circumstances and protection rights in others. The commentators are far from agreement, however, when defining those circumstances.[20]

---

[15] *Id.* at 919–47; *see also,* Gardner, *supra* § 6.04, note 46.

[16] *Supra* § 6.06, text accompanying note 76.

[17] *See Stanford v. Kentucky,* discussed at *supra* § 6.05, notes 27–33 and accompanying text.

[18] *Thompson, supra* § 6.05 notes 17–26 and accompanying text. For a discussion of the relationship between personhood as a prerequisite for punishment, see M. Gardner, *Punitive Juvenile Justice: Some Observations on a Recent Trend,* 10 INT'L J.L. & PSYCHIATRY 129 (1987).

[19] Davis & Schwartz, *supra* § 3.02, note 51, at 52.

[20] For a sample of the commentary, see generally *supra* notes 1, 6, and 7, as well as C. Espenoza, *Good Kids, Bad Kids: A Revelation About the Due Process Rights of Children,* 23 HASTINGS CONST. L.Q. 407 (1996); W. Fitzgerald, *Maturity, Difference, and Mystery: Children's Perspectives and the Law,* 36 ARIZ. L. REV. 11 (1994); B. Hafen, *Individualism and Autonomy in Family Law: The Waning of Belonging,* 1991 B.Y.U. L. REV. 1; R. Keiter, *Privacy, Children, and Their Parents: Reflections On and Beyond the Supreme Court's Approach,* 66 MINN. L. REV. 459 (1982); F. McCarthy, *The Confused Constitutional Status and Meaning of Parental Rights,* 22 GA. L. REV. 975 (1988); M. Minow, *What Ever Happened to Children's Rights?,* 80 MINN. L. REV. 267 (1995); Richards, *supra* § 1.01, note 1; and S. Rush, *The Warren and Burger Courts on State, Parent, and Child Conflict Resolution,* 36 HASTINGS L.J. 461 (1985).

# Part Three
## THE JUVENILE JUSTICE SYSTEM

# Chapter 7

# THE JUVENILE COURT MOVEMENT

## § 7.01 OVERVIEW

Until the late nineteenth century, juveniles who committed crimes were dealt with through the same criminal justice system that addressed the offenses of adults. While minors were afforded a defense of infancy,[1] they received no other legally recognized special attention. However, functionaries in the criminal justice system no doubt exercised discretion from time to time in favor of lenient treatment for youthful offenders. Young people who engaged in untoward or self-destructive conduct that was non-criminal in nature were subjected to no public intervention of any sort.

This all changed with the emergence of juvenile courts at the turn of the twentieth century. Reformers saw the need for a non-punitive *parens patriae* alternative to the criminal justice system for juvenile criminal offenders. As juvenile court statutes became ubiquitous, the bulk of juvenile criminal offenses were dealt with in juvenile court, although mechanisms existed to "waive" certain cases to adult criminal court. Juvenile court jurisdiction was not limited to criminal misbehavior, however, but also extended to so-called "status offenses," non-criminal behavior deemed harmful to the juvenile actor's healthy growth and development. In exercising either its criminal ("delinquency") or status offense jurisdiction, the juvenile courts, untrammeled by rigorous procedural rules, sought to impose dispositions beneficial to the individual young person appearing before the court.

In the mid-twentieth century, the United States Supreme Court began to scrutinize juvenile courts and, in a series of cases, imposed many of the same procedural protections constitutionally mandated for criminal cases. While the Court spoke directly only to procedural requirements in delinquency adjudications, its rulings are arguably relevant to other aspects of the juvenile justice system. Moreover, subsequent to, and perhaps in part because of, the Supreme Court's review, many juvenile justice systems have increasingly become more blatantly punitive in their treatment of youthful offenders.

This Chapter examines the historical evolution of the juvenile courts and traces the Supreme Court decisions in the area of juvenile justice. The cases considered in this Chapter speak specifically to the juvenile justice system *per se*. The Court's cases in the areas of pretrial detention and interrogation will be examined in a later Chapter addressing preadjudication issues.

## § 7.02 THE EMERGENCE OF JUVENILE COURTS

### [A] The Common Law

From early times, the law has differentiated between children and adults who violate criminal rules. Under Roman law, children enjoyed immunity from criminal liability until reaching seven years of age.[1] While the Mosaic Code prescribed severe penalties, including death, against children committing certain offenses

---

[1] *See infra* § 7.02, notes 1–11 and accompanying text.

[1] F. Ludwig, *Rationale of Responsibility for Young Offenders*, 29 NEB. L. REV. 521, 524 (1950).

against their parents, the severity of these penalties was mitigated in practice and later the Code explicitly required mitigation.[2] Children were afforded similar leniency under Moslem law.[3]

Prior to its recognition as a substantive defense, infancy operated in early English law as a basis for pardoning the actions of the offending child.[4] By the sixteenth century, the common law infancy defense had taken definite form.[5] The defense embodies a series of presumptions reflecting children's incapacity to take responsibility for their actions.[6] Under the infancy defense, children under the age of seven are conclusively presumed incapable of criminal responsibility, while those over the age of fourteen are regarded as adults and presumed capable of committing crimes.[7] Children between the ages of seven and fourteen are presumed to lack criminal capacity and can be punished only if the prosecution shows that the particular child defendant knew and understood the consequences of his act.[8]

The infancy defense, like the insanity defense, is a vehicle for avoiding unjust punishment.[9] Because punishment entails the purposeful infliction of suffering and

---

[2] *Id.* at 523; F. Ludwig, Youth and the Law 12 (1995). The Talmud deliminated criminal responsibility through a tripartite division of infancy (infancy, from birth to age six; impubescence, from age six to puberty; and adolescence, from puberty (age 12 for females, age 13 for males) to majority at age 20).

[3] Ludwig, *supra* note 1.

[4] A. Kean, *The History of the Criminal Liability of Children*, 53 Law Q. Rev. 364 (1937).

[5] F. Sayre, *Mens Rea*, 45 Harv. L. Rev. 974, 1009 (1932); F. Woodbridge, *Physical and Mental Infancy in the Criminal Law*, 87 U. Pa. L. Rev. 426, 427–37 (1939).

[6] The use of presumptions in infancy doctrine is explained:

> An infant's guilt depended upon his mental state; but in a day when the defendant accused of felony was not allowed to take the stand, the determination of his mental capacity and discretion was naturally sought through legal presumptions and through the consequent drawing of somewhat arbitrary age lines when infants would be conclusively presumed to possess or to lack the necessary "discretion."

Sayre, *supra* note 5, at 1009.

[7] LaFave & Scott, *supra* § 5.06, note 2, at 398–99. Adults are presumed to possess the general capacity to commit crimes. *See* J. Eule, *The Presumption of Sanity: Bursting the Bubble*, 25 UCLA L. Rev. 637 (1978).

[8] LaFave & Scott, *supra* note 7; R. Perkins & R. Boyce, Criminal Law 938 (3d ed. 1984).

[9] The exculpatory aspect of the infancy defense derives from the limited ability of children to appreciate the risks of doing certain things and to appreciate the significance of resulting harm. Full responsibility requires "social intelligence" that the young are only in a process of developing. H. Gross, A Theory of Criminal Justice 151 (1979).

While most defenses assume the general capacity of the defendant to obey the law, infancy and insanity "absolve[ ] a person precisely because his deficiencies of temperament, personality or maturity distinguish him so utterly from the rest of us to whom the law's threats are addressed that we do not expect him to comply." S. Kadish, *The Decline of Innocence*, 26 Cambridge L.J. 273, 275 (1968). Infancy and insanity are thus general "status defenses" that exclude individuals in these classes from legal liability. M. Moore, Law and Psychiatry 65 (1984); *see also* H. Fingarette & A. Hasse, Mental Disability and Criminal Responsibility 25–28 (1979); J. Jeffries, P. Low & R. Bonnie, Criminal Law, Cases and Materials 627–28 (1982); S. Morse, *Crazy Behavior, Morals and Science: An Analysis of Mental Health Law*, 51 S. Cal. L. Rev. 527, 640, n.249 (1978); A. Platt & B. Diamond, *The Origins of the Right and Wrong Test of Criminal Responsibility and Its Subsequent Development in the United States: An Historical Survey*, 54 Cal. L. Rev. 1227, 1232–34, 1257–58 (1966).

characteristically connotes blameworthiness,[10] it is unjustly applied if an offender lacks responsibility for his conduct. The infancy defense excuses the harmful actions of young people deemed to be unfit recipients of the criminal sanction.[11]

Thus, at common law juvenile criminal offenders were either punished for their actions, theoretically at least in the same manner as adults,[12] or excused under the infancy defense. Public law paid little attention to troubled youngsters who did not commit criminal acts,[13] at least so long as they were adequately supported by a parent or guardian.[14]

## [B]  Statutory Reform

Juvenile law reform began quietly in 1825 pursuant to New York legislation creating a "House of Refuge," a place to receive vagrant juveniles or those convicted of criminal offenses.[15] The House of Refuge was the result of efforts of Quaker reformers who directed their humanitarian attention to troubled children by offering food, shelter, and education to the needy and removing youthful offenders from the company of adult offenders.[16]

In 1899, the Illinois legislature created the first juvenile court system, immediately triggering an international movement so extensive that by 1945 every United States jurisdiction, state and federal, as well as most European countries had created their own juvenile justice alternatives to the traditional criminal law.[17] While these new systems handled the bulk of juvenile crime, virtually from their inception they provided mechanisms to waive juvenile court jurisdiction to the criminal court in certain cases.[18] The courts also asserted jurisdiction over "status

---

[10] *See* M. Gardner, *Punishment and Juvenile Justice: A Conceptual Framework for Assessing Constitutional Rights of Youthful Offenders,* 35 VAND. L. REV. 791, 797–822 (1982).

[11] *See supra* note 9.

[12] Not surprisingly, however, sentencing discretion was often exercised in favor of youthful offenders. "[C]olonial and post-colonial period sentencing practices appear to have shielded most juveniles from especially harsh dispositions and included such creative sentencing alternatives as lengthy apprentice-ships in lieu of strict reliance upon more traditional sanctions." C. Thomas & S. Bilchik, *Prosecuting Juveniles in Criminal Courts: A Legal and Empirical Analysis,* J. CRIM. L. & CRIMINOLOGY 439, 444 n.12 (1985). On the other hand, 287 juveniles, ages 10 to 17, were executed for criminal offenses between 1642 and 1964. V. Strieb, *Death Penalty for Children: The American Experience with Capital Punishment for Crimes Committed While Under Age Eighteen,* 36 OKLA. L. REV. 613, 618–19 (1983).

[13] However, some jurisdictions, Massachusetts for example, passed rare criminal statutes applicable only to children, that punished them for, among other things, being "stubborn and rebellious." *See, e.g.,* Commonwealth v. Brasher, 270 N.E.2d 389 (Mass. 1971) (upholding a statute punishing "stubborn children" with up to six months imprisonment); *See also* I. Rosenberg & Y. Rosenberg, *The Legacy of the Stubborn and Rebellious Son,* 74 MICH. L. REV. 1097 (1976).

[14] *See supra* § 2.02[C], note 9 and accompanying text.

[15] The House of Refuge development marked the beginning of institutionalized attempts at juvenile justice reform. S. Fox, *Juvenile Justice Reform: An Historical Perspective,* 22 STAN. L. REV. 1187 (1970).

[16] *Id.* at 1188–89.

[17] Thomas & Bilchik, *supra* note 12, at 451.

[18] In 1903, only four years after its establishment, the Chicago juvenile court transferred fourteen children to the adult criminal system. S. Wizner, *Discretionary Waiver of Juvenile Court Jurisdiction: An Invitation to Procedural Arbitrariness,* 3 CRIM. JUST. ETHICS 41, 42 (1984). Such a trend continued until by the 1970s every American jurisdiction had laws authorizing or requiring criminal prosecution of certain minors in adult courts. *Id.*; *see also* B. Feld, *Reference of Juvenile Offenders for Adult Prosecution: The Legislative Alternative to Asking Unanswerable Questions,* 62 MINN. L. REV. 515, 516

offenders" whose conduct or predicament, while not criminal, evidenced a need for supervision.[19]

As a by-product of the sociological jurisprudence movement,[20] the juvenile courts were created as tools of the social sciences to help vulnerable, deviant, and wayward youth whose problems were regarded as primarily social in nature.[21] Reliance was thus placed on social workers, probation officers, psychologists, psychiatrists, and physicians to provide the court with information about the child, her background, and environment that was deemed useful in assessing and treating the problems of each individual child.[22] The juvenile court movement was founded on the ideal of rehabilitating troubled youth[23] by offering individualized and non-punitive dispositions according to the minor's needs without the encumbrances of the adversarial model familiar to the criminal law. Under the guise of *parens patriae*, juvenile court functionaries were to promote the welfare of the offender, thus rendering unnecessary, indeed counterproductive, the procedural protections of the criminal system.[24]

---

n.5 (1978). Waiver is generally reserved for those youths whose "highly visible, serious, or repetitive criminality raises legitimate concern for public safety or community outrage." B. Feld, *Juvenile Court Legislative Reform and the Serious Young Offender: Dismantling the 'Rehabilitative Ideal,'* 65 MINN. L. REV. 165, 171 (1980) On the other hand, many youths committing minor offenses are dealt with in criminal court, perhaps because of the unavailability of fines as a juvenile court sanction. *See* Wizner, *supra* at 44–45.

[19] Kramer, *supra* § 3.03, note 15, at 245.

[20] The major thrust of sociological jurisprudence was that law was simply a means for attaining certain social ends. Davis, *supra* § 2.02, note 9, at 1–2.

[21] *Id.* at 1–2, 1–3.

[22] *Id.*

[23] The fundamental concern of juvenile courts towards child offenders was with "what is he, how has he become what he is, and what had best be done in his interest and in the interest of the state to save him from a downward career." J. Mack, *The Juvenile Court*, 23 HARV. L. REV. 104, 119–20 (1909). In adopting reformation as its goal, the juvenile court movement eschewed retributivist notions of guilt and blameworthiness. F. McCarthy, *The Role of the Concept of Responsibility in Juvenile Delinquency Proceedings*, 10 U. MICH. J.L. REF. 181, 207 (1977).

The rehabilitative objectives of the juvenile system were characterized by a system of indeterminate sentencing in which the type and duration of sanction were dictated by the "best interests" of the offender rather than the seriousness of the offense. S. Wisner & M. Keller, *The Penal Model of Juvenile Justice: Is Juvenile Court Delinquency Obsolete?*, 42 N.Y.U. L. REV. 1120, 1121 (1977). *But see* Fox, *supra* note 15, arguing that the juvenile court movement was primarily motivated by interests in preserving traditional values against the threat of rising urbanization and industrialism rather than by concerns about the welfare of children.

[24] Traditionally, juvenile courts dispensed with juries, lawyers, rules of evidence, and formal procedures. B. Feld, *Criminalizing Juvenile Justice: Rules of Procedure for the Juvenile Court*, 69 MINN. L. REV. 141, 150–51 (1984).

> The child — essentially good, as [the early reformers] saw it — was to be made "to feel that he is the object of (the state's) care and solicitude," not that he was under arrest or on trial. The rules of criminal procedure were therefore altogether inapplicable. The apparent rigidities, technicalities, and harshness which they observed in both substantive and procedural criminal law were therefore to be discarded. The . . . procedures were to be "clinical" rather than punitive.

*In re* Gault, 387 U.S. 1, 15–16 (1967). The infatuation with procedural informality was explained by an early court:

> To save a child from becoming a criminal . . . the Legislature surely may provide for the

The conceptual underpinnings of the juvenile court movement assume not only that children are malleable and thus prime subjects for rehabilitation, but also that they are unfit subjects for punishment because their immaturity renders them not responsible, or at least not fully responsible, for their conduct.[25] Thus, juvenile justice has traditionally disavowed punitive dispositions. The proceedings are conceptualized as civil and not criminal.[26] Moreover, to avoid the stigma attached to the criminal system, juvenile justice systems employ unique terminology. Juvenile proceedings are triggered by "petitions" rather than "indictments" or "informations," juveniles commit acts of "delinquency" rather than "crimes," are subjected to "adjudications" rather than "trials," discover their fate in "disposition" rather than "sentencing" proceedings, and may be sent to "training schools" rather than "prisons."[27]

While juvenile court systems are still generally conceptualized in terms of the rehabilitative model,[28] many policymakers are rethinking the mission of juvenile justice and have begun to embrace explicitly punitive sanctions as appropriate for delinquent offenders.[29] This shift in theoretical principle can be accounted for through a variety of converging factors including: a loss of faith in the juvenile

---

salvation of such a child . . . by bringing it into one of the courts of the state *without any process at all*. . . . When the child gets there, and the court, with the power to save it, determines on its salvation, and not its punishment, *it is immaterial how it got there*.

Commonwealth v. Fisher, 62 A. 198, 200 (Pa. 1905) (emphasis added).

For a discussion of *parens patriae* as the authority for state intervention through juvenile courts, see Fox, *supra* note 15, at 1192–93.

[25] S. Fox, *Responsibility in the Juvenile Court*, 11 WM. & MARY L. REV. 659, 661–64 (1970); Mack, *supra* note 23, at 109. For a discussion of the relationship between immaturity and criminal responsibility, see *supra* note 9.

[26] Davis, *supra* note 20, at 1–3.

[27] Feld, *supra* note 24; Kramer, *supra* note 19, at 244.

[28] Kramer, *supra* note 19, at 246.

[29] This rethinking is examined in Gardner, *supra* § 6.07, note 18, at 133–38. Punitive theory is manifested by the movement towards holding juveniles accountable for their delinquent acts through proportioning sanctions to the seriousness of the offense. *See, e.g.*, Wash. Rev. Code Ann. § 13.40.010(2)(c)(d) (West 1993) (which aims, *inter alia*, to "[m]ake the juvenile offender accountable for his or her criminal behavior" by "[p]rovid[ing] for punishment commensurate with the age, crime, and criminal history of the juvenile offender"); *see also* Minn. Stat. Ann. § 260B.001, Subd. 2 (West Supp. 2002) (seeking, *inter alia*, to "develop[ ] individual responsibility for lawful behavior"); R. Dawson, *The Third Justice System: The New Juvenile Criminal System of Determinate Sentencing for the Youthful Violent Offender in Texas*, 19 ST. MARY'S L.J. 943 (1988) (new determinate sentencing scheme for juvenile courts in Texas which imposes determinate sentencing for six serious, violent offenses). For a discussion of New York's move toward a system of punishment, see Note, *Rehabilitation vs. Punishment: A Comparative Analysis of the Juvenile Justice Systems in Massachusetts and New York*, 21 SUFFOLK U. L. REV. 1091, 1107–15 (1987). For a detailed list of jurisdictions adopting punitive, or partially punitive, models of juvenile justice, see A. Walkover, *The Infancy Defense in the New Juvenile Court*, 31 UCLA L. REV. 503, 523 n.82 (1984). The standards promulgated by the Joint Commission on Juvenile Justice of the American Bar Association and the Institute of Judicial Administration systematically reject rehabilitation as the primary goal of the juvenile justice system and adopt instead, *inter alia*, as a general purpose "to reduce juvenile crime by maintaining the integrity of the substantive law proscribing certain behavior and by developing individual responsibility for lawful behavior." Institute of Judicial Admin. & American Bar Ass'n, Juvenile Justice Standards, Dispositions 1.1, at 5 (1980). For commentary on the Standards, see F. McCarthy, *Delinquency Dispositions Under the Juvenile Justice Standards: The Consequences of a Change of Rationale*, 52 N.Y.U. L. REV. 1093 (1977); Wizner & Keller, *supra* note 23.

justice system's ability to rehabilitate; the Supreme Court's "criminalization" of juvenile court proceedings;[30] a general rebirth of retributive theories of punishment throughout the legal system;[31] an expanded view of children's capacity for responsibility;[32] and perceived increases in the rate of serious crime committed by juveniles.[33] Responding to these factors, some legislatures have adopted systems incorporating principles of personal responsibility and accountability, foreign to the traditional premises of juvenile justice, in order to give offending minors their "just deserts."[34] In light of these concerns and developments, some commentators argue for the total abolition of juvenile courts.[35] For young criminal offenders, such abolition would mean a return to a single justice system for adults and minors, and, for "status offenders," the total abandonment of judicial intervention until such time as they commit a criminal act or come to a court's attention as a possible victim of neglect or abuse.

Since the early 1990s, "problem-solving courts," as distinct from traditional juvenile courts, have been created in many jurisdictions to address issues such as juvenile delinquency, drug abuse, mental illness, and domestic violence (issues that often involve repeat offenders).[36] These courts are unique because they utilize a rehabilitative approach and emphasize solving the underlying problem and

---

[30] *See infra* § 7.03; Gardner, *supra* note 29, at 133–34.

[31] *See* M. Gardner, *The Renaissance of Retribution — An Examination of Doing Justice,* 1976 WIS. L. REV. 781; Gardner, *supra* note 29, at 135–37.

[32] "Psychological research concerning legal socialization, internalization of social and legal expectations, and ethical decision making . . . indicates that by about age fourteen a youth has acquired most of the legal and moral values that will guide his behavior through later life." B. Feld, *The Decision to Seek Criminal Charges: Just Deserts and the Waiver Decision,* 3 CRIM. JUST. ETHICS 27, 37 (1984). Therefore, some conclude: "There is no compelling or convincing evidence that persons [in late adolescence] differ significantly from persons [over the age of majority] in their capacity to understand the outcomes and consequences of their acts. . . . [S]erious crime should be treated seriously regardless of the offender's age." Confronting Youth Crime, Report of the Twentieth Century Fund Task Force on Sentencing Policy Toward Young Offenders 25 (1979); *see* Gardner, *supra* note 29, at 137–39.

[33] Gardner, *supra* note 29, at 140.

[34] The term "just deserts" describes the retributive justice model of punishment which proportions sanctions to the gravity of the offense. *See generally* A. Von Hirsch, Doing Justice (1976). While the sentencing aims of the juvenile penal codes seldom expressly define sentencing policy in terms of the "just deserts" rubric, the concept seems implicit in many of the requirements for proportionality. *E.g.,* Institute of Judicial Admin. & American Bar Ass'n, *supra* note 29, at 6 ("In choosing among statutorily permissible dispositions, the court should employ the least restrictive . . . disposition that is appropriate to the seriousness of the offense, as modified by the degree of culpability"); Minn. Stat. Ann. § 260B.001 subd. 2 (West Supp. 2002). It must be emphasized, however, that none of the new juvenile justice models totally reject such utilitarian concerns as deterrence, incapacitation, and even rehabilitation. *See, e.g.,* Wash. Rev. Code Ann. § 13.40.010(2)(a), (f), (g), (j) (West 1993) (in addition to any retributive considerations, the system must "[p]rotect the citizenry from criminal behavior, provide community-based dispositions whenever 'consistent with public safety,' and respond to the needs of youthful offenders").

[35] *See, e.g.,* J. Ainsworth, *Re-Imagining Childhood and Reconstructing the Legal Order: The Case for Abolishing the Juvenile Court,* 69 N.C. L. REV. 1083 (1991); K. Fedele, *The Abolition of the Juvenile Court: A Proposal for the Preservation of Children's Rights,* 16 J. CONTEMP. L. 23 (1990); B. Feld, *The Transformation of Juvenile Court,* 75 MINN. L. REV. 691, 722–25 (1991); Wizner & Keller, *supra* note 23. *But see* I. Rosenberg, *Leaving Bad Enough Alone: A Response to the Juvenile Court Abolitionists,* 1993 WIS. L. REV. 163.

[36] P. Casey & D. Rottman, *Problem-Solving Courts: Models and Trends,* 26 JUST. SYS. J. 35, 35 (2003).

decreasing recidivism, rather than just punishing the offender.[37] A disposition in one of these courts typically involves treatment, the provision and coordination of community resources, and monitoring by the court.[38] Examples of problem-solving courts are mental health courts, adult and juvenile drug courts, and domestic violence courts. The availability of the specific type of problem-solving court depends upon the jurisdiction; but many cases involving juveniles, as well as adults, are now being heard in these courts.[39]

## § 7.03  SUPREME COURT OVERSIGHT

### [A]  The Pre-*Gault* Era

Until the 1966 United States Supreme Court decision in *Kent v. United States*,[1] the juvenile courts operated without legal oversight or monitoring.[2] In *Kent*, the Court considered "disturbing" questions concerning procedures, or lack thereof, for waiving juveniles from juvenile to criminal court.[3] Morris Kent, age sixteen and on juvenile court probation, was apprehended by District of Columbia law enforcement on suspicion of burglary and rape. Because he was a minor, Kent was subject to the "exclusive jurisdiction" of the juvenile court which under the District of Columbia statute could, after "full investigation," waive jurisdiction of particular juveniles committing felonies to adult criminal court.[4] The juvenile court judge waived jurisdiction to criminal court without holding a hearing or considering a motion by Kent's counsel that he should remain under the jurisdiction of the juvenile court in order to receive needed psychiatric care. Kent was eventually convicted of six counts of housebreaking and robbery, sentenced to thirty to ninety years in prison, and acquitted by reason of insanity of several counts of rape. The juvenile court judge made no findings nor stated any reasons in support of his decision to waive jurisdiction. Moreover, the judge made no mention of, and denied Kent's counsel's request for access to, a social report prepared by probation authorities describing Kent's rapidly deteriorating mental condition. Kent appealed the judge's waiver order and the Supreme Court eventually granted *certiorari.*

The Supreme Court found that the order waiving jurisdiction was invalid under "basic requirements of due process and fairness as well as with the statutory requirement of a 'full investigation' " prior to waiver to criminal court.[5] While the Court conceded that juvenile court judges are allowed a "substantial degree of discretion as to the factual considerations to be evaluated, the weight to be given them, and the conclusion to be reached," the courts do not possess "a license for

---

[37]  B. Winick, *Therapeutic and Problem Solving Courts*, 30 FORDHAM URB. L. J. 1055, 1055–56 (2003).

[38]  *Id.* at 1060–61.

[39]  For statistics and descriptions of various types of problem-solving courts, see V. Flango, National Center for State Courts, *Families and Problem-Solving Courts*, http://www.ncsconline.org/WC/Publications/Trends/2007/ProSolTrends2007.pdf (last visited May 25, 2008).

[1]  383 U.S. 541 (1966).

[2]  Wadlington, Whitebread & Davis, *supra* § 3.02, note 34, at 198.

[3]  383 U.S. at 542–43.

[4]  The statute allowed for waiver to criminal court of minors sixteen years of age or older charged with offenses that "would amount to felonies in the case of an adult" if the judge so decides after "full investigation." *Id.* at 547–48.

[5]  *Id.* at 553.

arbitrary procedure" in deciding the "critically important" question of whether a child should be deprived of the "special protections" of the juvenile justice system, available, incidentally, to minors only until they reach the age of majority.[6] The Court noted that there is no place in our system of law for reaching a result of such tremendous consequences "without ceremony." The Court concluded that as a condition to a valid waiver order, Kent was entitled to a hearing with access to his counsel and to the relevant social report, although the hearing need not conform to "all the requirements of a criminal trial or even of the usual administrative hearing."[7]

The Court examined the underpinnings of the juvenile justice system and found that governmental exercise of *parens patriae* authority is "not an invitation to procedural arbitrariness."[8] Without citing any specific evidence, the Court expressed skepticism about the ability of the juvenile courts to perform their mission successfully:

> While there can be no doubt of the original laudable purpose of juvenile courts, studies and critiques in recent years raise serious questions as to whether actual performance measures well enough against theoretical purpose to make tolerable the immunity of the process from the reach of constitutional guaranties applicable to adults. There is much evidence that some juvenile courts, including that of the District of Columbia, lack the personnel, facilities and techniques to perform adequately as representatives of the State in a *parens patriae* capacity, at least with respect to children charged with law violation. There is evidence, in fact, that there may be grounds for concern that the child receives the worst of both worlds: that he gets neither the protections accorded to adults nor the solicitous care and regenerative treatment postulated for children.[9]

Finally, the District of Columbia statute authorizing waivers to criminal court contained no specific standards for judges to apply in making their "full investigations" under the statute. Consequently, the Court attached as an appendix to its opinion a "policy memorandum" prepared by lower federal court judges which formulated criteria for waiving jurisdiction. The criteria allowed for waiver if a given offense had "prosecutive merit and if it is heinous or of an aggravated character, or — even though less serious — if it represents a pattern of repeated offenses which indicate that the juvenile may be beyond rehabilitation under

---

[6] *Id.* The Court assessed the importance of the waiver decision to Kent as follows:

> The net, therefore, is that petitioner — then a boy of 16 — was by statute entitled to certain procedures and benefits as a consequence of his statutory right to the "exclusive" jurisdiction of the Juvenile Court. In these circumstances, considering particularly that decision as to waiver of jurisdiction and transfer of the matter to the District Court was potentially as important to petitioner as the difference between five years' confinement and a death sentence, we conclude that . . . petitioner is entitled to [the enumerated procedural protections].

*Id.* at 557.

[7] *Id.* at 554. Because Kent had counsel, the Court did not find a denial of a right to counsel. The *Kent* Court specifically embraced lower court decisions requiring counsel in federal waiver proceedings. *Id.* at 561 (dictum).

[8] *Id.* at 555.

[9] *Id.* at 555–56.

Juvenile Court procedures, or if the public needs the protection afforded by such action."[10]

The *Kent* Court based its decision on its interpretation of the federal statute "read in the context of constitutional principles relating to due process."[11] Because the decision was grounded, in part at least, in federal statutory law, *Kent's* bearing on state systems of juvenile justice was somewhat uncertain. Whatever the uncertainties, however, the Court quickly took steps to clarify matters with its landmark decision, *In re Gault,*[12] handed down approximately one year after *Kent.*

## [B]  In re *Gault*

*In re Gault* marked the first major effort by the United States Supreme Court to relate constitutional principles to the juvenile justice system. The Court reviewed the constitutionality of the commitment of fifteen-year-old Gerald Gault to the Arizona State Industrial School for a period not to exceed Gault's twenty-first birthday. Gault's commitment was the result of a delinquency adjudication, conducted without procedural formality,[13] at which it was determined that he had

---

[10] *Id.* at 566. The memorandum elaborates:

> The determinative factors which will be considered by the Judge in deciding whether the Juvenile Court's jurisdiction over such offenses will be waived are the following:
> 1. The seriousness of the alleged offense to the community and whether the protection of the community requires waiver.
> 2. Whether the alleged offense was committed in an aggressive, violent, premeditated or willful manner.
> 3. Whether the alleged offense was against persons or against property, greater weight being given to offenses against persons especially if personal injury resulted.
> 4. The prospective merit of the complaint, *i.e.*, whether there is evidence upon which a Grand Jury may be expected to return an indictment (to be determined by consultation with the United States Attorney).
> 5. The desirability of trial and disposition of the entire offense in one court when the juvenile's associates in the alleged offense are adults who will be charged with a crime in the U.S. District Court for the District of Columbia.
> 6. The sophistication and maturity of the juvenile as determined by consideration of his home, environmental situation, emotional attitude and pattern of living.
> 7. The record and previous history of the juvenile, including previous contacts with the Youth Aid Division, other law enforcement agencies, juvenile courts and other jurisdictions, prior periods of probation to this Court, or prior commitments to juvenile institutions.
> 8. The prospects for adequate protection of the public and the likelihood of reasonable rehabilitation of the juvenile (if he is found to have committed the alleged offense) by the use of procedures, services and facilities currently available to the Juvenile Court.

*Id.* at 566–67.

[11] *Id.* at 557.

[12] 387 U.S. 1 (1967). The discussion of *Gault* and its progeny in this text draws from previous work of the author. *See* Gardner, *supra* § 7.02, note 10, at 823–33.

[13] After a complaint by a neighbor that Gerald Gault had made an obscene phone call, Gault was taken into custody by police. The arresting officer initiated the adjudication proceeding by filing a petition in juvenile court alleging only that Gerald Gault was "under the age of eighteen years, and is in need of the protection of this Honorable Court; [and that] said minor is a delinquent minor." 387 U.S. at 5. The petition alleged no factual basis for the judicial action proposed and was never served on Gerald or his parents. Gerald appeared without counsel at a hearing that was held on the petition. The complaining neighbor did not attend and no record of the proceedings was prepared. The juvenile judge questioned Gerald about the neighbor's complaint as related to the judge by the arresting officer to

made an obscene phone call. The Court held that Gault and others in similar situations who risk incarceration in state correction facilities if found to be delinquents are constitutionally entitled to the following rights in their adjudication proceedings: notice of the charges, assistance of counsel, rights of confrontation and cross-examination, and the protections afforded by the privilege against self-incrimination.[14]

The *Gault* Court questioned the traditional appeal to *parens patriae* as a justification for denying juveniles procedural protections in juvenile courts:

> The right of the state, as *parens patriae*, to deny to the child procedural rights available to his elders was elaborated by the assertion that a child, unlike an adult, has the right "not to liberty but to custody." He can be made to attorn to his parents, to go to school, etc. If his parents default in effectively performing their custodial functions — that is, if the child is "delinquent" — the state may intervene. In doing so, it does not deprive the child of any rights, because he has none. It merely provides the "custody" to which the child is entitled. On this basis, proceedings involving juveniles were described as "civil" not "criminal" and therefore not subject to the requirements which restrict the state when it seeks to deprive a person of his liberty.
>
> Accordingly, the highest motives and most enlightened impulses led to a peculiar system for juveniles, unknown to our law in any comparable context. The constitutional and theoretical basis for this peculiar system is — to say the least — debatable. And in practice, the results have not been entirely satisfactory.[15]

After reviewing studies showing high recidivism rates among juveniles channeled through the juvenile justice system, the Court concluded that the system had, despite the lofty motives and enlightened goals of its founders, effectively failed to attain its rehabilitative goals.[16] Not only was the system unsuccessful as a benign dispenser of rehabilitation, but the Court concluded that it might actually have become a mechanism for visiting harm upon youthful offenders by stigmatizing them as "delinquents"[17] and severely restricting their liberty.[18] Thus, the *Gault* Court found that the essentials of due process and fair treatment under the Fourteenth Amendment entitled juveniles to increased procedural protections.

The Court found that the traditional absence of procedural protections in juvenile court had resulted in systematic "arbitrariness, inaccurate findings of fact

---

whom Gault apparently had admitted making the obscene call. Six days later, at a hearing at which Gault was again unrepresented by counsel, the judge sentenced Gault to the State Industrial School "for the period of his minority [until 21], unless sooner discharged by due process of law." *Id.* at 7–8.

[14] *Id.* at 31–57. The Court chose not to rule on whether juvenile courts are required to provide transcripts of their proceedings to appealing litigants or whether juvenile proceedings are even subject to appellate review. *Id.* at 57–58. The Court did find, however, that the juvenile's parents, as well as the juvenile, are entitled to notice of the charges. *Id.* at 41.

[15] *Id.* at 17–18.

[16] *Id.* at 21–23.

[17] "[Supposedly,] one of the important benefits of the special juvenile court procedures is that they avoid classifying the juvenile as a 'criminal.' The juvenile offender is now classed as a 'delinquent.' . . . [T]his term has come to involve only slightly less stigma than the term 'criminal' applied to adults." *Id.* at 23–24.

[18] *Id.* at 27.

and unfortunate prescriptions of remedy."[19] Furthermore, the Court found that the observance of due process standards would not be inconsistent with the "substantive benefits of the juvenile process."[20] The Court added that the "commendable principles relating to the processing and treatment of juveniles separately from adults are in no way . . . affected by the procedural" protections the Court imposed.[21] In fact, the Court noted that studies suggest that "the appearance as well as the actuality of fairness, impartiality and orderlines — in short, the essentials of due process — may" actually promote the rehabilitation of the juvenile offender.[22]

By relying on the concept of fair treatment under the Due Process Clause as the basis for imposing procedural protections, the Court did not specifically find that juvenile sanctions such as those imposed upon Gerald Gault were punitive — even though such a finding would have provided an alternative basis for engrafting the *Gault* protections upon the juvenile system. The Court averted the complete criminalization of delinquency adjudications by avoiding a specific finding that confinement of juvenile delinquents constitutes punishment.[23] The more flexible "fair treatment" standard permitted the Court to impose certain procedural requirements upon the juvenile system without necessarily imposing the full panoply of Fifth, Sixth, and Eighth Amendment rights available to criminal defendants.[24] The *Gault* Court, however, deviated from the due process fairness approach by relying directly upon the Fifth Amendment and its specific application to "criminal cases" in holding that the privilege against self-incrimination applied to state delinquency adjudications.[25] The Court based its analysis of the applicability of the privilege on the view that the juvenile system is the functional equivalent of the criminal system.[26] Thus, the Court's position seems to be not that due process fairness requires the application of the privilege, but that juvenile proceedings are essentially "criminal" proceedings for purposes of the privilege.[27]

---

[19] *Id.* at 19–20.

[20] *Id.* at 21.

[21] *Id.* at 22.

[22] *Id.* at 26.

[23] Criminal defendants are afforded special procedural protections under the United States Constitution such as the right to be free from double jeopardy, the right to counsel, and the right to trial by jury. U.S. Const. amends. V and VI. The United States Supreme Court traditionally defined "criminal" proceedings in terms of the presence of a punitive sanction. G. Fletcher, Rethinking Criminal Law 409 (1978). *See* Gardner, *supra* note 12, at 797–818.

[24] *See, e.g.*, McKeiver v. Pennsylvania, 403 U.S. 528 (1971) (no right to jury trials for juveniles in delinquency adjudications). For a discussion of *McKeiver*, see *infra* notes 40–53 and accompanying text.

[25] 387 U.S. at 47–49. "[J]uvenile proceedings to determine 'delinquency,' which may lead to commitment in a state institution, must be regarded as 'criminal' for purposes of the privilege against self-incrimination." *Id.* at 49.

[26] I. Rosenberg, *The Constitutional Rights of Children Charged with Crime: Proposal for a Return to the Not So Distant Past*, 27 UCLA L. Rev. 656, 665–71 (1980).

[27] The *Gault* Court specifically noted that the privilege against self-incrimination protects values other than those values protected by due process fundamental fairness. While the latter generally speak to accurate factfinding in legal proceedings, *see* Rosenberg, *supra* note 26, at 677, "[t]he roots of the privilege are . . . far deeper. They tap the basic stream of religious and political principle because the privilege reflects the limits of the individual's attornment to the state and — in a philosophical sense — insists upon the equality of the individual and the state." 387 U.S. at 47; *see also supra* notes 25–26 and accompanying text.

Because the Court consistently has viewed the dispensation of punishment as the defining characteristic of criminal law,[28] the *Gault* Court appears to have implicitly held that the juvenile system is punitive, at least in some aspects and for some purposes. At several points in its opinion, the Court intimated that the discomfort experienced by involuntarily confined juveniles is itself sufficient to constitute a finding of punishment. Because adjudications favorable to the state often result in significant restrictions of liberty in both juvenile and adult criminal proceedings, the Court equated the two proceedings. "A proceeding where the issue is whether the child will be found to be 'delinquent' and subjected to the loss of his liberty for years is comparable in seriousness to a felony prosecution."[29] In the same vein, the Court stated,

> Ultimately, however, we confront the reality of that portion of the Juvenile Court process with which we deal in this case. A boy is charged with misconduct. The boy is committed to an institution where he may be restrained of liberty for years. It is of no constitutional consequence — and of limited practical meaning — that the institution to which he is committed is called an Industrial School. The fact of the matter is that, however euphemistic the title, a "receiving home" or an "industrial school" for juveniles is an institution of confinement in which the child is incarcerated for a greater or lesser time. His world becomes "a building with white-washed walls, regimented routine and institutional hours. . . ." Instead of mother and father and sisters and brothers and friends and classmates, his world is peopled by guards, custodians, state employees, and "delinquents" confined with him for anything from waywardness to rape and homicide.[30]

While *Gault* appears far-reaching in its implications for juvenile justice, the Court perhaps limited its holding by specifically noting that it was speaking to the "delinquency adjudication" stage of the juvenile process.[31] Thus, it is uncertain whether the *Gault* protections extend to pre- or post-adjudication delinquency proceedings or to the nondelinquency, status offense, context. Moreover, the *Gault* Court did not specify the types of deprivations of liberty that are sufficient to trigger the *Gault* procedural protections. The risk of "incarceration against one's will" clearly suffices, but the Court also suggested that any "threatened . . . deprivation of . . . liberty" may also be enough to entitle the juvenile to the *Gault* protections.[32]

Finally, the *Gault* Court offered no view regarding whether the disposition handed Gerald Gault would have been permissible had he been afforded the required procedural protections. The Court noted, however, that "if Gerald had been over 18, he would not have been subject to Juvenile Court proceedings. For the particular offense immediately involved, the maximum punishment would have been a fine of $5 to $50, or imprisonment in jail for not more than two months. Instead, he was committed to custody for a maximum of six years."[33]

---

[28] *See supra* note 23.

[29] 387 U.S. at 36.

[30] *Id.* at 27.

[31] *Id.* at 13, 27 (pre-judicial and dispositional stages of juvenile proceedings thus not necessarily touched by *Gault*).

[32] *Id.* at 50.

[33] *Id.* at 29.

# [C] *Gault's* Progeny

The Supreme Court continued to expand the protections applicable to delinquency adjudications in *In re Winship*.[34] In *Winship*, the Court held that juveniles charged in delinquency proceedings with acts that would be crimes if committed by adults are entitled as a matter of due process right to the reasonable doubt standard of proof. The Court noted that the reasonable doubt standard is constitutionally required in adult criminal cases to minimize the risks of subjecting innocent persons to the stigma and loss of liberty inherent in criminal conviction and punishment.[35] Similar risks require that the same standard be applied in delinquency proceedings. "[Judicial] intervention cannot take the form of subjecting the child to the stigma of a finding that he violated a criminal law and to the possibility of institutional confinement on proof insufficient to convict him were he an adult."[36] As in *Gault*, the *Winship* Court avoided any explicit finding that the juvenile process was punitive and, therefore, governed by the full panoply of procedural protections unique to the criminal system. Instead, the Court focused on two aspects of juvenile dispositions — the potential for stigma and the potential for severely restricting liberty — as the reasons for requiring the reasonable doubt standard.

The *Winship* Court rejected the argument that affording juveniles the protection of proof beyond a reasonable doubt would "risk destruction of beneficial aspects of the juvenile process."[37] The reasonable doubt standard would not impair "the informality, flexibility, or speed" of the hearing at which factfinding takes place.[38] Moreover, after adjudications of delinquency beyond a reasonable doubt, the opportunity during the dispositional stage of juvenile proceedings for a "wide-ranging review of the child's social history and for his individualized treatment will remain unimpaired."[39]

One year after *Winship*, the Court held in *McKeiver v. Pennsylvania*[40] that juveniles are not entitled to jury trials in adjudication hearings. The *McKeiver* Court denied this right even though the offenses involved would be criminal offenses if committed by adults[41] and the consequences of adjudications unfavorable to the juveniles entailed possible confinement in state institutions. Reasoning that neither *Gault* nor *Winship* compelled the conclusion that delinquency proceedings are "criminal prosecutions" for purposes of the Sixth Amendment right to jury trial,[42] a plurality of the Court concluded that due process fundamental fairness would not be offended if juries were excluded from the adjudication process.[43] Unlike the *Gault/Winship* rights of notice, counsel, confrontation, cross-examination and proof beyond a reasonable doubt, which all

---

[34] 397 U.S. 358 (1970).

[35] *Id.* at 363.

[36] *Id.* at 367.

[37] *Id.* at 366.

[38] *Id.*

[39] *Id.*

[40] 403 U.S. 528 (1971).

[41] *McKeiver* and its companion cases concerned a variety of criminal conduct ranging from robbery and assault to willfully impeding traffic and making riotous noise. *Id.* at 534–36.

[42] "[T]he juvenile court proceeding has not yet been held to be a 'criminal prosecution' within the meaning of the Sixth Amendment." *Id.* at 541.

[43] Justices Blackmun, Stewart, and White, and Chief Justice Burger comprised the plurality. Justice

emphasize accurate factfinding, the plurality found that juries are not necessary to achieve that interest.[44] Moreover, juries in juvenile cases might actually be counterproductive. "If the jury trial were to be injected into the juvenile court system as a matter of right, it would bring with it the traditional delay, the formality, and the clamor of the public trial,"[45] possibly resulting in an "effective end to what has been the idealistic prospect of an intimate, informal, protective proceeding."[46] If these consequences were to befall the juvenile courts "there [would be] little need for [their] separate existence."[47]

The plurality refused to see juvenile justice as a complete failure and totally unable to accomplish its rehabilitative goals.[48] Finding that the system still holds "promise," the plurality felt that imposing jury trials would impede the ability of the states "to experiment further and seek in new and different ways the elusive answers to the problems of the young."[49] Moreover, the plurality observed that past abuses in juvenile justice "relate to the lack of resources and of dedication rather than to inherent unfairness."[50]

Noticeably absent from the *McKeiver* plurality's discussion was any attempt to explain *Gault's* application of the privilege against self-incrimination to delinquency adjudications.[51] By failing to list the privilege among the other *Gault/ Winship* rights, all of which were fundamental fairness requirements to achieve "accurate factfinding," the plurality apparently recognized that the theoretical underpinnings of the privilege rested neither in a concern for accurate factfinding nor in a notion of fundamental fairness.[52] The *McKeiver* plurality, like the *Gault*

---

Harlan concurred in the judgment and filed a separate opinion. Justice Brennan concurred in part and dissented in part. Justices Douglas, Black, and Marshall dissented.

[44] 403 U.S. at 543. The plurality discounted arguments that juries are necessary in juvenile actions because judges as fact-finders routinely have access to prejudicial material.

> Concern about the inapplicability of exclusionary and other rules of evidence, about the juvenile court judge's possible awareness of the juvenile's prior record and of the contents of the social file; about repeated appearances of the same familiar witnesses in the persons of juvenile and probation officers and social workers — all to the effect that this will create the likelihood of pre-judgment — chooses to ignore it seems to us, every aspect of fairness, of concern, of sympathy, and of paternal attention that the juvenile court system contemplates.

*Id.* at 550.

[45] *Id.*

[46] *Id.* at 545.

[47] *Id.* at 551. The dissent pointed out that juries in juvenile cases might actually promote the system's rehabilitative aims. "The child who feels that he has been dealt with fairly and not merely expediently or as speedily as possible will be a better prospect for rehabilitation." *Id.* at 566 (Douglas, J., dissenting).

[48] *Id.* at 547.

[49] *Id.*

[50] *Id.* at 547–48.

[51] The plurality apparently did not see *Gault's* inclusion of the privilege against self-incrimination as grounded in due process. "Due process [in *Gault*] was held to embrace adequate written notice; advice as to the right to counsel, retained or appointed; confrontation; and cross-examination. The privilege against self-incrimination was also held available to the juvenile." *Id.* at 532. At another point in the opinion, the plurality did not mention the privilege when discussing the due process dimensions of *Gault* and *Winship*. "As that standard [fundamental fairness] was applied in those two cases, we have an emphasis on factfinding procedures. The requirements of notice, counsel, confrontation, cross-examination, and standard of proof naturally flowed from this emphasis." *Id.* at 543.

[52] *Supra* notes 27, 51.

majority, apparently saw juvenile adjudications as functionally equivalent to criminal cases within the meaning of the Fifth Amendment itself. Apart from suggestions that juries might be counterproductive in the juvenile system — an argument which might be made with similar force against *Gault's* extension of the privilege against self-incrimination to juvenile defendants[53] — the plurality left unexplained why the system is characterized as criminal for purposes of the Fifth Amendment privilege but not for the Sixth Amendment right to jury trial.

In *Breed v. Jones*,[54] the Supreme Court held that the Fifth Amendment's Double Jeopardy Clause prohibits the trial of juveniles in criminal court if they have been subjected previously to a delinquency hearing on the same charge. Jeopardy describes "the risk that is traditionally associated with a criminal prosecution."[55] Indeed, "the risk to which the term jeopardy refers is that traditionally associated with 'actions intended to authorize criminal punishment.' "[56] In assessing delinquency adjudications in terms of such risks, the Court stated:

> [I]t is simply too late in the day to conclude . . . that a juvenile is not put in jeopardy at a proceeding whose object is to determine whether he has committed acts that violate a criminal law and whose potential consequences include both the stigma inherent in such a determination and the deprivation of liberty for many years.[57]

Thus, "in terms of potential consequences, there is little to distinguish an adjudicatory hearing such as was held in this case from a traditional criminal prosecution."[58] Both proceedings are designed "to vindicate [the] very vital interest in enforcement of criminal laws."[59] The Court concluded, therefore, that the juvenile respondent was put in jeopardy at the delinquency adjudication hearing,[60] and was protected from twice being subjected to the "anxiety and heavy personal strain" inherent in the trial process.[61]

The Court's analysis in *Breed* does not refer to the fundamental fairness standard employed in *Gault, Winship,* and *McKeiver.* Instead, the case rests entirely on the conclusion that delinquency dispositions are the functional equivalents of criminal punishments and are thus governed by the Fifth Amendment ban against double jeopardy.

The *Breed* Court maintained that its holding did not significantly interfere with the ability of juvenile systems to waive jurisdiction to criminal court. Such waivers are permissible under *Breed* so long as the waiver proceeding precedes juvenile court adjudication of the offense.[62] Because waiver hearings are not proceedings at

---

[53] Justice Harlan made this argument in his concurring opinion in *In re Gault*, 387 U.S. 1, 74–77 (1967) (Harlan, J., concurring).

[54] 421 U.S. 519 (1975).

[55] *Id.* at 528.

[56] *Id.* at 530.

[57] *Id.*

[58] *Id.*

[59] *Id.*

[60] *Id.*

[61] *Id.* at 531.

[62] *Id.*

which "jeopardy" attaches, juveniles are not twice placed in jeopardy by being subjected to a waiver hearing and subsequent criminal trial or juvenile court adjudication.[63]

In considering the double jeopardy implications of delinquency adjudications, the *Breed* Court, similar to its predecessor in *Gault*, expressed disillusionment with the ability of juvenile justice to achieve its aims, noting that "there is a gap between the benign conception of the system and its realities."[64] These concerns notwithstanding, the Court, similar to the *McKeiver* plurality, reaffirmed a modicum of hope for the system: "That the system has fallen short of the high expectations of its sponsors in no way detracts from the broad social benefits sought or from those benefits that can survive constitutional scrutiny."[65]

## [D]  Summary

With the exception of *McKeiver*, the Supreme Court's juvenile justice cases take a skeptical look at *parens patriae* as a basis for state deprivations of young people's liberty. *Kent, Gault, Winship,* and *Breed* may all be read to recognize the rights of young people to be treated as persons under the Constitution, at least in the context of delinquency adjudications. On the other hand, *McKeiver* appears to assess juvenile rights in terms of protectionist principles, allowing the state to make judges, rather than juries, the fact-finders in delinquency cases in an effort to effectuate the rehabilitation of juvenile offenders. Moreover, to the extent that procedural protections can be viewed as conducive to rehabilitation,[66] the Court's cases granting such protections may be at home with protectionist principles.

At a more technical level, *McKeiver* is difficult to reconcile with *Breed* and the privilege against self-incrimination analysis of *Gault*. If juvenile justice is punitive and thus the functional equivalent of the criminal law for purposes of the Fifth Amendment (the privilege in *Gault*[67] and the double jeopardy ban in *Breed*[68]), why not also for the Sixth Amendment right to trial by jury in *McKeiver? McKeiver* may perhaps be distinguished from *Gault* and *Breed* because, unlike the rights recognized in those two cases, the *McKeiver* plurality opined that jury trials may frustrate whatever rehabilitative potential the juvenile justice system possesses. Moreover, *Breed* and *McKeiver* may be further distinguished in light of the fact that *Breed* arose through a challenge to a state criminal conviction and thus was not a true "delinquency" case after the state had abandoned its rehabilitative efforts and relinquished the juvenile to the criminal system.[69] On the other hand, *McKeiver* took place entirely within the "rehabilitative" juvenile court context.

---

[63] *Id.* In a later case, *Swisher v. Brady*, 438 U.S. 204 (1978), the Court upheld against double jeopardy attack a state procedure permitting the state to file exceptions with the juvenile court to proposed findings and recommendations made by a master of that court even if the master proposed a finding of nondelinquency or recommended a lenient disposition. The procedure at issue in *Swisher* permitted the juvenile court judge to act only on the basis of the record made before the master unless the parties agreed to permit additional evidence. The Court found that such a procedure is analogous to the common and permissible procedure in criminal cases where evidence is presented and recorded in proceedings conducted by one not authorized to declare guilt.

[64] 421 U.S. at 528.

[65] *Id.* at 529.

[66] *See supra* note 22 and accompanying text.

[67] *See supra* notes 25–30 and accompanying text.

[68] *See supra* text accompanying note 61.

[69] Rosenberg, *supra* note 26, at 681.

The Court's cases, from *Kent* to *Breed*, illustrate that the juvenile system reflects a mixture of rehabilitative and punitive elements. As the cases suggest, and as will be explored at various points throughout the remainder of this book, to the extent the system is punitive, important constitutional consequences follow.

# Chapter 8
# JURISDICTION

## § 8.01 OVERVIEW

Early juvenile justice theory drew no distinction between offending and victimized children.[1] *Parens patriae* provided the conceptual justification for coercive court actions for both neglected and criminal children.[2]

These original jurisdictional grounds are retained in many juvenile court systems where courts hear child neglect and abuse cases as well as cases alleging that a child is "in need of supervision" or has committed either a criminal or status offense.[3] This book addressed the issues of neglect and abuse in earlier chapters[4] and will not revisit those matters here. Attention instead will be limited to juvenile court jurisdiction over delinquency (acts by minors that would be criminal if committed by adults)[5] and status offenses (offenses such as truancy and running away that are prohibited only for children and status conditions such as being "wayward" or "in need of supervision" that trigger judicial intervention).[6]

Early in the juvenile court movement, the distinction between the concepts of delinquency and status offense carried little legal importance. Recently, however, as the United States Supreme Court has addressed delinquency adjudications,[7] the distinction has taken on constitutional significance.[8] Moreover, it is now common for legislatures and courts to draw a variety of distinctions between the processing of delinquency and status offense cases.[9] In light of these considerations, it is useful to separately examine the delinquency and status offense categories. Before attending to these categories, however, the relevance of age as a jurisdictional issue will be discussed.

---

[1] Fox, *supra* § 7.02, note 15, at 1192–93.

[2] *Id.*

[3] Davis, *supra* § 2.02, note 9, at 2-12.

[4] *See supra* § 3.03 &Chapter 4.

[5] Davis, *supra* note 3, at 2-14.

[6] *Id.* at 2-12, 2-13.

[7] *See supra* § 7.03.

[8] Davis, *supra* note 3, at 2-15.

[9] *Id.*

## § 8.02  AGE

### [A]  Maximum Age

#### [1]  Generally

All juvenile court systems establish a maximum age below which children are deemed subject to the ameliorative processes of the court.[1] Generally, the age, usually eighteen,[2] is the same for delinquency or status offense jurisdiction.[3] Some states set the age at seventeen,[4] while a few lower it to sixteen, at least for cases of alleged delinquency.[5]

#### [2]  Gender Distinctions

Historically, some states drew statutory age distinctions based on gender, setting a higher jurisdictional age for females than for males.[6] The justification for such statutes, to the extent any was ever provided,[7] rested on the view that because young women face the risk of pregnancy throughout their post-pubescent lives, the state has an interest in extending the protective cloak of juvenile court jurisdiction to females until well into their adolescence in order to avoid the evils of out-of-wedlock pregnancies and births.[8] Such a rationale provided little explanation of why young men were excluded from the benefits of juvenile court jurisdiction at a younger age.

Not surprisingly, the courts have invalidated statutes setting different jurisdictional ages for males and females. Thus, the Tenth Circuit Court of Appeals struck down as violative of equal protection an Oklahoma statute that set the jurisdictional age at sixteen for males and eighteen for females.[9] The court found the gender distinction without rational explanation, rejecting the state's claim that the statute permissibly reflected "demonstrated facts of life," the meaning and content of which completely escaped the court. Likewise, the New York Court of Appeals struck down a New York statute containing an age-sex distinction[10] similar to that invalidated in the Oklahoma case. The New York Court found no basis for imposing juvenile court jurisdiction for girls until age eighteen while eliminating it at sixteen for boys. "Girls in that age bracket are no more prone than boys to truancy, disobedience, incorrigible conduct and the like, nor are they more

---

[1] Davis, *supra* § 2.02, note 9, at 2-1.

[2] R, Mnookin & D. Weisberg, Child, Family, and State: Problems and Materials on Children and the Law 761 (2005).

[3] Davis, *supra* note 1, at 2-1. *But see* Vt. Stat. Ann. tit. 33, § 5502(a)(1) (2001) (setting jurisdictional age at 16 for delinquent children, but at age 18 for children in need of supervision).

[4] *See, e.g.*, Ga. Code Ann. § 15-11-2(2)(A), (C) (Harrison 2001).

[5] *See, e.g.*, Conn. Gen. Stat. Ann. § 46b-120 (West Supp. 2000).

[6] 2 D. Kramer, Legal Rights of Children 313 (2d rev. ed. 2005).

[7] See the discussion of *Lamb v. Brown*, 456 F.2d 18 (10th Cir. 1972), *infra* note 9 and the accompanying text.

[8] *See* Patricia A. v. City of New York, 286 N.E.2d 432 (N.Y. 1972), discussed *infra* notes 10-12 and accompanying text.

[9] Lamb v. Brown, 456 F.2d 18 (10th Cir. 1972).

[10] Patricia A. v. City of New York, 286 N.E.2d 432 (N.Y. 1972).

in need of rehabilitation and treatment by reason of such conduct."[11] Moreover, the court rejected arguments that the risk of pregnancy supported setting an older jurisdictional age for females than males:

> The argument that discrimination against females on the basis of age is justified because of the obvious danger of pregnancy in an immature girl and because of out-of-wedlock births which add to the welfare relief burdens of the State and city is without merit. It is enough to say that the contention completely ignores the fact that the statute covers far more than acts of sexual misconduct. But, beyond that, even if we were to assume that the legislation had been prompted by such considerations, there would have been no rational basis for exempting, from [juvenile court jurisdiction], the 16 and 17-year-old boy responsible for the girl's pregnancy or the out-of-wedlock birth. As it is, the conclusion seems inescapable that lurking behind the discrimination is the imputation that females who engage in misconduct, sexual or otherwise, ought more to be censured, and their conduct subject to greater control and regulation, than males.[12]

The United States Supreme Court has never considered the constitutionality of rules setting different jurisdictional ages for girls than for boys. However, a plurality of the Court has suggested that statutes similar to those struck down in the Oklahoma and New York cases might be constitutional as attempts to address the problem of pregnancy if the state criminally punished males, exempted from juvenile court jurisdiction, for the male-only crime of statutory rape. The plurality observed: "Because virtually all of the significant harmful and inescapably identifiable consequences of teenage pregnancy fall on the young female, a legislature acts well within its statutory authority when it elects to punish only the [male] participant who, by nature, suffers none of the consequences of his conduct."[13] The plurality further supported this view by noting that the risk of pregnancy itself constitutes a deterrence to young females while the criminal sanction imposed solely on males arguably provides an equalizing deterrent.[14]

## [3]   Age at the Time of Offense or at the Commencement of Proceedings?

All juvenile justice systems grant jurisdiction to juvenile courts to hear cases of minors who commit offenses and are proceeded against while under the specified jurisdictional age.[15] However, in cases where the offender commits an offense while a juvenile but is not proceeded against until after he has reached the age of

---

[11] *Id.* at 434–35.

[12] *Id.* at 435. *See also* People v. Ellis, 311 N.E.2d 98 (Ill. 1974) (gender discrimination in juvenile court act struck down on state constitutional grounds). For a discussion of sexual bias in juvenile justice generally, see S. Davis & S. Chaires, *Equal Protection for Juveniles: The Present Status of Sex-Based Discrimination in Juvenile Court Law,* 7 Ga. L. Rev. 494 (1973); S. Kedia, *Creating an Adolescent Criminal Class: Juvenile Court Jurisdiction Over Status Offenders,* 5 Cardozo Pub. L. Pol'y & Ethics J. 543, 552 (2007); K. Taylor-Thompson, *Girl Talk — Examining Racial and Gender Lines in Juvenile Justice,* 6 Nev. L.J. 1137 (2006). See also the discussion of the issue of sex discrimination in the application of status offense jurisdiction, *infra* § 8.04, notes 11-16 and the accompanying text.

[13] Michael M. v. Superior Court, 450 U.S. 464, 473 (1981).

[14] *Id.*

[15] Fox, *supra* note 2, at 33–37.

majority, the jurisdictions split; some deny juvenile court jurisdiction[16] and others permit it to extend beyond the jurisdictional age.

In the states that permit actions against offenders beyond the jurisdictional age, some statutes specifically authorize such proceedings, but specify the maximum age above which juvenile court jurisdiction finally terminates. For example, Texas sets its jurisdictional age at seventeen but permits juvenile court proceedings against persons "under eighteen years of age" who commit offenses "before becoming seventeen years of age."[17] The Juvenile Justice Standards set the jurisdictional age at seventeen but permit juvenile proceedings to be brought against persons "not more than twenty years of age" who have committed offenses under the age of seventeen.[18] Some states that permit juvenile actions to be brought against persons older than the general cut-off age do so through judicial construction of statutes that do not specifically speak to the issue.[19] Other state statutes appear to embrace open-ended juvenile court jurisdiction for any person committing an act of delinquency while under the jurisdictional age.[20] In interpreting such statutes, the courts sometimes, nevertheless, deny jurisdiction to persons who at the time proceedings are initiated are well over the age of majority but who were minors at the time of their offense.[21]

Some courts have denied jurisdiction to criminal courts in situations where prosecutors purposely delay bringing criminal proceedings until such time as the defendant reaches the age of majority.[22] In such a situation, some cases require a remand to juvenile court with the possibility of waiver of the proceedings back to criminal court.[23] Other courts suggest that in situations of purposeful prosecutorial delay so as to invoke criminal court jurisdiction, the case need not be transferred to juvenile court but may simply be dismissed because of failure to adhere to the defendant's right to a speed trial.[24]

---

[16] Davis, *supra* note 3, at 2-8 to 2-12.

[17] Tex. Fam. Code Ann. § 51.02(2)(A), (B) (West 1996).

[18] Institute of Judicial Admin. & American Bar Ass'n, Juvenile Justice Standards, Juvenile Delinquency and Sanctions 14 (1980).

[19] *See, e.g.,* People v. Taylor, 391 N.E.2d 366 (Ill. 1979) (court interprets statutes defining "delinquents" as juveniles committing criminal acts "prior to their 17th birthday" and "minors" as "persons under the age of 21" thereby permitting juvenile court jurisdiction over a person who is 16 when he commits crimes but 17 when juvenile proceedings were initiated).

[20] *See, e.g., In re* Braswell, 294 So. 2d 896 (La. Ct. App. 1974) (interpreting statute granting juvenile court jurisdiction over "child[ren]," defined as "person[s] over 17 . . . who commit acts of delinquency before attaining the age of 17 years," court permits jurisdiction in case of 17-year-old who committed acts of delinquency while under the age of 17). Note, however, that juvenile courts do not have jurisdiction to impose dispositions upon individuals who have reached the age of majority. *Id.*

[21] *See, e.g.,* Application of Johnson, 178 F. Supp. 155 (D.N.J. 1957) (age 27 is beyond juvenile jurisdiction).

[22] *See, e.g.,* State v. Scurlock, 593 P.2d 1159 (Or. 1979).

[23] *Id.*

[24] *See In re* S.V., 296 N.W.2d 404 (Minn. 1980) (dicta).

## [B]   Minimum Age

Most juvenile statutes do not specify a minimum jurisdictional age.[25] As discussed in Chapter 7,[26] the common law infancy defense, still available to children who are tried in adult criminal court,[27] imposed immunity from jurisdiction for children under age seven. Some jurisdictions follow the common law rule for delinquency jurisdiction,[28] some have lowered the age,[29] and others have raised it.[30] Some jurisdictions specify a minimum age for delinquency cases but impose no limit for status offense jurisdiction.[31] On the other hand, some states perceive the juvenile justice system as a protective civil law alternative to the criminal system and thus deny the infancy defense in juvenile proceedings. Because the infancy defense provides a mechanism for avoiding unjust punishment,[32] it is thought to have no place in, and may actually frustrate the purposes of, a system aimed at helping troubled youth whatever their age.[33] Thus, some states embracing such views appear to impose no minimum age for juvenile court jurisdiction.[34]

---

[25] Fox, *supra* note 2, at 28. States uniformly impose no minimum age for juvenile court jurisdiction over neglected and abused children. *Id.* at 27; *see supra* § 3.03 & Chapter 4.

[26] *See supra* § 7.02[A].

[27] *See, e.g.*, State v. S.P., 746 P.2d 813 (Wash. App. 1987) (statutory presumption of incapacity of children over eight but less than twelve rebutted by clear and convincing evidence that ten-year-old charged with taking indecent liberties understood the wrongfulness of his conduct), *rev'd on other grounds*, 756 P.2d 1315 (Wash. 1988). Note that Washington has statutorily modified the common law presumption of incapacity applicable to children between seven and fourteen. *See supra* § 7.02, notes 5-8 and accompanying text.

[28] *See, e.g.*, Mass. Gen. Laws Ann. ch. 119, § 52 (West 1993) ("delinquent child" is a child between seven and seventeen who commits a criminal offense).

[29] *See, e.g.*, N.C. Gen. Stat. § 7B-1501(7),(27)(a) (2001) (age six is minimum age for juveniles alleged to be delinquent or undisciplined).

[30] *See, e.g.*, Tex. Fam. Code Ann. § 51.02(2)(A) (1996) (age ten is minimum age).

[31] *See, e.g.*, N.Y. Fam. Ct. Act §§ 301.2(1), 712(a) (McKinney Supp. 2002) (setting minimum age at seven for delinquency jurisdiction but setting no minimum for "persons in need of supervision").

[32] *See supra* § 7.02.

[33] *See, e.g.*, *In re* Tyvonne M., 558 A.2d 661, 666 (Conn. 1989) (common law presumption of incapacity of children between seven and fourteen not applicable in delinquency proceedings); State v. D.H., 340 So. 2d 1163 (Fla. 1976) (common law presumption of incapacity inapplicable in juvenile court proceedings).

[34] *See, e.g.*, *In re* Dow, 393 N.E.2d 1346 (Ill. App. Ct. 1979) (statutory provision imposing immunity from criminal prosecution for children under age thirteen (raised from common law standard of age seven) not applicable to eleven and nine-year-old juveniles charged with acts of delinquency in juvenile court). *See also supra* note 33.

While cases involving very young children committing delinquent acts are rare, a California case raised the prospects of a six-year-old being adjudicated a delinquent. A petition was filed in juvenile court charging the boy with the attempted murder of a 5-week-old infant (later reduced to assault with intent to injure and trespassing) after he and two 8-year-old boys allegedly entered a neighbor's home, tried to steal a tricycle, and beat the infant with fists and a stick. Believing that the boy suffered from mental problems that precluded his competency to stand trial, the juvenile court referee suspended the proceedings while the boy underwent intensive counselling. Star Tribune (Minneapolis-St. Paul), July 12, 1996, at 13A; *All Things Considered: Trial of 6-Year-Old Raises Questions About Development* (NPR radio broadcast May 8, 1996). It is not uncommon for children under age six to commit acts of arson even though delinquency proceedings are rarely pursued. L. Montgomery Knight, *In 1994: 110,000 Children Under 13 Arrested for Felonies*, Roanoke Times & World News, April 28, 1996, at 1. For a

Age factors also sometimes surface even after a juvenile court has properly asserted initial jurisdiction over a young person. The age of the juvenile is relevant and sometimes decisive when deciding whether or not to waive jurisdiction to criminal court. Furthermore, in juvenile court delinquency adjudications, the applicability of the common law presumption of incapacity of juveniles between the ages of seven and fourteen has become a controversial matter. These issues are considered in later sections of this book discussing waiver proceedings and substantive defenses in delinquency adjudications.[35]

## § 8.03  DELINQUENCY

Juvenile courts have jurisdiction over "delinquent" conduct.[1] In the early days of the juvenile court movement, the term "delinquency" was often used broadly to describe not only criminal misbehavior but also any form of misconduct that reflected negatively on the child's physical, mental, and moral well-being.[2] Most modern juvenile codes, however, limit the use of the concept of delinquency to describe conduct in violation of state, federal, or local law.[3] The "delinquency" classification thus operates as a supposedly less stigmatic euphemism for criminal conduct while at the same time functions to differentiate and destigmatize noncriminal, status offense, jurisdiction.[4]

Some jurisdictions continue to include noncriminal misbehavior within the term "delinquency." Texas, for example, defines "delinquent conduct" to include "conduct other than a traffic offense that violates a penal law" as well as conduct that violates conditions of probation.[5] Probation violators who have not committed criminal acts have argued that the statute discriminates against them in violation of the Equal Protection Clause. However, the Texas courts have rejected this argument and held the statute constitutional.[6]

Unlike the Texas model, other state statutes specifically preclude findings of delinquency in cases where a minor violates conditions of probation initially imposed for a noncriminal status offense.[7] Such provisions thus prevent "bootstrapping" a finding of "delinquency" without first establishing the commission of a criminal act.

Finally, some jurisdictions do not specifically employ the term "delinquency" in defining juvenile court jurisdiction. Nebraska, for example, provides for jurisdiction over any juvenile who commits a "misdemeanor," other than a "traffic offense," or an "act which would constitute a felony under the laws of this state."[8]

---

discussion of age issues in juvenile justice, see S. Davis, *The Jurisdictional Dilemma of the Juvenile Court*, 51 N.C. L. Rev. 195 (1972).

[35] *See infra* § 8.03, notes 9-22 and accompanying text & § 9.05[A].

[1] Davis, *supra* § 2.02, note 9, at 2-14.

[2] *Id.*

[3] *Id.*

[4] *Id.*

[5] The Texas statutes permit probation as a disposition for status offenses such as truancy and running away from home as well as for criminal violations. Tex. Fam. Code Ann. §§ 51.03(a), (b), 54.04 (West 1996). It is thus theoretically possible for a juvenile on probation for a status offense to subsequently be found "delinquent" for merely violating a condition of probation.

[6] *In re* D.L.S., 520 S.W.2d 442 (Tex. Civ. App. 1975).

[7] *See, e.g.*, Fla. Stat. Ann. § 985.03(9) (West Supp. 2000).

[8] Neb. Rev. Stat. § 43-247 (Reissue 1998).

## [A] Exclusive Jurisdiction

Although juvenile justice is premised on the theory that youthful offenders should be dealt with outside the criminal system, minors committing criminal acts do not necessarily avoid criminal court. In some states, juvenile courts have exclusive jurisdiction over some crimes, generally misdemeanors, committed by minors regardless of their age.[9] Some of these states subject juveniles accused of felony offenses, or certain specified felonies, to possible waiver to criminal court[10] regardless of the age of the juvenile.[11] The remainder of these states permit waivers of juvenile court jurisdiction only if the minor charged with a felony has reached a certain age.[12] Some statutes also preclude waivers of first time offenders.[13]

Other states afford original jurisdiction to juvenile courts over all cases alleging criminal activity by a minor but, because of statutory provisions permitting waivers to criminal court regardless of the crime, deny exclusive juvenile court jurisdiction over any specific category of crime.[14] In some such states, waivers are limited to juveniles who have reached a certain age,[15] but other states permit waivers regardless of age.[16]

In yet another group of states, statutes grant exclusive jurisdiction to criminal courts in cases where minors are charged with designated offenses, generally serious felonies.[17] Some such statutes impose age minimums, as low as age thirteen.[18] Some statutes limit exclusive criminal jurisdiction to minors who have a record of prior convictions.[19] Finally, some statutes impose original jurisdiction over certain offenses in criminal court, but permit transfers to juvenile court in certain circumstances.[20]

## [B] Concurrent Jurisdiction

In a few jurisdictions, prosecutors have authority to commence certain cases in either juvenile or criminal court. Nebraska, for example, specifies concurrent jurisdiction over juveniles charged with felonies, juveniles who are sixteen or seventeen and charged with misdemeanors other than traffic offenses, and

---

[9] See, *e.g.*, the Alabama and Colorado provisions described in Feld, *supra* § 2.02, note 12, at 505.

[10] For examples of states permitting waivers in all felony cases, see the Alabama and Colorado models. *Id.* Other states, Maine, Montana, and New Jersey for example, permit waivers only in cases of certain specified felonies. *Id.* at 506.

[11] See, *e.g.*, the New Hampshire and Oklahoma provisions (waivers permitted in any felony case with no age minimum). *Id.* Where statutes do not specify a minimum age for criminal prosecution, the common law infancy doctrine would arguably exempt children under age seven from prosecution.

[12] The ages range from 12 in Montana to as high as 16 in a number of jurisdictions. *Id.*

[13] See, *e.g.*, the Massachusetts provisions. *Id.* at 506, 508 n.10.

[14] This appears to be the model favored in nearly a majority of jurisdictions. *Id.* at 505–7.

[15] See, *e.g.*, the California and Idaho provisions which limit waivers to children over age 16 and 14 respectively. *Id.* at 505.

[16] See, *e.g.*, the Alaska and Arizona provisions. *Id.*

[17] See, *e.g.*, the Illinois and New York provisions. *Id.* at 512–13.

[18] *Id.*

[19] *Id.* at 511–13.

[20] See, *e.g.*, the discussion of the Maryland provisions in Davis, *supra* note 1, at 2-18, 2-23, 2-24.

juveniles charged with traffic offenses.[21] Under the Nebraska statutes, in cases originating in criminal court, jurisdiction is not exclusive since provisions permit waiver of jurisdiction to juvenile court.[22] Other models grant concurrent jurisdiction over a smaller category of cases. In the District of Columbia, for example, the United States Attorney has discretion to bring cases involving certain enumerated felonies in either juvenile or criminal court.[23]

## [C]  Waivers of Jurisdiction

As the above discussion suggests, juvenile court jurisdiction throughout the United States takes on a variety of forms and interacts in a variety of ways with the criminal justice system. To understand this interaction, it is useful to examine in some detail the mechanisms for "waiving" jurisdiction from one system to the other. Because the juvenile justice movement historically assumed that the vast majority of juvenile crime cases would be dealt with in juvenile court, traditionally juvenile courts in the overwhelming majority of states possessed original jurisdiction over delinquency cases with juvenile judges empowered to waive certain cases to criminal court.[24] This traditional model has been altered in many jurisdictions, however, by a recent legislative movement toward restricting judicial discretion in order to encourage the removal of certain cases from juvenile court. Some statutes go further and deny judicial discretion altogether by legislatively placing certain categories of juvenile crime exclusively within the jurisdiction of the criminal court.

## [1]  Judicial Waivers

In virtually all jurisdictions, the most prevalent method for transferring juvenile offenders from juvenile to criminal court is the judicial waiver model wherein a juvenile court judge decides whether a particular youngster should remain in the juvenile system or be sent to adult court.[25] As the previous discussion of *Kent v. United States*[26] suggests, juvenile judges traditionally possessed broad discretion, sometimes with few or no guidelines, in making waiver decisions. Where legislatures do specify guidelines, they generally adopt criteria similar to those approved by the *Kent* Court.[27]

Faced with the perception of an increasing rate of violent juvenile crime, legislatures in a majority of states have, since 1970, amended their statutes in hopes of structuring judicial discretion. These statutes specify the minimum level of offense for which waiver can operate or prescribe special handling in particular cases after reviewing the category of offense and the juvenile's prior record.[28] Some jurisdictions effectively create a presumption in favor of waiving cases in the

---

[21]  Neb. Rev. Stat. § 43-247 (Reissue 1998).

[22]  *Id.* § 43-261. Nebraska does not allow for waivers from juvenile to criminal court.

[23]  D.C. Code Ann. § 16-2301(3)(A) (2001). See the discussion of the statute in *United States v. Bland*, *infra* notes 37-39 and accompanying text.

[24]  A few states employing concurrent jurisdiction systems deviated from this original jurisdiction model, at least for some crimes. *See supra* notes 21-23 and accompanying text.

[25]  Feld, *supra* note 9, at 488.

[26]  *See supra* § 7.03[A], notes 1-10 and accompanying text.

[27]  Feld, *supra* note 9, at 490. Waiver proceedings and the substantive criteria applied therein are discussed *infra* § 9.05.

[28]  Feld, *supra* note 9, at 503–4. The Juvenile Justice Standards propose a model limiting waivers to

designated categories by placing the burden on the youth charged with such offense to prove that he is a fit candidate for the juvenile system.[29] Other jurisdictions apply no explicit presumptions but mandate hearings in all cases where a youth allegedly has committed an offense within the category specified by the statute.[30] Some jurisdictions go so far as requiring transfers to criminal court once the juvenile judge is satisfied that there is probable cause to believe that the juvenile has committed a designated offense.[31] On the other hand, statutes in roughly half the states permit juvenile judges to waive any offense, regardless of its seriousness.[32]

## [2] Legislative Waivers

Some legislatures have taken the matter out of the hands of juvenile court judges altogether by statutorily placing certain cases involving serious offenses within the exclusive jurisdiction of the criminal courts.[33] Such statutes effectively remove or "waive" jurisdiction over cases formerly heard in juvenile court and place them within the jurisdiction of the criminal justice system. Many jurisdictions supplement such statutes with judicial waiver statutes that permit judges the authority to waive jurisdiction to criminal court for offenses that are not statutorily excluded.[34]

Some jurisdictions exclude from juvenile court jurisdiction only youths who commit offenses punishable by death or life imprisonment. Others exclude juveniles committing other serious offenses such as sexual assault, armed robbery, or kidnapping.[35] Some states exclude juveniles charged with repeat offenses.[36]

Legislative waiver models have been challenged for failing to provide the procedural protections of *Kent*. Statutory exclusions of juvenile court jurisdiction preclude individualized judicial hearings to determine the propriety of subjecting particular juveniles to the jurisdiction of the criminal courts. In a leading federal case,[37] the Court of Appeals for the District of Columbia Circuit upheld post-*Kent* amendments to the District of Columbia juvenile code which effectively removed from juvenile court jurisdiction minors between the ages of sixteen and eighteen charged with murder, forcible rape, burglary in the first degree, armed robbery or assault with intent to commit any such offense.[38] The statute required that such offenses be brought in criminal court and thus avoided the individualized waiver hearing required by *Kent*. The court distinguished *Kent*, finding it applicable only to statutory models placing original jurisdiction in juvenile courts with possible judicial waiver to criminal court. To require a hearing on the merits of the

---

fifteen-, sixteen-, or seventeen-year-olds who commit a crime punishable by death, life imprisonment, or by five or more years imprisonment. Institute of Judicial Admin. & American Bar Ass'n, Juvenile Justice Standards, Transfer Between Courts 10, 27–28 (1980).

[29] Feld, *supra* note 9, at 508–9.

[30] *Id.* at 508.

[31] *Id.*

[32] *Id.* at 504–7. The procedures and criteria for judicial waivers are considered in detail *infra* § 9.05.

[33] Feld, *supra* note 9, at 511–14.

[34] *Id.* at 511.

[35] *Id.* at 511–14.

[36] *Id.*

[37] United States v. Bland, 472 F.2d 1329 (D.C. Cir. 1972), *cert. denied*, 412 U.S. 909 (1973).

[38] *Id.* at 1331.

prosecutorial decision to charge one of the offenses statutorily relegated to criminal court would offend longstanding separation of powers principles. Moreover, the court found the legislative exclusions from juvenile court jurisdiction to be a constitutionally permissible response to "the rise in the number of serious crimes committed by those 16 years of age and over coupled with a growing recidivist rate among that group."[39] Numerous state courts have upheld legislative waiver statutes attacked as violating procedural due process under *Kent*.[40]

In addition to procedural due process challenges, legislative waivers have also been challenged as creating arbitrary legislative classifications in violation of the Equal Protection Clause. The courts have uniformly rejected such arguments.[41]

## [a]   Statutes Excluding Gang Activity

The problem of youth street gangs has precipitated recent legislation in some states that excludes gang activity from juvenile court jurisdiction. Such statutes may become increasingly attractive if legislators perceive a continuing increase in crime associated with gang activity.[42]

In 1988, California passed the Street Terrorism Enforcement and Protection Act (STEP), becoming the first state to enact a special criminal statute aimed at street gangs.[43] While the California STEP Act was scheduled to remain in effect only through 1996,[44] other states have enacted legislation that generally follows the California model.[45] Although some statutes in the past specifically employed age criterion in defining "gang members,"[46] apparently no jurisdiction presently includes age provisions in their definitions. Clearly, however, all the statutes are

---

[39]   *Id.* at 1334.

[40]   *See, e.g.,* People v. Sprinkle, 307 N.E.2d 161 (Ill. 1974), *cert. denied,* 417 U.S. 935 (1974); Jackson v. State, 311 So. 2d 658 (Miss. 1975); State v. Grayer, 215 N.W.2d 859 (Neb. 1974).

[41]   *See, e.g.,* Myers v. District Court, 518 P.2d 836 (Colo. 1974); Johnson v. State, 314 So. 2d 573 (Fla. 1975).

[42]   For a discussion of the crime problem associated with gang activity, see Note, *The Jets and the Sharks Are Dead: State Statutory Responses to Criminal Street Gangs,* 73 Wash. U. L.Q. 683, 684–85, 691–705 (1995); T. Gest & V. Pope, *Crime Time Bomb: Rising Juvenile Crime, and Predictions That It Is Going to Get Worse, Are Prodding Cities, States and Congress to Seek a Balance Between Tougher Laws and Preventive Measures,* U.S. News & World Report, March 25, 1996, at 28.

The literature on the gang phenomena is extensive. For a sampling, consider: J. Howell, *Recent Gang Research: Program and Policy Implications,* 40 Crime & Delinq. 495 (1994); J. Hagedorn, *Homeboys, Dope Fiends, Legits and New Jacks,* 32 Criminology 197 (1994); J. Meyer, *Individual Moral Responsibility and the Criminalization of Youth Gangs,* 28 Wake Forest L. Rev. 943 (1993); G. Curry & I. Spergel, *Gang Homicide, Delinquency, and Community,* 26 Criminology 381 (1988); F. Zimring, *Kids, Groups, and Crime: Some Implications of a Well-Known Secret,* 72 J. Crim. L. & Criminology 867 (1981).

[43]   Note, *supra* note 42, at 686.

[44]   Cal. Penal Code § 186.22(g) (West 1999).

[45]   Note, *supra* note 42, at 688.

[46]   See, *e.g.,* Fla. Stat. Ann. § 874.03(2)(b), which, among other things, defined a "criminal street gang member" as "a youth under the age of 21 years who is identified as a criminal street gang member by a parent or guardian." The Florida statute has been amended removing the age provision. Fla. Stat. Ann. § 874.03(2)(b) (West 2000).

intended to include juveniles, even those of grade-school age.[47] The California statute defines a "criminal street gang" as follows:

> [A] "criminal street gang" means any ongoing organization, association, or group of three or more persons, whether formal or informal, having as one of its primary activities the commission of one or more of the criminal acts enumerated in [subsection (e)], having a common name or common identifying sign or symbol, whose members individually or collectively engage in or have engaged in a pattern of criminal gang activity.[48]

The statute creates a new substantive crime of participating in a criminal street gang activity:

> Any person who actively participates in any criminal street gang with knowledge that its members engage in or have engaged in a pattern of criminal gang activity, and who willfully promotes, furthers, or assists in any felonious criminal conduct by members of that gang, shall be punished by imprisonment in a county jail for a period not to exceed one year, or by imprisonment in the state prison for 16 months, or 2 or 3 years.[49]

In addition, the statute establishes enhanced sentences for gang-related felonies,[50] provides for forfeiture of gang weapons,[51] and allows buildings used for gang activities to be declared nuisances.[52]

The courts have upheld anti-gang statutes against constitutional attacks on vagueness and overbreadth grounds.[53] The courts have been similarly unsympathetic to arguments that the statutes violate First Amendment freedom of association.[54]

## [b] Policy Considerations

Historically, the juvenile justice system promised to provide a non-punitive, rehabilitative, alternative to the criminal system. The juvenile courts were intended to individualize treatment for youthful offenders, meeting the particular needs of each. The system was thus aimed at helping offenders rather than punishing offenses.

The recent legislative measures encouraging judicial waivers to criminal court or statutorily mandating criminal court jurisdiction for certain offenses suggest a dramatic shift from traditional offender-based dispositions towards an offense-based model imposing punitive sanctions. While *parens patriae* and protectionism might continue to explain the rationale for dispositions of juveniles who remain within the jurisdiction of the juvenile court, such theories provide a less accurate, if not an altogether inadequate, basis for characterizing the plight of juveniles waived to criminal court.

---

[47] Some street gangs recruit members who are still in grade school. Note, *supra* note 42, at 702.

[48] Cal. Penal Code § 186.22(f) (West 1999).

[49] *Id.* § 186.22(a).

[50] *Id.* § 186.22(b).

[51] *Id.* § 186.22a(f).

[52] *Id.* § 186.22a(a).

[53] *See, e.g.,* People v. Green, 278 Cal. Rptr. 140 (Cal. Ct. App. 1991), *abrogated on other grounds by* People v. Castenada, 97 Cal. Rptr. 2d 906, 913 (Cal. Ct. App. 2000); Jackson v. State, 634 N.E.2d 532 (Ind. Ct. App. 1994).

[54] *See, e.g.,* Helton v. State, 624 N.E.2d 499 (Ind. Ct. App. 1993).

Sending juveniles to criminal court is a controversial matter.[55] Yet, such a decision appears to be increasingly attractive to policy makers who perceive an expansion of serious crime committed by young people with high rates of recidivism, and who are becoming more willing to attribute moral responsibility to youthful offenders.[56]

## § 8.04  STATUS OFFENSES

In addition to delinquency jurisdiction, the juvenile courts have authority to deal with children who do not commit criminal offenses. Statutes defining so-called "status offense" jurisdiction characteristically proscribe certain actions or omissions, such as running away from home or failing to attend school, that are wrongful for children because of their "status" as children.[1] The statutes often also grant juvenile court jurisdiction over troubled youths who merely manifest undesirable traits or states of being, such as being "wayward" or "ungovernable," that do not necessarily entail any particular conduct, neither action nor omission.[2] Because this category of "pure status" jurisdiction does not focus on conduct, the statutory language is often imprecise and open-ended and thus subject to attack as unconstitutionally vague. These considerations suggest it is useful to distinguish non-criminal misconduct from conduct that relates only to undesirable status conditions when describing status offense jurisdiction.

### [A]  Noncriminal Misconduct

Juvenile court jurisdiction extends to a variety of noncriminal misconduct. Statutes routinely proscribe truancy, running away from home,[3] or violating curfews.[4] In some jurisdictions, possession or use of alcohol, or use of tobacco subjects offending juveniles to the jurisdiction of the juvenile court.[5] Some

---

[55] *See, e.g.*, Davis, *supra* note 1, at 2-23, 2-24; Rosenberg, *supra* § 7.02, note 35.

[56] The motivations behind legislative reforms of traditional waiver provisions are discussed by Feld, *supra* note 9, at 519–28.

[1] Georgia, for example, provides the following definition of "status offender":

> "Status offender" means a child who is charged with or adjudicated of an offense which would not be a crime if it were committed by an adult, in other words, an act which is only an offense because of the perpetrator's status as a child. Such offenses shall include, but are not limited to, truancy, running away from home, incorrigibility, and unruly behavior.

Ga. Code Ann. § 15-11-2(11) (Harrison 2001).

[2] Ohio, for example, defines an "unruly child" as:

> Any child who does not subject to the reasonable control of the child's parents, teachers, guardian, or custodian, by reason of being wayward or habitually disobedient; . . . Any child who behaves in a manner as to injure the child's own health or morals or the health or morals of others; . . .

Ohio Rev. Code Ann. § 2151.022 (Anderson Supp. 2002).

[3] Davis, *supra* § 2.02, note 9, at 2-13. The statutes sometimes passively define the proscribed misconduct. *See, e.g.*, Ohio Rev. Code Ann. § 2151.022(B) (Anderson Supp. 2002) ("unruly child" defined as, among other things, "[a]ny child who is an habitual truant from home or school").

[4] *See, e.g.*, Cal. Welf. & Inst. Code § 601 (West Supp. 1998) (juvenile court jurisdiction extends to persons under 18 years who violate a "curfew based solely on age").

[5] *See, e.g.*, Cal. Bus. & Prof. Code § 25662 (West 1997); Cal. Welf. & Inst. Code § 602 (West Supp. 2002) (possession of or attempt to purchase alcoholic beverages); Neb. Rev. Stat. §§ 28-1418, 43-247

jurisdictions employ catch-all statutes to subject all misconduct by youth to the jurisdiction of the juvenile court. For example, a California statute provides: "Any person who is under the age of 18 years when he or she violates any law of this state or of the United States or any ordinance of any city or county of this state defining crime . . . based solely on age, is within the jurisdiction of the juvenile court."[6]

## [B]  Undesirable Status Conditions

Status offense jurisdiction extends beyond the kinds of misconduct just described. Virtually all juvenile codes also include provisions permitting juvenile court intervention if a minor's situation fits within a statutorily designated category of undesirable status conditions. Such categories include being an "undisciplined," "wayward," or "unruly" child.[7] Thus, typical statutes lump doing certain things (running away from home, for example) with being a certain kind of child (one "in need of supervision," for example)[8] as predicates for juvenile court jurisdiction. Nebraska, for example, grants juvenile court jurisdiction over any juvenile who "by reason of being wayward or habitually disobedient, is uncontrolled by his or her parent, guardian, or custodian; who deports himself or herself so as to injure or endanger seriously the morals or health of himself, herself, or others; or who is habitually truant from home or school."[9]

## [C]  Constitutional Issues

Statutes imposing status offense jurisdiction have been attacked as unconstitutional on several grounds. A wide majority of courts have upheld the statutes.

## [1]  Equal Protection Challenges

### [a]  Discrimination Against Juveniles

Status offense statutes have been attacked as violating the Equal Protection Clause on the theory that the statutes subject juveniles to the risk of sanctions for certain non-criminal behaviors while adults face no similar risk.[10] The courts universally reject such arguments, finding that because juveniles are in need of supervision and control, juveniles are not similarly situated to adults and may thus

---

(Reissue 1995, Reissue 1998) (misdemeanor for minors under age 18 to smoke or use tobacco; juvenile court jurisdiction over minors under age 16 who commit misdemeanors).

[6]  Cal. Welf. & Inst. Code § 602 (West 2002).

[7]  *See supra* note 2 & *infra* note 8.

[8]  Several states utilize the classifications "person in need of supervision" or "child in need of supervision" to describe troubled children under juvenile court jurisdiction. *See, e.g.,* N.Y. Fam. Ct. Act § 712(a) (McKinney 1998) ("person in need of supervision" includes children who are "incorrigible, ungovernable or habitually disobedient and beyond the lawful control of parent"); Miss. Code Ann. § 43-21-105(k) (Supp. 2001) ("child in need of supervision" includes a child who "is habitually disobedient of reasonable . . . commands of his parent . . . and is ungovernable").

[9]  Neb. Rev. Stat. § 43-247(3)(b) (2001 Supp.). *See also* N.C. Gen. Stat. § 7B-1501(27) (2002) ("undisciplined juvenile" is one who "is unlawfully absent from school; or is regularly disobedient and beyond the disciplinary control of the juvenile's parent . . . or has run away from home for a period of more than 24 hours").

[10]  *See, e.g., In re* Walker, 191 S.E.2d 702 (N.C. 1972).

be treated differently. The courts conclude that status offense jurisdiction reflects permissible *parens patriae* power affording juveniles protection, care, and guidance.

## [b]  Discrimination Against Females

As discussed earlier in this Chapter, historically some jurisdictions adopted status offense statutes that set a higher jurisdictional age for females than males.[11] While the courts have struck down age distinctions between the sexes, other gender discrimination issues remain even when the statutes apply the same jurisdictional age for males and females.

A variety of empirical studies have suggested that status offense jurisdiction is more often invoked against girls than boys,[12] probably in part at least for the reasons discussed in the age discrimination cases.[13] As discussed above, it is unclear whether protecting against pregnancy provides adequate justification for applying status offense jurisdiction over girls more often than over boys.[14]

For some, this situation suggests that status offense jurisdiction is employed to enforce a double standard of permissible moral behavior for girls as opposed to boys.[15] Indeed, one court has opined in *dicta* that the present application of status offense jurisdiction discriminates against females, perhaps in violation of the Equal Protection Clause:

> [I]t should be noted that status offender legislation discriminates invidiously against females. It is apparent that status offense petitions can easily be used to bring under control young women suspected by their parents or by other authorities of promiscuous behavior. Our society tends to condemn female promiscuity more severely than male promiscuity, and this tendency may explain why females often are unfairly classified and treated as status offenders. This Court offers no explanation for this phenomenon, nor do we make any normative judgements regarding the wisdom of such a distinction; however, we recognize its existence and its discriminatory effect on female status offenders. The control of sexual behavior may be accomplished by other means.[16]

## [2]  Void for Vagueness

Status offense statutes, particularly the provisions describing undesirable status conditions, have also been attacked in several jurisdictions as unconstitutionally vague under the Due Process Clause. A clear majority of courts have rejected the void for vagueness arguments.[17] One court, for example, found no undue vagueness

---

[11] *See supra* § 8.02[A][2], notes 12-23 and accompanying text.

[12] *See, e.g.,* C. Alder, *Gender Bias in Juvenile Diversion,* 30 Crime & Delinq. 400 (1984); M. Chesney-Lind, *Judicial Paternalism and the Female Status Offender: Training Women to Know Their Place,* 23 Crime & Delinq. 121 (1977); Note, *Ungovernability: The Unjustified Jurisdiction,* 83 Yale L.J. 1383, 1386–89 (1974).

[13] *See supra* § 8.02[A][2], notes 21-23 and accompanying text.

[14] *Id.*

[15] *See, e.g.,* A. Sussman, *Sex-Based Discrimination and PINS Jurisdiction, in* L. Teitelbaum & A. Gough, Beyond Control: Status Offenders in the Juvenile Courts 179, 182 (1977).

[16] State v. Calendine, 233 S.E.2d 318, 326 (W. Va. 1977).

[17] Davis, *supra* note 3, at 2-17; *see supra* § 7.02, note 13.

in a statute imposing jurisdiction over minors "living in circumstances of manifest danger of falling into habits of vice or immorality."[18] The court found that the rigorous specificity requirements of criminal statutes were inapplicable in the *parens patriae* context of status offense legislation. "Just as the natural parent may substitute the will and judgment of the parent for that of the child . . . and thus constrain the child's will for his own protection, so also may the State."[19] Because the purpose of status offense jurisdiction is "salvation, not punishment . . . the due process requirements of the Constitution must be equated to this *sui generis* proceeding and not to a criminal proceeding."[20] The court went on to conclude that the statute was not unduly vague because those subject to its application were not relegated to merely guessing at its possible application.[21]

In addition to generally upholding the statutes against vagueness attacks, the courts routinely find no overbreadth problems with language employed in status offense provisions. Thus, for example, one court upheld a statute imposing juvenile court jurisdiction over children "beyond the control of [their] parents" or who "habitually deport[] [themselves] so as to injure or endanger the health or morals of [themselves] or others."[22] The court rejected the argument that the statute chilled the exercise of constitutional rights, specifically denying that children might be found "beyond the control of their parents" for engaging in religious practices or expressing political views contrary to the parents' wishes.[23]

On the other hand, at least one court has found a status offense statute unconstitutionally vague.[24] The New York statute in question permitted jurisdiction over juveniles who were "morally depraved or . . . in danger of becoming morally depraved." In reviewing the provision, the court expressed skepticism about whether status offense dispositions are indeed rehabilitative as alleged by the state. Because such dispositions pose at least a risk of being punitive, the court subjected the statute to scrutiny similar to that applied to criminal statutes.[25] The court found the concept of "morality" to be inherently vague, especially when compared to less vague terminology that had nevertheless been struck down as vague in other cases.[26] Moreover, the court found Eighth Amendment problems with the statute under Supreme Court caselaw holding the Cruel and Unusual Punishments Clause violated when a state punishes one for his "status" rather than for his wrongful "acts."[27] Because the New York statute asserted jurisdiction over, and imposed possible punishment for, a status condition (being "morally depraved" or being at risk of becoming so), the court found it constitutionally impermissible to impose sanctions for the status conditions designated in the statute.

---

[18] S.S. v. State, 299 A.2d 560 (Me. 1973).

[19] *Id.* at 568.

[20] *Id.*

[21] *Id.*

[22] *In re* Napier, 532 P.2d 423 (Okla. 1975).

[23] *Id.* at 426.

[24] Gesicki v. Oswald, 336 F. Supp. 371 (S.D.N.Y. 1971).

[25] *Id.* at 374–75.

[26] For example, the Court noted that criminal statutes prohibiting "annoying conduct" and addressing "suspicious persons" had been struck down as vague but were "modes of precision" compared to the New York statute. *Id.*

[27] *Id.* at 376 (citing Robinson v. California, 370 U.S. 660 (1962)).

## [D]  Policy Implications

Status offense jurisdiction has proven to be a controversial aspect of the juvenile court movement. Because the statutes typically employ broad and open-ended language, wide discretion in enforcement is permitted, often resulting in claims of discriminatory and arbitrary application of the statutes.[28] Moreover, critics find little evidence of successful rehabilitation flowing from the dispositions commonly imposed against status offenders.[29]

These and other concerns have led some to propose the elimination of status offense jurisdiction with sole reliance on programs of voluntary, non-judicial, social service assistance for troubled youths and their families. The Juvenile Justice Standards Project favors this position[30] as do a variety of commentators.[31]

On the other hand, defenders of juvenile court status offense jurisdiction point to the need for an enforcement authority to assure that treatment programs are implemented and followed in situations where the parties in need of help do not voluntarily seek, or are not willing to accept, treatment.[32] Often parents themselves seek out the coercive power of the juvenile courts as a means of assisting them in rearing and disciplining their children who are otherwise beyond their control.[33] For such parents the juvenile courts may provide an important and sometimes effective tool in assisting their parenting.

---

[28] See supra notes 10-15 and accompanying text; see also O.W. Ketcham, Why Jurisdiction Over Status Offenders Should Be Eliminated, 57 B.U. L. Rev. 645 (1977); Note, supra note 12.

[29] See, e.g., Note, For Troubled Youth-Help, Not Jail, 31 Hastings L.J. 539 (1979).

[30] Institute of Judicial Admin. & American Bar Ass'n, Juvenile Justice Standards, Standards Relating to Noncriminal Misbehavior 1-2 (1982). The Standards do provide for temporary official intervention in cases of runaways or where youths are in immediate jeopardy. Id.

[31] See, e.g., Ketcham, supra note 28; A. Sussman, Judicial Control Over Noncriminal Misbehavior, 52 N.Y.U. L. Rev. 1051 (1977).

[32] See, e.g., L. Arthur, Status Offenders Need a Court of Last Resort, 57 B.U. L. Rev. 631 (1977); J. Polier, Dissenting View, Institute of Judicial Admin. & American Bar Ass'n, Juvenile Justice Standards, Standards Relating to Noncriminal Misbehavior 67 (1982).

[33] See Fox, supra § 8.02, note 2, at 54; Wadlington, Whitebread & Davis, supra § 3.02, note 34, at 648.

# Chapter 9
# THE PRE-ADJUDICATION PROCESS

## § 9.01  OVERVIEW

This cChapter examines the events and procedural stages that precede the adjudication phase of the juvenile justice system. Law enforcement agencies are often involved initially in investigating the activities of young people, gathering evidence against them, and physically bringing them within the jurisdiction of the juvenile court. On the other hand, other young people come to the attention of the court without the direct activity of the law enforcement community. In any event, once a suspected delinquent or status offender is brought within the system, a series of procedures determine whether juvenile court proceedings will be pursued and, if so, whether the juvenile will be officially detained until initial proceedings run their course.

## § 9.02  POLICE INVESTIGATION

The police are involved in the juvenile justice system in a variety of ways. Law enforcement officers routinely encounter juveniles suspected as delinquents or status offenders. Such encounters often trigger more extensive investigations which raise Fourth Amendment issues when the police search for and seize evidence and take suspects into custody. Furthermore, when police interrogate juveniles or subject them to identification lineups, Fifth and Sixth Amendment issues are commonly raised.

### [A]  Searches and Seizures

As discussed in Chapter 5, the Supreme Court has recognized that young people possess Fourth Amendment rights.[1] While students arguably enjoy minimal protection against searches and seizures at the hands of educators,[2] the courts have generally recognized, at least theoretically, the same Fourth Amendment protections for juveniles against police intrusions occurring outside of school as are enjoyed by adults under similar circumstances.[3] However, because juveniles, unlike adults, are subject to impositions of status offense jurisdiction, the potential for state interference with their privacy through enforcement of status offense statutes is much greater than that faced by most adults.[4]

Neither adults nor children enjoy absolute protection of their privacy interests under the Fourth Amendment. The Fourth Amendment protects privacy only in the sense of requiring the government to follow rules and observe procedures that operate to justify invasions of privacy.[5]

---

[1] *Supra* § 6.04.

[2] *Id.*; Gardner, *supra* § 6.04, note 5.

[3] Davis, *supra* § 2.02, note 9, at 3–4.

[4] See, *e.g.*, *In re* J.B., 328 A.2d 46 (N.J. Juv. & Dom. Rel. Ct. 1974), discussed at *infra* notes 28–36 and accompanying text.

[5] For a general discussion of the circumstances in which governmental invasions of privacy are permissible under the Fourth Amendment, see Gardner, *supra* § 6.04, note 9, at 806–11.

## [1]  Taking Into Custody

When the police use their legal authority to deprive a person of his liberty, their action constitutes an "arrest" — a "seizure" of the person under the Fourth Amendment.[6] Under common law and in most jurisdictions, a police officer can legally arrest a person for a felony without obtaining an arrest warrant if the officer has probable cause to believe the person committed the offense and the arrest occurs in a public place.[7] Warrants are generally required if the police enter private premises to make arrests.[8] The common law rule for misdemeanor arrests, still followed in some jurisdictions, requires arrest warrants except for breaches of the peace occurring in the presence of the arresting officer.[9] Many jurisdictions presently permit warrantless arrests for any misdemeanor occurring in the officer's presence.[10]

Brief "seizures" of the person, less intrusive than arrests, often referred to as "*Terry* stops," are permissible so long as the officer making the stop has "reasonable suspicion" to believe that criminal activity is afoot.[11] The reasonable suspicion standard is less demanding than the probable cause requirement for arrests and is satisfied if the officer provides "some minimal level of objective justification."[12]

### [a]  Caselaw

Because the law of arrest speaks to police intrusions based on suspicion of "criminal" activity, its applicability to the "civil" juvenile system is questionable, and was particularly so in the pre-*Gault* era. Indeed, early cases held that police could take juveniles into custody "for their own good" under circumstances that would constitute an illegal arrest if an adult.[13] For example, an Ohio court found no impropriety in the actions of police officers who physically and forcibly took a resisting seventeen-year-old into custody after a complaint that the youth had been using obscene language and had been preventing children from using a swing at a public park.[14] The officers did not personally observe the conduct alleged in the complaint but, after the minor refused to give the officers his name and a scuffle ensued (resulting in injuries requiring hospital treatment for both the youth and one of the police officers), the officers took the minor into custody. The court rejected the juvenile's argument that he had been illegally arrested and instead held that "the law of arrest does not apply to the taking into custody of minors."[15]

---

[6]  W. LaFave & G. Israel, Criminal Procedure 168 (2d ed. 1992).

[7]  United States v. Watson, 423 U.S. 411 (1976) (warrantless arrest when supported by probable cause permissible when occurring in a restaurant).

[8]  Payton v. New York 445 U.S. 573 (1980) (arrest warrant required to enter suspect's home to make an arrest except under exigent circumstances).

[9]  LaFave & Israel, *supra* note 6, at 169.

[10]  *Id.*

[11]  *Id.* at 168–69; J. Dressler, Understanding Criminal Procedure 188 (1991).

[12]  I.N.S. v. Delgado, 466 U.S. 210, 217 (1984).

[13]  *See, e.g., Ex Parte* Sharp, 96 P. 563, 564 (Idaho 1908) (although not specifically raising Fourth Amendment issues, the court observed "to save a child . . . the Legislature surely may provide for the salvation of the child . . . by bringing it into one of the courts of the state without any process at all").

[14]  *In re* James L., 194 N.E.2d 797 (Ohio Juv. Ct. 1963).

[15]  *Id.* at 798.

The court identified juvenile court proceedings as noncriminal actions dispensing "care, guidance, and control" of the child.[16] The court sustained the officers' actions under a statutory provision that permitted "any police officer [or] probation officer" to "take into custody any child who . . . is reasonably believed to be a fugitive from his parents or from justice, or whose surroundings are such as to endanger his health, morals, or welfare."[17] The court noted that "certainly the minor herein was found in such surroundings as to endanger his welfare."[18]

Traditionally, the distinction between the criminal system and the "civil" juvenile court alternative was reflected in statutes and court opinions that euphemistically referred to juveniles being "taken into custody" rather than "arrested."[19] Whatever else its connotation, the euphemism suggested an understanding that the Fourth Amendment law of search and seizure did not apply to juveniles in the way it did to adults.

This traditional understanding has changed. Although neither *Gault* nor *T.L.O.*[20] speaks directly to the issue, courts and legislatures now commonly require the Fourth Amendment requirements for permissible seizures of the person in situations where juveniles are taken into custody.[21] At least in cases of suspected delinquency, *Gault* increasingly is coming to be understood to require the police to observe the same rules as are required for seizing adults suspected of criminal activity.

For example, a Texas court found that after *Gault* it is now "settled that the Fourth Amendment is to some undetermined extent applicable to juvenile proceedings."[22] At issue in the case was whether the police could take into custody a juvenile suspected of burglary pursuant to an order of the juvenile court authorizing the taking of his fingerprints. The police arrested the minor at his high school and took him to the police station where he was fingerprinted and thereby implicated in the burglary. After his case was waived to criminal court and he was convicted, the minor appealed contending that his arrest was illegal because the fingerprint order was not supported by probable cause. The appellate court agreed, holding that the probable cause requirement applies to the arrest of juveniles.[23] The court based its holding in part on the realization that, however benign its traditional purposes, "the [juvenile] system is clearly far more punitive than rehabilitative."[24] Even so, the court observed that "rehabilitation and child protection remain . . . the pervasive and uniform themes of the Texas juvenile system."[25] In language suggesting recognition of a mixture of rehabilitative and

---

[16] *Id.*

[17] *Id.* at 799.

[18] *Id.*

[19] Fox, *supra* § 8.02, note 2, at 89.

[20] See *supra* § 6.04 for a discussion of *T.L.O.*

[21] Davis, *supra* note 3.

[22] Lanes v. State, 767 S.W.2d 789, 791 (Tex. Crim. App. 1989).

[23] As a consequence of an illegal arrest, evidence seized as a result of the arrest is inadmissible, but the arrest does not deny jurisdiction to convict the arrestee of the offense if such can be achieved by evidence obtained independent of the illegal arrest. Brown v. Illinois, 422 U.S. 590 (1975) (confession obtained pursuant to suspect's illegal arrest inadmissible); United States v. Crews, 445 U.S. 463, 474 (1980) (illegal arrest does not bar subsequent prosecution).

[24] 767 S.W.2d at 799.

[25] *Id.* at 795.

punitive aspects within the juvenile justice system, the court appealed to both a child's right to rehabilitation (a protectionist right) and to autonomy (a personhood right) as support for its holding:

> One of the fundamental goals of the juvenile system is rehabilitation. Essential to a rehabilitative environment is the proper attitudinal setting. Children have the strongest sense of justice — a product of youth, energy, and innocence. Such an inherent sense of justice, however, is fragile and can easily be turned to cynicism, helplessness, disillusionment and disrespect. Not only would such an attitude be contra-rehabilitative, but it could breed dissention and reactionary criminal behavior.
>
> A child arrested without valid reason by a seemingly all-powerful and challengeless exercise of police power would instantly intuit the injustice and react accordingly. Even a juvenile who has violated the law, but is unfairly arrested will feel deceived and thus resist any rehabilitative efforts.
>
> Inherent in youth is a malleable nature, and example can be the most formidable teacher. We must institutionalize justice in order to engender it among our youth. Affording a child the essentials of basic human dignity and announcing a respect for their autonomy through the extension of constitutional privacy protections can only further these efforts.[26]

The Texas case just considered reflects a clear trend in the direction of applying the law of arrest to juveniles in the same manner in which it is applied to adults.[27] However, even if the law is "equally applied," it does not follow that young people enjoy the same scope of substantive privacy protection as adults. Indeed, because they are subject to status offense jurisdiction, as a practical matter, minors enjoy far less privacy protection than adults.

A New Jersey case[28] illustrates this point. The court applied the "same criteria" in assessing the legality of the "arrest" of the juvenile as is applied to adult arrests:[29] warrantless arrests for misdemeanors are unlawful unless the offense is committed in the presence of the arresting officer, while warrantless arrests for felonies are lawful if the arresting officer has probable cause to arrest.[30]

The New Jersey case involved a situation where the police detained a juvenile, J.B., because he matched witnesses' descriptions of the driver of a car involved in a "hit and run" collision with an unoccupied, parked car. After stopping J.B. and obtaining inconsistent and suspicious accounts of his appearance, noticing minor physical injuries, and recognizing his presence in a neighborhood not likely to be his own,[31] the police searched J.B., looking for the key to the ignition of the car involved

---

[26]  *Id.* at 795–96.

[27]  Davis, *supra* note 3.

[28]  *In re* J.B., 328 A.2d 46 (N.J. Juv. & Dom. Rel. Ct. 1974).

[29]  *Id.* at 51.

[30]  *Id.* at 50.

[31]  J.B. was a 15-year-old white boy walking in a black neighborhood several blocks from the accident site. His lip was bleeding, his right arm appeared to be hurt, and his clothes were wet (bushes near the accident site were wet from an earlier rain). When police asked J.B. to account for himself, he gave three inconsistent stories. *Id.* at 49. After searching J.B. in the field, the police took him to the hospital where they conducted a more extensive search, uncovering more marijuana.

in the collision. Instead of finding the key, the police found marijuana which was subsequently used as evidence against J.B. in a delinquency proceeding.[32]

The admissibility of the marijuana hinged on the legality of the arrest.[33] The suspected offense, the misdemeanor of "leaving the scene of an accident," was not committed in the arresting officer's presence. Therefore, the warrantless arrest for that offense was unlawful. But because J.B. was a juvenile, he also could be taken into custody for "engaging in conduct defined by law as juvenile delinquency."[34] "Juvenile delinquency" was defined to include "idly roaming the streets at night" and "deportment endangering the morals, health or general welfare of [a child under 18 years of age]."[35]

The court found that the arresting officer possessed probable cause to believe that J.B. was engaging in a delinquent act by "idly roaming" the streets. Moreover, the court found that the officer possessed probable cause to arrest J.B. for conduct that "endanger[ed] his morals, health or general welfare" by leaving the scene of an accident he had just caused after incurring his apparent injuries. Had J.B. been an adult, his arrest would have been unlawful, but because of his youthful status the invasion of his privacy was permissible even though the Fourth Amendment doctrine applied to him was the same as that applicable to adults.[36]

The New Jersey case above suggests the possibility that police may rely on status offense statutes to take into custody juveniles they suspect of criminal activity in circumstances where they could not otherwise make arrests for want of

---

[32] *Id.* After searching J.B. in the field, the police took him to the hospital where they conducted a more extensive search, uncovering more marijuana. While the *J.B.* case permitted the evidentiary use of the marijuana found in the hospital, this aspect of *J.B.* has been rejected by later New Jersey case law. *See, In re* J.M., 771 A.2d 651 (N.J. Super. Ct. App. Div. 2001). Arguably, however, the *J.M.* case does not call into question the initial field search permitted by the *J.B.* court.

[33] Warrantless searches of the person are permissible incident to the lawful arrest of that person. United States v. Robinson, 414 U.S. 218 (1973).

[34] 328 A.2d at 54.

[35] *Id.*

[36] As discussed in *supra* § 8.04[C][2], the courts have traditionally upheld against vagueness attacks statutes which provide law enforcement broad discretion to take juveniles into custody in order to protect their moral well-being. Therefore, the statute in *J.B.* likely is constitutional. As applied to adults, however, such a statute would be unconstitutionally vague. See *Papachristou v. City of Jacksonville*, 405 U.S. 156 (1972), where the Court invalidated a city ordinance which provided:

Rogues and vagabond, or dissolute persons who go about begging, common gamblers, persons who use juggling or unlawful games or plays, common drunkards, common night walkers, thieves, pilferers or pickpockets, traders in stolen property, lewd, wanton and lascivious persons, keepers of gambling places, common railers and brawlers, persons wandering or strolling around from place to place without any lawful purpose or object, habitual loafers, disorderly persons, persons neglecting all lawful business and habitually spending their time by frequenting houses of ill fame, gaming houses, or places where alcoholic beverages are sold or served, persons able to work but habitually living upon the earnings of their wives or minor children shall be deemed vagrants and, upon conviction in the Municipal Court shall be punished as provided for Class D offenses.

*Id.* at 156–57.

Thus, had J.B. been an adult he could not have been arrested for "idly roaming." Nor could he have been arrested for the hit and run offense. The misdemeanor offense — leaving the scene of an accident — was not committed in the arresting officer's presence and the arrest would be, therefore, unlawful without a warrant. *See supra* text accompanying note 30.

probable cause.[37] In such cases, status offense intervention becomes a pretext for circumventing rules governing the investigation of crime.

In other cases, however, the police may make good faith status offense interventions which fortuitously reveal delinquent activity. This action may, in turn, eventually trigger a waiver to criminal court. For example, in a California case,[38] police officers observed a young person whom they believed to be of school age carrying a bookbag and walking on a sidewalk during school hours. The officers stopped the youth pursuant to a statute permitting peace officers to "arrest or assume temporary custody, during school hours, of any minor subject to compulsory education . . . who is absent from school without valid excuse."[39] After stopping the youth, the officers asked him for identification and for an explanation of where he had been and where he was going. The youth replied that he had no identification, had been at a friend's house whose name he could not remember, and was on his way to a bus stop. The youth appeared nervous and suddenly shoved his hand beneath his jacket. The officers then patted his outside clothing for weapons and upon feeling a hard object attempted to remove it from the pocket. The youth resisted and the officers restrained him and removed the object which turned out to be a hairbrush. In removing the hairbrush, the officers inadvertently removed an envelope containing a piece of paper with green dots which the officers recognized as LSD. The officers then arrested the youth, and later discovered that he was seventeen-years-old, a high school graduate, and thus not subject to the compulsory education law applicable only to youths under eighteen who have not graduated from high school.

The youth moved to suppress the LSD as the fruit of an illegal seizure. The trial court granted the motion and the case eventually reached the California Supreme Court which reversed and remanded suggesting that the officers had "reasonable suspicion" to stop the youth initially and that the youth may have consented to the various intrusions.[40] Under either of these conclusions, the LSD would be admissible evidence.[41] Notwithstanding this possible consequence, the court described the governmental intervention in *parens patriae* terms:

---

[37] See, *e.g.*, In re *Daniel R.*, 79 Cal. Rptr. 247, 250 (Cal. Ct. App. 1969), where the police took a juvenile into custody on suspicion of selling marijuana. The minor was eventually adjudicated "a person in danger of leading a dissolute life" on the basis of his admission that he had sold marijuana. The court in *Daniel R.* eventually reversed the adjudication because the evidence did not satisfy the standard required for proving delinquency. However, some jurisdictions apply less rigorous standards of proof for status offenses than for acts of delinquency. *See infra* § 10.03[A][5][b]. In such jurisdictions, it is therefore possible to rely on criminal conduct as the basis for adjudicating a juvenile a status offender in circumstances where he could not be adjudicated a delinquent for the same conduct.

[38] *In re* James D., 741 P.2d 161 (Cal. 1987), *cert. denied*, 485 U.S. 959 (1988).

[39] *Id.* at 163.

[40] For a discussion of the relevance of consent in juvenile search and seizure cases, see *infra* § 9.02[B][3].

[41] If the juvenile consented, the evidence is admissible. *See* M. Gardner, *Consent as a Bar to Fourth Amendment Scope: A Critique of a Common Theory*, 71 J. Crim. L & Criminology 286 (1975). If the officers had "reasonable suspicion" to initially stop the minor, they likely also had "reasonable suspicion" to "frisk" him for weapons when he suddenly shoved his hand in his jacket. *See* Terry v. Ohio, 392 U.S. 1 (1968) (warrantless "frisk" for weapon permissible if supported by "reasonable suspicion"). Upon feeling the object in the pocket, the officers were entitled to remove it if they reasonably feared it might be a weapon. *Id.* When the officers inadvertently came upon the LSD — in "plain view" once it happened to fall out of the minor's pocket — they could seize the LSD which provided probable cause to arrest the minor for possessing illegal drugs. *See* Coolidge v. New Hampshire, 403 U.S. 443 (1971) (criminal

The effect of [a truancy detention] is very different from the effect of a typical criminal arrest. The emphasis is not on punishment but on correction of truancy, *i.e.*, to promote attendance in order that students may be educated. A minor so restrained is to be delivered "either to the parent, guardian, or other person having control, or charge of the minor or to the school from which the minor is absent," or to other designated persons whose role is that of counselor. The Education Code establishes a comprehensive mechanism for dealing with truants ranging from resort to various community programs, to special mediation programs. Truants are not, except in aggravated circumstances involving "habitual" offenders, subject to the jurisdiction of the juvenile courts.[42]

Moreover, the court minimized the intrusiveness of the police intervention:

On balance, we find the degree of interference with personal liberty occasioned by a "truancy detention" to be slight. Questioning must, of course, be strictly limited to the purpose of the stop. The sole purpose of a truancy "arrest" is to return the absent student to school as expeditiously as possible. . . . Likewise, the sole purpose of a truancy *detention* is to investigate whether a particular person is a truant, and if he is in fact a truant, to place him under "arrest" in order to return him to school. We are unwilling to conclude that the limited and brief intrusion required for such an investigative detention outweighs the legitimate governmental interest here involved.[43]

## [b]   Statutes

Statutes in some jurisdictions appear at first glance to exclude juvenile arrests from the purview of the Fourth Amendment. Illinois, for example, provides that law enforcement officers "may, without a warrant, take into temporary custody a minor . . . whom the officer with reasonable cause believes to be a delinquent minor."[44] Moreover, the statutes declare that the "taking of a minor into temporary custody . . . is not an arrest."[45] While such language would suggest Fourth Amendment non-applicability to pre-*Gault* courts,[46] the Illinois courts now interpret "reasonable cause" as synonymous with "probable cause," thus finding the Fourth Amendment applicable to juvenile "arrests."[47]

Statutes in other states expressly recognize that the Fourth Amendment applies when juveniles are taken into custody. Some statutes provide that taking a juvenile into custody is not an arrest for purposes other than determining the validity of the

---

evidence or contraband in "plain view" may be seized without a warrant); Adams v. Williams, 407 U.S. 143 (1972) (discovery of concealed weapon pursuant to "frisk" for weapon based on "reasonable suspicion" constituted probable cause to arrest for illegal possession of weapon).

[42]   741 P.2d at 163.

[43]   *Id.* at 167.

[44]   Ill. Ann. Stat. ch. 705, para. 405/5-401(1)(a) (Smith-Hurd 1999).

[45]   *Id.* para. 405 5-5(3).

[46]   *See, e.g., supra* notes 13–18 and accompanying text.

[47]   *See, e.g., In re* Williams, 333 N.E.2d 674, 675 (Ill. App. Ct. 1975) ("reasonable cause" synonymous with "probable cause"); *In re* Marsh, 237 N.E.2d 529 (Ill. 1968) (minors in juvenile proceedings receive the same Fourth Amendment protection as do their adult counterparts); *In re* R.S., 418 N.E.2d 195 (Ill. App. Ct. 1981) (Fourth Amendment applies when juveniles are taken into custody).

actions of the person taking custody under the United States Constitution.[48] The Juvenile Justice Standards allow juveniles "the same safeguards available to adults in the criminal justice system" as they relate to stops of the person and arrests.[49] Some states, Texas for example, provide that a "child may be taken into custody . . . pursuant to the laws of arrest."[50]

New York has adopted a provision permitting police to take children into custody "in cases in which [the officer] may arrest a person for a crime."[51] This provision apparently precludes police from taking children into custody for status offenses, thus placing reliance on the less coercive summons process as the means for bringing status offenders before the court.[52] Furthermore, the New York provisions require adherence to the Fourth Amendment, which may be interpreted to mean that a status offense summons must be supported by a probable cause belief that the summoned juvenile is a status offender.[53]

Once a minor is taken into custody, legislation in most states requires that he be taken to a juvenile facility rather than a jail.[54] The statutes also routinely require the arresting officer to notify the child's parents and, in some instances, a probation officer.[55] The statutes in many jurisdictions permit the police to release the child to his parents if they agree to bring him to court on a designated date.[56] In many jurisdictions, the child must be released to his parents unless compelling reasons support continued detention of the child.[57] The issues surrounding the continued detention of juveniles not immediately released to their parents will be examined later in this Chapter.[58]

## [2]  Searches and Seizures of Evidence

With the recognition that the Fourth Amendment applies to the juvenile system, suspected delinquents or status offenders enjoy protection under the same rules proscribing unreasonable searches and seizures as govern their adult

---

[48] *See, e.g.,* Ga. Code Ann. § 15-11-45(b) (Harrison 2001); Iowa Code Ann. § 232.2(55) (West 2008); Neb. Rev. Stat. § 43-249 (Reissue 1998); Ohio Rev. Code Ann. § 2151.31(B)(1) (Anderson 2002).

[49] Institute of Judicial Admin. & American Bar Ass'n, Juvenile Justice Standards, Police Handling of Juvenile Problems 6 (1980). Note that the Juvenile Justice Standards do not adopt status offense jurisdiction, *supra* § 8.04, note 30.

[50] Tex. Fam. Code Ann. § 52.01(a)(2) (West 1996).

[51] N.Y. Fam. Ct. Act § 305.2(2) (McKinney 1998).

[52] Davis, *supra* note 3, at 3–11 to 3–12.

[53] *Id.* The New York statutes do permit the police to take children into custody who are in immediate danger or peril. N.Y. Fam. Ct. Act § 1024 (McKinney 1998).

[54] Fox, *supra* note 19, at 107.

[55] Davis, *supra* note 3, at 3–57. Some courts hold that failure to adhere to a parental notification provision constitutes a violation of due process as well as statutory rights. *See, e.g.,* Palmer v. State, 626 A.2d 1358 (Del. 1993). Other courts see no due process requirement that parents be immediately notified of their child's arrest. *See, e.g.,* United States v. Watts, 513 F.2d 5 (10th Cir. 1975) (due process standards recognized in *Gault* relating to notice to child's parent constitute merely a prophylactic rule designed to protect the child's right to notice of charges against him).

[56] Fox, *supra* note 19, at 112.

[57] *See, e.g.,* Minn. Stat. Ann. § 260C.176 (West Supp. 2002); N.Y. Fam. Ct. Act § 305.2 (McKinney 1998).

[58] *Infra* § 9.03.

counterparts.[59] Moreover, the courts have held that the consequences of Fourth Amendment violations are the same for juveniles and adults: illegally obtained evidence is inadmissible in juvenile court adjudications to the same extent it is excluded from criminal trials.[60]

This is not to say, however, that the scope of actual Fourth Amendment protection is the same for juveniles as for adults. Because minors are subject to being "arrested" more readily than are adults,[61] they risk more extensive invasions of personal privacy than do adults. Moreover, the police may search arrested persons and areas immediately surrounding them "incident to the arrest" without a search warrant or even a suspicion that such searches will reveal weapons or criminal evidence.[62] Consequently, the police have more extensive power to search juveniles and their property than they do the persons and property of adults. Of course, any evidence discovered pursuant to searches incident to arrest may be seized and used as evidence.

## [3] Consensual Searches and Seizures

It has long been understood that a person, and under certain circumstances third persons, can consent to governmental intrusions into the person's private life. Voluntary consent eliminates the necessity for the government to support the intrusion with a warrant or, for that matter, with any level of belief that the intrusion is justified.[63] Governmental agents may seize without a warrant any criminal evidence they discover within the scope of consensual intrusions.[64]

Consensual intrusions are generally understood as beyond the scope of the Fourth Amendment. By consenting to an intrusion into his otherwise private life, the consenter relinquishes any claims that the intrusion invades his "reasonable expectations of privacy." Therefore the consensual intrusion is not a "search or seizure" under the Fourth Amendment.[65]

The Supreme Court has held that valid consent to a search or seizure exists where, in light of the totality of the circumstances, one is not coerced into permitting the intrusion.[66] Valid consent can be given without a showing that the consenter knew he could legally withhold consent.[67] This doctrine has been criticized as permitting the police to "conduct what will inevitably be a charade for consent. If they display any firmness at all, a verbal expression of consent will undoubtedly be forthcoming."[68] Moreover, because many people do not realize that

---

[59] Davis, *supra* note 3, at 3–19. For a discussion of the extensive caselaw defining "unreasonable searches and seizures" under the Fourth Amendment, see generally W. LaFave, Searches and Seizures (2d ed. 1987).

[60] Davis, *supra* note 3, at 3–16 to 3–21.

[61] *See supra* notes 28–43 and accompanying text.

[62] *See* Chimel v. California, 395 U.S. 752 (1969) (warrantless search of immediate area around arrestee permitted to secure possible weapons or evidence); United States v. Robinson, 414 U.S. 218 (1973) (warrantless search of the person of arrestee permitted to secure possible weapons or evidence).

[63] *See* Gardner, *supra* note 41.

[64] *Id.*

[65] *Id.*

[66] Schneckloth v. Bustamonte, 412 U.S. 218, 248–49 (1973).

[67] *Id.*

[68] *Id.* at 284 (Marshall, J., dissenting).

they are not obligated to consent to warrantless police intrusions, the doctrine affords the police the opportunity "to capitalize on the ignorance of citizens so as to accomplish by subterfuge what they could not achieve by the knowing relinquishment of constitutional rights."[69]

Although such concerns would appear to be especially relevant in assessing the issue of consent by juveniles, the courts apply the same consent doctrine applicable to adults except that age becomes a relevant factor in assessing voluntariness under the totality of the circumstances. Although the courts sometimes recognize "the special vulnerability of juveniles to intimidation by figures of authority," that does not justify a presumptive rule invalidating consent by juveniles.[70]

Routinely, the courts consider consent to be an issue of fact and thus largely a matter within the discretion of the trial court.[71] Some appellate courts, however, attempt to structure discretion by requiring the trial court to make explicit findings on the record concerning the effect of age and relative immaturity on the voluntariness of the juvenile's consent. This is true particularly when the police do not inform the juvenile that he may legally withhold consent.

A District of Columbia case imposed such a requirement.[72] The case involved a situation where plain clothes police boarded a bus during a rest stop and announced to the passengers that they were drug interdiction officers interested in discovering whether any drugs were being carried on the bus. After questioning other passengers, an officer approached J.M., a fourteen-year-old black youth traveling alone on the bus. The officer asked J.M. if he could search a bag J.M. was carrying. J.M. consented and after searching and finding nothing in the bag, the officer asked J.M. if he could frisk his outer clothing for drugs. In response, J.M. turned to the officer and raised his arms. The officer patted him down, felt a hard object on J.M.'s side, lifted J.M.'s shirt, and discovered and seized a plastic bag of crack cocaine taped to J.M.'s body.

At subsequent delinquency adjudication proceedings, J.M. admitted to consenting to the search of the bag because he knew it contained nothing illegal and feared if he did not consent the police would become suspicious and investigate further. J.M. denied consenting to the frisk but claimed he made no effort to stop it because, again if he had, the officer would have become more suspicious. The trial court concluded that J.M. had consented to the seizure of the cocaine, offering no explanation for its conclusion other than the fact that J.M. acted out of a desire to deflect suspicion from himself. J.M. appealed, contesting the validity of his consent.

The District of Columbia Court of Appeals remanded the case, requiring the trial court to make explicit findings that J.M. possessed "maturity and understanding of his right."[73] As for the basis for the trial court's conclusion, the court observed:

A desire to "deflect suspicion" from oneself by feigning cooperation may reveal sophistication and knowledge even by a fourteen-year-old, particularly one trusted to ferry a large amount of drugs by interstate transportation. But it may also reflect merely a belief by an inexperienced youth

---

[69] *Id.* at 288 (Marshall, J., dissenting).

[70] *In re* J.M., 619 A.2d 497, 502–3 (D.C. 1992).

[71] *See, e.g., In re* V., 517 P.2d 1145, 1148 (Cal. 1974).

[72] *In re* J.M., 619 A.2d 497 (D.C. 1992).

[73] *Id.* at 503.

rightly conditioned, like most young people, to obey authority that a search will be conducted regardless of his consent — so that his only real "choice" is to pretend cooperation. [And this could remain true even though a youngster believing the police intend to search him without consent might wonder why they bothered to request it.] Which of these hypothesis fits J.M.'s apparent cooperation must depend on an explicit evaluation of his maturity and knowledge in all the circumstances including as one factor the failure of the police to tell him he could refuse consent.[74]

While the law is clear that police advice of the right to refuse is not necessary for valid consent, the court found that the absence of such advice may be "highly relevant" in assessing the validity of juvenile consent.[75]

### [a]  Consent While in Custody

Where juveniles are in police custody, some courts hold that their consent to searches is invalid unless their parent or guardian also consents.[76] Such conclusions are judicial extensions of statutes, applicable in a few jurisdictions, that condition the admissibility of confessions obtained through police interrogation on the presence of the minor's parent or guardian during interrogation.[77] Where no statute addresses the situation, cases apply the totality of the circumstances approach and consider custody as one factor relevant in determining voluntariness.

### [b]  Third Party Consent

A child, in certain circumstances may give valid consent to searches of her parents' property where the premises are accessible to the child.[78] A parent generally is legally capable of consenting on behalf of a child to searches of the child's living quarters and other areas accessible to all family members.[79] On the other hand, parents may lack authority to consent to the search of an area of the family home accessible only to the child.[80] The same principles apply to searches of personal property. If the parent and the child share access to the property, the parent can consent to its search even though the child enjoys general possessory rights. However, where access is limited to the child and the parent possesses no proprietary interest in the property or its contents, parental consent to search is invalid.[81]

---

[74] Id. at 503–04.

[75] Id. at 504 n.9.

[76] See, e.g., In re S.J., 778 P.2d 1384 (Colo. 1989).

[77] Id.; see infra § 9.02[B][3][b].

[78] LaFave & Israel, supra note 6, at 242 (the older the child, the more likely consent will be valid); see, e.g., United States v. Clutter, 914 F.2d 775 (6th Cir. 1990), cert. denied, 499 U.S. 947 (1991) (12- and 14-year-old children gave valid consent to search their absent parents' home where children were "mature," had access to all areas of the house, and often were left in the exclusive control of the house); People v. Jacobs, 729 P.2d 757 (Cal. 1987) (11-year-old incapable of giving valid consent to search of family home).

[79] LaFave & Israel, supra note 6, at 242; See, e.g., United States v. Stone, 401 F.2d 32 (7th Cir. 1968); Taylor v. State, 491 So. 2d 1042 (Ala. Crim. App. 1986), aff'd 548 So. 2d 521 (Ala. Crim. App. 1988).

[80] LaFave & Israel, supra note 6, at 242. See, e.g., People v. Flowers, 179 N.W.2d 56 (Mich. Ct. App. 1970) (no authority for parent to consent to search his 17-year-old son's bedroom even though son did not possess exclusive control of the room).

[81] See, e.g., In re Scott K., 595 P.2d 105 (Cal. 1979) cert. denied, 444 U.S. 973 (1979) (parent lacked

## [4]  Policy Implications

The scope of juvenile court jurisdiction affords law enforcement officers broad authority to intervene in the lives of young people. Such discretion invites extensive intrusion into areas of juvenile privacy, which in turn raises a host of policy issues, some of which will be noted here.

For personhood theorists, assuring juvenile privacy rights is central to the right to be treated as a person.[82] Broad discretion to interfere with privacy unduly risks abrogation of theses rights. For such theorists, coercive paternalistic *parens patriae* interventions against adolescent persons are highly questionable, particularly where the intervention leads to the discovery of evidence later used against the minor in a delinquency or criminal action.[83] Where punitive sanctions are possible, the breadth of juvenile court jurisdiction poses the specter of state interventions supposedly on behalf of the child which instead serve as the mechanism for causing the child to suffer unpleasant and perhaps debilitating consequences.[84]

Policy makers interested in protecting juvenile privacy interests have several alternatives available to more tightly control the discretion of law enforcement officers in their confrontations with young people. One radical alternative would be to abolish status offense jurisdiction altogether and thus eliminate its potential for infringing privacy interests.[85] A more moderate approach might follow the New York model and limit arrests to the delinquency context,[86] thus effectively affording juveniles the same privacy protection enjoyed by adults. A third approach might restrict the dispositional alternatives available for *parens patriae* interventions to *parens patriae* dispositions. Thus, if the police intervene to help a suspected status offender, evidence obtained as a consequence of such intervention would be inadmissible as the basis for generating subsequent criminal, or even delinquency, charges that trigger punitive dispositions. Finally, the exercise of

---

authority to consent to search of his child's locked toolbox where parent lacked property right to toolbox or its contents).

[82] Privacy protection is often linked to the right to be treated as a person. *See, e.g.*, E. Bloustein, *Privacy as an Aspect of Human Dignity*, 39 N.Y.U. L. REV. 962, 974 (1964); Note, *Formalism, Legal Realism and Constitutionally Protected Privacy Under the Fourth and Fifth Amendments*, 90 HARV. L. REV. 945, 987 (1977) ("The right to privacy [in the Fourth Amendment] deserves primary recognition . . . because of its close connection with the uniqueness of the person and human dignity.").

Some courts have recognized the personhood theory as the basis for children's privacy protection. Justice Reynoso of the California Supreme Court expressed the theory as follows:

> It is well settled that minor students are "persons" under our state and federal Constitutions and therefore possess fundamental constitutional rights which the state must respect. . . . Among these rights is the guarantee of freedom from unreasonable searches and seizures contained in the Fourth Amendment. . . . [T]his guarantee is inferable from minors' constitutional rights to privacy . . . .
>
> . . . Homage to personhood is the foundation for individual rights protected by our state and national Constitutions. The privacy of a student, the very young or the teenager must be respected.

*In re* William G., 709 P.2d 1287, 1290, 1294–95 (Cal. 1985).

[83] *See supra* notes 28–43 and accompanying text.

[84] M. Paulsen, *The Expanding Horizons of Legal Services — II*, 67 W. VA. L. REV. 267, 269 (1965).

[85] *See supra* § 8.04[D], notes 30–31 and accompanying text.

[86] *Supra* notes 51–53 and accompanying text.

police discretion may be sensitized to the privacy interests of young persons by structuring appropriate police departmental regulations.[87]

Those sensitive to protecting the privacy interests of juveniles may also be concerned about the consent doctrine. Civil libertarians have long complained that valid consent should entail a showing that the consenter, regardless of age, understood that she had a right to withhold consent.[88] While the Supreme Court has not imposed such a requirement, states could, of course, adopt it either statutorily or under their state constitutions.[89] For those favoring an approach that requires individuals to understand their rights as a prerequisite to valid consent, there would be little reason to limit the requirement to consent by juveniles.

Policy makers would understand, of course, that any accommodations enhancing the privacy interests of juveniles probably entail law enforcement costs. Increases in privacy protection likely decrease the ability of police to gather criminal evidence and bring offenders to justice.

If juvenile rights are understood on protectionist rather than personhood grounds, there may be less concern with enhancing the protection of young people's privacy. Indeed, whether the right to be protected includes any accommodation to the value of privacy is debatable. As "persons in the making," young people are entitled to grow to maturity in an environment manifesting love, affection, discipline, guidance, and any other factor conducive to the development of those traits essential to responsible adulthood.[90] Privacy does not necessarily play a role in this environment.

A cluster of institutions — most predominantly the family and the school — perpetually exercise legal duties to shape the lives of youngsters who, by definition, stand in constant need of care, protection, and guidance. A violation of "protection rights" occurs when these institutions fail in their responsibilities to their youthful charges. Thus, to the extent juvenile justice delivers on its promise to help young people, affronts to privacy incurred as the system delivers its protection would create no special cause for alarm, and may in fact be perfectly acceptable.

On the other hand, the protection rights theory might itself incorporate privacy protection as a value in its own right. Some commentators view privacy as an

---

[87] See Davis, *supra* note 3, at 3–13 to 3–14.

[88] See *supra* notes 68–69 and accompanying text.

[89] LaFave & Israel, *supra* note 6, at 93–94 (states free to impose through their own constitutions limitations on governmental power beyond those demanded by the federal guarantees).

[90] In *People v. D.*, 315 N.E.2d 466, 469 (N.Y. 1974), Judge Breitel offered a summary of protection rights theory in the constitutional context:

> Children may not be equated with adults for all constitutional purposes . . . . Their natural limitations, varying with age, and the obligation of those, in whose charge they are, to protect, guide, and if need be, discipline them, are recognized in every kind of society. At the same time, in a civilized society it is also recognized that the obligations and powers of those charged with the care of children should be limited by standards shaped by the conditions which require them. Thus, the imposition of authority over children may not exceed the causes which give rise to that authority. Moreover, the spill-over from permissible substitute parental authority into the drastic action more restrictedly allowed the State is present. . . . When the drastic consequences flowing from State action occur, then the behavior of agents of the State may be circumscribed by similar limitations which circumscribe them in an adult frame of reference.

important component for the healthy psychological development of young people[91] in that threats to the privacy of adolescent and pre-adolescent children function as threats to self-esteem.[92] If experiencing privacy is essential to healthy maturation, privacy protection finds a significant niche within general protection rights theory.

Moreover, protectionists may afford youngsters privacy rights as a means of teaching them the precepts of our democratic system. Fostering an appreciation for freedom from arbitrary governmental intrusions into the private lives of citizens is a civic value some may hope is engrained at an early age.[93]

Finally, protectionists might worry that the invasions of privacy inherent in police encounters may themselves be psychologically harmful to young people, particularly if the police employ heavy-handed techniques.[94] However, even where the police act in a civil and professional manner, their encounters may be embarrassing and humiliating to the young people they confront.[95]

Concerns for protecting juvenile privacy might lead some protectionists to favor structuring the exercise of police discretion, perhaps along the lines discussed in the above consideration of personhood rights. Privacy issues aside, however, protectionists might be particularly troubled by the prospect that many youngsters caught within the net of juvenile court jurisdiction might end up not being helped or cared for. Thus, protectionists who conclude that punitive sanctions are inappropriate for juveniles might oppose the present system which permits *parens patriae* interventions to discover criminal evidence that is, in turn, used to trigger punitive dispositions.[96] These concerns may lead some to favor denying juveniles the ability to consent to police searches, or at least require that consent be given in the presence of a parent or guardian.[97]

On the other hand, some protectionists might favor fewer, rather than more, protections from the consequences of police encounters than those afforded adults. Some may wonder whether it is a good idea to apply the exclusionary rule in juvenile cases where an obviously guilty youngster is allowed to go free. For example, in the Texas case considered above,[98] some may argue that the most significant consequence of suppressing the fingerprint evidence is simply to reinforce to an impressionable juvenile, who may already possess feelings of invulnerability common to adolescents, that he can commit serious crime with impunity (assuming that there exists insufficient evidence to convict without the suppressed evidence). Because the Supreme Court has never decided whether the exclusionary rule applies to evidence obtained through illegal searches and

---

[91] *See, e.g.*, M. Wolfe, *Childhood and Privacy, in* Children and the Environment 175, 189 (I. Altman & J. Wohlwill eds., 1978).

[92] *See, e.g.*, G. Melton, *Minors and Privacy: Are Legal and Psychological Concepts Compatible?*, 62 Neb. L. Rev. 455, 488 (1988).

[93] Gardner, *supra* note 2, at 902.

[94] *Id.* at 902–3.

[95] *See* Davis, *supra* note 3, at 3–15 to 3–16.

[96] *See supra* note 90.

[97] Such a position would, of course, be consistent with the views of protectionists that juveniles lack general competence and maturity to make important decisions. *See supra* § 2.02. For an argument favoring special protections for minors in search and seizure situations, see Note, *Minors and the Fourth Amendment: How Juvenile Status Should Invoke Different Standards for Searches and Seizures on the Street*, 71 N.Y.U. L. Rev. 762 (1996).

[98] *Supra* notes 22–26 and accompanying text.

seizures of juveniles,[99] it is at least arguable that it would be constitutionally permissible to permit use of such evidence.[100] If so, other remedies instead may be imposed against government officials who violate the Fourth Amendment[101] rights of juveniles, especially where the evidence is used to trigger dispositions deemed beneficial to the youthful offender.

## [B]  Interrogations

The process of interrogating suspects, juvenile or adult, is governed by several doctrinal provisions of the Constitution. In a series of cases, the United States Supreme Court has subjected police interrogations to scrutiny under the Due Process Clause of the Fourteenth Amendment, the Right to Counsel Clause of the Sixth Amendment, and eventually to the provision against self-incrimination under the Fifth Amendment.

## [1]  Fourteenth Amendment Due Process

Prior to the Supreme Court's decision in *Miranda v. Arizona*,[102] police interrogation at the state level[103] was initially regulated by due process principles that precluded governmental use of coerced confessions.[104] The due process doctrine subjectively focused on the will of the suspect and denied the use of confessions that were "involuntary" in light of the "totality of the circumstances."[105] As an alternative to the subjective approach, the doctrine embodied an additional, objective, standard that rendered confessions inadmissible if the police engaged in "certain coercive techniques" likely to induce involuntary confessions in a substantial number of cases, regardless of the subjective effects of the techniques on the particular defendant before the court.[106]

While the Supreme Court applied the same standard — voluntariness in light of the totality of the circumstances — to the admissibility of statements obtained from juveniles and adults, in early cases the Court paid significant deference to age

---

[99] *Supra* § 6.04, note 22.

[100] For a case suggesting that evidence obtained from an illegal search of a high school student by a school official may nevertheless be used in a criminal case brought against the student, see *State v. Young*, 216 S.E.2d 586 (Ga. 1975), *cert. denied*, 423 U.S. 1039 (1975).

[101] For a discussion of whether the exclusionary rule, as opposed to some alternative remedy, is constitutionally mandated even for illegally obtained evidence from adults, see M. Gardner, *The Emerging Good Faith Exception to the* Miranda *Rule*, 35 Hastings L.J. 429, 432–40 (1984).

[102] 384 U.S. 436 (1966) The *Miranda* decision is discussed at *infra* notes 119–32 and accompanying text.

[103] Confessions obtained from interrogations by federal authorities were subjected early on to the rigors of the Fifth Amendment privilege against self-incrimination. Bram v. United States, 168 U.S. 532 (1897).

[104] See LaFave & Israel, *supra* note 6, at 291–99, for a general discussion of the pre-*Miranda* due process era.

[105] *See, e.g.*, Culombe v. Connecticut, 367 U.S. 568, 620–21 (1961) (holding that defendant's confession was not voluntary when he had a mental age of nine years and was detained and questioned for four nights and five days); Fikes v. Alabama, 352 U.S. 191, 197–98 (1957) (reversing conviction on due process grounds because a black defendant of "low mentality or mentally ill" was questioned while in custody over a two week period).

[106] W. White, *Police Trickery in Inducing Confessions*, 127 U. Pa. L. Rev. 581, 583–84 (1979); *see* Ashcraft v. Tennessee, 322 U.S. 143, 153 (1944) (confession was not voluntary where defendant was questioned for thirty-six hours without sleep or rest by relays of officers and investigators).

as a factor that cast doubt upon the voluntariness of statements given by juveniles. For example, in *Haley v. Ohio*[107] the Court held that in a criminal case the state could not use a statement made by a fifteen-year-old after hours of intensive custodial interrogation by the police conducted while the youth was isolated from his family and legal counsel. The Court focused on the age factor as crucial to its decision, noting that the facts of the case "would make us pause for careful inquiry if a mature man were involved."[108] But "when as here, a mere child — an easy victim of the law — is before us, special care in scrutinizing the record must be used."[109] The Court elaborated:

> No friend stood at the side of this 15-year-old boy as the police, working in relays, questioned him hour after hour, from midnight until dawn. No lawyer stood guard to make sure that the police went so far and no further, to see to it that they stopped short of the point where he became the victim of coercion. No counsel or friend was called during the critical hours of questioning.[110]

While the due process coerced confession doctrine continues to play an important role in regulating the interrogation process,[111] the perceived inadequacy of the due process approach as the sole constitutional check on police interrogation is well-documented.[112] The vagueness of the voluntariness standard left the police with little guidance as to how to conduct interrogation so as to assure the admissibility of confessions resulting therefrom.[113] By the same token, the courts were confined to case-by-case assessments of whether or not the particular suspect's "will was overborne," an issue hardly susceptible to objective analysis.[114] Moreover, because station house interrogation is always conducted in secret,[115] defendants routinely experience difficulty at trial recreating the interrogation process resulting in an inevitable "swearing contest" that is generally won by the police.[116] Such a police-dominated atmosphere creates the obvious risk of undue pressure being exerted upon suspects by zealous interrogators bent on solving crime.

---

[107] 332 U.S. 596 (1948).

[108] *Id.* at 599.

[109] *Id.*

[110] *Id.* at 600.

[111] *See, e.g.,* Colorado v. Connelly, 479 U.S. 157 (1986) (due process voluntariness test applied to test admissibility of confession by one not in police custody).

[112] *See, e.g.,* Y. Kamisar, Police Interrogation and Confessions: Essays in Law and Policy 1–76 (1980) (arguing that the "voluntariness" test which *Miranda* replaced was unworkable and ineffective); S. Schulhofer, *Confessions and the Court,* 79 Mich. L. Rev. 865, 867–78 (1981) (outlining six defects in the due process voluntariness test); *see also* J. Grano, *Voluntariness, Free Will, and the Law of Confessions,* 65 Va. L. Rev. 859 (1979) (defending a revitalized due process doctrine, proposed as the sole basis for regulating police interrogations).

[113] Schulhofer, *supra* note 112, at 869.

[114] *Id.* at 869–70.

[115] Kamisar, *supra* note 112, at 27–32.

[116] Y. Kamisar, W. LaFave & J. Israel, Modern Criminal Procedure 457 (8th ed. 1994).

## [2]  Sixth Amendment Right to Counsel

For a brief period, the Court addressed the perceived inadequacies of the due process approach by applying the right to counsel provision of the Sixth Amendment to custodial interrogations. Thus, in *Escobedo v. Illinois*[117] the Court forbade use of a confession obtained from a suspect after the police denied his requests for access to his lawyer and interrogated him without informing him of any of his possible legal rights. The *Escobedo* Court suggested that Sixth Amendment rights to counsel may be implicated whenever the police focus their suspicion on a particular suspect and subject him to interrogation without informing him of his rights, particularly his right to remain silent.[118]

The Court's flirtations with the Sixth Amendment were short-lived, however. Only two years after *Escobedo*, the Court decided *Miranda v. Arizona*[119] which replaced Sixth Amendment principles[120] with an approach that scrutinized custodial interrogations under the privilege against self-incrimination provision of the Fifth Amendment.

## [3]  Fifth Amendment Privilege Against Self-Incrimination: *Miranda*

In a case going "to the roots of our concepts of American criminal jurisprudence," the United States Supreme Court in *Miranda* considered the admissibility of statements obtained from suspects subjected to custodial police interrogation without the presence of counsel and who were not informed of their constitutional rights. The Court held that admitting these statements would violate a suspect's Fifth Amendment right not to "be compelled in any criminal case to be a witness against himself."[121] The Court found that the atmosphere of custodial interrogation was inherently coercive and this "exacts a heavy toll on individual liberty and trades on the weakness of individuals" by inducing their confessions.[122] Therefore, "unless adequate protective devices are employed to dispel the compulsion inherent in custodial surroundings, no statement obtained from the defendant can truly be the product of his free choice."[123] The "protective devices" articulated by the Court are the now-famous warnings: informing the suspect that she has a right to remain silent; that any statement she makes may be used in evidence against her; and that she has a right to counsel during interrogation, at state expense if she is indigent.[124] The Court found that without such warnings prior to interrogation, the privilege against self-incrimination, long cherished as a protection of defendants' rights in judicial proceedings, degenerates into "a form of words" and is effectively overridden by police practices aimed at inducing statements from suspects held incommunicado at the station house.[125] This

---

[117] 378 U.S. 478 (1964).

[118] *Id.* at 490–91.

[119] 384 U.S. 436 (1966).

[120] *See* Beckwith v. United States, 425 U.S. 341 (1976) (Court rejected Sixth Amendment approach in custodial interrogations in favor of *Miranda* approach).

[121] U.S. Const. amend. V.

[122] *Miranda*, 384 U.S. at 455, 467.

[123] *Id.* at 458.

[124] *Id.* at 444.

[125] *Id.*

compromises the central constitutional interests aimed at promoting government respect for "human dignity," maintaining a "fair state-individual balance," and assuring an accusatorial system of criminal justice.[126]

While certainly suspicious of police practices, the *Miranda* Court did not absolutely prohibit station house interrogation as a legitimate law enforcement tool. Indeed, so long as the police provide adequate warnings, they may freely interrogate suspects and any statement or confession obtained will later be admissible in evidence, provided the suspect "knowingly and intelligently" chooses to forego her rights to silence or to the presence of counsel during interrogation.[127] However, the Court emphasized that the government must meet a "heavy burden" to establish that the suspect waived her rights.[128]

The Court detailed the consequences of continued interrogation after a suspect asserts either her right to silence or to counsel. "If . . . [the suspect] indicates in any manner . . . that he wishes to consult with an attorney before speaking there can be no questioning. Likewise, if the individual is alone and indicates in any manner that he does not wish to be interrogated, the police may not question him"[129] at least until such time as "he has consulted with an attorney and thereafter consents to be questioned."[130] The Court continued:

> Once warnings have been given the subsequent procedure is clear. If the individual indicates in any manner, at any time prior to or during questioning, that he wishes to remain silent, the interrogation must cease. At this point he has shown that he intends to exercise his Fifth Amendment privilege; any statement taken after the person invokes his privilege cannot be other than the product of compulsion, subtle or otherwise. Without the right to cut off questioning, the setting of in-custody interrogation operates on the individual to overcome free choice in producing a statement after the privilege has been once invoked. If the individual states that he wants an attorney, the interrogation must cease until an attorney is present. At that time, the individual must have an opportunity to confer with the attorney and to have him present during any subsequent questioning. If the individual cannot obtain an attorney and he indicates that he wants one before speaking to police, they must respect his decision to remain silent.

> This does not mean, as some have suggested, that each police station must have a "station house lawyer" present at all times to advise prisoners. It does mean, however, that if police propose to interrogate a person they must make known to him that he is entitled to a lawyer and that if he cannot afford one, a lawyer will be provided for him prior to any interrogation. If authorities conclude that they will not provide counsel during a reasonable period of time in which investigation in the field is carried out, they may refrain from doing so without violating the person's Fifth Amendment privilege so long as they do not question him during that time.[131]

---

[126] *Id.* at 460.

[127] *Id.* at 478–79. Voluntary confessions by persons not in police custody remained admissible. *Id.* at 477–78.

[128] *Id.* at 475.

[129] *Id.* at 444–45.

[130] *Id.* at 445.

[131] *Id.* at 473–74.

The Court explicitly articulated at least some of the possible consequences of continued interrogation once the suspect asserts her rights. Failure to "scrupulously honor" the assertion results in the inadmissibility of any statement subsequently given.[132]

Although the Supreme Court has never ruled directly on the applicability of *Miranda* to juvenile proceedings, the lower courts have interpreted *Gault* as requiring the *Miranda* safeguards in delinquency cases[133] and a number of states have statutorily implemented the safeguards.[134] Some states require that the warnings be given not only to the juvenile, but also to his parent or guardian.[135] Moreover, some statutes specify that interrogation take place only in "suitable places"[136] and not at all if the police have "unduly delayed" delivering the minor to the appropriate juvenile authorities and notifying his parents.[137]

While there is little dispute that *Miranda* applies to custodial interrogations of juveniles regardless of whether they are eventually tried as criminals or delinquents, considerable controversy surrounds the waiver of rights issue. Shortly after *Miranda*, some lower courts held that the government was constitutionally precluded from using statements or confessions against a juvenile unless he had not only been given the *Miranda* warnings but had also had the opportunity to consult with his parents, guardian, or attorney as to whether or not he wished to waive his rights.[138] Such consultation was thought necessary because juveniles "lack the capacity and responsibility to realize the full consequences of their actions."[139] The consultation would thus assure "some equalization of the pressures borne by a juvenile and an adult" in the "unfamiliar and hostile" environment surrounding police interrogations.[140]

## [a] *Fare v. Michael C.*

When the Supreme Court eventually addressed the issue of juvenile waivers of *Miranda* rights, it saw no need to impose special protections for minors. In *Fare v. Michael C.*,[141] the Court held, among other things, that juvenile waivers may constitutionally be assessed by the same standard applicable to adults. Waivers are

---

[132] *Id.* at 479.

[133] *See, e.g., In re* Creek, 243 A.2d 49 (D.C. 1968); Leach v. State, 428 S.W.2d 817 (Tex. Civ. App. 1968).

[134] *See, e.g.,* Cal. Welf. & Inst. Code §§ 625, 627.5 (West 1998); N.C. Gen. Stat. § 7B-2101 (2002).

[135] *See, e.g.,* Colo. Rev. Stat. § 19-2-511 (1999); N.Y. Fam. Ct. Act § 305.2(7) (McKinney 1998) (parent or guardian "if present" must be warned of juvenile's rights).

[136] *See, e.g.,* N.Y. Fam. Ct. Act § 305.2(4)(b) (McKinney 1998).

[137] *See* Davis, *supra* note 3, at 3–70, 3–72.

[138] *See, e.g.,* Lewis v. State, 288 N.E.2d 138 (Ind. 1972), *superseded by statute,* Ind. Code § 31–6–7–3 (1998) (current version at Ind. Code § 31–32–5–1 (West 2008)), *as recognized in* Whipple v. State, 523 N.E.2d 1363 (Ind. 1998). *Lewis* was essentially codified by the Indiana statute, except that under *Lewis* a juvenile could waive his constitutional rights by himself, but under the Indiana Code, an unemancipated juvenile may do so only in conjunction with an attorney, parent, guardian, custodian, or guardian ad litem. *Whipple,* 523 N.E.2d at 1370.

[139] *Id.* at 141.

[140] *Id.* at 142–43.

[141] 442 U.S. 707 (1979).

valid if done "knowingly and intelligently" under the "totality of the circumstances."[142] The Court explained its position as follows:

> This totality-of-the-circumstances approach is adequate to determine whether there has been a waiver even where interrogation of juveniles is involved. We discern no persuasive reasons why any other approach is required where the question is whether a juvenile has waived his rights, as opposed to whether an adult has done so. The totality approach permits — indeed, it mandates — inquiry into all the circumstances surrounding the interrogation. This includes evaluation of the juvenile's age, experience, education, background, and intelligence, and into whether he has the capacity to understand the warnings given him, the nature of his Fifth Amendment rights, and the consequences of waiving those rights.

> Courts repeatedly must deal with these issues of waiver with regard to a broad variety of constitutional rights. There is no reason to assume that such courts — especially juvenile courts, with their special expertise in this area — will be unable to apply the totality-of-the-circumstances analysis so as to take into account those special concerns that are present when young persons, often with limited experience and education and with immature judgment, are involved.[143]

The *Fare* Court reached the waiver issue because it found that sixteen-year-old Michael C. had not invoked either his right to silence or to counsel when he requested to see his probation officer after having been given the *Miranda* warnings by police who were questioning him about a murder. The police denied Michael's request, continued to question him, and eventually obtained incriminating statements. The Court noted that the statements would be inadmissible *per se* under *Miranda* if they were obtained as a product of continued police interrogation after Michael had invoked his rights. The Court, however, distinguished between requests for attorneys and probation officers for *Miranda* purposes, apparently taking the position that a suspect invokes his right to counsel only by specifically requesting an attorney. The Court explained:

> [T]he probation officer is not in a position to offer the type of legal assistance necessary to protect the Fifth Amendment rights of an accused undergoing custodial interrogation that a lawyer can offer. The Court in *Miranda* recognized that "the attorney plays a vital role in the administration of criminal justice under our Constitution." . . . It is this pivotal role of legal counsel that justifies the *per se* rule established in *Miranda*, and that distinguishes the request for counsel from the request for a probation officer, a clergyman, or a close friend. A probation officer simply is not necessary, in the way an attorney is, for the protection of the legal rights of the accused, juvenile or adult. He is significantly handicapped by the position he occupies in the juvenile system from serving as an effective protector of the rights of a juvenile suspected of a crime.

> . . . The fact that a relationship of trust and cooperation between a probation officer and a juvenile might exist, does not indicate that the probation officer is capable of rendering effective legal advice sufficient to protect the juvenile's rights during interrogation by the police, or of

---

[142] *Id.* at 724–25.

[143] *Id.* at 725.

providing the other services rendered by a lawyer.[144]

Notwithstanding the *Fare* Court's language suggesting that only a request for an attorney effectively invokes the juvenile's right to counsel under *Miranda*, some courts take the position that a request to see a parent or other trusted family member during interrogation constitutes an invocation of the juvenile's *Miranda* rights.[145] Courts taking this view read *Fare* as leaving open the issue whether a request for access to a family member, one who lacks the "official ambivalence" of the probation officer, is tantamount to a request to see an attorney.[146] Other courts, however, interpret *Fare* as holding that only a request to see an attorney invokes the juvenile's *Miranda* rights.[147]

Subsequent to *Fare*, the Supreme Court decided another case raising *Miranda* issues as they relate to juveniles. In *Yarborough v. Alvarado*,[148] the Court addressed the question of whether courts must take into account a juvenile's age in deciding whether or not a young person is "in custody" for purposes of determining the necessity of *Miranda* warnings. The Court rejected the lower court's conclusion that courts must attend to the age and inexperience, where present, of particular juveniles questioned by police when deciding whether they were in custody for *Miranda* purposes. Instead, the Court specified that the custody issue was an "objective" one satisfied when, under the circumstances, "a reasonable person would [feel] at liberty to leave,"[149] without requiring courts in all cases to factor in the person's age or experience with the legal system in making custody determinations.

## [b] State Law Protections

Some state legislatures have gone beyond the requirements of the federal Constitution as interpreted in *Fare* and extended special protections for juvenile waiver of *Miranda* rights. For example, a Colorado statute makes a parent's or

---

[144] *Id.* at 722. The Court further explained its position:

> [I]t cannot be said that the probation officer is able to offer the type of independent advice that an accused would expect from a lawyer retained or assigned to assist him during questioning. Indeed, the probation officer's duty to his employer in many, if not most, cases would conflict sharply with the interests of the juvenile. For where an attorney might well advise his client to remain silent in the face of interrogation by the police, and in doing so would be "exercising [his] good professional judgment . . . to protect to the extent of his ability the rights of his client," a probation officer would be bound to advise his charge to cooperate with the police. . . .

> By the same token, a lawyer is able to protect his client's rights by learning the extent, if any, of the client's involvement in the crime under investigation, and advising his client accordingly. To facilitate this, the law rightly protects the communications between client and attorney from discovery. We doubt, however, that similar protection will be afforded the communications between the probation officer and the minor. Indeed, we doubt that a probation officer, consistent with his responsibilities to the public and his profession, could withhold from the police or the courts facts made known to him by the juvenile implicating the juvenile in the crime under investigation.

*Id.* at 721–22.

[145] *See In re* Patrick W., 163 Cal. Rptr. 848 (Ct. App. 1980), *cert. denied*, 449 U.S. 1096 (1981).

[146] *Id.*

[147] *See, e.g.*, State *ex rel.* Juvenile Dep't v. Gibson, 718 P.2d 759 (Or. Ct. App. 1986).

[148] 541 U.S. 652 (2004).

[149] *Id.* at 659, 665.

guardian's presence at interrogation a prerequisite for the admissibility of any statement made by a juvenile during custodial interrogation.[150] Some courts have adopted similar requirements under state constitutional provisions.[151] Moreover, some jurisdictions strongly suggest the presence of an attorney is a precondition to a valid waiver.[152]

In jurisdictions where no special protections have been adopted, courts assess waivers under the "totality of the circumstances" taking the age factor into account. The younger the child the heavier the state's burden in showing a valid waiver.[153] While the waiver issue is essentially *ad hoc* in such jurisdictions, some courts attempt to set forth the circumstances to be considered in determining the waiver issue. For example, one court listed the following factors as relevant to the inquiry:

> 1) age of the accused; 2) education of the accused; 3) knowledge of the accused as to both the substance of the charge, if any has been filed, and the nature of his rights to consult with an attorney and remain silent; 4) whether the accused is held incommunicado or allowed to consult with relatives, friends or an attorney; 5) whether the accused was interrogated before or after formal charges had been filed; 6) methods used in interrogation; 7) length of interrogations; 8) whether *vel non* the accused refused to voluntarily give statements on prior occasions; and 9) whether the accused had repudiated an extra judicial statement at a later date.[154]

### [c]  Policy Implications

Advocates of special protections for juveniles who face the decision whether or not to waive their *Miranda* rights appeal to a body of social science research suggesting that minors, especially those under fifteen, do not comprehend the meaning of the *Miranda* warnings as well as adults.[155] Some would remedy this problem by providing simplified *Miranda* warnings for juveniles.[156] Others favor requiring the presence of a parent or other interested adult during interrogation.[157] Still others argue for a requirement that counsel be present during interrogation.[158] Some evidence suggests that the presence of parents during interrogation provides an impetus for the child to confess.[159]

---

[150] *See* Colo. Rev. Stat. § 19-2-210(1) (Supp. 1996).

[151] *See, e.g., In re* E.T.C., 449 A.2d 937 (Vt. 1982); Commonwealth v. A Juvenile (No. 1), 449 N.E.2d 654 (Mass. 1983).

[152] *See, e.g.,* Ezell v. State, 489 P.2d 781 (Okla. Crim. App. 1971).

[153] Davis, *supra* note 3, at 3–82; Wadlington, Whitebread & Davis, *supra* § 3.02, note 34, at 334.

[154] West v. United States, 399 F.2d 467, 469 (5th Cir. 1968), *cert. denied,* 393 U.S. 1102 (1969).

[155] *See* Grisso, *Juvenile's Capacity supra* § 2.01, note 7; T. Grisso, Juvenile's Waiver of Rights (1981); T. Grisso, *Juveniles' Consent in Delinquency Proceedings, in* Children's Competence to Consent 131 (G. Melton, G. Koocher & M. Saks eds., 1983).

[156] *See, e.g.,* L. Holtz, Miranda *in a Juvenile Setting: A Child's Right to Silence,* 78 J. Crim. L. & Criminology 534 (1987).

[157] *See, e.g.,* Note, *Waiver of* Miranda *Rights by Juveniles: Is Parental Presence a Necessary Safeguard?,* 21 J. Fam. L. 725 (1983).

[158] *See, e.g.,* Grisso, *Juvenile's Capacity supra* note 153; Institute of Judicial Admin. & American Bar Ass'n, Juvenile Justice Standards, Police Handling of Juvenile Problems 69–70 (1980).

[159] *See, e.g.,* Y. Hassin, *Presence of Parents During Interrogation of Their Children,* Juv. & Fam. Ct. J., Aug. 1981 at 33, 40.

In light of such social science data, some personhood theorists who otherwise recognize the competence of children to make important decisions, may, somewhat ironically, favor implementing mechanisms to protect children from making ill-informed choices in the context of *Miranda* waivers. On the other hand, other personhood theorists may see confessing as a manifestation that the youthful offender takes personal responsibility for his actions.[160] The latter may see no particular virtue in protections that encourage silence and noncooperation.

For protectionist theorists, the desirability of implementing special protections for *Miranda* waivers likely depends on one's view of the overall effectiveness of the juvenile justice system or, given the possibility of waiver of jurisdiction, the criminal justice system to provide help for young people. For those with faith that guilty juveniles receive meaningful rehabilitation, special protections during police interrogation may be unnecessary or even undesirable. Such theorists may favor a system where children are encouraged to confess as a first step towards their rehabilitation. Indeed, on such a view, *Miranda* warnings are an undesirable impediment that prevents some children who stand on their rights from entering a system that would otherwise provide them needed help. On the other hand, protectionists skeptical of the ability of the juvenile justice system to deliver meaningful rehabilitation would likely favor imposing special protections for juveniles waiving *Miranda* rights. Such concerns for shielding juveniles are heightened considerably where juveniles make incompetent choices to confess and, as a result, they are waived into criminal court.

## [C]  Lineups

The United States Supreme Court has held that pretrial confrontations between suspects and their accusers are "critical stages" for purposes of the Sixth Amendment right to counsel so long as official proceedings have been initiated against the suspect at the time of the confrontation.[161] Thus, the suspect has a right to have counsel present at any lineup or identification procedure occurring after the filing of formal charges.[162]

The courts have generally held that the same lineup protections available to adults are available to juveniles.[163] Some courts have suggested, however, that because juvenile proceedings are not "criminal prosecutions" under the Sixth Amendment, the counsel protections might not be available to pre-adjudication identifications of juvenile suspects by their accusers.[164]

---

[160] Encouraging suspects to admit guilt is not inconsistent with respecting their dignity and personhood so long as force is not visited upon the suspect. *See* M. Gardner, *Section 1983 Actions Under Miranda: A Critical View of the Right to Avoid Interrogation*, 30 Am. Crim. L. Rev. 1277, 1318–19 (1993).

[161] The cases are discussed in LaFave & Israel, *supra* note 6, at 352–74. The Court has also held that highly suggestive identification procedures may offend due process even where the proceedings occur before the filing of formal charges.

[162] *Id.*

[163] Davis, *supra* note 3, at 3–95.

[164] *See* Jackson v. State, 300 A.2d 430, 435 (Md. Ct. Spec. App. 1973) (in dicta, the court posited that because lineup was conducted prior to the filing of formal charges no right to counsel existed under the Sixth Amendment even if Sixth Amendment protections applied).

## § 9.03  INTAKE AND DIVERSION

Most juveniles taken into custody will be released before they ever see a judge.[1] Through an informal screening process, often described as "intake" and administered by the police or by intake officials, juveniles may be 1) released outright, with or without a warning; 2) released after an official record of the contact is made; or 3) referred to juvenile authorities for further action.[2] Often, the case is not referred if the juvenile committed a minor offense.[3]

In cases where the minor is not released, probation officials meet with the child, his parents, and sometimes with police officers and complaining witnesses involved in the case. The probation officer then determines whether to pursue the matter in court, divert the juvenile to a non-court social service agency, place the child on informal probation, or simply dismiss the case.[4] The decision to proceed to court or divert the case elsewhere obviously may have a profound effect on the child and his family.[5]

While many jurisdictions permit virtually unfettered discretion by police and probation officers making intake decisions,[6] some states attempt to structure such discretion.[7] The Juvenile Justice Standards call for imposing the "least restrictive" of the various nonjudicial dispositions "depending upon the circumstances."[8] The Standards also encourage police agencies to formulate administrative policies to structure the discretion of police at intake and elsewhere.[9]

Even where a juvenile is placed in a diversion program, probation officials retain control over his activities and possess authority to terminate diversion and return him to the juvenile court for possible adjudication.[10] Thus, even decisions to divert implicate possible restrictions on the youngster's liberty interests. Moreover, in

---

[1] Note, *Juvenile Delinquents: The Police, State Courts, and Individualized Justice*, 79 Harv. L. Rev. 775, 776 (1966).

[2] *Id.* at 777. Data suggests that up to one half of all status offense cases are closed by intake officers. Kramer, *supra* § 3.03, note 15, at 216.

[3] Note, *supra* note 1, at 778–79; Fox, *supra* § 8.02, note 2, at 143.

[4] Wadlington, Whitebread & Davis, *supra* § 3.02, note 34, at 338.

[5] *Id.*

[6] E. Ferster & T. Courtless, *The Intake Process in the Affluent County Juvenile Court*, 22 Hastings L.J. 1127, 1133–35 (1971). The most important factors in evaluating the desirability of referring the matter to juvenile court include the seriousness of the act; prior record and age of the juvenile; the attitude of the juvenile and his parents; parental control over the youth; the juvenile's school, employment and psychiatric status; and the willingness of the juvenile and his parents to participate in a diversion program. *Id.*; Wadlington, Whitebread & Davis, *supra* note 4, at 342.

[7] *See* California Juvenile Court Deskbook Guidelines, *reproduced in* Wadlington, Whitebread & Davis, *supra* note 4, at 342–45. Texas statutes permit police to release minors taken into custody without referral to juvenile court if "guidelines . . . have been issued by the law-enforcement agency in which the officer works" and the guidelines have been approved by the juvenile court. Tex. Fam. Code Ann. § 52.03 (West 1996).

[8] Institute of Judicial Admin. & American Bar Ass'n, Juvenile Justice Standards, Police Handling of Juvenile Problems 4 (1980).

[9] *Id.* at 5.

[10] F. Miller, et al., The Juvenile Justice Process 265 (3d ed. 1985).

some jurisdictions statements made by a juvenile at intake may be admissible in any subsequent court proceedings.[11]

Notwithstanding the important interests that are at stake at the intake stage, the courts hold that juveniles possess no constitutional right to counsel at intake proceedings.[12] The fear is that the presence of counsel might convert the informal intake conference to "a formal rigid adversarial proceeding."[13] Although some state statutes specifically assure a right to counsel at intake[14] and others appear sufficiently broad to permit such,[15] it appears that the practice virtually everywhere is to conduct intake proceedings without the presence of counsel[16] except in cases where the juvenile has retained an attorney who decides to participate.[17] The Juvenile Justice Standards provide juveniles an unwaivable right to the assistance of counsel at intake in connection with any interrogation or discussion regarding diversion.[18]

## § 9.04 DETENTION AND BAIL

As mentioned earlier, state statutes routinely specify procedures dictating how juveniles taken into custody are to be handled.[1] Parent notification requirements are common as are statutes requiring release of the child to parental custody once parents agree to produce the child to the court at the designated time.[2] Continued

---

[11] Ferster & Courtless, *supra* note 6, at 1146. *But see* Ill. Ann. Stat. ch. 705 para. 405/2-12(4) (Smith-Hurd 1999); N.Y. Fam. Ct. Act § 735(k) (McKinney 1998) (forbidding the use of statements made in intake proceedings in subsequent adjudication proceedings).

[12] *See, e.g., In re* H., 337 N.Y.S.2d 118 (N.Y. Fam. Ct. 1972).

[13] *In re* Anthony S., 341 N.Y.S.2d 11, 15 (N.Y. Fam. Ct. 1973).

[14] Wash. Rev. Code Ann. § 13.40.080(10) (West Supp. 2002).

[15] *See, e.g.,* Colo. Rev. Stat. § 19-1-105(2) (1999).

[16] Fox, *supra* note 3, at 144 (there does not appear to be statutory authority for courts to appoint counsel for juveniles at intake proceedings).

[17] Wadlington, Whitebread & Davis, *supra* note 4, at 349.

[18] Institute of Judicial Admin. & American Bar Ass'n, Juvenile Justice Standards, The Juvenile Probation Function 12 (1980). For general discussion of the intake process, see Ferster & Courtless, *supra* note 6, and R. Shepherd, *The Juvenile Court Intake Process*, 5 A.B.A. Sec. Crim. Just. 26 (Summer 1990).

[1] *Supra* § 9.02, notes 53–56 and accompanying text.

[2] *Id.*, Davis, *supra* § 2.02, note 9, at 3–55. The following statutes are examples of preventive detention statutes:

Unless otherwise ordered by the court pursuant to the provisions of this chapter, a child lawfully taken into custody as an allegedly dependent or delinquent child or a child in need of supervision shall immediately be released, upon the ascertainment of the necessary facts, to the care, custody and control of such child's parent, guardian, custodian or other suitable person able and willing to provide supervision and care for such child, except in situations where:

(1) The child has no parent, guardian, custodian or other suitable person able and willing to provide supervision and care for such child;

(2) The release of the child would present a clear and substantial threat of a serious nature to the person or property of others where the child is alleged to be delinquent;

(3) The release of such child would present a serious threat of substantial harm to such child; or

(4) The child has a history of failing to appear for hearings before the court.

detention of the child is generally justified only if necessary to protect the minor, assure his appearance at subsequent proceedings, or prevent his commission of additional offenses.[3]

In cases where a juvenile is taken into custody without an arrest warrant, detention cannot be continued without a timely judicial determination of probable cause to believe that the juvenile committed an offense.[4] While a probable cause hearing is required under the Fourth Amendment, the hearing may be informal and does not entail rights to counsel, confrontation, or other protections associated with adversarial proceedings.[5] While the Supreme Court has held that a probable cause hearing within forty-eight hours of arrest is sufficiently timely in the case of an adult arrestee,[6] some lower courts have upheld longer periods for juveniles, up to seventy-two hours, in light of "the fundamental differences between adult and juvenile proceedings."[7] The relevant "differences" center on the fact that decisions to detain juveniles involve complex inquiries into matters of personal and public safety and family situation not applicable in adult detention decisions.[8]

## [A]  Preventive Detention

One aspect of juvenile justice which historically distinguished it from the criminal system is the ubiquitous statutory authority to detain youthful suspects if they are perceived to pose a danger of committing further offenses if released.[9] While preventive detention provisions have begun to appear as grounds for pretrial detention of adults accused of crime, express appeal to preventing subsequent offenses by adults has only recently appeared, and then only in some jurisdictions.[10] On the other hand, preventive detention has been an aspect of juvenile justice from its inception. Some statutes specifically include the minor's past record as relevant to the detention decision[11] while others provide the court with less specific criteria.[12]

---

Ala. Code § 12-15-59(a) (1995).

> If a child is taken into custody . . . the parent, guardian, or custodian of the child shall be notified as soon as possible. Unless there is reason to believe that the child would endanger self or others, not return for a court hearing, run away from the child's parent, guardian, or custodian or otherwise not remain in the care or control of the person to whose lawful custody the child is released, or that the child's health or welfare would be immediately endangered, the child shall be released to the custody of a parent, guardian, custodian, or other suitable person.

Minn. Stat. Ann. § 260C.176 (West Supp. 2002).

[3] See the Alabama and Minnesota provisions cited in *supra* note 2.

[4] *See, e.g.*, Bell v. Superior Court, 574 P.2d 39 (Ariz. Ct. App. 1977).

[5] Gerstein v. Pugh, 420 U.S. 103 (1975).

[6] County of Riverside v. McLaughlin, 500 U.S. 44 (1991).

[7] *See, e.g.*, Alfredo A. v. Superior Court, 865 P.2d 56, 58 (Cal. 1994), *cert. denied*, 513 U.S. 822 (1994).

[8] *Id.* at 62–63.

[9] Schall v. Martin, 467 U.S. 253, 266–67 (1984) ("[e]very state, as well as the United States in the District of Columbia, permits preventive detention of juveniles accused of crime").

[10] LaFave & Israel, *supra* § 9.02, note 6, at 606–7. The Supreme Court upheld adult preventive detention in *United States v. Salerno*, 481 U.S. 739 (1987).

[11] *See, e.g.*, Texas Family Code Annotated § 53.02(b) (West Supp. 2002), which provides:

## [1]　*Schall v. Martin*

In *Schall v. Martin*,[13] the United States Supreme Court addressed the constitutionality of preventive detention in the juvenile justice system. The Court upheld a New York provision authorizing pretrial detention of accused delinquents if they pose a "serious risk" of committing an act before the court date "which if committed by an adult would constitute a crime." The Court rejected arguments that preventive detention violated due process because it constituted punishment without proof of guilt,[14] and that the statutory procedures inadequately protected against erroneous and unnecessary deprivations of liberty.[15]

The Court saw the preventive detention statute as furthering legitimate state interests in "protecting the child and society from the potential consequences of his criminal acts."[16] While recognizing the juvenile's interest in freedom from institutional restraints, the Court minimized the possible infringements of protected liberty by noting that the New York system permitted preventive detention for only a maximum of seventeen days[17] and, in any event, "juveniles, unlike adults are always in some form of custody."[18] Moreover, "[c]hildren, by definition, are not assumed to have the capacity to take care of themselves" and "are assumed to be subject to the control of their parents, and if parental control falters, the State must play its part as *parens patriae*."[19] Thus "the juvenile's liberty interest may, in appropriate circumstances, be subordinated to the State's *parens patriae* interest in preserving and promoting the welfare of the child."[20] The Court determined that the child's welfare was jeopardized by his criminal activity because of the "potential for physical injury which may be suffered when a victim fights back or a policeman attempts to make an arrest and from the downward spiral of criminal activity into which peer pressure may lead the

---

A child taken into custody may be detained prior to hearing on the petition only if:

(1) the child is likely to abscond or be removed from the jurisdiction of the court;

(2) suitable supervision, care, or protection for the child is not being provided by a parent, guardian, custodian, or other person;

(3) the child has no parent, guardian, custodian, or other person able to return the child to the court when required;

(4) the child may be dangerous to himself or the child may threaten the safety of the public if released; or

(5) the child has previously been found to be a delinquent child or has previously been convicted of a penal offense punishable by a term in jail or prison and is likely to commit an offense if released.

---

[12]　See the statutory provisions cited in *supra* note 2.

[13]　467 U.S. 253 (1984).

[14]　*Id.* at 269–70. The Court concluded that preventive detention was motivated by "non-punitive" concerns for protecting society and the detainee from harm. For a discussion of the distinction between punishment and preventive detention, see Gardner, *supra* § 7.02, note 10, at 809–15.

[15]　467 U.S. at 274.

[16]　*Id.* at 264.

[17]　*Id.* at 270.

[18]　*Id.* at 265.

[19]　*Id.*

[20]　*Id.* (quoting Santosky v. Kramer, 455 U.S. 745, 766 (1982)).

child."[21] In the interest of protecting the child from his "own folly,"[22] the Court cited with apparent approval the observations of the New York Court of Appeals:

> Our society recognizes that juveniles in general are in the earlier stages of their emotional growth, that their intellectual development is incomplete, that they have had only limited practical experience, and that their value systems have not yet been clearly identified or firmly adopted. . . .

> For the same reasons that our society does not hold juveniles to an adult standard of responsibility for their conduct, our society may also conclude that there is a greater likelihood that a juvenile charged with delinquency, if released, will commit another criminal act than that an adult charged with crime will do so. To the extent that self-restraint may be expected to constrain adults, it may not be expected to operate with equal force as to juveniles. Because of the possibility of juvenile delinquency treatment and the absence of second-offender sentencing, there will not be the deterrent for the juvenile which confronts the adult. Perhaps more significant is the fact that in consequence of lack of experience and comprehension the juvenile does not view the commission of what are criminal acts in the same perspective as an adult. . . . There is the element of gamesmanship and the excitement of "getting away" with something and the powerful inducement of peer pressures. All of these commonly acknowledged factors make the commission of criminal conduct on the part of juveniles in general more likely than in the case of adults.[23]

## [2] Policy Implications

*Schall* has been criticized by some commentators as paying inadequate attention to the liberty interests of juveniles and as being at odds with the Court's decisions in *Gault, Winship,* and *Breed*.[24] On the other hand, *Schall* appears at home with other Supreme Court cases, *T.L.O.* and *Acton* for example,[25] which embrace protectionist principles.

Preventively detaining persons who are considered likely to cause harm in the future is controversial, whether children or adults, given the difficulty of courts, or anyone else for that matter, to accurately predict future dangerousness.[26] Affording judges open-ended discretion to detain the dangerous[27] invites overpredictions of dangerousness with concomitant unjustified restrictions of liberty.[28] For protectionists who share the *Schall* Court's view that preventive detention is merely another form of the custody in which juveniles constantly live, the phenomenon of overpredicting dangerousness may not be particularly troubling. On the other hand, protectionists who see detention as creating risks to the well-being of the detainee may join personhood theorists in seeking ways to

---

[21] *Id.* at 266.

[22] *Id.*

[23] *Id.* at 265–66 n.15 (quoting People *ex rel.* Wayburn v. Schupf, 350 N.E.2d 906, 908–9 (1976)).

[24] *See, e.g.*, I. Rosenberg, Schall v. Martin : *A Child is a Child is a Child*, 12 AM. J. CRIM. L. 253 (1984).

[25] *Supra* § 6.04.

[26] *See* G. Melton et al., Psychological Evaluations for the Courts 193–207 (1987).

[27] See, *e.g.*, the Minnesota provision quoted, *supra* note 2, allowing courts to detain juveniles who might "endanger themselves or others." *See also* Tex. Fam. Code Ann. § 53.02(b)(4), *supra* note 11.

[28] Melton et al., *supra* note 26, at 194–207.

limit discretion in order to avoid unnecessary restrictions of liberty. While it is impossible to formulate criteria which, when applied in particular cases, will yield totally accurate predictions of dangerousness, provisions that require a finding of high likelihood that the juvenile will commit a serious offense[29] offer some greater protection of liberty than statutes granting courts authority to confine whomever they consider a "danger."[30] Some personhood theorists may favor abolishing preventive detention altogether.[31]

## [B] Bail

Juvenile court legislation typically dictates that if the child is not immediately released to his parents upon being taken into custody, the child is to be taken to a juvenile detention facility.[32] The initial detention decision is made by the police in some jurisdictions and by intake and probation officers in others.[33] As mentioned earlier, the statutes require a timely judicial hearing to determine the necessity of continued detention.[34]

A few jurisdictions statutorily assure juveniles the same right to release on bail as is enjoyed by adults.[35] Others grant juvenile court judges discretion to release on bail.[36] Still other jurisdictions specifically deny juveniles a right to release on bail.[37]

The courts have found that juveniles do not have a right to bail under either federal or state constitutional provisions extending the right to persons accused of crimes.[38] The cases generally focus on release provisions, common to juvenile statutes,[39] as providing adequate alternatives to bail.[40] For example, the Supreme Court of Alaska found sufficient alternatives to bail release in statutory provisions requiring timely release unless detention is necessary "to protect the juvenile from others," from "caus[ing] harm to himself or others," or from being "[un]available for subsequent court proceedings."[41] Moreover, the court noted that "blanket application of the right to bail" raises "certain problems" peculiar to juvenile proceedings:[42]

> In some cases, a parent whose child had become involved in delinquency proceedings may be unwilling to take the child back into the home pending

---

[29] See, e.g., subsection (2) of the Alabama provision, supra note 2, which permits detention where "the release of the child would present a clear and substantial threat of a serious nature to the person or property of others where the child is alleged to be a delinquent."

[30] See supra note 27.

[31] See, e.g., J. Fagen & M. Guggenheim, Preventive Detention and the Judicial Prediction of Dangerousness for Juveniles: A Natural Experiment, 86 J. Crim. L. & Criminology 415 (1996).

[32] Fox, supra § 8.02, note 2, at 147.

[33] Id. at 148–49.

[34] Supra notes 1–8 and accompanying text.

[35] See, e.g., Ga. Code Ann. § 15-11-47(d) (Harrison 2001).

[36] See, e.g., Neb. Rev. Stat. § 43-253 (Reissue 1998).

[37] See, e.g., Or. Rev. Stat. § 419C.179 (2001).

[38] Fox, supra note 32, at 150.

[39] See supra note 2.

[40] Wadlington, Whitebread & Davis, supra § 3.02, note 34, at 379.

[41] Doe v. State, 487 P.2d 47 (Alaska 1971).

[42] Id. at 52.

an adjudication hearing. In other cases, a child may not wish to return to his home, or facts adduced at a detention inquiry may show that he should not return home, because the child fears he will be in danger of abuse at the hands of his parents. But the existence of these problems does not mean that the right to remain free pending an adjudication proceeding should be denied to children. Other courts have found that the children's rules can be construed and applied so that children are provided with an adequate substitute for bail.

. . . We believe, . . . because of the peculiarities of children's proceedings, that the present adult bail system would be practically unsuitable as a device for securing the child's future appearance before the court, and would not necessarily result in the child's release. Because contracts entered into by minors have been held to be voidable, a bail bondsman surely would be unwilling to deal directly with a child in providing a bail bond. Unless the child's parents are willing and financially able to secure the bond, the child's right to bail will not result in release. Where the child's parents are not able to assure the bail bondsman of their financial security, the often criticized injustices of the adult bail system as applied to indigents would be visited upon the child.[43]

Some courts have recognized that juveniles possess a right to counsel at detention hearings,[44] even though no such federal constitutional right exists at hearings where the issue is simply whether probable cause exists to believe the juvenile committed an offense.[45] Many legislatures have enacted a statutory right to counsel at detention hearings.[46]

# § 9.05 JUDICIAL WAIVER OF JURISDICTION

As discussed earlier, most jurisdictions authorize juvenile courts to waive jurisdiction over certain youthful offenders to criminal court.[1] While a few states permit "reverse waivers" from criminal to juvenile court, the majority of jurisdictions employ models in which the case originates in juvenile court.[2]

## [A] Criteria For Waiver

Waiver criteria vary from state to state. While some jurisdictions provide few guidelines,[3] others follow the legislative trend towards adopting specific criteria, often similar to those appended to the *Kent* case.[4] Most jurisdictions require that

---

[43] *Id.*

[44] *Id. But see* T.K. v. State, 190 S.E.2d 588 (Ga. Ct. App. 1972) (no right to counsel at detention hearing).

[45] *See supra* note 5 and accompanying text.

[46] *See, e.g.,* Va. Code Ann. § 16.1-266 (Michie 1999).

[1] *See supra* § 8.03[C].

[2] *Id.*

[3] *See, e.g.,* Nev. Rev. Stat. § 62B.390(1) (LexisNexis 2007) (permitting waivers of children over fourteen charged with felonies after "full investigation"). See also the discussion of the judicial interpretation of the Nevada statute, *infra* notes 8–10 and accompanying text.

[4] *See supra* § 8.03, notes 26–27 and accompanying text; Wadlington, Whitebread & Davis, *supra* § 3.02, note 34, at 409.

the child be over a certain age and charged with a serious offense.[5] Some jurisdictions permit waiver of jurisdiction of children over a certain age regardless of the nature of the offense charged.[6]

## [1] Vagueness of the Criteria

Waiver statutes have been attacked as unconstitutionally vague, both in jurisdictions which provide no waiver criteria and in those which articulate the relevant factors to be taken into account in making the waiver decision. Some courts have struck down provisions that provide no criteria while generally upholding statutes that specify the factors to be taken into account by the court.

Thus, the Louisiana Supreme Court struck down as unconstitutionally vague a waiver provision that permitted transfer to criminal court of any case involving a fifteen-year-old where the court found that there was probable cause to believe the juvenile had committed homicide, rape, armed robbery, aggravated burglary, or aggravated kidnapping.[7] The court found the measure unduly vague in failing to provide definite standards to govern the judge's determination. The court specifically found fault with the absence of any statutory requirement that the court consider the child's amenability to treatment in juvenile court before waiving jurisdiction to criminal court.

On the other hand, other courts have upheld statutes silent as to waiver criteria, sometimes supplying the criteria themselves. The Nevada Supreme Court, for example, upheld a waiver statute requiring only that the court conduct a "full investigation" in determining whether to waive jurisdiction over sixteen- and seventeen-year-olds charged with felonies.[8] After initially adopting the *Kent* criteria as the guiding principles,[9] the court eventually determined that the sole criterion for waiving jurisdiction is "whether the public interest requires that the youth be placed within the jurisdiction of the adult courts."[10] In making that determination, the court identified three factors to be taken into account: 1) the nature and seriousness of the crime; 2) the presence or absence of past offenses; and 3) the juvenile's age, maturity, character, personality, and family situation.[11]

Void for vagueness attacks on statutes that do provide some criteria for waiver have been less successful. For example, the California Supreme Court upheld a statute permitting waivers of a child if he is "not amenable" and "not a fit and proper subject" to be treated under facilities of the juvenile justice system.[12] In finding that such criteria provides sufficient guidance to courts in making waiver decisions, the court observed that "[s]ince proper operation of the Juvenile Court Law is predicated on treating each minor as an individual, any attempt to explicate

---

[5] Davis, *supra* § 2.02, note 9, at 4-3.

[6] *Id.* at 4–5.

[7] State *ex rel.* Hunter, 387 So. 2d 1086 (La. 1980). The *Hunter* case was subsequently superceded by constitutional amendment. *See* State v. Perow, 616 So.2d 1336, 1344 (La. App. 1993).

[8] Lewis v. State, 478 P.2d 168 (Nev. 1970).

[9] *Id.*; *see also* Davis v. State, 297 So. 2d 289 (Fla. 1974) (upholding State waiver statute but requiring *Kent* waiver criteria).

[10] *In re* Seven Minors, 664 P.2d 947, 952 (Nev. 1983).

[11] *Id.*

[12] Donald L. v. Superior Court, 498 P.2d 1098 (Cal. 1972).

the standards with greater particularity appears not merely unnecessary, but undesirable as likely to set up mechanical categories which the spirit of the law forbids."[13]

## [2]  Applying the Criteria

Regardless of the criteria chosen, juvenile courts possess broad discretion in making waiver decisions. In jurisdictions without explicit criteria, the discretion is virtually unfettered, while it is perhaps only slightly less so under the rather extensive list provided by *Kent* or other statutory provisions specifying some waiver criteria.[14] Where criteria are provided, courts seldom direct the weight to be applied to each criterion or resolve issues created when the criteria are in conflict with one another.

While trial courts possess broad discretion in making waiver decisions, their actions are subject to reversal when discretion is abused. For example, in a Maryland case,[15] the juvenile court faced a decision whether to waive jurisdiction over a sixteen-year-old young woman charged with negligent homicide when she carelessly drove her boyfriend's car without a license and unintentionally ran over and killed a toddler. The Maryland statute directed the court to consider five factors in making its waiver decision: "1) Age of child; 2) Mental and physical condition of child; 3) The child's amenability to treatment in any institution, facility, or program available to delinquents; 4) The nature of the offense; and 5) The safety of the public."[16] In applying the criteria, the juvenile court decided to waive the case to criminal court emphasizing the seriousness of the offense as the basis for the waiver. The court also discounted the "amenability to treatment" factor in light of uncontested evidence that the young woman was a good student who attended school regularly and participated in a variety of extra-curricular and community activities, was an active member of her church, was a responsible and caring person with no prior record of being in trouble with the law, and felt great remorse for the harm she had caused. The young woman appealed the waiver decision to the appellate court which found that the trial court had abused its discretion by being "unduly influenced" by the "nature of the offense" criterion and failing to adequately weigh the other four factors. Regarding the juvenile court's assessment of the "amenability to treatment" factor, the court observed:

> It is specious to argue that because Miss Johnson is not in need of rehabilitative measures that she should be charged as an adult. Such an argument is the inverse of the legislative will, and injects into waiver hearings the anomalistic proposition that waiver should be granted because the juvenile is too good for rehabilitation, and, as such, should be subjected to the regular criminal procedures. It creates a penalty for good conduct.[17]

---

[13]  *Id.* at 1104.

[14]  See the *Kent* criteria, *supra* § 7.03, note 10.

[15]  *In re* Johnson, 304 A.2d 859 (Md. Ct. Spec. App. 1973).

[16]  *Id.* at 861–62.

[17]  *Id.* at 863–64. For a case upholding a waiver decision based primarily on the seriousness of the offense, see *In re* Mathis, 537 P.2d 148 (Or. Ct. App. 1975).

## [B]  Procedures

Prior to *Kent*,[18] few jurisdictions provided procedural protections at the waiver of jurisdiction stage of the juvenile justice system.[19] *Kent* involved an interpretation of an act of Congress governing the District of Columbia. The Court did not limit itself to statutory analysis, however, but also appealed to due process concepts in reaching its conclusion. Thus, immediately after the decision it was unclear whether *Kent* applied to the states or was no more than an exercise of the Supreme Court's supervisory power over the administration of justice in the District of Columbia.[20] With *Gault's* references to the constitutional underpinnings of *Kent*,[21] the matter is now settled in the minds of the courts who hold that the rights mandated in *Kent* (right to hearing, right to access to juvenile's social record, and right to statement of reasons supporting any waiver of jurisdiction) are applicable to state waiver proceedings.[22]

Although the issue of whether juveniles are entitled to the right to counsel was not before the *Kent* Court,[23] subsequent cases have read *Kent* and *Gault* as recognizing a constitutionally mandated right to counsel at "critically important" waiver proceedings.[24] Some cases find waiver proceedings to be "critical stages" thus triggering the right to counsel required directly under the Sixth Amendment.[25] Other courts follow *Gault's* example regarding counsel rights at adjudication by grounding the right to counsel at the waiver stage in fundamental fairness principles under the Due Process Clause.[26] Moreover, most jurisdictions now statutorily provide for the right to counsel, as well as the *Kent* protections, at waiver proceedings.[27] As with waivers of *Miranda* rights,[28] juveniles may waive their right to counsel.[29]

In addition to the rights recognized in *Kent*, courts and legislatures require that the child, his parents, and counsel receive notice of the waiver hearing sufficiently in advance of its occurrence to provide a reasonable opportunity for preparation.[30] The jurisdictions split on the effect of failure to provide notice: some find that the defect invalidates any subsequent waiver[31] and others hold that the defect is waivable where the required parties receive actual notice and appear at the proceedings.[32]

---

[18] *See supra* § 7.03, notes 1–11 and accompanying text.

[19] Davis, *supra* note 5, at 4–9.

[20] Fox, *supra* § 8.02, note 2, at 253; Wadlington, Whitebread & Davis, *supra* note 4, at 208.

[21] *See supra* § 7.03, notes 12–13 and accompanying text.

[22] Davis, *supra* note 5, at 4–10.

[23] *See supra* § 7.03, note 7.

[24] *See supra* § 7.03, note 6; Davis, *supra* note 5, at 4–15.

[25] *See, e.g.*, Kemplen v. Maryland, 428 F.2d 169 (4th Cir. 1970).

[26] *See, e.g.*, Inge v. Slayton, 395 F. Supp. 560 (E.D. Va. 1975).

[27] Davis, *supra* note 5, at 4–10, 4–15.

[28] *See supra* § 9.02[B][3].

[29] *See* Wadlington, Whitebread & Davis, *supra* note 4, at 394. On the other hand, the Juvenile Justice Standards impose a non-waivable right to counsel at waiver proceedings. Institute of Judicial Admin. & American Bar Ass'n, Juvenile Justice Standards, Transfer Between Courts 46 (1980).

[30] *See, e.g.*, State v. McArdle, 194 S.E.2d 174 (W. Va. 1973).

[31] *Id.*

[32] *See, e.g.*, Turner v. Commonwealth, 222 S.E.2d 517 (Va. 1976).

The courts have recognized that juveniles have a right to produce witnesses and records when contesting attempts to waive their cases to criminal court.[33] The Juvenile Justice Standards recommend that the juvenile be provided access to the services of expert witnesses, paid for by the court, if the juvenile desires such and is unable to afford the costs, unless the court finds that the expert witness is "not necessary."[34]

Evidentiary rules applicable in criminal trials and delinquency adjudications are not followed in waiver proceedings on the theory that waiver decisions are dispositional rather than adjudicatory in nature.[35] Hearsay, particularly in the form of social reports, is admissible so long as it is not totally unreliable. Moreover, illegally obtained evidence, inadmissible at trial or adjudication, is also admissible in considering the issue of whether the juvenile is amenable to the services of the juvenile system.[36] Where waiver proceedings require findings of probable cause to believe the juvenile committed the alleged delinquent act, some jurisdictions permit the use of illegally obtained evidence[37] while others statutorily preclude its use,[38] perhaps on the theory that using evidence that will eventually be inadmissible wastes the waiver court's time.[39]

Some jurisdictions also forbid use at trial or adjudication of statements or confessions made by a minor during waiver proceedings[40] except for purposes of impeaching the minor's testimony should he testify at trial or adjudication.[41] The purpose of statutes suppressing trial use of confessions given at waiver is to encourage the juvenile to be forthcoming at the waiver stage in hopes that his rehabilitation might be enhanced.[42]

The standard of proof applied at waiver proceedings varies from jurisdiction to jurisdiction. Except in certain jurisdictions adopting presumptive waivers of certain types of cases,[43] the state carries the burden of persuading the court to waive jurisdiction to criminal court.[44] Some states adopt a "substantial evidence" standard, others require "clear and convincing" evidence, while a majority employ the traditional "preponderance of the evidence" standard.[45]

---

[33] *See, e.g., In re* Doe, 519 P.2d 133 (N.M. Ct. App. 1974); *In re* Brown, 183 N.W.2d 731 (Iowa 1971).

[34] Institute of Judicial Admin. & American Bar Ass'n, *supra* note 29, at 12.

[35] Davis, *supra* note 5, at 4–27 to 4–28.

[36] *Id.* at 4–28.

[37] *Id.*

[38] *Id.*

[39] *See* Institute of Judicial Admin. & American Bar Ass'n, *supra* note 29, at 37–38.

[40] *See, e.g.,* Commonwealth v. Ransom, 288 A.2d 762 (Pa. 1972); Mo. Ann. Stat. § 211.271(3) (Vernon 1996).

[41] *See, e.g.,* Shiela O. v. Superior Court, 178 Cal. Rptr. 418 (Ct. App. 1981).

[42] State v. Ross, 516 S.W.2d 311 (Mo. Ct. App. 1974).

[43] *See supra* § 8.03[C][1]; Sheila O. v. Superior Court, 178 Cal. Rptr. 418 (Ct. App. 1981) (upholding provision placing burden on juvenile to show amenability to juvenile court treatment).

[44] Fox, *supra* note 20, at 255.

[45] Davis, *supra* note 5, at 4–26 to 4–27; Wadlington, Whitebread & Davis, *supra* note 4, at 397–99.

# Chapter 10
# ADJUDICATION

## § 10.01  OVERVIEW

Adjudication proceedings are fact-finding hearings to determine the existence or nonexistence of the allegations specified in the petition. Where the petition alleges an act of delinquency, the court must determine whether the child committed the act. In such cases, the adjudication phase of juvenile justice is in many ways synonymous with the trial stage of the criminal system. As previously discussed, *Gault, Winship,* and *Breed* impose many of the protections of the criminal justice system on delinquency adjudications.[1]

Moreover, many of the same affirmative defenses applicable in criminal trials are available to juveniles in delinquency adjudications.[2] On the other hand, where the petition alleges a status offense, the procedural rules are sometimes more relaxed as some courts and legislatures apply *Gault* and its progeny only to delinquency, and not to status offense, adjudications.[3] Furthermore, a different, and sometimes more limited, array of defenses are available to juveniles charged with status offenses than to those alleged to be delinquents.[4]

## § 10.02  DELINQUENCY

As discussed in Chapter 8, juvenile courts have jurisdiction over minors charged with acts of delinquency. The term "acts of delinquency" is generally understood to mean acts which would be crimes if committed by an adult.[1] Finding that the juvenile in fact committed the alleged act(s) is a necessary precondition to a subsequent disposition, whether rehabilitative or punitive.

### [A]  Procedural Aspects

*Gault* and its progeny articulated procedural protections in "delinquency adjudications" where "loss of liberty" is a possible consequence.[2] It is theoretically possible that the *Gault* line of cases may be inapplicable if the disposition for an act of delinquency does not entail a loss of liberty.[3] The courts and legislatures, however, have generally applied at least the *Gault* right to counsel to all delinquency adjudications regardless of the possible disposition.[4] In any event, the issue of whether the procedural protections identified by the Supreme Court apply

---

[1] *Supra* § 7.03[B], [C].

[2] *Infra* § 10.02[B].

[3] *Infra* § 10.03[A].

[4] *Infra* § 10.03[B].

[1] *Supra* § 8.03.

[2] *Supra* § 7.03, notes 29, 32, 36, 56, 57 and accompanying text.

[3] At least one court has possibly taken this position. *See* State *ex rel.* Maier v. City Court of Billings, 662 P.2d 276 (Mont. 1982) (no right to counsel for traffic offense with no possibility of jail sentence). Note, however, that the Montana Youth Court Act does not apply to traffic offenses which are brought in city court and not in juvenile court.

[4] *See* Kramer, *supra* § 3.03, note 15, at 273–74. The provision of counsel rights to juveniles in situations where incarceration is not possible provides greater protection for juveniles than the Supreme Court has allowed for adults under the Sixth Amendment. *See* Scott v. Illinois, 440 U.S. 367 (1979) (no

is moot in most jurisdictions given that incarcerative commitments are authorized as possible dispositions for acts of delinquency.[5]

In addition to the rights identified by the United States Supreme Court (right to notice, counsel, confrontation, protection against self-incrimination and double jeopardy, and proof of charges beyond a reasonable doubt),[6] all jurisdictions recognize a variety of other protections associated with the criminal system as equally applicable to delinquency adjudications.

## [1] Notice

*Gault* requires that the juvenile and his parents receive notice of the alleged charges. The Court specified:

> Notice, to comply with due process requirements, must be given sufficiently in advance of scheduled court proceedings so that reasonable opportunity to prepare will be afforded, and it must "set forth the alleged misconduct with particularity." . . .
>
> [Due process requires] that the child and his parents or guardian be notified, in writing, of the specific charge or factual allegations to be considered at the hearing, and that such written notice be given at the earliest practicable time, and in any event sufficiently in advance of the hearing to permit preparation. Due process of law requires notice of the sort we have described — that is, notice which would be deemed constitutionally adequate in a civil or criminal proceeding.[7]

Most jurisdictions have enacted statutes requiring timely notice specifying the charges against the juvenile. Notice is deemed inadequate if it is either untimely or insufficiently specific.

The timeliness requirement is addressed in many jurisdictions by statutes providing that notice must be made at least twenty-four hours in advance of the scheduled hearing in situations where the persons to be notified are personally served.[8] Where service is by mail, the statutes typically require that notice be mailed at least five days before the scheduled date of the hearing.[9] Some states require earlier notice if the juvenile is detained prior to adjudication.[10] Moreover, the statutes often permit a period of time, ten days or so, between the filing of the petition and the scheduling of the hearing to enable the juvenile's lawyer to prepare for the hearing.[11]

Regarding the requirement that notice specifically describe the offense charged, some courts have required the same specificity required in a criminal indictment or

---

Sixth Amendment right to counsel for adult misdemeanants who receive non-jail sanctions, in this case a $50 fine).

[5] *See* Fox, *supra* § 8.02, note 2, at 234–35.

[6] *Supra* § 7.03, notes 14, 34, 35, 54, 55 and accompanying text.

[7] *In re* Gault, 387 U.S. 1, 33 (1967).

[8] *See, e.g.*, N.D. Cent. Code § 27-20-23 (1974). A Minnesota rule requires that notice be served at least five days before the hearing. Minn. R. Juv. P. 25.03.

[9] See, *e.g.*, the Minnesota and North Dakota provisions cited *supra* note 8.

[10] *See, e.g.*, Cal. Welf. & Inst. Code § 660(a)(b) (West Supp. 2002) (5 days before hearing if juvenile is detained).

[11] *See, e.g.*, Tex. Fam. Code Ann. § 53.05 (West 1996) (10 days).

information,[12] including reference to the particular criminal statute allegedly violated.[13] Other courts hold that while the petition need not meet all the technical requirements of an indictment, it must "contain sufficient factual details to inform the juvenile of the nature of the offense and . . . provide data adequate to enable the accused to prepare his defense."[14] Such requirements are statutorily required in many jurisdictions.[15]

The courts generally hold that a variance between the allegations contained in the petition and the proof adduced at the hearing denies due process.[16] Some courts permit amendments to the petition in order to avoid the problem of a variance between the facts pleaded and those charged so long as the juvenile is not surprised by the amendment and therefore handicapped in his defense by the new material.[17]

While *Gault* appears to require notice to both the juvenile and his parents, some courts have held that failure to provide parental notification does not invalidate an adjudication of delinquency against a juvenile who was properly notified and who was represented by counsel at all material times.[18] Courts taking this view see the parental notice requirement as a mere prophylactic safeguard aimed at protecting the juvenile's rights.[19]

On the other hand, some jurisdictions statutorily exempt very young children from the notice requirement so long as their parents or guardian have been adequately notified.[20] Absent explicit statutory exemption, some courts require serving notice to all children charged with acts of delinquency even though "personal service of process on extremely young children will be an empty form."[21]

Some statutes specifically permit juveniles to waive defective notice, usually only after advice of counsel.[22] Some courts reach a similar result absent statutory authorization for waiver so long as the minor had actual notice and was represented by counsel who failed to raise the issue of defective notice at the adjudication stage.[23]

---

[12] *See, e.g., In re* Dennis, 291 So. 2d 731 (Miss. 1974).

[13] *See, e.g.,* Tex. Fam. Code § 53.04(d)(1) (West 1996).

[14] *See, e.g.,* T.L.T. v. State, 212 S.E.2d 650, 653 (Ga. Ct. App. 1975).

[15] *See, e.g.,* Neb. Rev. Stat. § 43-274 (Reissue 1998) (petition must have same specificity as a criminal complaint).

[16] *See, e.g.,* L.G.R. v. State, 724 S.W.2d 775 (Tex. 1987); D.P. v. State, 200 S.E.2d 499 (Ga. Ct. App. 1973).

[17] *See, e.g., In re* Steven G., 556 A.2d 131 (Conn. 1989); Carrillo v. State, 480 S.W.2d 612 (Tex. 1972) (holding that amended pleadings violated due process because juvenile's counsel was taken by surprise and prejudiced by the amendment).

[18] *See, e.g.,* United States v. Watts, 513 F.2d 5 (10th Cir. 1975).

[19] *Id.*

[20] *See, e.g.,* Cal. Welf. & Inst. Code § 658 (West 1998) (requiring that minors above 8 years of age be served with petition); Ga. Code Ann. § 15-11-39(b) (Harrison 2001) (summons must be served on juveniles above 14 years of age).

[21] RLR v. State, 487 P.2d 27, 41 (Alaska 1971).

[22] *See, e.g.,* Ga. Code Ann. § 15-11-39(e) (Harrison 2001).

[23] *See, e.g.,* RLR v. State, 487 P.2d 27 (Alaska 1971).

## [2]  Discovery

Prior to *Kent,* juvenile courts were presumed to conduct nonadversarial proceedings where parties from both sides pooled their information in promoting the welfare of the child.[24] *Kent* ushered in the beginning of adversarial juvenile justice, thus creating the necessity to confront issues of discovery. The discovery process is governed by rules defining the circumstances under which one adversary must provide the other with information in the possession of the providing party.[25]

Although specifically addressing the stage of the proceedings at which waiver to criminal court is considered, *Kent* also introduced discovery issues into juvenile justice. *Kent* required that the juvenile's lawyer must be provided the same access to social records concerning her client which had been provided to the court to assist the waiver decision-making process. After *Kent,* some courts and legislatures fashioned rules providing counsel access to social service and other court records[26] even though *Kent* has not been read as creating a constitutional right to discovery.[27] Some courts, however, have recognized a right of access to material relied on by juvenile court judges under the right to the effective assistance of counsel.[28]

Absent statutory authorization, some courts have asserted inherent judicial power in ordering discovery to the extent it is allowed in criminal cases.[29] Even where statutes explicitly provide that civil discovery rules apply to juvenile courts,[30] some courts hold that discovery is restricted to the extent allowed in criminal cases.[31] Some statutes, on the other hand, expressly apply criminal discovery rules to the juvenile system.[32]

## [3]  Counsel

In discussing the importance of counsel in juvenile adjudications, the *Gault* Court stated:

> A proceeding where the issue is whether the child will be found to be "delinquent" and subjected to the loss of his liberty for years is comparable in seriousness to a felony prosecution. The juvenile needs the assistance of counsel to cope with problems of law, to make skilled inquiry into the facts,

---

[24]  Fox, *supra* note 5, at 169.

[25]  *Id.* at 169–70.

[26]  *See, e.g.,* Minn. Stat. Ann. § 260B.171 Subd. 4(d) (West Supp. 2002); N.D. Cent. Code § 27-20-51 (Supp. 2001).

[27]  *See* District of Columbia v. Jackson, 261 A.2d 511 (D.C. 1970) (no due process right for juveniles to discovery because adults enjoy no right to discovery in criminal cases).

[28]  *See, e.g.,* Baldwin v. Lewis, 300 F. Supp. 1220 (E.D. Wis. 1969), *rev'd on other grounds,* 442 F.2d 29 (7th Cir. 1971).

[29]  *See, e.g.,* Joe Z. v. Superior Court, 478 P.2d 26 (Cal. 1970). *But see* People *ex rel.* Hanrahan v. Felt, 269 N.E.2d 1 (Ill. 1971) (holding that juvenile courts have discretion to apply civil discovery provisions).

[30]  For a discussion of the contrast between civil and criminal discovery, see LaFave & Israel, *supra* § 9.02, note 6, at 836–96. For discussion of discovery issues in juvenile justice, see D. Geraghty, *Juvenile Discovery: A Developing Trend and a Word of Caution,* 7 Pepp. L. Rev. 897 (1980); Institute of Judicial Admin. & American Bar Ass'n, Juvenile Justice Standards, Pre-Trial Court Proceedings 59–64 (1980).

[31]  *See, e.g.,* T.P.S. v. State, 590 S.W.2d 946, 954 (Tex. Civ. App. 1979).

[32]  La. Children's Code Ann. art. 866 (West 1995).

to insist upon regularity of the proceedings, and to ascertain whether he has a defense and to prepare and submit it.

  . . . .

We conclude that the Due Process Clause of the Fourteenth Amendment requires that in respect to proceedings to determine delinquency which may result in commitment to an institution in which the juvenile's freedom is curtailed, the child and his parents must be notified of the child's right to be represented by counsel retained by them, or if they are unable to afford counsel, that counsel will be appointed to represent the child.[33]

In the wake of *Gault*, many state legislatures enacted statutes affording a right to counsel,[34] often at "all stages" of the proceedings,[35] even though *Gault* specifically addressed only the adjudication stage.[36]

While it is now widely agreed that juveniles enjoy a right to counsel at delinquency adjudications, controversy surrounds the issue of how, if at all, the right is waived. As discussed in Chapter 9, juveniles are deemed capable of waiving their rights to counsel under *Miranda*,[37] in many jurisdictions without a requirement that consultation with a lawyer or parent precede the waiver.[38] At the adjudication stage, however, courts and legislatures generally take a stricter view of waivers of counsel. Some cases permit waivers only upon the advice of counsel,[39] while some statutes permit waivers only after the court informs the juvenile and his parents of the risks of proceeding without counsel including the possible dispositions.[40] At least one state stands in agreement with the position of the Juvenile Justice Standards and denies waivers of counsel altogether at adjudication.[41]

Notwithstanding the importance of counsel at delinquency adjudications, some data establishes that nearly half of the juveniles adjudicated as delinquent do not have lawyers.[42] Moreover, the evidence suggests, perhaps ironically, that adjudicated delinquents with lawyers receive harsher dispositions than those without lawyers regardless of the types of offenses with which they are charged.[43]

Although juveniles clearly enjoy a right to counsel at adjudication, questions surround the role the lawyer should play. While *Gault* suggests a traditional

---

[33] *In re* Gault, 387 U.S. 1, 36, 41 (1967).

[34] *See, e.g.*, Minn. Stat. Ann. § 260B.163 (West Supp. 2002).

[35] A "large number" of statutes take this form. Wadlington, Whitebread & Davis, *supra* § 3.02, note 34, at 457. *See, e.g.*, 42 Pa. Const. Stat. Ann. § 6337 (2000); Utah Code Ann. § 78-3a-913(1)(a) (Supp. 2001).

[36] *See supra* § 7.03[B], notes 31–32 and accompanying text.

[37] *See supra* § 9.02, notes 127–43 and accompanying text.

[38] *Id.*

[39] *See, e.g.*, State *ex rel.* J.M. v. Taylor, 276 S.E.2d 199 (W. Va. 1981); *In re* Appeal No. 544, 332 A.2d 680 (Md. Ct. Spec. App. 1975).

[40] *See, e.g.*, Ark. Code Ann. § 9-27-317 (Michie 2002).

[41] Tex. Fam. Code Ann. § 51.10(b) (West 1996); Institute of Judicial Admin. & American Bar Ass'n, *supra* note 30, at 88–95 (permitting juveniles to proceed *pro se* "in exceptional circumstances" so long as stand-by counsel is appointed).

[42] B. Feld, In re Gault *Revisited: A Cross-State Comparison of the Right to Counsel in Juvenile Court*, 34 CRIME & DELINQ. 393 (1988).

[43] *Id.*; *see also* B. Feld, *The Right to Counsel in Juvenile Court: An Empirical Study of When Lawyers Appear and the Difference They Make*, 79 J. CRIM. L. & CRIMINOLOGY 1185 (1989).

criminal defense role,[44] some lawyers may feel hesitant in functioning as a zealous adversary if they feel their clients are either factually guilty of the offense or innocent but in need of the rehabilitative services available to adjudicated delinquents.[45] In such circumstances, many lawyers may feel that it is their role to assume a non-adversarial posture and cooperate with the court to assure that the client is adjudicated a delinquent. To the extent juvenile justice actually delivers meaningful rehabilitation, lawyers who cooperate in assuring such rehabilitation for their needy clients arguably act in a professional manner in representing the best interests of the client.[46]

## [4] Evidentiary Issues

### [a] Rules of Evidence

Although prior to *Gault*, jurisdictions typically applied no formal rules of evidence to juvenile proceedings, today, the rules of evidence, including the rule against hearsay, apply in delinquency adjudications.[47] Some states specifically apply the rules applicable in criminal trials[48] while others apply the rules utilized in civil proceedings.[49]

### [b] Standard of Proof

As mentioned above, in order to minimize the risks of subjecting innocent persons to the stigma and loss of liberty often inherent in being adjudicated a delinquent, the United States Supreme Court in *Winship* found that due process required the government to prove the commission of acts of delinquency beyond a reasonable doubt. In analogizing juvenile delinquency to criminal conviction, the Court observed:

> The reasonable-doubt standard plays a vital role in the American scheme of criminal procedure. It is a prime instrument for reducing the risk of convictions resting on factual error. The standard provides concrete substance for the presumption of innocence — that bedrock "axiomatic and elementary" principle whose "enforcement lies at the foundation of the administration of our criminal law." . . .

> The requirement of proof beyond a reasonable doubt has this vital role in our criminal procedure for cogent reasons. The accused during a criminal prosecution has at stake interests of immense importance, both because of the possibility that he may lose his liberty upon conviction and because of the certainty that he would be stigmatized by the conviction. Accordingly,

---

[44] *See supra* note 33 and accompanying text.

[45] *See* R. Kay & D. Segal, *The Role of the Attorney in Juvenile Court Proceedings: A Non-Polar Approach*, 61 Geo. L.J. 1401, 1409–15 (1973).

[46] *Id.; see also* Mnookin & Weisberg, *supra* § 1.02, note 8, at 1186–1201; M. Guggenheim, *A Paradigm For Determining the Role of Counsel for Children*, 64 Fordham L. Rev. 1399, 1421–24 (1996); R. Shepherd & S. England, *"I Know the Child is My Client, But Who Am I?"*, 64 Fordham L. Rev. 1917 (1996).

[47] Davis, *supra* § 2.02, note 9, at 5-26 to 5-27.

[48] *See, e.g.*, Cal. Welf. & Inst. Code § 701 (West 1998).

[49] *See, e.g.*, Mo. Ann. Stat. § 211.171(7) (Vernon Supp. 2002) (equity practice and procedure applicable in juvenile court).

a society that values the good name and freedom of every individual should not condemn a man for commission of a crime when there is reasonable doubt about his guilt. . . .

Moreover, use of the reasonable-doubt standard is indispensable to command the respect and confidence of the community in applications of the criminal law. It is critical that the moral force of the criminal law not be diluted by a standard of proof that leaves people in doubt whether innocent men are being condemned. It is also important in our free society that every individual going about his ordinary affairs have confidence that his government cannot adjudge him guilty of a criminal offense without convincing a proper factfinder of his guilt with utmost certainty.

Lest there remain any doubt about the constitutional stature of the reasonable-doubt standard, we explicitly hold that the Due Process Clause protects the accused against conviction except upon proof beyond a reasonable doubt of every fact necessary to constitute the crime with which he is charged.[50]

Many states have statutorily mandated the *Winship* requirement.[51]

## [c] Self-Incrimination, Confrontation, and Cross Examination

*Gault*'s recognition of the applicability of the privilege against self-incrimination at adjudication hearings has been codified in some jurisdictions.[52] Some statutes require that the juvenile and his parents be advised of the right against self-incrimination at the adjudication hearing.[53] Application of the privilege means, among other things, that failure to testify at the hearing cannot be considered as evidence of guilt.[54] Juveniles are, of course, permitted to testify and to admit guilt if they so choose. As in adult criminal cases, guilty pleas are valid so long as the record shows that the plea is made knowingly and voluntarily.[55]

*Gault* also recognized a juvenile's right to confrontation, stating that "absent a valid confession, a determination of delinquency and an order of commitment to a state institution cannot be sustained in the absence of [confrontation and] sworn testimony subjected to the opportunity for cross-examination."[56] In light of these requirements, the courts have held that confrontation and cross-examination rights are violated if courts consider hearsay evidence that does not fall within one of the recognized exceptions to the hearsay rule.[57] Along these lines, courts have held that a juvenile's confrontation rights are violated if the court considers a social report, largely hearsay, at the adjudication stage of the proceedings.[58] Again, the

---

[50] *In re* Winship, 397 U.S. 358, 363–64 (1970).

[51] Davis, *supra* note 47, at 5-23. *See, e.g.,* Cal. Welf. & Inst. Code § 701 (West 1998).

[52] *Supra* § 7.03, notes 24–27 and accompanying text; *see, e.g.,* Ga. Code Ann. § 15-11-7(b) (Harrison 2001).

[53] *See, e.g.,* Tex. Fam. Code Ann. § 54.03(b)(3) (West 1996).

[54] *See* State *ex rel.* D.A.M., 333 A.2d 270 (N.J. Super. Ct. App. Div. 1975).

[55] *In re* Chavis, 230 S.E.2d 198 (N.C. Ct. App. 1976).

[56] *In re* Gault, 387 U.S. 1, 56–57 (1967).

[57] *See, e.g., In re* Dennis H., 96 Cal. Rptr. 791 (Cal. Ct. App. 1971).

[58] *See In re* Gladys R., 464 P.2d 127 (Cal. 1970).

rights to confrontation and cross-examination have been statutorily codified in some jurisdictions.[59]

## [5] Jury Determinations

As discussed above, the *McKeiver* Court held that juveniles are not constitutionally entitled to jury determinations at delinquency adjudications.[60] While the majority of jurisdictions conduct delinquency proceedings without juries,[61] some states statutorily provide for jury trials in delinquency cases.[62]

Under Supreme Court caselaw recognizing a Sixth Amendment right to trial by jury in criminal cases punishable by six months or more imprisonment,[63] some courts have recognized a similar right in juvenile systems that impose punitive incarceration for terms in excess of six months. Thus, a New York court found a Sixth Amendment right to a jury trial for "designated felony" cases brought under provisions of the New York statutes.[64] Although labeling the actions "juvenile proceedings," the New York State Legislature imposed fixed periods of confinement, either for six-month or twelve-month intervals, for juveniles committing certain enumerated offenses who were found to be in need of restrictive placement. The New York court analyzed the confinement issue by distinguishing punishment and rehabilitation. The court cited *McKeiver* for the proposition that there is no requirement of jury trials in juvenile proceedings in which the disposition is "rehabilitative and nonpenal."[65] "When, however, . . . what is actually a punishment is characterized as a treatment, an abuse of constitutional dimension has occurred, and, a jury trial is required before punishment, although appropriate, may be inflicted."[66] The court found that the New York provisions were punitive because they premised the length of confinement upon "the act committed rather than [upon] the needs of the child."[67] Moreover, the court found the mandatory nature of the confinement to be inconsistent with the "philosophy of treatment," which requires that juveniles be released when rehabilitation occurs.[68] "Indeterminate sentencing is based upon notions of rehabilitation, while determinate sentencing is based upon a desire for retribution or punishment."[69]

---

[59] *See, e.g.*, Conn. Gen. Stat. Ann. § 46b-135(a) (West 1995).

[60] *Supra* § 7.03, notes 40–53 and accompanying text.

[61] Davis, *supra* note 47, at 5-19.

[62] *See, e.g.*, Tex. Fam. Code Ann. § 54.03(c) (West 1996).

[63] Baldwin v. New York, 399 U.S. 66 (1970).

[64] *In re* Felder, 402 N.Y.S.2d 528 (N.Y. Fam. Ct. 1978).

[65] *Id.* at 531.

[66] *Id.*

[67] *Id.* at 533.

[68] *Id.*

[69] *Id.* While the court found the sanction to be punitive and not therapeutic, it refrained from ordering a jury trial which it found could not be ordered without statutory authorization. Instead, the court forbade restrictive placements in designated felony proceedings tried without juries. Adopting a similar analysis, the Kansas Supreme Court held that changes in the Kansas Juvenile Justice Code had rendered the Kansas juvenile system more akin to a punitive adult criminal system than a paternalistic juvenile justice system, thus warranting a juvenile's right to a jury trial under the Sixth and Fourteenth Amendments to the United States Constitution and under the Kansas Constitution. *In re* L.M., 186 P.3d 164, 170 (Kan. 2008). Recent changes to the Kansas code had included, *inter alia*, extensive removal of

On the other hand, other New York courts have reached the opposite conclusion, finding that despite the punitive nature of the designated felony provisions, juveniles charged with such felonies enjoy no right to a jury determination.[70] Moreover, the Washington Supreme Court has held that although the presumptive sentencing scheme adopted by that state's legislature may be punitive, the Sixth Amendment right to trial by jury does not apply, in part because "punishment [may do] as much to rehabilitate, correct and direct an errant youth as does the prior philosophy of focusing upon the particular characteristics of the individual juvenile."[71]

## [6]  Speedy Trials

The speedy trial provision of the Sixth Amendment has been held applicable to juvenile courts.[72] Some jurisdictions have statutes codifying speedy trial principles.[73] The Juvenile Justice Standards provide for adjudication within fifteen days of arrest or filing of charges, whichever occurs first, for juveniles detained by the court for more than twenty-four hours and within thirty days for all others.[74]

## [7]  Public Trials

### [a]  Rights of Juveniles

Historically, juvenile proceedings were not open to the public. Indeed, statutes in most states currently exclude the general public from hearings in juvenile court although the courts are often allowed discretion to admit persons with significant interests in the proceedings.[75]

On the other hand, the Sixth Amendment guarantees a right to a public trial in all criminal prosecutions.[76] The underlying rationale of the public trial right has been explained as follows:

> Essentially, the public-trial guarantee embodies a view of human nature, true as a general rule, that judges, lawyers, witnesses, and jurors will perform their respective functions more responsibly in an open court than

---

euphemisms that had previously been used to avoid stigma (*e.g.*, "State youth center" became "Juvenile correctional facility"), alignment of the juvenile sentencing guidelines with the adult guidelines, adoption of presumptive sentencing, and nearly unrestricted disclosure of juvenile records. *Id.* at 160–70.

[70] *See* People v. Young, 416 N.Y.S.2d 171 (N.Y. Fam. Ct. 1979); William M. v. Harold B., 393 N.Y.S.2d 535 (N.Y. Fam. Ct. 1977).

[71] State v. Lawley, 591 P.2d 772, 773 (Wash. 1979).

[72] *See, e.g., In re* C.T.F., 316 N.W.2d 865 (Iowa 1982); *In re* Anthony P., 430 N.Y.S.2d 479 (N.Y. Fam. Ct. 1980). For a discussion of the federal constitutional right to a speedy trial, see LaFave & Israel, *supra* note 30, at 786–806.

[73] *See, e.g.*, Ark. Code Ann. § 9-27-327(b) (Michie 2002) (adjudication hearing to be held within 14 days of detention hearing); 52 Minn. Stat. Ann., Rules of Juv. Proc. 13.02 (West Supp. 2002) (trial within 30 days of date of demand for speedy trial for juveniles held in detention; trial within 60 days from date of demand for speedy trial for all others).

[74] Institute of Judicial Admin. & American Bar Ass'n, Juvenile Justice Standards, Interim Status 89–90 (1980).

[75] Wadlington, Whitebread & Davis, *supra* note 35, at 504; *see, e.g.*, Ga. Code Ann. § 15-11-78(b) (Harrison 2001) (but general public admitted to adjudications involving designated felonies or juveniles previously adjudicated delinquent).

[76] U.S. Const. amend. VI.

in secret proceedings. . . . A fair trial is the objective, and "public trial" is an institutional safeguard for attaining it.

Thus the right of "public trial" is not one belonging to the public, but one belonging to the accused, and inhering in the institutional process by which justice is administered.[77]

Although the Supreme Court has suggested that juveniles might be entitled to the presence of their friends and relatives at delinquency adjudications,[78] the Court has not addressed the issue of whether the public trial provision applies to juvenile courts. The *McKeiver* plurality's rejection of jury trials as the possible harbingers of "public trials" frustrating the traditional "intimacy" of juvenile proceedings[79] suggests that the Court might deny juveniles the right to a public trial. Indeed, the lower courts that have confronted the issue have denied a federal constitutional right to public trial[80] or, for that matter, to a private one.[81] However, the Alaska Supreme Court has recognized a state constitutional right to a public trial in juvenile proceedings.[82] In holding that juveniles possess a right to demand the presence of the "press, friends, or others,"[83] the court said:

The reasons for the constitutional guarantees of public trial apply as much to juvenile delinquency proceedings as to adult criminal proceedings. Delinquency proceedings as much as adult criminal prosecutions can be used as instruments of persecution, and may be subject to judicial abuse. The appellate process is not a sufficient check on juvenile courts, for problems of mootness and the cost of prosecuting an appeal screen most of what goes on from appellate court scrutiny. We cannot help but notice that the children's cases appealed to this court have often shown much more extensive and fundamental error than is generally found in adult criminal cases, and wonder whether secrecy is not fostering a judicial attitude of casualness toward the law in children's proceedings.[84]

The Juvenile Justice Standards provide for a right to a public trial, waivable by the juvenile upon consultation with counsel.[85] When the right is waived, the judge has discretion to admit members of the public, including the news media.[86] Even

---

[77] Estes v. Texas, 381 U.S. 532, 588 (1965) (Harlan, J., concurring).

[78] *See In re* Oliver, 333 U.S. 257, 265 n.12 (1948) (dicta) (courts favor openness and even juvenile proceedings have never wholly excluded "parents, relatives or friends" of the accused minor). At least one lower court has held that accused juveniles are statutorily entitled to have their parents present at delinquency proceedings. Hopkins v. Youth Court, 227 So. 2d 282 (Miss. 1969).

[79] *Supra* § 7.03, notes 45–47 and accompanying text.

[80] *See, e.g., In re* Burrus, 167 S.E.2d 454 (N.C. Ct. App. 1969), *aff'd,* 403 U.S. 528 (1971).

[81] *See, e.g., In re* Chase, 446 N.Y.S.2d 1000 (N.Y. Fam. Ct. 1982) (juvenile has no right to exclude press, court applies presumption of open trial proceedings).

[82] R.L.R. v. State, 487 P.2d 27 (Alaska 1971).

[83] *Id.* at 39. The Alaska statute in place at the time provided that "[c]hild hearings shall not be open to the general public," but permitted the court "in its discretion after due consideration for the welfare of the child and of the public interest, [to] admit particular individuals to the hearing." *Id.* at 38–39.

[84] *Id.* at 38.

[85] Institute of Judicial Admin. & American Bar Ass'n, Juvenile Justice Standards, Adjudication 70–72 (1980).

[86] *Id.* at 72.

after waiving his right to a public trial, the juvenile retains a right to specify persons he wishes to attend the proceedings.[87]

## [b]  Rights of the Press

In addition to juvenile defendants who sometimes seek open proceedings, representatives of the press have raised First Amendment challenges to delinquency adjudication closure rules. The United States Supreme Court has held that in criminal cases the press enjoys a general First Amendment right of access to trial proceedings[88] as a means of enhancing "the quality and safeguard[ing] the integrity of the factfinding process, with benefits to both the defendant and to society as a whole" as well as "foster[ing] an appearance of fairness, thereby heightening public respect for the judicial process."[89] With *Gault's* analogy of juvenile justice to criminal justice, the press is arguably entitled access to juvenile proceedings for the same reasons applicable to criminal trials.

The Vermont Supreme Court rejected the argument that the First Amendment afforded a newspaper a right of access to juvenile proceedings that had been ordered closed by the trial court.[90] The court refused to apply to the juvenile courts the United States Supreme Court cases requiring access of the press to criminal cases.

> [The Supreme Court] held that the combination of the unbroken tradition of open criminal trials at common law and the fact that openness of criminal trials serves important First Amendment goals requires public access, absent overriding interests. That limited holding, however, does not extend to the case at hand.
>
> Far from a tradition of openness, juvenile proceedings are almost invariably closed. . . . Further, juvenile proceedings are not criminal prosecutions, a fact which makes at least some of the First Amendment purposes served by open criminal trials inapplicable. Finally, inherent in the very nature of juvenile proceedings are compelling interests in confidentiality which the Supreme Court itself has endorsed and which we hold override any remaining First Amendment goals which access might serve.[91]

The court went on to note that juvenile courts conduct "protective" proceedings "concerned with the welfare of the child" that "are not punitive."[92] Therefore, a juvenile action is "so unlike a criminal prosecution that the . . . right of access [recognized by the Supreme Court in criminal cases] does not govern."[93] Finally, the court observed:

---

[87]  The right to permit certain persons to attend is also enjoyed by the juvenile's attorney and family. *Id.* at 73.

[88]  Globe Newspaper Co. v. Superior Court, 457 U.S. 596 (1982) (holding unconstitutional a statute requiring closure of courtroom during testimony of child victim witness). The Court has permitted some exceptions to the right of access of the press to criminal proceedings. *See* LaFave & Israel, *supra* note 30, at 985–1007.

[89]  457 U.S. at 606.

[90]  *In re* J.S., 438 A.2d 1125 (Vt. 1981).

[91]  *Id.* at 1127.

[92]  *Id.*

[93]  *Id.* at 1128.

The punitive purpose of criminal proceedings raises First Amendment issues which are not present here. There, public access serves as a check against unjust conviction, excessive punishment and the undeserved taint of criminality. . . . The juvenile proceeding, by contrast, involves no criminal conviction, no punishment, and, when confidential, no taint of criminality. Thus fewer First Amendment interests are at stake here than [in criminal cases]. [In addition] [c]onfidential proceedings protect the delinquent from the stigma of conduct which may be outgrown and avoids the possibility that the adult is penalized for what he used to be, or worse yet, the possibility that the stigma becomes self-perpetuating, thereby making change and growth impossible.[94]

The courts generally have upheld laws maintaining closure of juvenile proceedings. The United States Supreme Court has held, however, that states cannot impose criminal penalties on newspapers that publish the lawfully obtained names of juvenile offenders. In *Smith v. Daily Mail Publishing Co.*,[95] the Court found that a statute that prohibited publishing the names of juveniles charged with criminal offenses without approval of the court violated newspapers' First Amendment rights. The Court explained its decision as follows:

The sole interest advanced by the State to justify its criminal statute is to protect the anonymity of the juvenile offender. It is asserted that confidentiality will further his rehabilitation because publication of the name may encourage further antisocial conduct and also may cause the juvenile to lose future employment or suffer other consequences for this single offense. . . .

The magnitude of the State's interest in this statute is not sufficient to justify application of a criminal penalty to respondents. Moreover, the statute's approach does not satisfy constitutional requirements. The statute does not restrict the electronic media or any form of publication, except "newspapers," from printing the names of youths charged in a juvenile proceeding. In this very case, three radio stations announced the alleged assailant's name before the Daily Mail decided to publish it. Thus, even assuming the statute served a state interest of the highest order, it does not accomplish its stated purpose.

In addition, there is no evidence to demonstrate that the imposition of criminal penalties is necessary to protect the confidentiality of juvenile proceedings. As the Brief for Respondents points out, all 50 states have statutes that provide in some way for confidentiality, but only 5, including West Virginia, impose criminal penalties on nonparties for publication of the identity of the juvenile. Although every state has asserted a similar interest, all but a handful have found other ways of accomplishing the objective.[96]

## [8] Policy Implications

To some extent at least, *Gault* and its progeny have not delivered complete realization of the procedural protections promised by the United States Supreme Court. As noted above, apparently most juveniles who confront the juvenile justice

---

[94] *Id.* at 1128–29.

[95] 443 U.S. 97 (1979).

[96] *Id.* at 104–5.

system do so without the assistance of counsel.[97] Moreover, the presence of counsel appears to aggravate the sentence that juveniles receive.[98] This apparent bias against juveniles represented by counsel is a cause for concern, unless one sees juvenile dispositions, regardless of their severity, as inherently beneficial to their recipients. A leading commentator has called for further research on the delivery of legal services, the role and effect of counsel, and the relationship between procedural formality and sentencing severity in juvenile court.[99]

Moreover, some social science data suggests that juries acquit more readily than judges, thus making it easier to convict delinquents than similarly situated adults in criminal court.[100] To the extent this is true, policy makers who are skeptical of the ability of the juvenile system to deliver meaningful rehabilitation may consider joining the few jurisdictions that allow jury determinations in delinquency adjudications.

Along these same lines, concerns over the inadequacy of procedural safeguards may suggest a policy of open, rather than closed, adjudications. Exposing the system to public view may be an attractive move, particularly for those who see juvenile court dispositions as punitive or ineffective in their rehabilitative efforts.

## [B] Affirmative Defenses

Historically, the juvenile system was reluctant to afford juveniles all the defenses available to criminal defendants. For courts and legislatures convinced that young people benefit from the juvenile system, it was deemed undesirable to permit youngsters in need of help to avoid rehabilitative benefits by utilizing affirmative defenses to the charges to obtain acquittals.[101] Thus, all jurisdictions denied applicability of the defense of infancy,[102] many denied the defense of insanity,[103] and some avoided rigorous application of other defenses including self-defense.[104]

With the advent of *Gault* and *Winship*, however, most jurisdictions have begun to recognize affirmative defenses in delinquency adjudications. Indeed, as discussed below, juveniles in many jurisdictions are now permitted to invoke the same array of defenses available in criminal cases[105] with the exception of infancy,

---

[97] *Supra* note 42 and accompanying text.

[98] *Supra* note 43 and accompanying text; *see also* B. Feld, *Criminalizing the American Juvenile Court*, 17 CRIME & JUST. 197, 221–27 (1993).

[99] *Id.* at 227.

[100] *Id.* at 200. Note, however, that some jurisdictions allow for jury determinations in delinquency cases. *See supra*, note 62.

[101] *See* McCarthy, *supra* § 7.02, note 23, at 208–09.

[102] Fox, *supra* § 7.02, note 25, at 667 (unanimous rejection of the infancy defense in delinquency proceedings by every court that faced the issue prior to 1970).

[103] McCarthy, *supra* note 101; *In re* State *ex rel.* H.C., 256 A.2d 322 (N.J. Juv. & Dom. Rel. Ct. 1969) (denying insanity defense at adjudication), *overruled by*, State *in re* the Interest of R.G.W., 342 A.2d 869 (N.J. Super. Ct. App. Div. 1975), *aff'd*, 358 A.2d 473 (N.J. 1976) (pursuant to statute allowing juveniles all defenses available to an adult).

[104] McCarthy, *supra* note 101.

[105] See, *e.g.*, New Jersey Statutes Annotated § 2A:4A-40 (West 1987), which provides: "All defenses available to an adult charged with crime, offense or violation shall be available to a juvenile charged with committing an act of delinquency." For a complete discussion of criminal law defenses, see generally P. Robinson, Criminal Law Defenses (1984).

and to a lesser degree insanity, so long as adequate evidence supports raising the defense issue. The unavailability of the infancy defense in a majority of jurisdictions has become controversial as juvenile court dispositions become more punitive. Moreover, arguments have recently been raised for expanding self-defense to cover cases of battered children who kill their abusers under circumstances where the traditional doctrine precludes the defense. Similarly, youthful gang members have argued for an expanded defense of duress to excuse crimes they commit under pressure by gang members. As discussed below, at least one jurisdiction has recognized a more liberal self-defense doctrine for certain battered child defendants who kill their abusers, while the gang-duress defense has been universally rejected.

## [1]  Competency to be Adjudicated

Questions regarding a juvenile defendant's mental capacity may arise in various contexts of adjudicatory proceedings. Such questions may arise even prior to adjudication through inquiries into whether the defendant is competent to be adjudicated. The competency issue is generally viewed in the same terms as in adult criminal court, namely, whether the juvenile defendant understands the nature of the proceedings against him and can assist in his defense.[106]

Some jurisdictions statutorily provide for an incompetency defense.[107] In the absence of statute, some courts have held that juveniles are entitled to raise the incompetency issue as a matter of due process of law.[108]

At least one court has linked the incompetency issue to *Gault's* recognition of a right to counsel:

> Although this issue is one of first impression in Arkansas, the United States Supreme Court held, in the case of *In re Gault*, that while proceeding a juvenile court need not conform with *all* the requirements of a criminal trial, primarily because of the special nature of the proceedings, essential requirements of due process and fair treatment must be met. The Court, in *Gault*, specifically acknowledged a juvenile's right to constitution-ally adequate notice, the right against self-incrimination, and the right to cross-examine witnesses; further, the Court explicitly held that a juvenile must be afforded the right to counsel during these proceedings. Logically, this right to counsel means little if the juvenile is unaware of the proceedings or unable to communicate with counsel due to a psychological or developmental disability. Therefore, applying *Gault*, we hold that a juvenile *must* be allowed to assert incompetency and have his competency determined prior to adjudication.[109]

---

[106]  *See, e.g., In re* W.A.F., 573 A.2d 1264 (D.C. 1990); *In re* D.D.N., 582 N.W.2d 278 (Minn. Ct. App. 1998).

[107]  *See, e.g., In re* D.D.N., 582 N.W.2d 278 (Minn. Ct. App. 1998) (applying a rule of court setting the standard for juvenile competency.)

[108]  *See, e.g., In re* Y.C., 570 N.W.2d 36 (S.D. 1997).

[109]  Golden v. State, 21 S.W.3d 801, 802 (Ark. 2000). The majority's position in *Golden* did not go unchallenged, however. In his dissenting opinion, Justice Smith observed:

> . . . I would affirm the trial court's denial of a competency hearing. I do so because the distinctions that exist between juvenile court proceedings and adult criminal proceedings are substantial and are rationally based upon the differences between adults and children. Although according a juvenile the right to a competency hearing appears equitable, it is, I submit, unwise. It reflects the continued erosion of all distinction between juvenile court and

## [2]  The Insanity Defense

Legal insanity operates as a culpability defense that precludes the imposition of punitive sanctions. Because punishment entails the purposeful infliction of suffering and characteristically connotes blameworthiness, it is unjust to punish offenders who lack responsibility for their offenses.[110] Therefore, the law excuses offenders who commit offenses while suffering from a mental disease or defect that preludes them from acting rationally (or, in some jurisdictions, voluntarily), thus rendering them unable to function as moral agents.[111]

A successful insanity defense results in hospitalization of the acquittee until it is established that she is no longer mentally ill or that she poses little risk of danger to herself or others.[112] The length of confinement in the hospital is determined by the release criteria, not by the nature of the offense of which she was acquitted.[113]

If the juvenile justice system were indeed thoroughly rehabilitative in its dispositional responses to adjudicated delinquents, exculpatory defenses such as insanity would obviously be irrelevant at the adjudication stage. Indeed, in some jurisdictions the issue at adjudication is conceptualized simply in terms of whether the juvenile defendant committed the alleged act with the requisite intent without regard to whether or not any mental abnormality might have impaired his moral responsibility for its commission.[114] Therefore, in such jurisdictions the insanity

---

adult criminal courts. This erosion could ultimately lead to the irrelevance of juvenile codes in general.

Juveniles do not have a fundamental due process right to not be deprived of their liberty as a result of a hearing during which they were incompetent. The State's *parens patriae* interest, under proper circumstances subordinates the child's liberty interest. A juvenile has a liberty interest, which the U.S. Supreme Court describes as "substantial," but of which they also state that "that interest must be qualified by the recognition that juveniles, unlike adults, are always in some form of custody." The U.S. Supreme Court in this same opinion also states, "Children by definition are not assumed to have the capacity to take care of themselves. They are assumed to be subject to the control of their parents, and if parental control falters, the State must play its role as *parens patriae*."

The distinctions existing between juveniles and adults are recognized by the legislature in Ark. Code Ann. § 9-27-102, which states, "The General Assembly recognizes that children are defenseless and that there is no greater moral obligation upon the General Assembly than to provide for the protection of our children and that our child welfare system needs to be strengthened by establishing a clear policy of the state that the best interests of the children must be paramount and shall have precedence at every stage of juvenile court proceedings. . . ." This is consistent with the *parens patriae* interest as discussed in the U.S. Supreme Court cases. Implicit in the General Assembly's statement is the recognition that juveniles will not be competent in the sense adults would be, because they are assumed not to have the capacity to take care of themselves. In fact, the juvenile proceedings are designed to accomplish its ends without regard to the juvenile's competence because its absence is presumed.

*Id.* at 805 (Smith, J., dissenting).

For a discussion of the incompetency issue in juvenile justice, see V. Cowden & G. McKee, *Competency to Stand Trial in Juvenile Delinquency Proceedings — Cognitive Maturity and the Attorney-Client Relationship*, 38 U. LOUISVILLE J. FAM. L. 829 (1995).

[110] Gardner, *supra* § 4.02, note 11, at 654–67, 738.

[111] J. Dressler, Understanding Criminal Law 319–24 (2d ed. 1995).

[112] *Id.* at 324–26.

[113] *Id.* at 326.

[114] See, *e.g.*, In re *C.W.M.*, 407 A.2d 617, 622 (D.C. 1979), where the court said:

A juvenile delinquency proceeding concededly does not incorporate [an inquiry into

defense is not available at the adjudication stage; instead, issues of the juvenile's mental state are considered at the disposition stage where such matters are relevant to fashioning appropriate rehabilitation for adjudicated delinquents.[115]

On the other hand, other jurisdictions allow the insanity defense at adjudication sometimes to avoid unjust punishment where the court recognizes punitive aspects of juvenile court dispositions.[116] Other jurisdictions embrace the rehabilitative theory of juvenile justice but permit the insanity defense as a mechanism for providing needed care, given that successful insanity acquittees are hospitalized rather than released outright.[117]

## [3] The Infancy Defense

As discussed earlier, the infancy defense at common law played a role similar to the insanity defense with both providing a mechanism for avoiding unjust punishment.[118] The theoretical affinity of the defenses of infancy and insanity suggests that the respective defenses would play a similar role in juvenile justice. Such is not the case, however. While the insanity defense enjoys widespread applicability in the juvenile context, the infancy defense is recognized in only a few jurisdictions.[119]

The infancy doctrine presumes that children between the ages of seven and fourteen lack criminal responsibility and holds children under age seven immune from criminal liability.[120] Courts rejecting the infancy defense in juvenile court routinely do so on grounds that recognition of the defense would frustrate the rehabilitative mission of the juvenile courts.[121] Thus, on this view, if the state were required to rebut the presumption of incapacity of seven to fourteen-year-olds or were unable to try those under seven altogether, the result would be that more children would be denied the benefits of a court disposition.

---

responsibility for the defendant's actions once the government has proven he committed the criminal act with the requisite intent]. Nevertheless, it is well settled now that unlike a criminal trial a juvenile factfinding hearing does not result in a determination of criminal responsibility. Nor is the succeeding dispositional hearing intended to result in the imposition of any penal sanction on the child. Rather, the purpose is to determine the treatment required to rehabilitate him. Accordingly, the insanity defense would be superfluous in a juvenile delinquency proceeding.

[115] *Id.*

[116] *See, e.g.,* State *ex rel.* Causey, 363 So. 2d 472 (La. 1978) (recognizing right to plead insanity in delinquency proceedings in part because of "the underlying notion that an accused must understand the nature of his acts in order to be criminally responsible"); Winburn v. State, 145 N.W.2d 178, 182–84 (Wis. 1966) ("juvenile procedures, to some degree at least, smack of crime and punishment," and therefore, as in criminal cases, insanity is a defense to delinquency charges).

[117] *See, e.g., In re* Gladys R., 464 P.2d 127, 141–42 (Cal. 1970) (Burke, J., dissenting) (insanity defense available in juvenile proceedings because "[p]ermitting the defense of insanity . . . does not deprive the minor of needed care").

[118] *See supra* § 7.02, notes 4–11 and accompanying text.

[119] Mnookin & Weisberg, *supra* note 46, at 1113 ("small number of cases have held that the infancy defense is applicable to juvenile proceedings"). For a thorough discussion of the infancy defense in juvenile courts, see A. Walkover, *The Infancy Defense in the New Juvenile Court*, 31 UCLA L. Rev. 503 (1984); Fox, *supra* note 102.

[120] *Supra* note 118.

[121] *See, e.g., In re* Tyvonne, 558 A.2d 661 (Conn. 1989); State v. D.H., 340 So. 2d 1163 (Fla. 1976).

A few jurisdictions, on the other hand, recognize the infancy defense in delinquency adjudications. Some court cases conclude that juvenile justice is at least in part punitive, and thus apply the infancy defense in juvenile court for the same reasons the defense applies in criminal courts.[122] Other courts find the defense applicable based on statutory interpretation without explicitly reasoning that it is a vehicle to avert unjust punishment.[123]

## [4] Battered Children and Self-Defense

Under traditional self-defense doctrine, applicable in delinquency adjudications, persons are entitled to resort to deadly force if necessary to repel another who unlawfully threatens the defender with immediate deadly force.[124] Similarly, persons are excused when they employ force to resist the attacks of another whom the defender reasonably but mistakenly believes is imminently threatening the defender with unlawful deadly force.[125]

Some courts have relaxed the requirement that the threatened attack be imminent in cases where women kill men who abuse them but where no immediate threat of abuse exists. The battered woman may be psychologically conditioned to believe that her abuser will eventually kill her and that she has no alternative short of self-help. Under such circumstances, the battered woman resorts to deadly force to avoid being killed.[126] Thus, with the aid of the testimony of mental health experts explaining the "battered woman syndrome," women who kill their abusers in nonconfrontational circumstances are sometimes allowed to present self-defense claims which would otherwise be precluded because no "immediate threat of deadly force" existed at the time of the killing.[127]

Mental health professionals have also identified a "battered child syndrome," other aspects of which were discussed in Chapter 4,[128] which, like the battered woman syndrome, provides a psychological profile of abused children.[129] Similar to battered women, battered children typically feel powerless against their abusers and experience acute feelings of fear towards them. Moreover, because battered

---

[122] *In re* Andrew M., 398 N.Y.S.2d 824, 826 (N.Y. Fam. Ct. 1977) (because juvenile proceedings impose "almost criminal liability," traditional common law infancy defense must be available in delinquency adjudications); State v. Q.D., 685 P.2d 557 (Wash. 1984) (juvenile system now "akin" to criminal system); *In re* William A., 548 A.2d 130 (Md. 1988) (defense of infancy relates to the presence or absence of *mens rea* required for commission of a crime).

[123] *See, e.g., In re* Gladys R., 464 P.2d 127 (Cal. 1970).

[124] LaFave & Scott, *supra* § 5.06, note 2, at 454–60; Dressler, *supra* note 111, at 199–210.

[125] *Id.*

[126] Dressler, *supra* note 111, at 215–21.

[127] *Id.*

[128] *Supra* § 4.03[A][1].

[129] The psychological aspects of the battered child syndrome are discussed in B. Bjerregaard & A. Blowers, *Chartering a New Frontier for Self-Defense Claims: The Applicability of the Battered Person Syndrome as a Defense for Parricide Offenders*, U. Louisville J. Fam. L. 843 (1995); J. Moreno, *Killing Daddy: Developing a Self-Defense Strategy for the Abused Child*, 137 U. Pa. L. Rev. 1281 (1989); Note, *Self-Defense and the Child Parricide Defendant: Should Courts Make a Distinction Between Battered Women and the Battered Child?*, 44 Drake L. Rev. 351, 161–65 (1996); Note, *The Hazards of Using the "Battered Child Syndrome" as Evidence of Self-Defense When Children Kill in Non-Confrontational Situations*, 16 J. Juv. L. 91 (1995); and Note, *Nonconfrontational Killings and the Appropriate Use of Battered Child Syndrome Testimony: The Hazards of Subjective Self-Defense and the Merits of Partial Excuse*, 45 Case W. Res. L. Rev. 185 (1994).

children live in situations of pervasive abuse which may occur at any moment, they become "hypervigilant" in perceiving subtle cues from the abuser that not only create fear of impending abuse but also sometimes cause flashbacks to past abuse.[130]

Children who kill their abusers, usually parents, in nonconfrontational circumstances have fared less well than their battered women counterparts in maintaining self-defense claims. Most of the cases have arisen in criminal court.[131] Some courts refuse to admit expert testimony on battered child syndrome and refuse to instruct the jury on self-defense. For example, in a Wyoming case[132] a sixteen-year-old killed his father who had physically and psychologically abused his son for much of the son's life. On the night of his death, the father had engaged in a violent altercation with the son. The father then took the boy's mother out to dinner, but before leaving warned the son not to be home when the father and mother returned. While his parents were out to dinner, the son made preparations to kill his father, placing weapons in various parts of the family home as "backups" should his initial plan fail. The son then waited in the darkened garage with a shotgun and shot and killed his father when he returned home. The son was tried for murder and the trial court refused a proffer of evidence by a mental health expert that the defendant suffered from the battered child syndrome. The trial court also refused to instruct the jury on self-defense.

On appeal, the court upheld the trial court's actions, finding insufficient evidence to support a claim of self-defense and expressing skepticism about the scientific validity of the battered child syndrome. In any event, the court saw little relevance of the syndrome to a self-defense claim given the absence of any unlawful or deadly threat by the father at the time of the attack by the son. While the court noted the battered women cases, it rejected the notion that either abused women or children should have a "special defense" which justifies killing the abuser.[133] Finally, the court noted that the sole relevance of evidence of family abuse is to assist the jury in determining whether a defendant's belief that he was in danger of his life or serious bodily injury was reasonable under the circumstances. Finding insufficient evidence to support a claim of self-defense in the instant case, the court concluded that the proffered evidence of child abuse was properly excluded as irrelevant.[134]

On the other hand, Washington has recognized an expanded self-defense for battered children similar to that allowed battered women.[135] The case involved a situation where a seventeen-year-old, Andrew, killed his abusive stepfather after the stepfather had engaged in a prolonged and heated argument with Andrew's

---

[130] Note, *Self-Defense and the Child Parricide Defendant, supra* note 129; *see also* State v. Janes, 850 P.2d 495, 501–3 (Wash. 1993).

[131] *But see In re* Appeal in Maricopa County, Juvenile Action No. JV-506561, 893 P.2d 60 (Ct. App. Ariz. 1994) (12-year-old charged in juvenile court with murdering her mother, trial court permitted expert testimony on battered child syndrome on issue of whether child killed in "heat of passion" thus reducing the crime to manslaughter).

[132] Jahnke v. State, 682 P.2d 991 (Wyo. 1984), *abrogated on other grounds,* Vaughn v. State, 962 P.2d 149 (Wyo. 1998).

[133] *Id.* at 996.

[134] *See also* Whipple v. State, 523 N.E.2d 1363 (Ind. 1988) (court denied self-defense instruction because of insufficient evidence of imminent or impending danger where 17-year-old son killed his father, who had severely abused the son and his sister for years, while the father was sleeping — the killing occurred several days after the father severely beat the son for having candy bars in his room).

[135] State v. Janes, 850 P.2d 495 (Wash. 1993).

mother and then criticized Andrew "in a low voice" which the mother claimed was usually reserved for threats. The next day, after the stepfather had gone to work, Andrew awoke. His mother warned him that the stepfather was still angry. While his stepfather was still at work, Andrew made preparations to kill him. After drinking whiskey, smoking marijuana, and loading a gun, Andrew pondered how miserable his stepfather had made him and his mother. When the stepfather arrived home that afternoon, Andrew shot and killed him as he entered the front door.

At the murder trial, a mental health professional testified that Andrew, the defendant, suffered from "post-traumatic stress disorder" as a consequence of years of the stepfather's abuse. This caused the defendant, in the opinion of the expert, to be in a constant state of fear of attack by his stepfather. Notwithstanding this evidence, the trial court denied the defendant's request for a self-defense instruction, finding insufficient evidence of imminent danger.

Upon conviction of second degree murder, the defendant appealed, contesting the denial of a self-defense instruction. The Washington Supreme Court, drawing an analogy to its cases permitting battered woman syndrome evidence, held that the evidence of battered child syndrome was properly admitted in order to assist the jury to understand the "reasonableness of the defendant's perceptions."[136] Moreover, the court held that the trial court paid inadequate attention to Andrew's subjective fears in denying the self-defense instruction. In remanding the case to consider this issue, the court implied that if Andrew had actually feared an imminent attack by the stepfather at the time of the killing, a jury might conclude he killed in self-defense.

## [5] Gang Activity and the Duress Defense

The common law defense of duress excuses a person who commits any offense except murder if: 1) the offender, or a person near to the offender, was threatened with death or serious bodily injury by another unless the offender committed the offense; 2) the offender reasonably believed the threat was impending and credible; 3) the offender had no reasonable escape from the threat except to comply with the demands of the person posing the threat; and 4) the offender was not at fault in exposing himself to the threat.[137] While the traditional duress defense may be available in appropriate cases, some members of criminal gangs have unsuccessfully argued for an expanded defense, claiming that even though they may have been at fault in initially joining the gang, they should nevertheless be acquitted when the gang subsequently pressures them to commit a crime.[138] Others have been similarly unsuccessful in arguing that they were coerced into initially joining the gang and thus should enjoy a duress defense when gang pressures subsequently influence their criminal acts.[139]

---

[136] *Id.* at 503.

[137] *See* Dressler, *supra* note 111, at 273–76; *see also* Model Penal Code § 2.09 (Proposed Official Draft 1962) (not excluding operation of duress defense where coerced person commits murder).

[138] *See, e.g.*, Meador v. State, 664 S.W.2d 878 (Ark. Ct. App. 1984) (trial court properly rejected defendant's argument that duress defense could apply even if he had recklessly placed himself in a situation where it was reasonably foreseeable that he would be subjected to threatened force to commit a crime).

[139] *See, e.g.*, Williams v. State, 646 A.2d 1101 (Md. Ct. Spec. App. 1994), *cert. denied*, 651 A.2d 855 (Md. 1995).

While the courts have rejected a new gang-duress defense, some commentators support its recognition.[140] Citing evidence that some street gangs threaten physical injury as a means of initially recruiting members and subsequently induce criminal conduct, proponents argue that the underlying policies of the duress defense apply as readily to gang-induced crime as to traditional contexts where the defense is applicable.[141]

### [6] Policy Implications

To the extent that juvenile dispositions are punitive, both personhood and protectionist theorists would likely argue that juveniles in delinquency proceedings should enjoy access to the full array of culpability defenses available in criminal cases. Thus, for the same reasons they occupy an important place in criminal jurisprudence, the defenses of infancy and insanity should be applicable in juvenile courts. Moreover, theorists from both camps would likely permit evidence of the battered child syndrome to be considered in conjunction with self-defense claims in parricide cases, at least to the same extent the jurisdiction permits evidence of the analogous battered woman syndrome in self-defense arguments raised in criminal court. Whether juveniles should be allowed a broader arsenal of defense theories than adults (*e.g.*, a gang-duress defense for children coerced into joining street gangs who subsequently are influenced by gang pressures to commit crimes) depends upon whether one sees young people as uniquely vulnerable to outside influences and pressures that render them less culpable than adults engaging in similar conduct.

On the other hand, if juvenile justice is perceived as a system that affords meaningful help for adjudicated delinquents, protectionists may oppose allowing any excuse or justification defenses not constitutionally required by *Winship*'s holding that the prosecution prove each element of the offense beyond a reasonable doubt.[142] Protectionists may thus favor liberal avenues for directing troubled youngsters into the system rather than recognizing a host of defenses which effectively keep them out. In contrast, personhood theorists may favor a wide array of defenses as a means of avoiding the evils of unwanted paternalistic interventions even if dispositions of adjudicated delinquents are perceived as rehabilitative in nature.[143]

## § 10.03 STATUS OFFENSES

### [A] Procedural Aspects

In many respects, procedures to adjudicate a minor a status offender are the same as those employed in delinquency cases. The action begins by filing a petition alleging facts that specify non-criminal conduct or status conditions that place the

---

[140] *See, e.g.*, Student Article, *A Coercion Defense for the Street Gang Criminal: Plugging the Moral Gap in Existing Law*, 10 Notre Dame J.L. Ethics & Pub. Pol'y 137 (1996).

[141] *Id.* at 155–83, 206–26. For discussion of anti-gang legislation in general, see *supra* § 8.03[C][2][a].

[142] For a discussion of the distinction between the "failure of proof defenses" required by *Winship* and "affirmative defenses" (excuses and justifications) arguably not constitutionally mandated, see Gardner, *supra* note 110, at 667–743 and Robinson, *supra* note 105.

[143] *See supra* § 2.03, notes 3–9 and accompanying text.

child within the status offense jurisdiction of the juvenile court.[1] A discussion of the procedural aspects of status offense adjudication follows.

## [1]  Constitutional Protections

The *Gault* Court specifically applied its procedural protections to delinquency adjudications, thus leaving open the question whether the protections apply in status offense cases. Indeed, the lower court cases disagree on whether *Gault* and its progeny govern status offense adjudications, especially where "loss of liberty' in the form of an incarcerative commitment is not available as a direct disposition for status offenders.[2]

Some cases hold *Gault* inapplicable in status offense adjudications, sometimes on the basis of a perceived distinction between the stigmatic effect of being labeled a "delinquent" as opposed to a "status offender." In a Maryland case,[3] for example, a thirteen-year-old girl confessed to the police that she had escaped from her home by putting sleeping pills in her mother's coffee and subsequently engaged in various sexual acts with adults. The police questioned her and obtained a confesssion before giving the girl the *Miranda* warnings. Relying on the information provided by the confession, juvenile authorities brought an action against the girl, charging her as a "child in need of supervision" (CINS).[4] At her adjudication, the girl sought to exclude the confession, arguing that her privilege against self-incrimination rights under *Gault* and *Miranda* were denied. The trial court denied the girl's motion, permitted the confession to be admitted into evidence, proceeded to adjudicate the girl a CINS, and placed her in a foster home.

On appeal, the Maryland Supreme Court affirmed the actions of the lower court finding that *Gault* applies only if a two-pronged test is satisfied: 1) the juvenile must be charged with an act which would be a crime if committed by an adult; and 2) commitment to a state institution must be a possible result of adjudication for the act. Although the court noted that under the Maryland statute CINS children may not be confined in institutions designed for delinquent children,[5] it found it unnecessary to explore the second prong of the test as a possible basis for denying *Gault*'s applicability. Instead, the court found that it "is sufficient to hold that since appellant was not charged with an act which . . . would constitute a crime if committed by an adult, the privilege against self-incrimination is not applicable to these proceedings."[6]

Other courts define the applicability of *Gault* solely in terms of whether or not status offense adjudication carries the possibility of "commitment to an institution

---

[1] Davis, *supra* § 2.02, note 9, at 5-2 to 5-3. See *supra* § 8.04 for discussion of status offense jurisdiction.

[2] See *supra* § 10.02, notes 2–5 and accompanying text.

[3] *In re* Spalding, 332 A.2d 246 (Md. 1975).

[4] The petition initially also alleged some acts of delinquency (drug use) which were eventually dropped from consideration by the court.

[5] CINS children were subject to confinement in institutions so long as the institution was not designed for delinquent children. 332 A.2d at 259 (Eldridge, J., dissenting).

[6] *Id.* at 257; *see also In re* Potter, 237 N.W.2d 461 (Iowa 1976) (no due process violation where juvenile court applied "clear and convincing" evidence standard rather than *Winship*'s "proof beyond reasonable doubt" in a proceeding where juvenile was declared a "delinquent" as one "who habitually deports himself in a manner that is injurious to himself and others" (statute since repealed) and committed to training school).

in which the juvenile's freedom is curtailed."[7] Thus, for example, in a North Carolina case,[8] juvenile authorities initiated proceedings to determine whether a young woman was an "undisciplined child" for failing to obey her parents. The applicable statutory provisions made incarcerative commitments available dispositional alternatives only for "delinquents" (statutorily defined to include children who violate conditions of probation) and not for undisciplined children.

The trial court found the juvenile to be an undisciplined child and placed her on probation in a proceeding in which she was not represented by counsel. In a subsequent proceeding in which the juvenile was represented by counsel, the juvenile was charged with being a delinquent for violating her earlier probation. The juvenile's lawyer moved to vacate the earlier status offense adjudication and probation disposition because the minor was not represented by counsel in those proceedings. The trial court rejected the motion, finding *Gault* inapplicable because incarcerative dispositions were not a possible consequence of the status offense proceeding and therefore no right to counsel existed. The court adjudicated the young woman a delinquent for violating her probation and committed her to the custody of the state correctional officials. On appeal, the North Carolina Supreme Court affirmed the trial court's actions, rejecting the argument that the *Gault* protections were triggered at the status offense proceeding because it subjected the child to the risk of probation, a violation of which in turn subjected her to the risk of being adjudicated a delinquent with attendant confinement in a state institution.

Other courts, however, apply the *Gault* rights because of the risk of incarceration even though the disposition for the initial status offense did not entail the possibility of incarceration. Thus, a Florida court held that a juvenile could not be incarcerated pursuant to a statutory provision permitting incarceration for juveniles upon their second status offense adjudication when counsel was not available at the original status offense proceeding.[9] Nevertheless, the court held that juveniles charged with status offenses do not enjoy a right to counsel in initial status offense proceedings where no direct risk of incarceration exists.

While some courts hold that the procedural protections recognized by the United States Supreme Court's juvenile justice cases are inapplicable in status offense cases, some state statutes extend at least some of the protections to all status offense proceedings.[10] On the other hand, other legislatures provide *Gault* rights without specifying whether or not they apply to status offense as well as delinquency cases.[11] Moreover, many statutes limit *Winship* to delinquency cases by specifying that proof beyond a reasonable doubt is not required in status offense proceedings.[12]

---

[7] *Supra* § 10.02, note 33 and accompanying text; *see also supra* § 7.03, note 30 and accompanying text; *see, e.g., In re* K., 554 P.2d 180 (Or. Ct. App. 1976) (*Gault* not applicable in status offense proceedings where institutional confinement was not a possible disposition); State *ex rel.* Wilson v. Bambrick, 195 S.E.2d 721 (W. Va. 1973) (*Gault* protections must be afforded to "runaway children" who risk incarceration in state industrial school upon adjudication).

[8] *In re* Walker, 191 S.E.2d 702 (N.C. 1972).

[9] *In re* Hutchins, 345 So. 2d 703 (Fla. 1977).

[10] *See, e.g.,* Ga. Code Ann. §§ 15-11-6(b), 65(a) (Harrison 2001) (right to counsel, proof beyond reasonable doubt); Nev. Rev. Stat. § 62D.030 (2007) (right to counsel).

[11] *See, e.g.,* Neb. Rev. Stat. § 43-272(1) (Reissue 1998).

[12] Davis, *supra* note 1, at 5-23; *see, e.g.,* Cal. Welf. & Inst. Code § 701 (West 1998); N.M. Stat. Ann. § 32A-3B-14(B) (Michie 1999) ("clear and convincing evidence" required to find the child "in need of

## [2] Notice

As in delinquency cases, petitions alleging status offenses must be drawn with sufficient particularity to advise the juvenile of the nature of the charges.[13] Where the status offense takes the form of noncriminal misconduct such as truancy or running away from home,[14] notice is easily provided by specifying the particular dates the alleged acts occurred. On the other hand, where the status offense takes the form of an undesirable status condition, such as being a "wayward" or "unruly" child,[15] providing adequate notice may be problematic given the vagueness of the statutory categories.[16] Nevertheless, the petition should state with reasonable particularity occasions where the status condition was manifested.

In jurisdictions holding *Gault* inapplicable, notice requirements may be more lax, particularly where the state is responding to the child's troubled status rather than to specific acts of noncriminal misbehavior. Indeed, in such cases it can be argued that the object of the petition is not to notify the child, but rather to bring the case within the jurisdiction of the juvenile court in order for it to initiate needed help for the child.[17] Thus, petitions alleging that the child is a person in need of the court's care could be viewed as similar to petitions seeking to civilly commit mentally ill persons where the point of the petition is not aimed at notifying the defendant of his mental illness, but instead operates as a mechanism for bringing him before the court so that he might receive treatment among other things.

## [3] Discovery

As discussed above, the courts have generally applied criminal discovery rules to delinquency proceedings.[18] Some courts, on the other hand, apply civil discovery rules to juvenile proceedings not involving delinquent conduct.[19] To the extent the inquiry is directed to states of being and not particular acts, the proceeding may appear "civil" rather than "criminal" for purposes of applying discovery rules. Thus, greater discovery opportunities, including the taking of depositions, may be available in status offense cases, particularly those focusing on status conditions rather than on particular noncriminal acts.

---

court-ordered services"); Tenn. Code Ann. § 37-1-129(c) (2001) ("clear and convincing evidence" required to find child "unruly").

[13] Davis, *supra* note 1, at 5-7.

[14] *See supra* § 8.04[A].

[15] *See supra* § 8.04[B].

[16] *See supra* § 8.04[C][2].

[17] Statutes imposing jurisdiction over juveniles who manifest undesirable status conditions may be understood as "decision rules" addressed to the court as a vehicle for evaluating the state of being, rather than the conduct, of alleged status offenders. For a discussion of the distinction between "conduct rules" (addressed to the general public in order to guide its conduct) and "decision rules," see M. Dan-Cohen, *Decision Rules and Conduct Rules: On Acoustic Separation in Criminal Law*, 97 Harv. L. Rev. 625 (1984).

[18] *See supra* § 10.02[A][2].

[19] Davis, *supra* note 1, at 5-53.

## [4] Counsel

As mentioned above, many jurisdictions recognize a right to counsel in status offense adjudications, either by judicial recognitions of the applicability of *Gault* or by statute.[20] Defining the proper role to be played by available counsel is perhaps more difficult in status offense cases than in delinquency matters.[21] To the extent the label of status offender carries less stigma than being labeled a delinquent,[22] lawyers who represent juveniles in status offense cases may be even more prone to attempt to promote the welfare of their clients by cooperating with the state to obtain their adjudication than in delinquency cases where the adjudication itself is highly stigmatic. Lawyers may also be less zealous in seeking to avoid their client's adjudication as a status offender given the fact that, unlike delinquency cases, incarceration is often not available as a direct disposition for status offenders.[23]

## [5] Evidentiary Issues

### [a] Rules of Evidence

Apart from the issue of burden of proof where only about half the states apply the delinquency standard of proof, beyond a reasonable doubt,[24] many jurisdictions apply the same evidentiary rules in status offense and delinquency adjudications. Thus, most jurisdictions apply rules forbidding hearsay evidence.[25] For example, the Supreme Court of Vermont found prejudicial error where the trial court adjudicated a juvenile an "unmanageable child" based on the testimony of two social workers as to the contents of a social report drawn from interviews with third persons.[26] The court focused on the risk of possible confinement in a facility used for the treatment of delinquent children as a crucial factor in its rejection of hearsay in unmanageable child adjudications.

Some jurisdictions, on the other hand, permit hearsay evidence in status offense proceedings.[27] A New York court, for example, found no error when a trial court adjudicated a juvenile a truant and thus a "person in need of supervision" (PINS) solely on the basis of hearsay evidence composed of certified transcripts of school attendance records prepared by teachers from their roll books pursuant to state statutes that permitted truancy to be established in this manner.[28] Even though the teachers who prepared the roll books did not testify at the adjudication proceedings, the court found that the transcripts were inherently reliable and thus satisfied the "competent evidence" standard required in PINS cases. Furthermore,

---

[20] *Supra* notes 7–11 and accompanying text.

[21] See *supra* § 10.02, notes 44–46 and accompanying text for a discussion of the role of counsel in delinquency cases.

[22] See the discussion of *Spalding*, *supra* notes 2–6 and accompanying text.

[23] *See supra* notes 8–10 and accompanying text.

[24] Wadlington, Whitebread & Davis, *supra* § 3.02, note 34, at 630. See discussion of burden of proof, *infra* notes 32–35 and accompanying text.

[25] Davis, *supra* note 1, at 5-28.

[26] *In re* J.L.M., 430 A.2d 448 (Vt. 1981).

[27] Wadlington, Whitebread & Davis, *supra* note 24, at 630.

[28] *In re* R., 357 N.Y.S.2d 1001 (N.Y. Fam. Ct. 1974).

the court concluded that cross-examination of the teachers keeping the attendance records would add nothing to the reliability of the evidence.[29]

Another New York court held that PINS petitions may be based on hearsay allegations even though such allegations would not support a delinquency petition. The court gave the following explanation for the acceptability of hearsay in status offense adjudications:

> The basis for a PINS adjudication is somewhat imprecise, requiring, for example, findings such as that the respondent is "incorrigible" or "habitually disobedient." On the other hand, since a JD [juvenile delinquency] adjudication requires a finding that the respondent committed an act which, if committed by an adult, would have constituted a crime, the elements to be proved are precise and defined by the penal statutes. A PINS adjudication requires a finding that the respondent needs supervision or treatment while a JD adjudication requires a finding that the respondent needs supervision, treatment or confinement and secure detention is a dispositional alternative only in a JD proceeding. In view of the different nature of these proceedings, we find that the hearsay form of a PINS petition is consistent with the objective of providing a more informal procedure for those respondents whose conduct does not rise to the level of criminal conduct at issue in a JD proceeding.[30]

For courts finding *Gault* inapplicable in status offense proceedings, the Confrontation Clause poses no barrier to the admissibility of hearsay. Indeed, some courts see virtue in permitting hearsay evidence in status offense cases. One court explained:

> In juvenile cases, where the judge sits alone as the trier of fact and where it is his duty to become as knowledgeable and inquisitive as reasonably possible, it is better for him to admit hearsay "for what it's worth." He can make the determination whether responsible people would rely upon it in serious affairs when he makes his findings. He, by his experience in dealing with thousands of juveniles, being exposed to their statements, both forthright and delusive, will not be swayed, as a jury would, by hearsay which is not to be relied upon.
>
> Of course, we would not allow an adjudication of delinquency based on hearsay. Such a result would be in violation of a juvenile's right of confrontation.[31]

---

[29] While the court did not explicitly rely on the "business records" exception to the hearsay rule, a later decision from the same court appealed to this doctrine in permitting attendance records to prove truancy. *See In re* Kelly, 405 N.Y.S.2d 207 (N.Y. Fam. Ct. 1978); *see also In re* L.Z., 396 N.W.2d 214 (Minn. 1986); *In re* D.M.C., 503 A.2d 1280 (D.C. 1986) (business records exception applies regarding attendance records in truancy cases, even though elements of exception not met). For a New York truancy case holding admission transcripts inadmissible hearsay, violative of the juvenile's confrontation and due process rights, see In re *George C.*, 398 N.Y.S.2d 936 (N.Y. Fam. Ct. 1977).

[30] *In re* Keith H., 594 N.Y.S.2d 268, 272 (N.Y. App. Div. 1993).

[31] *In re* Farms, 268 A.2d 170, 175 (Pa. Super. Ct. 1970).

## [b] Standard of Proof

As mentioned above, the states differ as to the standard of proof in status offense cases.[32] About half the states employ the reasonable doubt standard in both delinquency and status offense adjudications.[33] Some jurisdictions lower the burden in status offense cases to the clear and convincing evidence standard,[34] while others utilize the preponderance of the evidence standard commonly employed in civil proceedings.[35]

## [c] Self-Incrimination

While some jurisdictions recognize the right against self-incrimination in status offense cases, either as constitutionally or statutorily required,[36] others find the right inapplicable.[37] An Iowa case,[38] for example, found that the privilege did not apply in a case alleging that a child was "wayward and habitually disobedient" and thus in need of special care which his mother could not provide.[39] The alleged violation of the privilege occurred when the child gave statements in response to questioning from a probation officer and from mental health professionals without being informed of his right to remain silent. The trial court found the child to be "uncontrolled," evidenced in part on the basis of his contested statements, and ordered the child to be placed in a juvenile institution. The child appealed and the Iowa Supreme Court found no violation of the privilege against self-incrimination. A four-member plurality of the court distinguished juvenile proceedings involving "public offenses," where the privilege is available, and the instant case where it was not. The plurality explained:

> [T]he purpose of juvenile proceedings is to help and assist the child, not to punish. The constitutional safeguard of "fundamental fairness" must be preserved in that setting. However, where there is no public offense charged we believe the requirement of advising the juvenile and his parents of his right to remain silent would frustrate the very purposes of the juvenile proceeding. Admittedly, upon the findings of the trial court the child may have to spend some time away from his home but such time will not be spent in a completely institutionalized setting. The record establishes visitation rights are lenient, and that the average stay for a child at the Home is about one year.

> We conclude, therefore, that in a juvenile proceeding where no public offense is charged, the question of self-incrimination is not presented.[40]

---

[32] *Supra* note 12 and accompanying text.

[33] *Supra* note 24; *see, e.g.*, Ga. Code Ann. § 15-11-65(a) (Harrison 2001); Tex. Fam. Code Ann. § 54.03(f) (West 1996 & Supp. 2002).

[34] *See, e.g.*, N.M. Stat. Ann. § 32A-3B-14(B) (Michie 1978); Tenn. Code Ann. § 37-1-129(c) (2001).

[35] *See, e.g.*, La. Children's Code Ann. art. 665 (West 1995); Md. Code Ann., Cts. & Jud. Proc. § 3-8A-18(e) (Supp. 2001).

[36] *See supra* note 11 and accompanying text.

[37] *See supra* notes 3–6 and accompanying text.

[38] *In re* Henderson, 199 N.W.2d 111 (Iowa 1972).

[39] *Id.* at 119.

[40] *Id.*

## [6]  Jury Determinations, Open Proceedings

As discussed above, jury trials are rare in delinquency cases.[41] In status offense cases, juries are utilized even less often. Because dispositions of status offenders are routinely perceived to be less punitive than those visited upon delinquents, there exists less impetus towards involving juries in status offense cases than in delinquency situations.

By the same token, while analogies to the criminal process lead very few jurisdictions to embrace public proceedings in delinquency cases,[42] status offense proceedings appear more at home with the traditional *parens patriae* premise of the juvenile justice movement and thus continue to remain closed.

## [7]  Policy Implications

In jurisdictions where the courts have held the federal constitutional provisions in the *Gault* line of cases inapplicable to status offense proceedings, policy makers are free to apply more relaxed procedural protections than those utilized in delinquency adjudications. Retaining the traditional informality of juvenile courts may appear attractive to protectionists who see the juvenile system as beneficial, or at least not harmful, to youngsters charged with status offenses. On the other hand, protectionists who see procedural formality as itself conducive to promoting rehabilitation[43] may favor employing the same protections as are applied in delinquency cases, even where juvenile dispositions are perceived as genuinely helpful to adjudicated status offenders.

Policy makers skeptical of the ability of juvenile justice to deliver on its promise of rehabilitation would likely see no reason to distinguish between the procedural aspects of status offense and delinquency adjudications. Some who hold this view of juvenile justice may, as in the context of delinquency, favor expanding the procedural protections available in status offense cases to include open proceedings with juries as fact finders.

## [B]  Affirmative Defenses

As mentioned above, juveniles were traditionally denied a broad arsenal of defenses in juvenile court proceedings.[44] While that situation has changed in the context of delinquency,[45] some jurisdictions continue to favor a narrow scope of available defense theories for defendants in status offense cases.

To understand the role of defenses in status offense cases, it is useful to distinguish cases where noncriminal misconduct is charged from those where jurisdiction is premised on an allegation that a juvenile manifests an undesirable status condition. In the latter category of cases, punitive dispositions cannot constitutionally be imposed[46] and thus culpability defenses such as insanity, infancy, and duress are theoretically inapposite. Indeed, all of the criminal law defenses relating to *mens rea* or *actus reus* may be considered irrelevant, given that the action is not premised on the claim that the juvenile intentionally or

---

[41] *Supra* § 10.02, notes 64–71 and accompanying text.

[42] *Supra* § 10.02, notes 82–84 and accompanying text.

[43] *See supra* § 7.03, note 22 and accompanying text.

[44] *Supra* § 10.02, notes 101–4 and accompanying text.

[45] *Supra* § 10.02, notes 105–38 and accompanying text.

[46] *See infra* § 11.04[D][b].

negligently engaged in statutorily proscribed acts of misconduct.[47] These ideas are reflected sporadically in the cases, some of which hold, for example, that the infancy defense is applicable in delinquency cases, where issues of punishment and *mens rea* are at stake, but not in cases addressing status issues such as whether a juvenile is a "person in need of supervision."[48]

In cases where a juvenile is alleged to have committed specific acts of noncriminal misconduct, such as running away from home or absenting himself from school, the *actus reus* and *mens rea* defenses available in delinquency actions are more clearly relevant.[49] Indeed, if punitive dispositions are imposed for such misconduct, denying the juvenile the full array of defenses available in criminal court is difficult to justify.

---

[47] *See supra* note 30 and accompanying text.

[48] *See, e.g., In re* William A., 548 A.2d 130 (Md. 1988) (holding infancy defense available in delinquency context, suggesting in *dicta* that the defense is not available in PINS cases).

[49] *See In re* L.Z., 396 N.W.2d 214 (Minn. 1986) (child permitted to introduce evidence that he did not "absent himself" from school through "volitional conduct").

# Chapter 11
# DISPOSITIONS

## § 11.01  OVERVIEW

While historically juvenile courts often considered the dispositional issue in the same proceeding which determined that the child had committed a status offense or an act of delinquency, the common practice today is to conduct adjudication and disposition in separate proceedings.[1] Through bifurcating the adjudication and disposition stages, jurisdictions routinely apply different procedures at disposition than those mandated by *Gault* and *Winship* or otherwise applied at the adjudication stage.[2]

Whether or not dispositional orders occur in a separate proceeding, they are among the most important matters decided by juvenile court judges. Traditionally, judges and legislatures drew no distinctions between delinquents and status offenders in evoking the goal of rehabilitation as the theoretical premise for all juvenile court dispositions.[3] In the post-*Gault* era, however, several jurisdictions have questioned the continuance of the rehabilitative ideal as the sole dispositional predicate, at least in delinquency cases.[4] Indeed, a variety of juvenile justice systems now adopt punitive sanctions for certain acts of delinquency as additions to, or alternatives for, traditional rehabilitative dispositions.[5] Some jurisdictions expressly appeal to theories of deterrence and retribution in systematically employing punitive dispositions,[6] while other jurisdictions impose pockets of punishment within systems that nominally disavow punitive dispositions as inconsistent with the traditional rehabilitative ideal.[7]

The emergence of punitive juvenile justice constitutes not only an important redirection of policy, but also entails a host of new legal issues not traditionally associated with the rehabilitative model of juvenile justice. Because punitive dispositions occur predominantly in the area of delinquency, and because many jurisdictions explicitly provide different dispositional alternatives for delinquents and status offenders, it is useful to distinguish between those two contexts in order to understand the law governing juvenile court dispositions. Therefore, after considering procedural matters, this chapter will separately examine delinquency and status offense dispositions.

## § 11.02  HEARING PROCEDURES

In *Gault*, the Court included a footnote suggesting that the holding of that case might have no application to the disposition phase of juvenile proceedings. The Court observed that "the problems of . . . postadjudication are unique to the

---

[1] Davis, *supra* § 2.02, note 9, at 6-1; Fox, *supra* § 8.02, note 2, at 211–12.

[2] *Supra* note 1.

[3] *Supra* § 8.01, notes 1–7 and accompanying text.

[4] Wadlington, Whitebread & Davis, *supra* § 3.02, note 34, at 516–24.

[5] *See supra* § 7.02, note 29 and accompanying text.

[6] *Id.*

[7] *See infra* § 11.03, notes 50–52 and accompanying text.

juvenile process; hence, what we hold in this opinion with regard to the procedural requirements at the adjudication stage has no necessary applicability to other steps of the juvenile process."[1]

Because the United States Supreme Court has not addressed constitutional issues at disposition, the states arguably are free to structure the process however they reasonably see fit. A state might, for example, merge the adjudication and disposition phases into a single proceeding so long as the *Gault* and *Winship* requirements are met. The clear trend, however, is towards a bifurcated process with fewer procedural formalities observed at the dispositional stage.[2]

## [A]  Right to a Hearing

In jurisdictions requiring separate proceedings for adjudications and dispositions, the courts have held that adjudicated juveniles have a right to a dispositional hearing,[3] except perhaps in cases where disposition decisions are based entirely on the gravity of the offense committed.[4] In fact, however, disposition decisions are generally based on a variety of considerations in addition to judgments assessing the gravity of the offense. Indeed, the disposition decision routinely involves determinations of how best to promote the child's welfare in a way consistent with the public interest.[5] Such judgments require courts to assess the child's background, environment, health, and family and educational situation. Thus, where disposition decisions consider such factors, the juvenile is entitled to be notified of the proceedings,[6] afforded the opportunity to be heard, and allowed to present any evidence relevant to the dispositional decision.[7]

On the other hand, in jurisdictions where separate dispositional proceedings are not statutorily required, the courts generally do not require a dispositional hearing.[8] In such jurisdictions, courts are permitted to make disposition decisions immediately upon finding that the juvenile is a delinquent or a status offender.[9]

## [B]  Right to Counsel

Notwithstanding *Gault*'s language suggesting the applicability of the case only to the adjudication phase, several courts have held that juveniles possess a due process right to counsel at disposition,[10] and sometimes even in status offense cases.[11] However, in jurisdictions that deny counsel rights at status offense

---

[1]  *In re* Gault, 387 U.S. 1, 31 n.48 (1967).

[2]  Davis, *supra* § 2.02, note 9, at 6-1 to 6-3; Fox, *supra* § 8.02, note 2, at 211–12.

[3]  Davis, *supra* note 2, at 6-2.

[4]  *See In re* J.L.P., 100 Cal. Rptr. 601, 603 (Cal. Ct. App. 1972) (suggesting in *dicta* that hearing might not be required if disposition decision were based solely on the gravity of the "crime").

[5]  Davis, *supra* note 2, at 6-4.

[6]  *See, e.g., In re* D.L.W., 543 N.E.2d 542 (Ill. App. Ct. 1989).

[7]  *See, e.g., In re* J.L.P., 100 Cal. Rptr. 601 (Cal. Ct. App. 1972).

[8]  Davis, *supra* note 2, at 6-3.

[9]  *Id.*

[10]  *See, e.g.,* A.A. v. State, 538 P.2d 1004 (Alaska 1975).

[11]  *See, e.g., In re* Cecilia R., 327 N.E.2d 812 (N.Y. 1975).

adjudications, a denial of counsel at disposition would also arguably be permitted, although there apparently are no reported cases addressing the issue.[12]

In a number of states, the child possesses a statutory right to counsel at adjudication.[13] In some of these states, the right is entailed in statutory language recognizing counsel rights at "all stages of the proceedings."[14]

## [C]  Rules of Evidence

Dispositional decisions are generally aimed at promoting the welfare of the child. That inquiry requires judicial access to as much information as possible regarding the child's background. As a consequence, any and all evidence relevant to the child's general situation is generally admissible at dispositional proceedings.[15] Thus, usual rules of evidence are not applicable. Hearsay, often in the form of a social report, is routinely considered by the court in making its dispositional decision.[16] Moreover, the exclusionary rule is generally inapplicable,[17] and some cases suggest that the juvenile may be interrogated by the court without observing the formalities otherwise necessary for effectuating waivers of the privilege against self-incrimination.[18]

On the other hand, in rare instances courts have recognized limited rights to cross-examination at disposition proceeding. For example, the Minnesota Supreme Court has held that a statutory provision affording juveniles the right "to cross-examine witnesses appearing at the hearing" was applicable to disposition, as well as adjudication, hearings.[19] The court held, however, that the right had not been denied to a juvenile who was permitted to cross-examine a witness at disposition only after the court approved the questions before being directed to the witness. The court opined that juveniles at disposition possess only minimal due process rights that are satisfied if the juvenile is given an opportunity to deny and explain material he deems adverse to his interests.

## § 11.03  DELINQUENCY CASES

As the *Gault* Court recognized, adjudicated delinquents often are subjected to custodial confinement in secure facilities. However, while institutional restraint is almost always a possible consequence of committing an act of delinquency, a variety of other, less restrictive, dispositions are also possible. These alternatives generally

---

[12] Fox, *supra* note 2, at 218.

[13] Davis, *supra* note 2, at 6-5.

[14] *Id.*

[15] *Id.* at 6-4.

[16] *Id.*; Fox, *supra* note 2, at 219–24.

[17] Fox, *supra* note 2, at 219; *see, e.g.*, *In re* Michael V., 223 Cal. Rptr. 503 (Cal. Ct. App. 1986) (illegally seized evidence suppressed at earlier hearing held admissible at disposition).

[18] Fox, *supra* note 2, at 219; *see, e.g.*, *In re* Smith, 337 N.E.2d 209 (Ill. App. Ct. 1975) (no error where trial judge informed juvenile that juvenile need not tell the judge anything, but then admonished the juvenile to divulge the whereabouts of a weapon, suggesting that such information may influence a disposition beneficial to the juvenile and thus arguably causing the juvenile to admit to selling the weapon).

[19] *In re* G.S.J., 281 N.W.2d 511 (Minn. 1979).

allow courts to impose probation, restitution, community service, and community-based institutionalization.[1]

While juvenile court judges have traditionally enjoyed broad discretion in imposing particular dispositions in individual cases,[2] some courts have found that the juvenile is entitled to the least drastic disposition consistent with the dispositional goals of the system.[3] Historically, those goals were defined in terms of promoting the welfare of the child.[4] In the post-*Gault* era, however, some jurisdictions have included crime prevention and dispensing just deserts as additional dispositional interests.[5] As a consequence, dispositional goals may differ from one jurisdiction to another.

## [A]   The Traditional Theory: Promoting the Child's Interests

At its inception, juvenile justice embraced the Progressive reform movement which adopted individualized dispositions aimed at rehabilitating deviant youngsters.[6] This approach eschewed uniform treatment or standardized criteria in an attempt to afford a case-by-case diagnosis of the causes of delinquency in order to effectuate a cure consistent with the individual needs of the particular juvenile.[7] Thus, juvenile court personnel were vested with broad discretion to promote the best interests of the child.[8] The overall inquiry paid little attention to the offense committed because it revealed little information relevant to the child's needs.[9] Therefore, the offense affected neither the intensity nor the duration of the disposition which the courts imposed for the duration of the child's minority.[10]

### [1]   Appellate Review of Judicial Discretion

The extent of judicial discretion to make dispositional decisions varies from jurisdiction to jurisdiction.[11] Some states continue the traditional practice of allowing judges broad discretion at disposition. Indeed, as discussed below, some courts permit virtually unfettered discretion[12] while others minimally review the actions of juvenile court judges and uphold their decisions unless there is evidence of clear abuse of discretion.[13] On the other hand, appellate courts in other

---

[1] *See* Wadlington, Whitebread & Davis, *supra* § 3.02, note 34, at 549–93; Kramer, *supra* § 3.03, note 15, at 370–71.

[2] *See infra* notes 11–21 and accompanying text.

[3] *See infra* notes 22–29 and accompanying text.

[4] *See infra* notes 6–31 and accompanying text.

[5] *See infra* notes 32–38 and accompanying text.

[6] B. Feld, *The Juvenile Court Meets the Principle of Offense: Punishment, Treatment, and the Difference it Makes*, 68 B.U. L. REV. 821, 823 (1988).

[7] *Id.* at 824.

[8] *Id.*

[9] *Id.* at 825.

[10] *Id.*

[11] *See* Miller, et al., *supra* § 9.03, note 10, at 885.

[12] See, *e.g.*, the discussion of *In re J.A.*, *infra* notes 15–16 and accompanying text.

[13] See, *e.g.*, the discussion of *In re S.J.*, *infra* notes 17–18 and accompanying text.

jurisdictions more rigorously scrutinize the actions of juvenile courts by affording full *de novo* review.[14]

Some appellate courts appear to grant absolute discretion to juvenile court judges who make dispositional decisions. For example, the Nebraska Supreme Court upheld a juvenile court's order committing a juvenile to institutional confinement without requiring the lower court to provide any explanation for its disposition.[15] The supreme court noted that "a juvenile court has broad discretion as to the disposition of a juvenile delinquent," but also observed that appellate courts review such actions "*de novo* on the record and [are] thus required to reach a conclusion independent of the juvenile court's finding" except where the evidence is in conflict, in which case the appellate court "may give weight to the juvenile court's observation of the witnesses and acceptance of one version of the facts over another."[16]

In the case at hand, the juvenile had admitted to one offense, disturbing the peace, after which the juvenile judge dismissed two other counts, obstructing a police officer and a second count of disturbing the peace. The juvenile court accepted the youth's admission and delayed disposition for approximately one month, during which time the juvenile allegedly had a fight with her mother, drank alcohol, and sniffed paint. After the juvenile admitted these additional allegations, the juvenile court, without explanation, issued an order committing the juvenile to the Youth Development Center. The juvenile appealed the order, arguing that the juvenile court must provide reasons for its disposition. The Nebraska Supreme Court affirmed and held that the disposition was justified solely by virtue of the fact that the juvenile court was statutorily authorized to impose a range of dispositions, including commitment to the Youth Development Center. Like the lower court, the supreme court offered no independent justification for the disposition, supplied no reasons of its own pursuant to its review powers, and simply ratified the institutional commitment.

Other appellate courts require the juvenile court to make dispositions consistent with applicable statutes, but uphold the dispositions unless they constitute a clear abuse of discretion. For example, the North Dakota Supreme Court upheld a juvenile court's commitment of a young woman to the State Industrial School after she was adjudicated a delinquent for committing the offense of robbery.[17] Before rejecting less severe alternatives, the juvenile court considered the array of available dispositions. The judge concluded, however, that the minor's past history indicated that she had difficulty adjusting to restrictions placed on her in her family home. On appeal, the supreme court found that the juvenile court's commitment to the Industrial School was consistent with the requirement that dispositions be in the best interests of the child. The court found that the "structured environment" of the State Industrial School would benefit the minor, adding that "[b]y placing her in the care, custody, and control of the Superintendent of the . . . School, the juvenile court has provided the means by which [the minor] may receive the necessary treatment, rehabilitation, and correction."[18]

---

[14] See, *e.g.*, the discussion of *In re Appeal No. 179*, *infra* notes 19–21 and accompanying text.

[15] *In re* J.A., 510 N.W.2d 68 (Neb. 1994).

[16] *Id.* at 72.

[17] *In re* S.J., 304 N.W.2d 685 (N.D. 1981).

[18] *Id.* at 686.

While juvenile courts routinely enjoy broad discretion in making dispositional decisions, their actions are nevertheless subject to scrutiny in some jurisdictions. In a Maryland case,[19] for example, a fifteen-year-old was adjudicated a delinquent as a result of his participation in a series of housebreakings and destruction of property therein. After reviewing a report from school officials indicating that the boy was an underachieving student with disciplinary problems and a report from a psychologist indicating that the boy had serious conflicts in his home with his father, the juvenile court ordered the boy committed to the appropriate state institution. The judge justified the disposition as a "loud and clear message" that a recent "epidemic of housebreakings" would not be countenanced.[20] The juvenile appealed and the appellate court vacated the juvenile court's order, finding it inconsistent with the statutory requirement that dispositions be premised on the "child's need for protection or rehabilitation." The court explained:

> [T]he juvenile act does not contemplate the punishment of children where they are found to be delinquent, but rather an attempt to correct and rehabilitate them in "a wholesome family environment whenever possible," although rehabilitation may have to be sought in some instances in an institution. . . .

> The record in the instant case does not justify uprooting the child from his parents' home and placing him in a training center or other juvenile institution.[21]

## [2] The Least Drastic Alternative

Increasingly, appellate courts have permitted commitments to state institutions only as a last resort.[22] Courts taking this view require the juvenile court to demonstrate that a given institutional commitment is the only dispositional alternative that adequately promotes the aims of the juvenile justice system.[23] Where "less drastic" alternatives to institutionalization are more or equally effective in achieving the dispositional goals, institutionalization is inappropriate and cannot be imposed in lieu of less severe dispositional alternatives.

The "less drastic alternatives" approach is illustrated by a California case[24] where a fifteen-year-old Mexican nonresident alien was adjudicated a delinquent for the offense of unlawful use of a motor vehicle. The youth had earlier admitted to a charge of attempted auto theft and had been turned over to immigration officials who returned him to Mexico. At the disposition hearing, probation officials recommended placement with the California Youth Authority (CYA), the most restrictive placement available in the state. The probation officer's opinion was that the two auto offenses revealed that the youth was probably making a living by stealing cars in California and selling them in Mexico. The court adopted the probation office recommendation after concluding that the youth was probably unamenable to treatment as evidenced by the fact that he reentered the United States and committed a criminal act after the immigration authorities had sent him back to Mexico.

---

[19] *In re* Appeal No. 179, 327 A.2d 793 (Md. Ct. Spec. App. 1974).

[20] *Id.* at 794.

[21] *Id.* at 795.

[22] Davis, *supra* § 2.02, note 9, at 6-12.

[23] *Id.*

[24] *In re* Jose P., 161 Cal. Rptr. 400 (Cal. Ct. App. 1980).

The youth appealed the order committing him to CYA and the appellate court reversed, finding that the juvenile court abused its discretion by not considering less drastic alternatives. The court emphasized that juvenile dispositions are meant to be rehabilitative, not punitive, and that confinement in CYA thrusts the detainee into custody with some offenders having lengthy involvement in violent activity. The court noted that the statute imposing juvenile court dispositions listed the alternatives in ascending order of severity, ranging from probation to commitment to CYA. This list suggested to the court a legislative plan of imposing progressively restrictive dispositions and requiring that CYA placements be deferred until "lesser remedies of probation or other placements have failed or are clearly inappropriate."[25] The court saw the sole reason for the trial judge's CYA order as an attempt to deter the juvenile from reentering the state. Moreover, the court found no evidence to support a conclusion that the juvenile could not benefit from a less severe disposition. Because "the record [did] not reveal the unavailability of suitable alternative dispositions,"[26] the CYA commitment could not stand and the court remanded the case directing the juvenile court to consider the viability of less restrictive alternative placements.

Some courts go further and hold that a child cannot be committed to a juvenile institution solely on the grounds that there are no suitable alternatives available. In an Illinois case,[27] for example, a thirteen-year-old was adjudicated a delinquent for committing a theft offense. Substantial evidence was presented at the disposition hearing indicating that the juvenile would likely respond well to rehabilitative placements outside institutional confinement. A variety of witnesses testified that the juvenile was doing well in a counseling program, that he attended school regularly and desired to continue to do so, and that he would receive maximum benefit from a residential treatment program. While all the evidence justified a community-based treatment disposition, no specific program was presented as an option for the juvenile and, seeing no other alternative, the court ordered the juvenile committed to the Department of Corrections.

The juvenile appealed and the appellate court reversed the disposition order. While recognizing that "the disposition of a minor rests within the discretion of the trial judge," the court nevertheless concluded that institutionalized commitments could be imposed "only when less severe placement alternatives would not be in the best interests of the minor and the public."[28] The court therefore remanded the case for "further investigation" of "all possible placement alternatives."[29]

In some states, legislatures specifically have required the courts to consider less drastic alternatives prior to imposing incarcerative commitments.[30] For example, an Arkansas provision directs the court to "give preference to the least restrictive disposition consistent with the best interests and welfare of the juvenile and the public."[31]

---

[25]  *Id.* at 404.

[26]  *Id.* at 405. For a case where an incarcerative commitment was upheld after the trial court had considered less drastic dispositions and rejected them as inadequate, see *In re* F.N., 624 N.E.2d 853 (Ill. App. Ct. 1993).

[27]  *In re* B.S., 549 N.E.2d 695 (Ill. App. Ct. 1989).

[28]  *In re* B.S., 549 N.E.2d 695, 698 (Ill. App. Ct. 1989).

[29]  *Id.* at 699.

[30]  Davis, *supra* note 22, at 6-12 n.38.

[31]  Ark. Code Ann. § 9-27-329(d) (Michie 2002).

## [B]   The New Theory: Social Protection and Punishment

While the rehabilitative model provided the traditional theoretical basis for juvenile justice, it probably never provided a totally accurate description of the dispositional practices of juvenile courts.[32] Arguably, the interest in protecting society from juvenile criminal activity has also been inherent in dispositions imposed in the name of rehabilitating the offender, at least where the disposition was intended to inhibit the commission of subsequent offenses.[33] Incarcerative dispositions, for example, not only addressed the rehabilitative needs of the offender but protected society from his possible recidivism during the period of incarceration. Moreover, despite disclaimers to the contrary, juvenile justice has probably always manifested punitive aspects.[34]

In any event, several jurisdictions have explicitly expanded their theory of juvenile justice, downplaying the role of rehabilitation. These jurisdictions have embraced dispositions aimed at incapacitating juveniles from committing subsequent offenses or punishing them in order to deter juvenile crime and hold offenders accountable for their wrongdoing.[35] Thus, in such jurisdictions, incapacitation and punishment have emerged as dispositional alternatives to the traditional goal of rehabilitating the child.

In other jurisdictions, dispositions are sometimes dispensed to achieve incapacitative or punitive purposes even though the relevant statutes espouse rehabilitation of the child as the sole dispositional goal.[36] Incapacitative dispositions are not necessarily inconsistent under the rehabilitative model, because juveniles who are incapacitated due to a perceived risk that they might commit future crime are also likely to be deemed in need of rehabilitation.[37]

On the other hand, punishment and rehabilitation are conceptually mutually exclusive penal goals.[38] Therefore, punitive dispositions are forbidden under systems that embrace rehabilitation as the sole purpose of juvenile dispositions. Moreover, as discussed in Chapter 10, the imposition of punishment arguably triggers jury trial rights not otherwise associated with delinquency adjudications.[39]

---

[32] *See* Fox, *supra* § 7.02, note 15, at 1193–1230.

[33] *Id.*

[34] *Id.*; Feld, *supra* note 6, at 837.

[35] Feld, *supra* note 6, at 842.

[36] *Id.* at 882.

[37] Incapacitation in the name of preventive detention and rehabilitation both address undesirable status conditions. *See* Gardner, *supra* § 7.02, note 10, at 809–18. On the other hand, theories of incapacitation and rehabilitation can be viewed as at odds with one another. Consider the following:

> [I]t is now generally recognized that caring for the juvenile and controlling the juvenile are often quite contradictory processes. Much of our juvenile law at the moment is predicated upon a healthy skepticism about the capacity of the State and its agents to help children when they are incarcerated in one of the juvenile detention facilities. Thus, the control of juveniles and the treatment of juveniles (if that expression can be used without conjuring Kafkaesque images) are frequently irreconcilable goals. Furthermore, children can be dangerous, destructive, abusive, and otherwise thoroughly anti-social, which prompts an entirely understandable expectation in society of protection, even if we have matured beyond expecting retribution.

State *ex rel.* D.D.H. v. Dostert, 269 S.E.2d 401, 408–9 (W. Va. 1980).

[38] Gardner, *supra* note 37, at 793–94, 815–16; Feld, *supra* note 6, at 833.

[39] *See supra* § 10.02, notes 63–71 and accompanying text.

Thus, the distinction between punitive and rehabilitative dispositions carries important legal consequences.

## [1]  Distinguishing Punishment and Rehabilitation

Punishment and rehabilitation are analytically distinct concepts. Punishment entails the purposeful imposition of suffering by an authority upon an offender because of his offense.[40] Punishment thus is a response to *past offenses* and is imposed to exact retribution, often in hopes of deterring future undesirable conduct.[41] Because it is connected to an offense, punishment is determinate and proportional to the seriousness of the offense and the blameworthiness of the offender.[42]

Rehabilitation, on the other hand, benefits its recipients by alleviating personal characteristics deemed undesirable.[43] This purportedly beneficial action is always subject to revision upon a showing that a different course of action would produce more benefit, or that the recipient's status has changed and thus eliminated the need for further action.[44] Rehabilitation thus responds to the present status of a person, rather than to any of his particular past acts, in order to improve his future welfare.[45] Being based on characteristics of the person rather than his offenses, rehabilitative dispositions are typically open-ended, non-proportional, and indeterminate.

## [2]  Punitive Juvenile Justice Legislation

Some jurisdictions have systematically embraced punitive juvenile justice. The State of Washington, for example, has revised its juvenile code to "[p]rovide for punishment commensurate with the age, crime, and criminal history of the juvenile offender" and to hold "him accountable for his . . . criminal behavior."[46] Consistent with these purposes, legislative guidelines impose a "presumptive sentencing" model with determinate dispositions proportional to the age of the offender, the seriousness of the offense, and the juvenile's prior record.[47] Under the guidelines, statutorily defined "serious offenders" must be institutionalized for 125 weeks to three years.[48] The Washington system is similar to the Juvenile Justice Standards model that eschews the rehabilitative ideal in favor of proportioning dispositions to the seriousness of the offense.[49]

As illustrated by the discussion in Chapter 10 of the "designated felony" provisions in New York,[50] other jurisdictions have mandated punitive dispositions

---

[40] *See* Gardner, *supra* note 37, at 798–817.

[41] *Id.*

[42] *Id.*; Feld, *supra* note 6, at 833.

[43] Gardner, *supra* note 37, at 817.

[44] *Id.*

[45] *Id.*; Feld, *supra* note 6, at 833.

[46] Wash. Rev. Code Ann. § 13.40.010(2)(d), (c) (West 1993). The Washington statute is also aimed at "responding to the needs of youthful offenders." *Id.* § 13.40.010(2).

[47] *See* Feld, *supra* note 6, at 853.

[48] *Id.* at 854.

[49] Institute of Judicial Admin. & American Bar Ass'n, Juvenile Justice Standards, Dispositions (1980).

[50] *See supra* § 10.02, notes 63–69 and accompanying text.

for certain offenses without adopting a totally systematic model of punitive juvenile justice. In addition, some states have simply redefined statutory purpose clauses to permit punitive dispositions at the discretion of the juvenile court. The California purpose clause, for example authorizes the juvenile court to impose "punishment that is consistent with . . . rehabilitative objectives," while taking into account the "public safety and protection" as well as the "best interests" of the minor.[51] Without expressly authorizing punitive dispositions, the Iowa statute requires the court to "specify the duration . . . of the disposition" and "enter the least restrictive dispositional order appropriate in view of the seriousness of the delinquent act, the child's culpability as indicated by the circumstances of the particular case, the age of the child and the child's prior record."[52]

## [3]  Legal Consequences of Punitive Dispositions

As mentioned earlier, it is sometimes necessary to distinguish punitive from rehabilitative dispositions in order to resolve legal issues. In systems that permit only rehabilitative dispositions, courts must differentiate between punishment and rehabilitation when a particular disposition is alleged to be punitive. Moreover, juveniles arguably have the right to a jury trial when they face possible punitive incarceration in excess of six months.[53] In addition, as will be discussed later, punitive dispositions may trigger scrutiny under the Cruel and Unusual Punishments Clause of the Eighth Amendment.[54]

The alleged presence of punishment within the juvenile justice system may also raise equal protection problems. In a California case, for example, a juvenile was adjudicated a delinquent for committing the offense of burglary.[55] The juvenile court committed the youth to the California Youth Authority for the maximum term of three years, without finding aggravating circumstances indicating that the burglary offense was especially serious.[56] The juvenile appealed the order, arguing that he was being punished for the offense in violation of the Equal Protection Clause because an adult offender could not receive the same three year sentence for the same offense without explicit judicial findings of aggravating circumstances.

The California Supreme Court reviewed the case under a statute directing that juveniles "not be held in physical confinement for a period in excess of the maximum term of imprisonment which could be imposed upon an adult convicted of the offense . . . which brought . . . the minor under the jurisdiction of the juvenile court."[57] The court granted that in the absence of a finding of aggravating circumstances, an adult would have received a sentence of two years, or perhaps less, for the offense of burglary. Nevertheless, the court found no equal protection problem with the juvenile's three-year commitment. The court noted that unlike an

---

[51]  Cal. Welf. & Inst. Code § 202 (West Supp. 2002).

[52]  Iowa Code Ann. § 232.52(1) (West 2000). The Iowa statute also requires that its juvenile justice provisions be "liberally construed to the end that each child under the jurisdiction of the court shall receive, preferably in the child's own home, the care, guidance and control that will best serve the child's welfare and the best interest of the state." *Id.* § 232.1.

[53]  *See supra* § 10.02[A][5].

[54]  *See infra* § 11.03[C][5][b]. See also *infra* § 11.04[D] for discussion of due process and cruel and unusual punishment issues in the status offense context.

[55]  *In re* Eric J., 601 P.2d 549 (Cal. 1979). The juvenile was also charged with contempt.

[56]  The juvenile received an additional six months confinement for the contempt offense. *Id.* at 550.

[57]  *Id.* at 552.

adult offender, the juvenile might be released on parole prior to serving the full three-year term. Moreover, the court found that because adult offenders were punished for their offenses but juveniles were not, criminal convicts and delinquents were not "similarly situated," thus precluding any equal protection violation.

> The first prerequisite to a meritorious claim under the equal protection clause is a showing that the state has adopted a classification that affects two or more similarly situated groups in an unequal manner. . . . Adults convicted in the criminal courts and sentenced to prison and youths adjudged wards of the juvenile courts and committed to the Youth Authority are not "similarly situated." The state does not have the same purpose in sentencing adults to prison that it has in committing minors to the Youth Authority. Adults convicted in the criminal courts are sentenced to prison as punishment while minors adjudged wards of the juvenile courts are committed to the Youth Authority for the purposes of treatment and rehabilitation . . . .[58]

The court did not explain how the juvenile court action linking the disposition to the offense rather than to the needs of the offender could be anything other than punitive.[59] Moreover, the court failed to consider whether recent amendments to the California statutes permitting dispositions "to protect the public from criminal conduct by minors," and "to impose on the minor a sense of responsibility for his own acts"[60] might support the conclusion that punitive juvenile justice had become a part of California law.

The reasoning in the California case just discussed is routinely adopted by courts in rejecting claims by juveniles who, as is commonly the case, receive incarcerative commitments for the period of their minority (unless released on parole) and who argue that the commitments are unconstitutional because they are longer, or at least potentially longer, than any prison term possible for adults who commit the same offense. In one case, for example, the court upheld a potential eight-year commitment of a juvenile who had been adjudicated a delinquent for stealing a bag of potato chips.[61] The court saw the commitment as an exercise of "paternal attention," and thus not analogous to criminal punishment.[62] In another case, the court upheld the commitment of a fifteen-year-old for an indeterminate period which could exceed the sentence permissible for an adult committing the same offense (LSD possession and transfer).[63] The court rejected the argument that the commitment was unconstitutional, finding that juvenile and adult offenders were not similarly situated. Unlike sentences of adult offenders, the "commitment of a juvenile is not for the purpose of penalty or punishment, but for the purpose of effecting a result that will serve the best interests of the child. . . ."[64]

---

[58] *Id.* at 553.

[59] *See supra* notes 40–45 and accompanying text.

[60] *See* Wadlington, Whitebread & Davis, *supra* note 1, at 542.

[61] *In re* Blakes, 281 N.E.2d 454 (Ill. App. Ct. 1972).

[62] *Id.* at 457.

[63] *In re* J.K., 228 N.W.2d 713 (Wis. 1975).

[64] *Id.* at 716.

## [C]  Dispositional Alternatives

In most juvenile systems, the dispositional alternatives essentially consist of probation, restitution, community service, community-based institutionalization, and custodial confinement in secure facilities.[65] Each of these alternatives is thought to promote the traditional rehabilitative aims of juvenile justice when properly imposed in particular cases. On the other hand, as discussed herein, most, if not all, of the alternatives may also be employed for punitive purposes.

## [1]  Probation

Probation, the most common disposition in delinquency cases, allows the juvenile to continue life within a familiar environment without being subjected to institutionalized confinement.[66] Judges who order probation specify conditions, tailored to the needs of the specific child, that must be observed in an attempt to provide structure to the child's "normal" life. Probation orders are generally monitored by probation officers who are expected to maintain regular contact with the child. Should the child fail to follow the imposed conditions, probation may be revoked and a more severe disposition imposed.[67]

Courts have discretion to impose probation regardless of the severity of the offense committed by the juvenile.[68] Although probation is generally considered to be the least restrictive of the various dispositional alternatives,[69] some juveniles have argued that it is unduly harsh in some circumstances. In a California case,[70] for example, a minor argued that the court violated his equal protection rights when it imposed an order of home probation after finding that the minor had committed a misdemeanor offense punishable by a $100 fine in criminal court. The minor argued that probation was a more onerous disposition than the sanction that would have been imposed on an adult in similar circumstances, thus violating equal protection. The court rejected this argument, finding that juvenile court probation, unlike the fine imposed in criminal court, is non-punitive and therefore places delinquents in a situation dissimilar to that of adult offenders. The court elaborated:

> One of the purposes of the Juvenile Court Law is to secure for each minor under the jurisdiction of the juvenile court such care and guidance, preferably in his own home, as will best serve his welfare and "preserve and strengthen the minor's family ties." Thus with this in mind, a comprehensive statutory scheme was devised to best provide for the placement and treatment of juveniles. It is apparent . . . that probation in a juvenile proceeding is not an act of leniency which a minor can refuse but the preferred disposition if warranted by the circumstances. . . .
>
> . . . Appellant's position ignores the nature and purposes of the Juvenile Court Law, the options available to the court in dealing with the youthful offender, and the involvement of the probation officer in virtually every phase of the juvenile court process, in particular, his role in representing

---

[65]  *See supra* note 1 and accompanying text.

[66]  Wadlington, Whitebread & Davis, *supra* note 1, at 580.

[67]  *See infra* § 11.03[C][1][b].

[68]  Fox, *supra* § 8.02, note 2, at 225.

[69]  *See supra* § 11.03[A][2].

[70]  *In re* Wayne J., 159 Cal. Rptr. 106 (Cal. Ct. App. 1979).

the interests of the minor and supplying the need for supervision and assistance of a trained counselor. The difference in treatment seems justified by the differing characteristics and needs of adult and juvenile offenders.

. . . [W]hatever test is used to analyze the distinction between placement in the parents' home under the supervision of the probation officer, and imposition of a fine and/or summary probation on the adult who violates the same statute, we find the distinction reasonable, and necessary to facilitate the purposes of the Juvenile Court Law and the rehabilitation of the minor. . . .

. . . The conditions of probation required the minor to do little more than that appropriate to any minor who resides at home (with the exception of obeying all orders of and reporting to the probation officer). The benefit of probation to the minor under the circumstances is that he is able to remain at home and is given needed guidance and discipline which his parents should, but in many cases cannot or will not give him, and he and his parents are afforded the assistance of a professional counselor in the person of the probation officer. The great advantage of this kind of counseling in such a case as this is the lasting effect it may have on molding the minor's attitudes for the better.[71]

## [a]　Conditions of Probation

Juvenile court judges enjoy broad discretion not only in choosing probation over other dispositional alternatives, but also in tailoring probation orders with obligatory conditions deemed beneficial to the particular juvenile.[72] Statutes routinely allow juvenile courts to impose "reasonable conditions" of probation, thus allowing judges virtually complete discretion to follow their personal judgment.[73]

The courts have upheld orders of probation, potentially extending for the entire period of the delinquent's minority, even though the underlying offense is a relatively minor misdemeanor.[74] Juvenile court judges routinely order regular school attendance as a condition of probation,[75] and may impose an additional requirement that the juvenile earn passing grades.[76] Similarly, other permissible and commonly-imposed probation conditions include obeying all laws, reporting to the probation officer, remaining within the jurisdiction, and obeying a curfew.[77] Moreover, the courts have upheld conditions permitting the juvenile to associate only with persons approved by his parents or probation officer,[78] and requiring his

---

[71] *Id.* at 108–10.

[72] Fox, *supra* note 68, at 227.

[73] *Id.*

[74] *See, e.g., In re* Westbrooks, 288 S.E.2d 395 (S.C. 1982) (shoplifting).

[75] *See, e.g., In re* Gerald B., 164 Cal. Rptr. 193 (Cal. Ct. App. 1980); Wadlington, Whitebread & Davis, *supra* note 1, at 583.

[76] *See, e.g., In re* Angel J., 11 Cal. Rptr. 2d 776 (Cal. Ct. App. 1992).

[77] Wadlington, Whitebread & Davis, *supra* note 1, at 583.

[78] *See, e.g., In re* Frank V., 285 Cal. Rptr. 16 (Cal. Ct. App. 1991). The courts have also upheld conditions prohibiting the probationer's presence at known gathering areas of gang activity and wearing of gang clothing and insignia. *In re* Laylah K., 281 Cal. Rptr. 6 (Cal. Ct. App. 1991).

consent to any searches of his person or property conducted in connection with his probation supervision.[79]

On the other hand, the courts have invalidated orders requiring attendance at church or Sunday School on the grounds that such orders violate the doctrine of separation of church and state.[80] Occasionally, courts strike down other probation conditions. In a Missouri case, for example, the court reversed an order of "shock probation," consisting of confinement in the county jail for a period of seven days, finding the order illegal "for whatever time or reason."[81] In another case, an Arizona court held that the juvenile court lacked authority to require juvenile sex offenders to furnish DNA samples to the state DNA identification system as a condition of probation.[82]

## [b] Probation Revocation

Alleged violations of probation conditions may result in revocation of probation. Often such actions are initiated by the probation officers who are authorized to take their probationers into custody when there is probable cause to believe a probationer has violated probation.[83]

Basic due process protections apply to revocation proceedings.[84] Summary revocations are thus impermissible and the juvenile is entitled to a hearing[85] with advance notice advising the probationer of the alleged violation.[86] Probation may be revoked if the probationer commits a crime, even if the probation order does not specifically list obeying the law as a probation condition.[87] Some courts have extended such "implied conditions" of probation to include any conduct that "the probationer clearly should have realized might result in revocation."[88]

Some jurisdictions follow the procedures applicable in adult probation revocation cases.[89] The probationer thus enjoys rights to present evidence,

---

[79] *See, e.g., In re* Curtis T., 263 Cal. Rptr. 296 (Cal. Ct. App. 1989), *cert. denied*, 498 U.S. 858 (1990).

[80] *See, e.g.,* L.M. v. State, 587 So. 2d 648 (Fla. Dist. Ct. App. 1991) (per curiam). *But see* L.M. v. State, 610 So.2d 1314 (Fla. Dist. Ct. App. 1992) (upholding probation condition that juvenile obey all lawful and reasonable demands of his mother including participation in the mother's church's youth program). *See also In re* A.H., 459 A.2d 1045 (D.C. 1983) (upholding a probation condition ordering the child to stay away from the Islamic Center, the place where he had been arrested in connection with incidents of violence occurring on those premises).

[81] *In re* L.L.W., 626 S.W.2d 261, 263 (Mo. Ct. App. 1981).

[82] *In re* Juvenile Action No. JV-508801, 901 P.2d 1205 (Ariz. Ct. App. 1995). *But see In re* James P., 510 N.W.2d 730 (Wis. Ct. App. 1993) (appellate court upheld an order by juvenile court requiring that juvenile undergo a blood test as a condition of probation as a precaution to placing him in the same home with his sister whom he had allegedly impregnated).

[83] Fox, *supra* note 68, at 229.

[84] *Id.* at 230.

[85] *See, e.g., In re* Gerald B., 164 Cal. Rptr. 193 (Cal. Ct. App. 1980) (no summary detention permitted where child violates legitimate probation condition requiring regular school attendance).

[86] *See, e.g., In re* Litdell, 232 So. 2d 733 (Miss. 1970).

[87] *Id.*

[88] *Id.* at 736 (citing with approval Note, *Legal Aspects of Probation Revocation*, 59 Colum. L. Rev. 311, 315 (1959)). *But see In re* G.G.D., 292 N.W.2d 853 (Wis. 1980) (juvenile's due process right to notice violated where probation revoked for juvenile's failure "to cooperate with his caseworker" where such was not an explicit condition of his probation).

[89] Fox, *supra* note 68, at 230.

confront opposing witnesses, and have counsel appointed where, under the facts of the particular case, counsel is needed to assure the effectiveness of the due process rights available at the hearing.[90] Although adult proceedings often do not require proof beyond a reasonable doubt,[91] statutes in some states impose that rigorous burden of proof in juvenile revocation proceedings.[92] Moreover, some jurisdictions apply the same rules to both adjudication and revocation proceedings, although the burden of proof is lowered in some states to the clear and convincing evidence standard for revocation.[93]

The court has discretion to determine the consequences of a violation of probation. Sometimes the court will continue the probation in spite of a probation violation.[94] If the court had originally committed the child to an institutionalized placement but suspended the commitment in order to put the child on probation, the court can revoke the suspension and commit the child to the institution without holding an additional disposition hearing.[95] Such a hearing might be necessary in some jurisdictions, however, if the court seeks to revoke the probation and institutionalize the child without having ordered an institutional commitment at the original disposition.[96]

## [c] Rehabilitation or Punishment?

While probation is almost always viewed as a means to promote the rehabilitation of the child,[97] it is theoretically possible for probation conditions to constitute punishment. Indeed, some tests for determining the permissibility of particular probation conditions seem to embrace a punitive model. For example, a California court[98] articulated the following test for determining the permissibility of probation conditions under a statute authorizing courts to "impose and require any and all reasonable conditions that it may determine fitting and proper to the end that justice may be done and the reformation and rehabilitation of the [juvenile] enhanced":[99]

A probation condition will not be held invalid unless it 1) has no relationship to the crime of which the offender was convicted, 2) relates to conduct which is not in itself criminal, and 3) requires or forbids conduct which is not reasonably related to future criminality. All three requirements must be met before the condition is invalidated.[100]

Thus, any condition that is "related" to the offense is permissible, apparently even if it is not conducive to the probationer's rehabilitative needs. If the relationship to the offense standard means simply that the onerousness of the condition must be proportional to the seriousness of the offense, the court has embraced a model of

---

[90] LaFave & Israel, *supra* § 9.02, note 6, at 524.

[91] *Id.* at 1091–92.

[92] Fox, *supra* note 68, at 230.

[93] *Id.*; Kramer, *supra* note 1, at 393.

[94] Fox, *supra* note 68, at 231.

[95] *Id.*

[96] *See supra* § 11.03[A][2].

[97] *See supra* notes 70–71 and accompanying text.

[98] *In re* Frank V., 285 Cal. Rptr. 16 (Cal. Ct. App. 1991).

[99] *Id.* at 21.

[100] *Id.*

punitive probation. Such a consequence appears consistent with the statutory aim of assuring that probation conditions "do justice."[101]

Occasionally the period of probation itself is linked to the underlying offense, again suggesting a theory more consistent with punishment than with rehabilitation.[102] New York, for example, permits a maximum period of two years probation for delinquents with the possibility of one additional year in "exceptional circumstances."[103] On the other hand, the New York statutes limit probation to one year for status offenders with the possibility of one additional year in "exceptional circumstances."[104] That the statutes limit the duration of probation and require the duration to be proportionate to the seriousness of the offense, implies a punitive rather than a rehabilitative dispositional model.[105]

## [2]   Restitution

In addition to the probation alternative, juvenile court judges are commonly authorized to order adjudicated delinquents to make restitution for the harm caused by their offense. In some jurisdictions, restitution is an outright disposition[106] while in others it is imposed as a condition of probation.[107] This distinction can have practical significance because probation and institutional confinement are often viewed as antithetical. Thus, where restitution is viewed as a component of probation, that disposition is sometimes found impermissible in cases where the minor is committed to an institution.[108] However, in jurisdictions where

---

[101] *Id.* Some courts have recognized that probation may be a form of punishment. "[P]robation is [not] meant to be painless. Probation has an inherent sting, and restrictions upon the freedom of the probationer are realistically punitive in quality." *In re* Buehrer, 236 A.2d 592, 596 (N.J. 1967). But see *In re Miller*, 611 N.E.2d 451, 453 (Ohio Ct. App. 1992), where the court invalidated probation conditions prohibiting the probationer from associating with a particular individual, going to a specified place of business, and dressing as a female. The probationer had admitted to acts of violence upon his brother and argued that the imposed conditions "had nothing to do with" the incidents with his brother. The court agreed, finding that valid probation conditions "must somehow relate to the offense for which the juvenile is charged." The court implied that the purpose of the "relationship to the offense" requirement was to make it less likely that the probationer would commit that particular offense again. On this view, the requirement that the probation condition be "related to" the offense is arguably consistent with rehabilitative concerns and does not necessarily belie a punitive orientation.

[102] See *supra* § 11.03[B][1] for a discussion of the distinction between punishment and rehabilitation.

[103] N.Y. Fam. Ct. Act § 353.2(6) (McKinney 1998).

[104] *Id.* § 757(b).

[105] *See supra* § 11.03[B][1]. The Juvenile Justice Standards allow for conditional release of the juvenile so long as the imposed conditions do not exceed in "severity or duration" the maximum disposition permissible for the offense. Such an offense-grounded model of probation reflects a punitive orientation. Institute of Judicial Admin. & American Bar Ass'n, *supra* note 49, at 7.

[106] For example, the Nebraska statute provides in one subsection that "the court may prescribe . . . an order of restitution of any property stolen or damaged when the same is in the interest of the juvenile's reformation or rehabilitation," while in a separate subsection the statute authorizes the court to "[p]lace the juvenile on probation." Neb. Rev. Stat. § 43-286(1)(a) (Reissue 1998).

[107] *See, e.g.,* N.Y. Fam. Ct. Act § 353.6(1)(a) (McKinney 1998) (authorizing, as a "condition of probation or conditional discharge, restitution in an amount representing a fair and reasonable cost to replace the property or repair the damage caused by the respondent, not, however, to exceed one thousand five hundred dollars").

[108] Davis, *supra* note 22, at 6-16.

restitution is itself an independent disposition, it may be ordered in conjunction with an order of commitment to an institution.[109]

Statutes in some states forbid restitution in cases where the juvenile does not have, and could not reasonably acquire, the means to pay restitution.[110] Where no such statutory provisions exist, courts sometimes impose similar limitations on the power of juvenile courts to order restitution.[111]

For restitution to be considered an appropriate disposition, there must be a showing that the juvenile's criminal conduct caused pecuniary damage.[112] Some statutes limit orders of restitution to property damage cases.[113] Other courts sometimes include orders to pay for the medical expenses of victims of delinquency where applicable statutes do not limit restitution to property damage.[114]

Furthermore, statutes and caselaw often hold juveniles jointly and severally liable for damage caused by their concerted criminal activity.[115] Some courts permit a rebuttable presumption of equal liability for individuals jointly responsible for the criminal conduct, but allow each individual party the opportunity to challenge the presumption.[116] Thus, minimally responsible parties may present arguments that they should pay less restitution than those with greater responsibility for causing the damage.[117] Apart from questions of comparative responsibility, the courts are sometimes urged to consider rehabilitative interests when considering whether to treat joint offenders equally insofar as restitution is concerned. One court put the matter this way:

> Bearing in mind the rehabilitative purpose of probation restitution [the court] may distinguish between culprit "A," let us say, existing in the most meager poverty, whose restitution, if any, will be rehabilitative because earned by the sweat of his brow; whereas as to culprit "B," perhaps the scion of a wealthy and supportive family, the same restitution requirement would be meaningless as a rehabilitative tool. In the latter case reparation in kind might be deemed more effective.[118]

---

[109] *See, e.g.*, People *ex rel.* A.R.M., 832 P.2d 1093 (Colo. Ct. App. 1992) (immediate ability to pay not required; juvenile given latitude to make restitution in the future after being released from confinement).

[110] *See, e.g.*, N.C. Gen. Stat. § 7B-2506(4) (2002).

[111] *See, e.g.*, *In re* Don Mc., 686 A.2d 269, 273 (Md. 1996) (interpreting the statutory language "age and circumstances of the child" to include the child's ability to pay and reversing the lower court's order of restitution); *In re* Carroll, 393 A.2d 993 (Pa. Super. Ct. 1978) (vacating a lower court order sentencing juvenile to incarceration when juvenile's mother could not afford to pay restitution); *In re* J.M., III., No. 13-02-140-CV, 2003 Tex. App. LEXIS 9083 (Oct. 23, 2003) (analogizing to adult criminal procedure statutes and holding inability of a minor to pay restitution was a defense to revocation of probation).

[112] Davis, *supra* note 22, at 6-18.

[113] *See, e.g.*, the Nebraska provision, *supra* note 106.

[114] *See, e.g.*, K.M.C. v. State, 485 So. 2d 1296 (Fla. Dist. Ct. App. 1986). Some statutes expressly authorize restitution for medical treatment for physical injury to persons and even for lost wages resulting from physical injury. *See, e.g.*, Wash. Rev. Code Ann. § 13.40.020(21) (West Supp. 2002).

[115] *See, e.g.*, N.C. Gen. Stat. § 7B-2506(4) (2002); Davis, *supra* note 22, at 6-18.

[116] *See, e.g.*, *In re* D.G.W., 361 A.2d 513 (N.J. 1976).

[117] *Id.* at 523–24.

[118] *Id.* at 524.

## [a]   Procedural Requirements

If restitution is to be imposed, the juvenile is entitled to a due process hearing[119] with the assistance of counsel, the right to confront witnesses and examine evidence, and the ability to present evidence in his own behalf.[120] At such hearing, the court determines the amount of restitution needed to restore the victim to his previous state in a manner that is consistent with the rehabilitative needs of the child.[121]

In determining the amount of damage caused by the juvenile, courts sometimes rely on damage figures derived by probation officers so long as the figures reflect "recognized methods of valuation" such as repair or replacement costs, market values, or reliable appraisals.[122] In assessing damages, courts in restitution cases need not conduct hearings approximating those conducted in tort actions where, for example, a defendant is permitted to contest the damage issue by raising defenses alleging the contributory fault of the injured party.[123]

## [b]   Rehabilitation or Punishment?

Historically, punitive dispositions were considered inappropriate in the juvenile justice system. Therefore, fines, a punitive sanction,[124] were impermissible as dispositional alternatives.[125] Some courts equated fines with orders to pay restitution and thus forbade both.[126]

While many jurisdictions continue to prohibit fines,[127] restitution has become a universally acceptable form of disposition in delinquency cases.[128] Courts routinely see restitution as nonpunitive and consistent with the traditional rehabilitative aims of the juvenile justice system,[129] benefitting both its recipients and the juvenile. One court offered the following cautious defense of the role of restitution in achieving the traditional aim of the juvenile courts "to make men out of errant boys"[130]:

> Restitution manifestly serves the interest of the public for it is not right that either victim [sic] or the public should bear the whole burden, let us say, of loss from extensive juvenile vandalism. *Quaere*: does an order for restitution so clearly disserve the "best interests" of the juvenile offender that it must be abandoned as a rehabilitative tool? We think not.[131]

---

[119] *Id.* at 520–21.

[120] *Id.*; Davis, *supra* note 22, at 6-18 to 6-19.

[121] Davis, *supra* note 22, at 6-19.

[122] *See, e.g., In re* D.G.W., 361 A.2d 513, 521–22 (N.J. 1976).

[123] *See, e.g.,* People v. Pettit, 276 N.W.2d 878 (Mich. Ct. App. 1979) (adult restitution).

[124] *In re* D.G.W., 361 A.2d 513, 516 (N.J. 1976) ("fines are essentially punitive in nature").

[125] *See, e.g., id.*; E.P. v. State, 203 S.E.2d 757 (Ga. Ct. App. 1973).

[126] *See, e.g.,* Bordone v. F., 307 N.Y.S.2d 527 (N.Y. App. Div. 1969).

[127] Davis, *supra* note 22, at 6-19.

[128] Fox, *supra* note 68, at 228.

[129] *Id.*

[130] *In re* D.G.W., 361 A.2d 513, 518–19 (N.J. 1976).

[131] *Id.* at 518.

Restitution arguably is nonpunitive because it is not aimed at making the offender suffer for what he has done;[132] rather, the purpose is to compensate his victim and, in the process, to help the offender learn from his mistakes. Fines, on the other hand, are punitive to the extent that they impose unpleasant consequences upon the offender because of, and in proportion to, the offense.[133] As a manifestation of the movement towards punitive juvenile justice,[134] statutes in some jurisdictions now permit fines,[135] thus reducing the legal significance of the distinction between fines and restitution.

### [3] Community Service

Judicial orders to perform public work or community service are dispositions similar to restitution and are imposed for similar reasons. As exercises of discretion, juvenile court judges commonly order delinquents to do a variety of work assignments aimed at benefitting the community and teaching the juvenile to accept responsibility for his actions in a context affording him work experience.[136] As with restitution, community service can operate as a separate disposition or as a condition of probation depending on the jurisdiction.[137]

The forms of work assignments vary. For example, the courts have ordered delinquents to work in rural cemeteries,[138] mountain parks, city parks, and zoos; to help in supervising recreational programs for young children; to work in county hospitals; and to do clerical and maintenance work for public agencies.[139] In each context, the juvenile is supervised by regular personnel and his work is evaluated in order to meet the court imposed criteria.[140]

The appellate courts have generally upheld contested juvenile court orders to perform community service.[141] Some cases, however, hold that the amount of time imposed for community service may not exceed the period of time for which the juvenile could have been committed to custodial confinement.[142]

Moreover, the courts have upheld community service against attacks under the Thirteenth Amendment to the United States Constitution which prohibits the imposition of "involuntary servitude except as a punishment for crime."[143] Some courts conclude that community service is punishment in the context of the particular state's juvenile justice system, and thus is not violative of the Thirteenth Amendment.[144] Other courts hold that while community service is rehabilitative in

---

[132] See *supra* § 11.03[B][1] for a discussion of the concept of punishment.

[133] *Id.*

[134] *See supra* § 11.03[B].

[135] Davis, *supra* note 22, at 6-19.

[136] Kramer, *supra* note 1, at 388.

[137] *Id.*; Davis, *supra* note 22, at 6-20.

[138] *In re* P.E.K., 558 N.E.2d 763 (Ill. App. Ct. 1990).

[139] Institute of Judicial Admin. & American Bar Ass'n, *supra* note 49, at 54–55.

[140] *Id.* at 55.

[141] Kramer, *supra* note 1, at 388.

[142] *See, e.g.*, M.G. v. State, 556 So. 2d 820 (Fla. Dist. Ct. App. 1990).

[143] U.S. Const. amend. XIII.

[144] *See, e.g.*, *In re* Erickson, 604 P.2d 513 (Wash. Ct. App. 1979).

nature, it nevertheless comes within the Amendment's punishment exemption.[145] The words of one court convey the obvious theoretical difficulty with the latter position: "[A] juvenile court order of [community service] would come within the constitutional exception as it is 'punishment for crime' even though it is rehabilitative rather than punitive."[146] This same court imposed one hundred hours of service to the county parks and recreation department as a condition of probation for a juvenile who had committed an act of vandalism. The court extolled the virtues of community service this way:

> The permeating premise of our statute is that juvenile offenders can be rehabilitated and transformed into productive citizens by a system specially designed to achieve those ends. One of the methods provided in that statute is probation. . . . The . . . designation of work of a public purpose for destruction of public property is akin to restitution and does not resemble a monetary penalty. . . . [U]seful services for the public good are in the pattern of probation, which is a specialized judicial tool and is helpful towards achieving the statute's pervading purpose of producing a good adult citizen. As the trial judge stated: "This is specific action designed to foster in him an understanding that he's got some responsibilities and what it takes to create something as opposed to going around destroying things." It is constructive rather than punitive. It comes within the statutory mandate that juvenile court judges are to make such disposition of a delinquent child as is "best suited to his treatment, rehabilitation, and welfare." . . .
>
> . . . [Community service is an] innovative and imaginative approach [that] seeks to avoid "a trauma left on the victim or the community" while aiming to give the offender a chance "for a sense of satisfaction and accomplishment that prison rarely offers."[147]

## [4]   Community-Based Institutionalization

In situations where it is deemed necessary or desirable to remove a delinquent child from the family home, courts may order placements in nonsecure facilities such as community-based group homes and foster care homes.[148] Such placements permit the child to continue to live in the community while at the same time receive needed structure and security.[149]

As with other dispositional alternatives, courts have discretion to order community-based institutionalization (CBI) when deemed necessary or desirable to promote the child's rehabilitative needs.[150] In jurisdictions that require courts to impose the least drastic alternative consistent with dispositional goals,[151] juveniles sometimes contest CBI placements as too severe in light of less drastic alternatives such as probation. For example, in a New York case,[152] a twelve-year-old was

---

[145] *See, e.g.*, M.J.W. v. State, 210 S.E.2d 842 (Ga. Ct. App. 1974).

[146] *Id.* at 844.

[147] *Id.* at 843–44.

[148] Kramer, *supra* note 1, at 397.

[149] *Id.*

[150] *Id.*

[151] *See supra* § 11.03[A][2].

[152] *In re* Jennifer M., 509 N.Y.S.2d 935 (N.Y. App. Div. 1986).

adjudicated a delinquent for assisting her mother in shoplifting various items from a department store. Although the child had no previous record, the court ordered the child placed in foster care for one year on the basis of the child's statement that it was "necessary to steal in order to live" and on evidence from a predispositional investigative report that the child drank alcohol and was frequently absent from school. The child appealed, arguing that the court should have imposed probation as the least restrictive alternative. The appellate court rejected this argument and found that under the circumstances the lower court's imposition of foster care constituted "the least restrictive alternative commensurate with the best interest of [the minor] and the community's protection."[153]

## [a] Foster Care

While foster care is clearly a less restrictive disposition than custodial confinement in secure facilities, it nevertheless constitutes substantial restraints on the child's liberty similar to those more ideally imposed by parents in functional families. Indeed, the courts have sometimes treated the relationship between foster parent and child as essentially the same as the natural parent/child relationship, even though foster parents are routinely licensed and paid by the state.

For example, in an Alaska case,[154] a juvenile was adjudicated a delinquent and placed in a foster home in which he subsequently possessed, and possibly trafficked in, illegal drugs. Suspecting that the juvenile might be engaging in illegal drug activity, his foster parent eavesdropped on the phone conversations by the juvenile during which he stated that his supply of marijuana was running low and that he needed to pick up more along with some pills. The foster parent subsequently searched the juvenile's room and clothing and discovered a bag of marijuana in his coat pocket. She seized the bag and turned it over to the social worker assigned to the juvenile's case, who transferred the evidence to the police, who in turn initiated new delinquency proceedings against the juvenile for possessing drugs. The juvenile sought to suppress the marijuana, arguing that its seizure violated his Fourth Amendment rights. The juvenile court rejected this argument, admitted the evidence, adjudicated the juvenile a delinquent, and committed him to a correctional facility for an indeterminate period not to exceed the date of his nineteenth birthday.

The juvenile appealed and the Alaska Supreme Court upheld the lower court action, finding that no illegal search or seizure occurred because the foster parent was acting essentially as a private person when she conducted her searches and seized the evidence, even though in some respects she was also an agent of the state.[155] The court explained the legal status of the foster parent this way:

> A foster parent is required both to assume temporarily the role of a natural parent to the child committed to his custody and to aid in the discharge of the government's obligation to care for and supervise those juveniles who have become the responsibility of the state. In substituting

---

[153] Id. at 937–38; see also In re Andrew M.M., 589 N.Y.S.2d 1008 (N.Y. App. Div. 1992) (placement with commissioner of social services rather than probation appropriate where child was in need of continuous supervision which could not be provided by the child's father who had manifested uncooperative attitudes towards probation authorities in the past).

[154] J.M.A. v. State, 542 P.2d 170 (Alaska 1975).

[155] The foster parent was licensed and paid by the state ($233 per child) for performing her duties as a foster parent. Id. at 172.

for a natural parent, the foster parent is no more an agent of the police than would be any natural parent. The actions of Mrs. Blankenship [the foster parent] were in no manner instigated by the police. She testified that she did not want her children to get into trouble with the police and that she sought to work out such problems without police involvement. In fact, even after discovering the marijuana, she contacted [the juvenile's] social worker rather than the police. There is no reason for regarding Mrs. Blankenship's actions undertaken while fulfilling this parental role, which did not involve collaboration with the police, as being any different from the actions of a private parent, and, therefore, not subject to fourth amendment constitutional restraints.

The second function undertaken by foster parents, that of caring for and supervising foster children on behalf of the state, quite obviously involves the foster parent in a relationship with the state which may be characterized as an agency relationship. At least insofar as the supervision of J.M.A. [the juvenile] is concerned, even as an agent of the state, we suggest without deciding that Mrs. Blankenship had the right to search J.M.A.'s room. He had previously been declared a delinquent and was placed in the Blankenship home as an alternative to placement in a correctional institution. Had he been placed in a correctional institution, his room would have been legally subject to searches. "In prison, official surveillance has traditionally been the order of the day."

Thus, if Mrs. Blankenship's relationship with J.M.A. is analogized to that of parent and child, the search did not violate the fourth amendment, and if the relationship were to be construed as similar to that involved had J.M.A. been placed in a correctional institution, again there would be no violation. In this instance, the operator of a foster home is in the extremely difficult position of endeavoring to fulfill the role of parent, and, at the same time, perform the task of supervising the activities of a minor found to be a delinquent. Under the circumstances of such a relationship, a search of the room can hardly be regarded as the type of unreasonable activity constitutionally prohibited. . . .

. . . In the instant case, a principal motivating factor of Mrs. Blankenship's actions must have been a desire to aid her foster child as well as to have her home free of illegal drugs and criminal activity. Excluding the evidence seized herein would do nothing to deter similar future conduct by the Blankenships and other foster parents as that interest is entirely separate from a desire to have a person convicted of a crime or adjudged a delinquent. Put another way, the incentive to make a search, under the circumstances here involved would not be lessened because of the likelihood that the evidence would be suppressed. In short, the primary purpose to be served by the exclusionary rule would not be served by its application in this case or ones similar to it.[156]

## [b]   The Problem of Runaways

The courts frequently encounter cases of juveniles who leave foster care and other CBI placements without permission. If a probation order is also in place, such activity may constitute a violation of probation resulting in a possible

---

[156] *Id.* at 175–76.

probation revocation and imposition of a more restrictive confinement.[157] The act of running away would also itself constitute a status offense should authorities seek to pursue the matter on that theory.[158]

In addition, leaving the premises of a CBI placement might itself represent a violation of statutes prohibiting escape from detention facilities thus constituting a new act of delinquency. The cases addressing this issue often determine whether or not the conduct is covered under escape statutes by assessing the level of security imposed by the institution from which the juvenile absconded. For example, in a Florida case,[159] a juvenile who had been committed to Duval House, a residential half-way house, attended a football game with a group from the facility as part of its rehabilitation program. The juvenile left the group during the game, returning to the facility the next day. After being adjudicated a delinquent for "escaping from a secure facility,"[160] the juvenile appealed, arguing that life in Duval House was not sufficiently restrictive to render it a "secure facility" under the statute. The appellate court agreed with the juvenile, finding that no evidence had been presented to show that Duval House imposed "24-hour awake supervision with a structured residential environment," the critical factor that distinguished "secure" facilities from others outside the scope of the escape statute.[161]

## [5]　Secure Confinement

Custodial confinement in secure facilities is the most restrictive disposition available in the juvenile justice system[162] and is generally considered a last resort to be used only when other alternatives are clearly unacceptable.[163] While statutes in a few states permit juvenile courts to commit delinquents to correctional facilities which also house adult offenders,[164] most delinquents are confined in facilities housing only juveniles.[165] The maximum period of such confinement is

---

[157] See supra § 11.03 [C][1][b].

[158] See supra § 8.04.

[159] K.A.N. v. State, 582 So. 2d 57 (Fla. Dist. Ct. App. 1991).

[160] The Florida statute made it a "felony of the third degree" to escape from any secure detention or any residential commitment facility of level VI or above. Id. at 59. The court defined a level VI commitment as one requiring "24-hour awake supervision." Id.

[161] Id. In Benitez v. Collazo, 584 F. Supp. 267, 269 (D.P.R. 1984) and Kramer, supra note 1, at 397 n.166, the court accepted the following definitions of "secure" as distinguished from "nonsecure" facilities, as stipulated to by the parties in the case:

> Secure Facility: one which is designed and operated so as to ensure that all entrances and exits from such facility are under the exclusive control of the staff of the facility, whether or not the person being detained has freedom of movement within the perimeters of the facility or which relies on locked rooms and buildings, fences, or physical restraints in order to control the behavior of its residents.

> Nonsecure Facility: a facility not characterized by the use of physically restricting construction, hardware or procedures and which provides its residents access to the surrounding community with minimal and/or no supervision as appropriate.

[162] Davis, supra note 22, at 6-10; Fox, supra note 68, at 231.

[163] Wadlington, Whitebread & Davis, supra note 1, at 564.

[164] Davis, supra note 22, at 6-8 to 6-12; Fox, supra note 68, at 233–34.

[165] In most jurisdictions, commitment of juveniles to adult penal or correctional institutions is prohibited. Kramer, supra note 1, at 401–02.

usually until the minor reaches the age of majority (release on probation prior to that time is common)[166] although the statutes in some jurisdictions permit confinement until age twenty-one[167] and even beyond in at least one state.[168]

Historically, confinement in secure facilities, commonly designated as "training schools" or "industrial schools," was for the purpose of rehabilitating the juvenile. While this rationale continues in many jurisdictions, the goal in others is to impose secure confinement as a means of punishment.

## [a]   The Right to Rehabilitation

Several cases have considered arguments that confinement of juveniles in secure institutions is impermissible because the facility offers no realistic possibilities for rehabilitation.[169] Some courts have been receptive to such claims in contexts where rehabilitation provided the sole underlying purpose for juvenile court dispositions. One court articulated the following as the theoretical basis for a federal constitutional "right to rehabilitation" in such circumstances:

> "[D]ue process requires that the nature and duration of commitment bear some reasonable relation to the purpose for which the individual is committed." . . . [W]hen a state incarcerates juveniles for the purpose of treatment or rehabilitation . . . due process requires that the conditions of confinement be reasonably related to that purpose.[170]

---

[166]   Fox, *supra* note 68, at 236, 239.

[167]   *Id.* at 238.

[168]   California permits delinquents to be confined beyond the age of majority for two-year periods, extending indefinitely, if release of the detainee "would be physically dangerous to the public because of the person's mental or physical deficiency, disorder or abnormality." Cal. Welf. & Inst. Code §§ 1800, 1802 (West 1998).

[169]   Although claims to a "right to rehabilitation" could plausibly be made in the context of non-incarcerative dispositions such as probation or community service, the cases considering the right to rehabilitation appear to have arisen entirely in the context of incarcerated youngsters. Fox, *supra* note 68, at 242.

[170]   Alexander S. v. Boyd, 876 F. Supp. 773, 796–97 n.43 (D.S.C. 1995) (quoting Jackson v. Indiana, 406 U.S. 715, 738 (1972)). Other courts have offered more elaborate versions of the right to rehabilitation. In an opinion subsequently reversed, a federal district court offered the following two-part theory:

> The first part of this theory holds that any non-trivial governmental abridgment of liberty must be justified in terms of some permissible governmental goal. The governmental goals or interests typically advanced are danger to self, danger to others, and the need for treatment, care, custody, or supervision. In the instant case, the state is charged with a statutory duty to provide "a program of constructive training aimed at rehabilitation and reestablishment in society of children adjudged to be delinquent." This basis for commitment — to rehabilitate and re-establish the juvenile in society — is clearly grounded in a *parens patriae* rationale. Thus, under the *parens patriae* theory, the juvenile must be given treatment lest the involuntary commitment amount to an arbitrary exercise of governmental power proscribed by the due process clause.
>
> Under the second part of the two-part due process theory, the government must afford a *quid pro quo* to warrant the confinement of citizens in circumstances in which the conventional limitations of the criminal process are inapplicable. The three central limitations on the government's power to detain are: (1) that detention be retribution for a specific offense; (2) that it be limited to a fixed term; and (3) that it be permitted only after a proceeding where fundamental procedural safeguards are observed. In their absence a *quid pro quo* must be extended by the government to justify confinement. As previously noted, the *quid pro quo* applicable here, by virtue of state statute, is rehabilitative treatment.

Morales v. Turman, 383 F. Supp. 53, 70–71 (E.D. Tex. 1974), *rev'd*, 535 F.2d 864 (5th Cir. 1976); *see also*

In addition to a federal right, the courts have also recognized a right to rehabilitation under state law where the juvenile statutes promise rehabilitative care. For example, a New Jersey court invoked a delinquent child's "right to treatment," under state statutes embracing "the *parens patriae* underpinnings of the juvenile court," as the basis for ordering state correctional officials to place the child in a private hospital for psychiatric treatment.[171] The court considered itself statutorily bound to provide the child with needed care. "It is this obligation which requires the court to assure itself that a juvenile adjudicated delinquent will get effective rehabilitative treatment, and to choose a dispositional alternative most likely to achieve that result."[172]

While the courts have recognized a right to rehabilitation, more specifically a right to *effective* rehabilitation, the cases have struggled when attempting to define whether or not a given rehabilitation program is "effective." In one famous example, a federal district court found that the Texas system inadequately rehabilitated juveniles confined within the various state institutions.[173] As a consequence, the court ordered wholesale renovations of the system, including the closing of two facilities, only to be reversed on procedural grounds on appeal.[174] In another case, the United States Court of Appeals for the Seventh Circuit found that the regimen of group therapy practiced at the Indiana Boys School by a bare bones staff of counselors lacking specialized mental health training[175] did not adequately satisfy the institutionalized juvenile's right to rehabilitation. The court suggested that the School employ more certified psychologists, and perhaps psychiatrists, in order to implement individualized treatment programs for each juvenile. Apart from this suggestion, the appellate court left it to "the competent district court" to

---

Morales v. Turman, 562 F.2d 993, 997–98 (5th Cir. 1977) (*dictum* rejecting constitutional right to rehabilitation for juveniles), *rev'd*, 430 U.S. 322 (1977).

　　Under the theory quoted directly above, the court apparently saw the absence of fixed term sentencing and trial by jury, characteristic of the juvenile justice system, to constitute denials of the "traditional limitations of the criminal process," thus requiring the *quid pro quo* of rehabilitation in return for the deprivation of liberty entailed in secure confinement in a juvenile institution. The *quid pro quo* doctrine has proven to be especially controversial, in part because the juvenile system has come to require so many of the "procedural safeguards" embodied as "traditional limitations of the criminal process." *See, e.g.*, Davis, *supra* note 22, at 6-35 to 6-38; *see also* Santana v. Collazo, 714 F.2d 1172, 1177 (1st Cir. 1983), *cert. denied*, 466 U.S. 974 (1984) (rejecting the *quid pro quo* theory).

[171] *See, e.g., In re* D.F., 351 A.2d 43, 47 (N.J. Juv. & Dom. Rel. Ct. 1975); *see also* Nelson v. Heyne, 355 F. Supp. 451, 459 (N.D. Ind. 1972), *aff'd*, 491 F.2d 35 (7th Cir. 1974), *cert. denied*, 417 U.S. 976 (1974) (court recognizes right to rehabilitation under both state and federal law).

[172] *In re* D.F., 351 A.2d at 47.

[173] Morales v. Turman, 383 F. Supp. 53 (E.D. Tex. 1974).

[174] Morales v. Turman, 535 F.2d 864 (5th Cir. 1976), *rev'd*, 430 U.S. 322 (1977) (holding that a three-judge district court should have considered the case). The case was subsequently remanded to the district court to consider whether subsequent changes in the Texas system removed the need for federal court intervention. Morales v. Turman, 569 F. Supp. 332 (E.D. Tex. 1983) (requiring several steps to be taken before court could approve proposed settlement agreement).

[175] Nelson v. Heyne, 491 F.2d 352 (7th Cir. 1974), *cert. denied*, 417 U.S. 976 (1984). The court noted a staff-to-juvenile ratio of one to thirty and observed that much of the staff time was spent on administrative paper work. One psychiatrist was available for "crisis" situations, but he played no role in developing or managing individual psychotherapy programs. Three uncertified staff psychologists, none of whom held graduate degrees, participated in supervising intake diagnostic services aimed at classifying incoming juveniles into one of four groups ("the inadequate, the neurotic, the aggressive, and the sub-cultural") in which similarly classified juveniles would subsequently live within the institution.

determine "the minimal treatment required to provide constitutional due process."[176]

Some courts do not recognize a right to rehabilitation, particularly where rehabilitation is not the sole statutory dispositional purpose. Thus, some courts find no constitutional right to rehabilitation where protection of society supplements rehabilitation as a dispositional goal.[177] Where secure confinement is imposed primarily as punishment, a right to rehabilitation can in fact be viewed as inconsistent with dispositional goals.[178]

Whether or not courts recognize a right to rehabilitation, they do subject conditions of confinement to federal constitutional scrutiny under the Due Process Clause. Thus, courts have held that incarcerated juveniles have rights to personal safety, to medical services, to adequate nourishment, to be free from the indiscriminate use of tear gas by institutional authorities,[179] and to due process hearings prior to being placed in disciplinary segregation for more than twenty-four hours.[180]

## [b]   Cruel and Unusual Punishment

As noted earlier, the United States Supreme Court has specifically left open the question of whether the Eighth Amendment applies to the context of punishment of youngsters confined in juvenile institutions.[181] After *Ingraham*, Eighth Amendment applicability would appear to depend not only on a determination that a given disposition constitutes "punishment," but also on whether the punishment is "sufficiently analogous to criminal punishments in the circumstances in which they are administered to justify application of the Eighth Amendment."[182]

Some courts have rejected arguments that general conditions of institutional confinement constitute cruel and unusual punishment on the theory that the confinement is rehabilitative and not punitive, and thus not governed by the Eighth Amendment.[183] Other courts have denied application of the Eighth Amendment on the view that confinement of juveniles is not "sufficiently analogous to criminal

---

[176] *Id.* at 360.

[177] *See, e.g.*, Santana v. Collazo, 714 F.2d 1172, 1176–77 (1st Cir. 1983), *cert. denied*, 466 U.S. 974 (1984). In addition to noting that there is no right to rehabilitation where the purpose of confinement is to protect society from the juvenile, the *Santana* court added: "In addition, even without treatment, simply removing a juvenile from a dangerous or unhealthy environment may be a legitimate exercise of the state's *parens patriae* authority." *Id.*

[178] *See supra* § 11.03[B][1]. Several courts have upheld punishment as a legitimate purpose of juvenile justice. See, *e.g.*, In re *Seven Minors*, 664 P.2d 947, 950 (Nev. 1983), which provides:

> By formally recognizing the legitimacy of punitive and deterrent sanctions for criminal offenses juvenile courts will be properly and somewhat belatedly expressing society's firm disapproval of juvenile crime and will be clearly issuing a threat of punishment for criminal acts to the juvenile population.

For commentary on the right to rehabilitation, see A. Gough, *The Beyond Control Child and the Right to Treatment: An Exercise in the Synthesis of Paradox*, 16 St. Louis U. L.J. 182 (1971); N. Kittrie, *Can the Right to Treatment Remedy the Ills of the Juvenile Process?*, 57 Geo. L.J. 848 (1969); Note, *A Right to Treatment for Juveniles?*, 1973 Wash. U. L.Q. 157.

[179] *See, e.g.*, Alexander S. v. Boyd, 876 F. Supp. 773, 786–89 (D.S.C. 1995).

[180] Gary H. v. Hegstrom, 831 F.2d 1430 (9th Cir. 1987).

[181] *See supra* § 6.05, note 11 and accompanying text.

[182] *Id.*

[183] *See, e.g.*, R.R. v. State, 448 S.W.2d 187 (Tex. Civ. App. 1969).

punishment" to justify application of the Eighth Amendment under the *Ingraham* dictum.[184] Other courts, however, have applied the Eighth Amendment in reviewing juvenile confinement. Some such courts find the confinement sufficiently punitive to justify Eighth Amendment applicability even though the articulated statutory dispositional purpose is rehabilitation and not punishment.[185] Other courts simply apply the Cruel and Unusual Punishments Clause without explicitly finding that nominally rehabilitative confinement is in fact punitive.[186] Moreover, in addition to assessing general conditions of confinement under the Eighth Amendment, the courts have sometimes found specific regimens imposed to maintain discipline within the institution to be cruel and unusual punishment.

## [i] General Conditions of Confinement

Several courts have applied Eighth Amendment scrutiny in cases where juveniles argued that the general conditions of their confinement constituted cruel and unusual punishment. Some courts have responded sympathetically to such arguments. For example, in a case pre-dating *Ingraham*, a federal district court applied the Eighth Amendment and found that certain physical conditions of the Rhode Island Boys Training School were constitutionally inadequate under "evolving standards of decency that mark the progress of a maturing society."[187] In particular, the court enjoined the School's use of cold, dark, solitary confinement cells containing only a mattress and toilet (flushed from outside the cell by School personnel).

In a post-*Ingraham* case, a federal court found that two juveniles were subjected to cruel and unusual punishment when an Ohio juvenile court judge committed them to an adult corrections facility in order "to frighten them away

---

Appellant . . . takes the position that the confinement of a delinquent child must be viewed as "punishment" for the purpose of determining the child's rights under the Eighth Amendment, even though the language of our juvenile statutes speaks in terms of treatment rather than punishment.

The record before us contains no evidence concerning the conditions at the state training schools. . . . In the absence of evidence that the dismal picture painted in *Gault* reflects the conditions in the institutions of this State and giving due consideration to the legislative declaration of policy and purpose, we are not prepared to condemn out of hand . . . the people working in this field.

*Id.* at 189–90.

[184] *See, e.g.,* Gary H. v. Hegstrom, 831 F.2d 1430, 1431–32 (9th Cir. 1987) (holding that the Due Process Clause, which "implicitly incorporates the cruel and unusual punishments clause standards as a constitutional minimum," is the appropriate standard for reviewing the "noncriminal and nonpenal" Oregon juvenile justice system); Alexander S. v. Boyd, 876 F. Supp. 773, 781, 796 (D.S.C. 1995) (holding that incarceration of juveniles is for "beneficent rather than punitive purposes," and that incarcerated juveniles have "not been convicted of a crime . . . but have merely been adjudicated to be juvenile delinquents" thus justifying application of "more stringent" due process protection rather than less stringent protection under the Cruel and Unusual Punishments Clause).

[185] *See, e.g.,* Inmates of Boys' Training School v. Affleck, 346 F. Supp. 1354, 1366 (D.R.I. 1972) ("the fact that juveniles are *in theory* not punished but merely confined for rehabilitative purposes does not [alter] the reality [that] confinement . . . is punishment" thus justifying application of the Eighth Amendment).

[186] *See, e.g.,* Morales v. Turman, 562 F.2d 993, 998 (5th Cir. 1977) (Eighth Amendment "applies to juvenile detention centers as well as to adult prisons" even where state chooses a "social policy . . . of rehabilitating juvenile offenders").

[187] Inmates of Boys' Training School v. Affleck, 346 F. Supp. 1354, 1366–67 (D.R.I. 1972) (citing Trop v. Dulles, 356 U.S. 86, 101 (1958)).

from a life of crime."[188] During their incarceration, both juveniles were assaulted and allegedly raped by other inmates while corrections officers were away from their posts. The court identified rehabilitation of the juvenile to be the sole dispositional purpose under the Ohio statutes while also finding that the adult facility to which the juveniles were sent did not provide a program of rehabilitation. These considerations led the court to observe:

> "[I]ncarceration of juveniles for rehabilitation violates the Eighth Amendment when the reality of the imprisonment is punishment not treatment. . . . Such imprisonment without treatment violates juveniles' Eighth Amendment rights."[189]

## [ii] Disciplinary Regimens

Several courts have applied the Eighth Amendment in assessing the constitutionality of disciplinary regimens imposed upon juveniles confined in secure facilities.[190] For example, in a pre-*Ingraham* case, the Seventh Circuit Court of Appeals[191] condemned two practices prevalent within the Indiana Boy's School: 1) corporal punishment with a "fraternity paddle" imposed for various violations of institutional rules,[192] and 2) the School's use of intramuscular tranquilizer injections to control the excited behavior of juvenile inmates.

Regarding the use of the paddle to punish offending inmates, the court found that the "uncontradicted authoritative evidence indicates that the practice does not serve as useful punishment . . . and that it actually breeds counter-hostility resulting in greater aggression by a child."[193] Therefore, the court found the "beatings presently administered are unnecessary and therefore excessive"

---

[188] Doe v. McFaul, 599 F. Supp. 1421 (E.D. Ohio 1984). The court also found the commitment offended the due process rights of the juveniles.

[189] *Id.* at 1430.

[190] See, *e.g.*, *State v. Werner*, 242 S.E.2d 907, 909–10 (W. Va. 1978), where the court invalidated under the Eighth Amendment the following inmate disciplinary practices employed by authorities at the West Virginia Industrial School for Boys:

1) Inmates thought guilty of serious disciplinary offenses, such as escape, were punished by confinement in small, windowless steel-walled cells (there are three cells) furnished with a combination toilet, wash basin and drinking fountain, a steel cot with flame-proof mattress, and a light. There is an aperture in the door about eight by eight inches through which food and other articles can be passed. The cells are about four feet wide, eight feet long and eight feet high. Youths placed in them were allowed to wear only their undershorts.

2) "Floor time" was a punishment whereby the inmate apparently was required to stand stiffly in one position for several hours each day without talking.

3) "Bench time" was a punishment that required the inmate to sit in a specified location with arms crossed for several hours each day and for several days without talking or moving.

4) Mace, a chemical irritant, was freely used by staff upon inmates whose behavior did not suit staff requirements.

The court also prohibited "slapping, kicking, and otherwise physically abusing juveniles in the absence of exigent circumstances." *Id.* at 910–11.

[191] Nelson v. Heyne, 491 F.2d 352 (7th Cir. 1974), *cert. denied*, 417 U.S. 976 (1974).

[192] As punishment for various offenses against institutional rules, juveniles were beaten with a paddle between one-half and two inches thick and twelve inches long with a narrow handle. The beatings were apparently ungoverned by extensive formal procedures and sometimes caused painful injuries. *Id.* at 354.

[193] *Id.* at 355.

punishment under the Eighth Amendment.[194] While the court disclaimed that it was "hold[ing] that all corporal punishment in juvenile institutions . . . is *per se* cruel and unusual,"[195] the empirical conclusion that corporal punishment is inherently counter-productive and thus cruelly excessive in fact implies a *per se* invalidation of corporal punishment. Any conclusion that corporal punishment is *per se* unconstitutional is, of course, highly questionable in light of *Ingraham*.[196]

The Seventh Circuit's analysis of the tranquilizer issue summarily rejected the School's claim that the Eighth Amendment did not apply because administering drugs does not constitute punishment.[197] The court simply assumed that the injections were punitive and went on to find them cruel and unusual punishment because of a variety of potential dangers inherent in misuse of the drugs.[198]

The Seventh Circuit Court of Appeals has also subjected disciplinary practices to Eighth Amendment scrutiny in cases decided subsequent to *Ingraham*. In one such case,[199] the court found a violation of the Cruel and Unusual Punishments Clause when a consulting psychologist of a Wisconsin facility for delinquent females refused to see a juvenile after she had been placed in solitary confinement for attempting to escape and for assaulting a staff person. The court found that the psychologist, who had been treating the juvenile, "caused cruel and unusual punishment to be imposed on [her]" when he informed her that he "chose" not to see her while she was in isolated confinement.[200] The court explained its conclusion as follows:

> Clearly, [the psychologist's] suspension of his regular program of treatment of [the juvenile] at a time she was deprived of all but minimal human contact . . . and his response at the time that he chose not to see her, could reasonably be found as intentional, needless infliction of pain.[201]

---

[194] *Id.*

[195] *Id.* at 355 n.6.

[196] *See supra* § 6.05[A].

[197] "We are not persuaded by defendants' argument that the use of tranquilizing drugs is not 'punishment.'" 491 F.2d at 357. For a discussion of whether or not the use of the drugs did indeed constitute punishment, see Gardner, *supra* note 37, at 844–46.

[198] The court found that drugs were occasionally administered to control the excited behavior of juvenile inmates. Apart from their effects as sedatives, the drugs possessed no significant psychotherapeutic benefits. Moreover, the drugs were capable of causing severe and dangerous side effects unless carefully monitored by trained medical personnel. The court also found that medical personnel did not monitor the administration of the drugs. At no time prior to or following the injections did medical professionals examine the youths to determine their individual tolerances for the drugs. Instead, the school administered standardized dosages pursuant to orders given by the school's only physician. 491 F.2d at 356–57.

The court intimated that the injections may have been permissible if they had been administered more carefully. "We do not intend that . . . reform institutional physicians cannot prescribe necessary tranquilizing drugs in appropriate cases. Our concern is with . . . potential abuses under policies where . . . drugs are administered to juveniles intramuscularly by the staff, without trying medication short of drugs and without medical guidance and prescription." *Id.* at 357.

[199] Mary and Crystal v. Ramsden, 635 F.2d 590 (7th Cir. 1980).

[200] *Id.* at 598.

[201] *Id.*

## [D] Boot Camps

During the last two decades of the twentieth century, many states created so-called "boot camps" as a secure confinement alternative to traditional training schools.[202] The camps are routinely designed to house delinquent offenders in a setting patterned after military basic training where the inmates are subjected to a rigorous regimen of discipline and physical exercise. The camps are sometimes viewed as a form of "shock incarceration," punitively imposed as a means of deterring future offenses and visiting just deserts upon offenders.[203] On the other hand, to the extent the camps teach self-discipline, respect for the law, and the value of work,[204] they may be perceived as vehicles aimed at rehabilitating the juveniles confined therein.[205]

## [E] "Blended Sentencing"

In the 1990s several states enacted "blended sentencing" or "extended jurisdiction" provisions aimed at balancing the interests of juvenile offenders with concerns for holding juveniles accountable for the crimes they commit. One type of blended sentencing provision allows the court to combine a juvenile disposition with a suspended adult sentence. If the offender is deemed rehabilitated at the conclusion of his juvenile disposition, the court can place him or her on probation. If, however, the juvenile violates the conditions set forth in the juvenile sentence or commits a new offense before completing the juvenile sentence, the court can then execute the stayed adult criminal sentence. Minnesota was the first to pass this kind of statute in 1995,[206] with several states following suit shortly thereafter.[207]

A different blended sentencing scheme has been adopted in some states which allows juvenile court judges to impose either a juvenile or criminal sentence upon certain classes of offenders who have been adjudicated in juvenile courts extending

---

[202] *See* P. Katel, M. Liu & B. Cohn, *Washington,* NEWSWEEK, Feb. 21, 1994, at 26.

[203] *Id.*

[204] *Id.*

[205] However, recidivism rates of camp graduates appear to be as high or higher as those of juveniles paroled from traditional training schools. *Id.; see also* D. MacKensie et. al., *Title,* National Institute of Justice Research in Brief (August 2001) at www.ncjrs.org/pdffiles/nig/187680.pdf at 2. Despite the data on recidivism, juveniles in boot camps apparently feel better prepared for release, believe they are given more therapeutic programming and are subjected to more structure and control, than those juveniles subject to confinement in traditional youth facilities. *Id.* at 4–7.

For commentary on boot camps, see, *e.g.,* D. Marlowe, *New Voices on the War on Drugs: Effective Strategies for Intervening with Drug Abusing Offenders,* 47 VILL. L. REV. 989 (2002); C. Conward, *Where Have All the Children Gone?: A Look at Incarcerated Youth in America,* 27 WM. MITCHELL L. REV. 2435 (2001); R. Smith, *Toward a More Utilitarian Juvenile Court System,* 10 U. FLA. J.L. & PUB. POL'Y 237 (1999).

[206] Minn. Stat. Ann. § 260B.130 (2001); M. Caulum, Comment, *Postadolescent Brain Development: A Disconnect Between Neuroscience, Emerging Adults, and the Corrections System,* 2007 WIS. L. REV. 729, 749. Under the Minnesota statute, juveniles were tried in juvenile court with the full array of procedural protections allowed in adult criminal court. Upon conviction, the court was empowered to impose both a juvenile court disposition and a stayed adult criminal sentence. A Minnesota appellate court held the statute unconstitutional on Equal Protection and Due Process Grounds. *In re* Welfare of T.C.J., 689 N.W.2d 787, 796 (Minn. App. 2004).

[207] *See, e.g.,* Ark. Code Ann. § 9-27-501-510 (2000); 705 Ill. Comp. Stat. Ann. 405/5-810(7) (West 2006 & Supp. 2007).

full adult criminal court procedural protections.[208] Depending on the judge's assessment of the offender's amenability to treatment, the judge is given sole discretion to impose an adult criminal sentence or a juvenile disposition with jurisdiction extended to age twenty-one.[209]

Other states employ a model in which the juvenile court retains jurisdiction and responsibility for adjudication of the case and has the authority to impose a sanction that would be in force beyond the age of the court's extended jurisdiction, usually twenty-one.[210] The juvenile court is then given the authority to determine whether the remainder of the sanction should be completed in an adult correctional facility. In particular, a juvenile court judge in Texas is given the authority to impose a one-to-forty year sentence for the commission of one of twelve named violent offenses. The sentence is begun in the juvenile correctional system until the age of eighteen, at which time transfer to an adult facility is authorized if deemed necessary after a court review. Transfer to an adult facility is mandatory at age twenty-one.[211]

Although the varying statutory schemes relating to the practice of "blended jurisdiction" differ in many respects, a common theme runs through these statutes. By providing youthful offenders with the procedural safeguards guaranteed adults in criminal court, the state retains the option to punish these juveniles to the fullest extent possible (as an adult convicted of a similar crime). Such statutes can be viewed as serving a variety of functions, from setting forth a get-tough-on-juvenile-crime mentality to providing a viable alternative to mandatory waiver to adult criminal court for those youths deemed to be amenable to treatment in the juvenile system. With a carrot and stick approach, the youthful offender is given one last chance to rehabilitate while at the same time possessing the knowledge that an adult sentence has been imposed and may be enforced at the state's discretion.[212]

## [F]　Policy Implications

Empirical data suggests that juvenile dispositions, particularly secure confinement, have not been successful in rehabilitating many delinquent offenders.[213] For some, this data suggests that more resources should be devoted to improve the effectiveness of rehabilitative programs.[214] For others, the data suggests that the traditional *parens patriae* juvenile court movement has failed and is beyond repair. In the face of evidence that the rate of violent juvenile crime

---

[208] *See, e.g.*, N.M. Stat. Ann. § 32A-2-3(C),(H)(1) (1993).

[209] *Id.*

[210] *See, e.g.*, Tex. Family Code Ann. § 54.04 (Supp. 2002).

[211] *Id.*

[212] For commentary on blended sentencing, see, *e.g.*, M. Caulum, *supra* note 206; Mark Ells, *A Brief Analysis of Some Elements of a Proposed Model Juvenile Code*, 28 HAMLINE J. PUB. L. & POL'Y 199 (2006); R. Henderson, *Blended Sentencing in Montana: A New Way to Look at an Old Problem*, 61 MONT. L. REV. 337 (2000); E. Moore, *Juvenile Justice: The Nathaniel Abraham Murder Case*, 41 U. MICH. J.L. REFORM 215 (2007); M. Spring, *Extended Jurisdiction Juvenile Prosecution: A New Approach to the Problem of Juvenile Delinquency in Illinois*, 31 J. MARSHALL L. REV. 1351 (1998); R. Smallheer, *Sentence Blending and the Promise of Rehabilitation: Bringing the Juvenile Justice System Full Circle*, 28 HOFSTRA L. REV. 259 (1999); C. Tanner, *Arkansas's Extended Juvenile Jurisdiction Act: The Balance of Offender Rehabilitation and Accountability*, 22 U. ARK. LITTLE ROCK L. REV. 647 (2000).

[213] Kramer, *supra* note 1, at 398 n.172.

[214] *Id.* at 398–99.

is rapidly increasing,[215] many now favor subjecting juvenile offenders to decidedly more punitive consequences in the form of lengthy incarcerative commitments.[216]

## § 11.04   STATUS OFFENDERS

In some states, the same array of dispositional alternatives available for delinquents, including secure confinement, may be employed against status offenders.[1] In some such states, however, legislatures and courts have imposed requirements that status offenders be segregated from delinquents when confined in secure confinement institutions.[2]

On the other hand, other jurisdictions prohibit the use of incarcerative confinement for status offenders, at least as an initial disposition.[3] The movement towards deinstitutionalizing status offenders is a consequence, in part at least, of federal actions begun in the 1970's aimed at encouraging the states to divert status offenders from the juvenile justice system whenever possible and to devise alternatives to incarcerative dispositions when status offenders are dealt with by the juvenile courts.[4] The opposition to secure confinement dispositions for status offenders is premised in large part on the view that secure confinement belies a punitive orientation inappropriate for youngsters who have not been shown to have committed a criminal act and who are thus appropriate candidates for *parens patriae* dispositions.[5] Moreover, punishment is unconstitutional when imposed in

---

[215] *See* F. Sherman & W. Talley, *Foreward, Symposium — Struggling for a Future: Juvenile Violence, Juvenile Justice*, 36 B.C. L. Rev. 889, 890–91 (1995).

[216] *Id.*; Kramer, *supra* note 1, at 399.

[1] Davis, *supra* § 2.02, note 9, at 6-21.

[2] *See infra* § 11.04[B][3].

[3] *See infra* § 11.04[B][1], [2].

[4] For discussion of the federal influence towards the deinstitutionalization movement, see Mnookin & Weisberg, *supra* § 1.02, note 8, at 1057–63; Wadlington, Whitebread & Davis, *supra* § 3.02, note 34, at 630–36.

[5] See, *e.g.*, the *Gault* Court's characterization of secure confinement, *supra* § 7.03, note 30 and accompanying text. One court expressed the concern with incarcerating status offenders this way:

> We are . . . concerned with incarceration of children for status offenses. Particularly . . . we are concerned with a child who is incorrigible, ungovernable, habitually disobedient and beyond the control of his parents, truant, repeatedly deserts his home or place of abode, engages in an occupation which is in violation of law, or frequents a place the existence of which is in violation of law. The Legislature has vested the juvenile court with jurisdiction over children who commit these status offenses so that the court may enforce order, safety, morality, and family discipline within the community. The intention of the law is laudable; however, the means employed to accomplish these ends are unconstitutional insofar as they result in the commitment of status offenders to secure, prison-like facilities which also house children guilty of criminal conduct, or needlessly subject status offenders to the degradation and physical abuse of incarceration.
>
> At the outset the Court should make clear that we are not impressed with euphemistic titles used to disguise what are in fact secure, prison-like facilities. We define a secure, prison-like facility, regardless of whether it be called a "home for girls," "industrial school," "forestry camp," "children's shelter," "orphanage," or other imaginative name, as a place which relies for control of children upon locked rooms, locked buildings, guards, physical restraint, regimentation, and corporal punishment. Somehow, it appears to us that if the State's purpose is to develop a society characterized by peace and love, that our institutions for children should reflect those qualities and not their opposite.

State *ex rel.* Harris v. Calendine, 233 S.E.2d 318, 324–25 (W. Va. 1977).

status offense cases where it is found that the child manifests an undesirable status condition rather than on a showing that she has engaged in a particular act of noncriminal misconduct.[6]

## [A] Non-Incarcerative Dispositions

As is true with delinquency, conditional probation is probably the most common disposition in status offense cases.[7] In appropriate cases, the courts may also order restitution or community service, even though the child has not been shown to have committed a criminal offense.[8] Likewise, courts routinely possess discretion to order community-based institutionalization when deemed desirable.[9] Where the least drastic alternative consistent with dispositional goals is required, courts must apply the standard to both status offense and delinquency cases.

## [B] Secure Confinement

### [1] Initial Disposition

Traditionally, secure confinement at a juvenile institution was perceived as a rehabilitation vehicle available for status offenders and delinquents alike. Some jurisdictions continue to embrace this position, seeing secure confinement as a viable dispositional option for status offenders to the same extent as for delinquents.[10] However, some such jurisdictions permit secure confinement as initial dispositions for status offenders only if less drastic rehabilitative alternatives are not realistically available.[11]

On the other hand, some jurisdictions statutorily prohibit secure confinement as an initial disposition for status offenders. For example, the Mississippi statute provides:

> In children in need of supervision cases, the disposition order may include any of the following alternatives or combination of the following alternatives, giving precedence in the following sequence:

---

[6] *See infra* § 11.04[D][2][b].

[7] Kramer, *supra* § 3.03, note 15, at 388. While probation is the most common disposition in status offense cases reaching the juvenile courts, many status offense cases are diverted from the courts altogether. *See* Wadlington, Whitebread & Davis, *supra* note 4, at 634–36.

[8] Restitution is routinely imposed in cases involving property loss or damage. While such infringements of property rights usually constitute acts of delinquency, they may also trigger status offense jurisdiction should juvenile authorities utilize them as evidence that the child is "unruly," "wayward," or the like, under a status offense statute.

[9] *See, e.g.*, Neb. Rev. Stat. § 43-284 (Cum. Supp. 1996).

[10] *See, e.g.*, Ga. Code. Ann. § 15-11-36 (Harrison 1994).

[11] *Id.* One court expressed the matter this way:

> [B]efore [a status offender] may be committed to a penal institution . . . [there] must be evidence on the record which clearly supports the conclusion, and the juvenile court must specifically find as a matter of fact, that no other reasonable alternative either is available or could with due diligence and financial commitment on the part of the State be made available to help the child, and that the child is so totally unmanageable, ungovernable, and anti-social that he or she is amenable to no treatment or restraint short of incarceration in a secure, prison-like facility.

State *ex rel.* Harris v. Calendine, 233 S.E.2d 318, 331 (W. Va. 1977).

(a) Release the child without further action;

(b) Place the child in the custody of the parent, a relative or other person subject to any conditions and limitations as the youth court may prescribe;

(c) Place the child under youth court supervision subject to any conditions and limitations the youth court may prescribe;

(d) Order terms of treatment calculated to assist the child and the child's parent, guardian or custodian which are within the ability of the parent, guardian or custodian to perform;

(e) Order terms of supervision which may include participation in a constructive program of service or education or restitution not in excess of actual damages caused by the child to be paid out of his own assets or by performance of services acceptable to the parties and reasonably capable of performance within one (1) year;

(f) Give legal custody of the child to any of the following but in no event to any state training school;

  (i) The Department of Human Services for appropriate placement which may include a wilderness training program; or

  (ii) Any private or public organization, preferably community-based, able to assume the education, care and maintenance of the child, which has been found suitable by the court. Prior to assigning the custody of any child to any private institution or agency, the youth court through its designee shall first inspect the physical facilities to determine that they provide a reasonable standard of health and safety for the child.[12]

In jurisdictions where statutes do not expressly preclude institutional confinement of status offenders, courts have sometimes imposed such limitations. In one such case, the Alaska Supreme Court invalidated the institutional commitment of a fourteen-year-old runaway girl, finding that the statutory distinction between "delinquents" and "child[ren] in need of supervision" permitted institutionalized confinement for delinquents only, even though the statutory language literally authorized both classes of juveniles to be committed to the Department of Health and Welfare for disposition.[13] The court noted provisions of the statutes specifying that in delinquency cases the courts have the option of placing minors under the care of the Department or ordering commitment to "a [juvenile] correctional school, detention home, or detention facility designated by the [D]epartment."[14] The court concluded:

Thus the only instance under children's laws authorizing institutionalization or incarceration is when the child has violated the laws of the state, or any of its political subdivisions, and in turn has been adjudged a delinquent minor. Since the runaway child in the case at bar was found to be a child in need of supervision, not a delinquent minor, no legal basis existed for her incarceration.[15]

---

[12] Miss. Code Ann. § 43-21-607 (Supp. 1996); *see also* Neb. Rev. Stat. § 43-287 (Cum. Supp. 1996).

[13] *In re* E.M.D., 490 P.2d 658 (Alaska 1971).

[14] *Id.* at 659–60.

[15] *Id.* at 660.

## [2] Secure Confinement as a Secondary Disposition

Some jurisdictions adhering to the position that only delinquent minors may be subjected to secure institutional confinement nevertheless permit courts to confine status offenders who violate their probation or run away from community-based dispositions. By definition, the minor becomes a "delinquent" by virtue of violating probation conditions, thus justifying secure confinement as a delinquent.[16]

Moreover, some courts find that juvenile court judges possess inherent authority to institutionalize status offenders for contempt without finding the juvenile a "delinquent" under statutory law, even though the legislature has mandated that status offenders not be placed in secure confinement facilities.[17] For example, the South Carolina Supreme Court recognized the "inherent judicial power [of juvenile courts] to punish contemners" in a case where the juvenile court had ordered the institutionalization of a young woman for contempt after she had initially been found to be a "runaway child" and subsequently absconded from a court ordered community-based commitment.[18] The supreme court noted that the minor had a previous history of truancy and running away. Moreover, the court observed that in its original disposition, the juvenile court had informed the minor that she would be held in contempt if she ran away again. The court explained the rationale for upholding the lower court's action as follows:

> The issue is whether a juvenile who commits criminal contempt by running away in violation of a court order may be given a disposition reserved for delinquents who have committed offenses which would be crimes if committed by an adult. We conclude that, under the most egregious circumstances as we have here, family courts may exercise their contempt power in such a manner that a status offender will be incarcerated in a secure facility.

> Although we have held that juvenile offenders may be punished only as prescribed by the South Carolina Children's Code, the Code specifically provides that it shall be interpreted in conjunction with all relevant laws and regulations. Therefore, when dealing with juveniles, family courts may look to their inherent powers as well as to the Children's Code. All courts possess the inherent power to punish contemnors. That power is essential to the preservation of order in judicial proceedings, and to the enforcement of the courts' judgments, orders and writs and consequently to the due administration of justice.[19]

---

[16] See, e.g., In re C.H., 683 P.2d 931 (Mont. 1984).

[17] See, e.g., In re Darlene C., 301 S.E.2d 136 (S.C. 1983).

[18] Id.

[19] Id. at 137. The South Carolina case described in the text permits juvenile courts to hold status offenders in contempt only in "egregious" circumstances. The court explained:

> Nevertheless, we hold that only under the most egregious circumstances should family courts exercise their contempt power in such a manner that a status offender will be incarcerated in a secure facility. Before a chronic status offender is placed in a secure facility, the record must show that all less restrictive alternatives have failed in the past. Additionally the following elements should exist: (1) the existence of a valid order directing the alleged contemnor to do or refrain from doing something and the court's jurisdiction to enter that order; (2) the contemnor's notice of the order with sufficient time to comply with it; and in most cases, (3) the contemnor's ability to comply with the order; and (4) the contemnor's willful failure to comply with the order. Furthermore, the record must reflect the juvenile understood that disobedience would result in incarceration in a secure facility.

On the other hand, a minority of jurisdictions hold that where statutes clearly prohibit placing status offenders in secure confinement, courts may not employ contempt power to incarcerate contemptuous status offenders.[20] A Pennsylvania case[21] provides an example of this minority view. A juvenile court judge held several juveniles in contempt for running away from an unrestricted facility to which they had been committed after being adjudicated status offenders. The juvenile court ordered the juveniles to be detained in secure facilities and they appealed, arguing, among other things, that the court lacked authority to hold them in contempt. The appellate court agreed[22] and vacated the lower court's actions. The court explained its position as follows:

> We sympathize with the well-intentioned efforts of the juvenile court judge to cope with the problems resulting from the revisions of the Juvenile Act removing status offenders from the ambit of a delinquency adjudication and providing for their separate treatment. However inconsistent it may seem to place a runaway in a nonphysically restrained setting, the legislature has ordained that this is the manner of treatment to be employed, and we must abide by their judgment. The responsibility for action to cure the problem of devising an effective method of treating chronic runaways from shelter care lies with the legislature and not with

---

*Id.* at 138.

Other courts have been less strict. In upholding the power of a juvenile court judge to incarcerate a status offender for fifteen days for contempt when she failed to abide by conditions of her original disposition, an Illinois court said:

> The minor's final argument is that the court did not have the power to sentence the minor to fifteen days detention in a secured facility. The minor argues that she was adjudicated a minor in need of supervision and not a delinquent. Since the Juvenile Act does not permit a minor to be detained in a secured facility unless the minor is a delinquent, she argues that the court could not so order in a contempt hearing. We disagree. A virtually identical issue was dealt with in In re *G.B.* In that case, the minor had violated his supervision order and the trial court found him guilty of contempt and sentenced him to one year probation with sixty days incarceration at a detention facility. On appeal, the court found that the trial court's inherent power extended to criminal contempt. In dealing with what sentence could be meted out for a finding of criminal contempt, the court stated:

> > We recognize the parallel procedures under the Juvenile Court Act and of citation for criminal contempt that were available when the minor violated the supervisory order. When, under those circumstances, the contempt route is selected, a criminal contempt is found to have taken place, and, as here, the court deems the conduct serious enough to require incarceration, we deem the appropriate procedure to ordinarily be for the court to sentence the contemnor to reasonable imprisonment.

> In the instant case, the trial court held the criminal contempt to be serious enough to require incarceration and we do not believe this finding to be against the manifest weight of the evidence. Therefore, we believe the trial court had the authority to sentence the minor to fifteen days incarceration.

*In re* R.R., 417 N.E.2d 237, 239 (Ill. App. Ct. 1981), *rev'd*, 442 N.E.2d 252 (Ill. 1982) (citations omitted) (failure of lower court to specify a term for the original disposition on which the contempt charge was based rendered the contempt order void); *see also In re* Walker, 191 S.E.2d 702 (N.C. 1972).

[20] Mnookin & Weisberg, *supra* note 4, at 1063–64.

[21] *In re* Tasseing H., 422 A.2d 530 (Pa. Super. Ct. 1980).

[22] The appellate court found that status offenders who violate court orders by running away are in civil, and not criminal, contempt. Thus their conduct cannot trigger findings of delinquency. *Id.* at 534–37.

this court.[23]

## [3]   Segregating Status Offenders and Delinquents

While a few jurisdictions prohibit the secure confinement of status offenders, either as an initial disposition or as a secondary sanction for contempt, most states have not altogether ruled out secure confinement for youngsters who enter the juvenile justice system as status offenders and subsequently violate conditions of probation. Some such jurisdictions permit status offenders and delinquents to be confined in the same facility.[24] Other jurisdictions, however, statutorily specify that status offenders not be confined in facilities used for the confinement of delinquents.[25]

The Juvenile Justice and Delinquency Prevention Act of 1974 (JJDP)[26] has been a major influence on state segregation of status offenders and delinquents, and on segregation of juveniles and adults, although juveniles do sometimes continue to be confined in adult institutions.[27] The JJDP mandates that juveniles have "sight and sound separation" from convicted adult prisoners and adults that are held awaiting trial.[28] This is to prevent adults from assaulting juveniles and from corrupting them with "adult prison culture."[29]

The JJDP also conditions state receipt of federal grants available for fighting juvenile delinquency on the state not placing status offenders in "secure detention facilities or secure correctional facilities."[30] For those states which prohibit the secure confinement of status offenders in detention facilities housing juvenile delinquents, many exceptions are available.[31] For example, a court may hold a juvenile in contempt and order secure confinement if the juvenile violates a court order requiring treatment.[32] A potential problem with prohibiting any status offender confinement is that a court's hands may be tied when it needs to deal with a runaway or homeless child and cannot order the child securely confined.[33]

The California Supreme Court expressed the rationale for segregating status offenders and delinquents in the following comments from an opinion which reversed earlier California law[34] and, for the first time, permitted secure

---

[23] *Id.* at 537–38; *see also* W.M. v. State, 437 N.E.2d 1028 (Ind. Ct. App. 1982) (under then current statute, juvenile courts lack contempt power to incarcerate child who repeatedly ran away from facility to which he had been committed for running away from home).

[24] Davis, *supra* note 1, at 6-21.

[25] *See, e.g.,* Md. Code Ann. Cts. & Jud. Proc. § 3-823(b) (1995) ("[a] child who is not delinquent may not be committed . . . to a facility used for the confinement of delinquent children").

[26] 42 U.S.C. § 5601 *et seq.*

[27] D. Abrams & S. Ramsey, Children and the Law: Doctrine, Policy, and Practice 1147 (2d ed. 2003); L. Harris & L. Teitelbaum, Children, Parents, and the Law 598–599 (2002).

[28] Abrams & Ramsey, *supra* note 27, at 1146.

[29] *Id.*

[30] 2 D. Kramer, Legal Rights of Children 345 (2d rev. ed. 2005 & Supp. 2007) (quoting 42 U.S.C. § 5602(a)(12)(a)).

[31] *Id.* at 346–47.

[32] Abrams & Ramsey, *supra* note 27, at 1035.

[33] *Id.* at 1041, n.3.

[34] *See In re* Ronald S., 138 Cal. Rptr. 387 (Cal. Ct. App. 1977) (courts could not use contempt powers to incarcerate contemptuous status offenders).

confinement of contemptuous status offenders so long as they did not comingle with delinquents:

It thus seems manifest that incarcerated status offenders must be segregated so as to avoid contact with others confined due to their criminal conduct.

We realize our decision permits the contemptuous status offender to suffer the major disadvantage heretofore reserved for [delinquents]: secure confinement during nonschool hours. However, the nature of the confinement suffered by the contemptuous status offender differs in at least one substantial respect: he cannot come in contact with [delinquent] wards who may be confined in the same facility. This limitation, as recognized by the juvenile court below, is important to ensure the status offender's problems, noncriminal at that time, are not exacerbated by mingling with delinquents. We thus avoid the unsavory situation whereby "the youngster whose only offense against society was that he could not get along with his parents, found himself cheek by jowl with the underage rapist, robber or heroin peddler."[35]

## [C]  The Right to Rehabilitation

As in the context of delinquency, status offenders subjected to secure confinement have raised arguments that such confinement without meaningful rehabilitation violates due process protections. Not surprisingly, the courts have been, if anything, more receptive to such claims by status offenders than by delinquents, given the tendency to see status offense dispositions as more centrally grounded in *parens patriae* principles than those visited upon at least some categories of delinquents. As discussed earlier, in many jurisdictions *parens patriae* considerations no longer provide the primary rationale for delinquency dispositions.[36] Thus, social protection might afford the basis for confining some delinquents, but that theory provides little justification for incarcerating youngsters who have not been shown to have committed a criminal offense. Moreover, while punishment theories might reasonably explain the basis for incarcerating some status offenders (for example, habitual runaways, truants, or minors acting in contempt of court orders), punitive incarceration generally appears more theoretically at home as a disposition for juveniles who have committed criminal acts than for status offenders. Thus, to the extent that rehabilitation of the offender provides the essential rationale for secure confinement of status offenders, the courts have scrutinized confinement devoid of rehabilitation. One court put the matter this way: "juveniles . . . who have not been convicted of crimes[] have a due process interest in freedom from

---

[35] *In re* Michael G., 747 P.2d 1152, 1163 (Cal. 1988); *see also* Lavette M. v. Corporation Counsel of the City of New York, 316 N.E.2d 314 (N.Y. 1974) (status offenders may be securely confined so long as the facility is for status offenders only); Doe v. Norris, 751 S.W.2d 834 (Tenn. 1988) (commingling status offenders and delinquents in secure facilities "punishes" status offenders and is unconstitutional under due process and equal protection principles). For criticism of the requirement that delinquents and status offenders be segregated, see C. Thomas, *Are Status Offenders Really So Different?*, 22 CRIME & DELINQ. 438 (1976); S. Fjeld, L. Newsome & M. Fjeld, *Delinquents and Status Offenders: The Similarity of Differences*, JUV. & FAM. CT. J., May 1981, at 3.

[36] *See supra* § 11.03[B].

unnecessary bodily restraint which entitles them to closer scrutiny of their conditions of confinement than accorded convicted criminals."[37]

A West Virginia case[38] illustrates the heightened judicial concern for the interests of status offenders subjected to secure confinement. The case involved a sixteen-year-old who had been committed to a forestry camp pursuant to a juvenile court order based on the court's finding that the boy was a habitual truant. At the time of the disposition, the juvenile had nearly reached the age after which school attendance was no longer required. Nevertheless, the court ordered the juvenile to be held for a period extending beyond the age compelling mandatory school attendance. The juvenile appealed the disposition to the state supreme court which found, among other things, that the order of the juvenile court violated the due process rights of the juvenile because it bore no rational relationship to the statutory dispositional goal of protecting the welfare of the child. The court explained its conclusion as follows:

> [T]he Court finds no rational connection between the legitimate legislative purposes of enforcing family discipline, protecting children, and protecting society from uncontrolled children, and the means by which the State is permitted to accomplish these purposes, namely incarceration of children in secure, prison-like facilities.
>
> It is generally recognized that the greatest colleges for crime are prisons and reform schools. The most egregious punishment inflicted upon a child incarcerated in a West Virginia penal institution is not the deprivation of his liberty but rather his forced association with reprehensible persons. Prisons, by whatsoever name they may be known, are inherently dangerous places. Sexual assaults, physical violence, psychological abuse and total degradation are the likely consequences of incarceration. If one hopes to find rehabilitation in a penal institution, his hopes will be confounded. . . . [W]hen the State is proceeding under color of its *parens patriae* authority, it must actually have fair prospects of achieving a beneficent purpose, otherwise the reason for the authority fails.
>
> . . . We find with regard to status offenders . . . that the State means, namely incarceration in secure, prison-like facilities, except in a limited class of cases, bears no reasonable relationship to legitimate State purposes, namely rehabilitation, protection of the children, and protection of society.[39]

## [D] Unconstitutional Punishment

While punitive dispositions are not theoretically unsound for certain classes of status offenders, for example habitual truants, runaways, or violators of court orders, *parens patriae* principles tend to provide the overriding dispositional rationale in status offender cases. Dispositions are generally aimed at providing care and rehabilitation for troubled children deemed in need of the state's beneficence. Punitive dispositions are often considered to be inconsistent with such *parens patriae* concerns.[40] Therefore, if the state in fact imposes punishment in the name of *parens patriae*, constitutional problems arise under the Due Process

---

[37] Santana v. Collazo, 714 F.2d 1172, 1179 (1st Cir. 1983), *cert. denied*, 466 U.S. 974 (1984).

[38] State *ex rel.* v. Calendine, 233 S.E.2d 318 (W. Va. 1977).

[39] *Id.* at 326–29.

[40] *See supra* § 11.03[B][1].

and the Cruel and Unusual Punishments Clauses. Moreover, punishment of "unruly" or "wayward" children who have not been shown to have committed a specific act of misconduct violates the Eighth Amendment.

## [1] Punishment Violative of Due Process

When the state promises a rehabilitative disposition but in fact imposes a punitive one, some courts see the disposition as not rationally related to the state interest sought to be achieved and thus violative of due process. For example, in a Tennessee case[41] the court considered an argument by status offenders that their confinement in the same juvenile facility housing delinquent offenders constituted punishment and was thus constitutionally inconsistent with the state's articulated purpose of providing them with *parens patriae* dispositions. The Tennessee Supreme Court agreed. The court noted that "the *parens patriae* interest possessed by the state allows the state to act for the preservation and promotion of the child's welfare, the child's liberty interest may be subordinated to the state's *parens patriae* interest, and the state may impose restrictions upon the child, including confinement."[42] The court specified, however, that "one purpose of confinement which the state may not assert when acting in its *parens patriae* capacity is retributive punishment."[43]

In deciding the issue of whether the confinement in the case at hand constituted punishment, the Tennessee Supreme Court noted that it must determine "whether the confinement is imposed for the purpose of punishment or whether it is an incident of a legitimate [nonpunitive] governmental purpose."[44] In answering this question, the court applied a test derived from a series of United States Supreme Court cases: "[W]here as here, no showing of an express intent to punish is made, 'that determination generally will turn on whether an alternative purpose to which [the restriction] may rationally be connected is assignable for it, and whether it appears excessive in relation to the alternative purpose assigned.'"[45] Because the nature of the confinement in the case at hand manifested little evidence of rehabilitation while belying aspects of punishment,[46] the court found it to

---

[41] Doe v. Norris, 751 S.W.2d 834 (Tenn. 1988).

[42] *Id.* at 839.

[43] *Id.*

[44] *Id.*

[45] *Id.* (quoting Bell v. Wolfish, 441 U.S. 520, 538 (1979) (quoting Kennedy v. Mandoza-Martinez, 372 U.S. 144, 168–69 (1963))).

[46] The court based its conclusion on the following factors:

> Status offenders are incarcerated at Spencer for an indefinite period of time. Once committed, these children are commingled with the delinquent in every respect. The status offenders and delinquents are housed in the same dormitories, follow the same daily routine, and are subject to the same disciplines. Misbehavior may be punished by isolation for a period up to 72 hours. Among the incidents of misconduct reported during a one week period in 1985 were 41 incidents of assault/battery; 27 incidents of threatening the staff; and 18 incidents of threatening a student. Other reported incidents include possession of a deadly weapon, burglary, theft, arson, extortion, and substance abuse. Although the facility provides counseling and a minimal educational program, the expert witnesses testified that status offenders and delinquents should not be housed together in secure correctional facilities. This practice of commingling status offenders with delinquents was also found to be psychologically and socially harmful to the status offenders.

*Id.* at 840.

constitute punishment because it appeared excessive in relation to the articulated state interest in providing rehabilitative care.[47]

## [2]   Cruel and Unusual Punishment

As discussed in the context of delinquency, the United States Supreme Court has explicitly left open the question of the applicability of the Eighth Amendment's Cruel and Unusual Punishments Clause to juvenile court dispositions.[48] Nevertheless, as in delinquency cases, the lower courts have sometimes scrutinized dispositions of status offenders under the Eighth Amendment. The cases fall into two main categories: 1) cases involving punishment where dispositions are supposedly grounded on nonpunitive considerations, and 2) cases where punishment is imposed as a response to the juvenile's status rather than to an act of misconduct.

## [a]   Punishment in "Nonpunitive" Dispositional Systems

Where the statutory dispositional theory is premised on providing rehabilitative care, courts have found that dispositions which are in fact punitive constitute cruel and unusual punishment under the Eighth Amendment.[49] The courts have been especially sensitive to claims of punishment when made by status offenders. One court observed the following:

> In the case before us we are confronted with a child who was obviously in need of help, and yet the State chose to degrade him, to humiliate him, and to punish him by sending him to institutions which fail to meet his needs and cannot help him.

> At the outset this Court acknowledges that the cruel and unusual punishment standard cannot easily be defined and certainly is not fixed; consequently, we feel the standard tends to broaden as society becomes more enlightened and humane. The standard ought to be especially broad in this application to status offenders, whom the State has pledged *not* to punish at all, but rather, to protect and rehabilitate. Furthermore, status offenders are not guilty of the criminal conduct which ordinarily serves to make society's exercise of the penal sanction legitimate.[50]

In determining whether a given disposition is in fact punitive, the courts routinely assess whether the disposition is excessive in relation to nonpunitive dispositional alternatives[51] along the lines of the analysis described above in the

---

[47] The court also found the confinement unconstitutional because it constituted punishing "unruly children" for their status, *see infra* § 11.04[D][2][b], and because it offended equal protection principles.

[48] *See supra* § 11.03[C][5][b].

[49] *See, e.g.,* State *ex rel.* Harris v. Calendine, 233 S.E.2d 318 (W. Va. 1977).

[50] *Id.* at 329–30.

[51] The following analysis from a case finding the cruel and unusual punishment of status offenders is representative:

> By definition, the nature of the class of offenses committed by status offenders is non-criminal. Accordingly, the status offender is located on the extreme end of a spectrum of juvenile misconduct running from most serious to least serious offenses. The nature of their offenses thus tends to indicate that status offenders incarcerated in secure, prison-like facilities along with children guilty of criminal conduct, are suffering a constitutionally disproportionate penalty.

> . . . [T]his Court is unable to discern any rational connection between the legitimate

discussion of due process doctrine.[52] Thus, one court concluded that under a system aimed at rehabilitation, status offenders are subjected to unconstitutional punishment under the Eighth Amendment if they are "held for 30 days or longer in secure confinement without 'treatment.' "[53]

## [b]  Punishment of Status

In *Robinson v. California*,[54] the United States Supreme Court held that a state imposes cruel and unusual punishment under the Eighth Amendment when it punishes persons merely because they manifest an undesirable status condition the state seeks to eliminate.[55] Thus, in *Robinson* the Court held that a state could not punish a person for being a heroin addict even though the person could be punished for such acts as using or possessing heroin.[56] Moreover, the Court suggested that the state may also subject drug addicts to involuntary therapy or rehabilitation.[57] Under *Robinson*, therefore, punishment is unconstitutional when imposed for a status condition rather than for a specific wrongful act.

Some courts have applied *Robinson* to status offender cases and found Eighth Amendment violations when punishment is imposed for such statuses as being an "unruly" or "wayward" child.[58] For example, one federal district court held that under a New York statute, incarceration in adult penal institutions of "wayward minors" found to be "morally depraved or in danger of becoming morally depraved" constituted unconstitutional punishment for a status.[59] The court found that the statutory language relating to "moral deprav[ity]" made no reference to

---

legislative purposes of enforcing family discipline, protecting children, and protecting society from uncontrolled children and the incarceration of status offenders in secure, prison-like facilities along with children guilty of criminal conduct.

*Id.* at 330.

[52] *See supra* notes 36–37 and accompanying text.

[53] Martarella v. Kelley, 359 F. Supp. 478, 481 (S.D.N.Y. 1973).

[54] 370 U.S. 660 (1962).

[55] *Id.* at 667. The *Robinson* Court utilized the Cruel and Unusual Punishments Clause to strike down a California statute that punished persons adjudged to be drug addicts with a sentence of ninety days in the county jail. The Eighth Amendment violation occurred because the statute punished the "status" of drug addiction rather than a specific criminal "act" such as possession or sale of an illegal drug. *Id.* at 664–67.

The majority simply assumed that the jail term constituted punishment. The Court said: "To be sure, imprisonment for ninety days is not, in the abstract, a punishment which is either cruel or unusual. But the question cannot be considered in the abstract. Even one day in prison would be a cruel and unusual punishment for the 'crime' of having a common cold." *Id.* at 667.

[56] *Id.* at 664.

[57] "[A] State might establish a program of compulsory treatment for those addicted to narcotics. Such a program of treatment might require periods of involuntary confinement." *Id.* at 665 (dicta).

[58] See *supra* § 8.04[B] for a discussion of status offense jurisdiction premised on findings that juveniles manifest undesirable status conditions without any necessary finding that they have committed any particular act of misconduct.

[59] Gesicki v. Oswald, 336 F. Supp. 371 (S.D.N.Y. 1971), *aff'd*, 406 U.S. 913 (1972). The court also found the statutory language referred to in the text to be impermissibly vague. *See also* Santana v. Collazo, 714 F.2d 1172, 1180 (1st Cir. 1983), *cert. denied*, 466 U.S. 974 (1984) (suggesting violation of Eighth Amendment under *Robinson* if the state punishes children on the basis that they are "deemed undisciplined").

any conduct but spoke only to "a condition or status of immorality."[60] The court rejected arguments by the state that it was affording *parens patriae* benefits for "wayward children" under the statute rather than punishing them. The court instead found that the presence of such "ameliorative treatment as remedial schooling and vocational training" available in the institutions did not belie the fact that they were essentially institutions of punishment. The fact that the children were housed in adult penal institutions and subjected to essentially the same conditions of confinement as adult criminals satisfied the court that the disposition was punitive.[61] The court noted that "it is not an acceptable answer to say that some minors found 'wayward' are in fact treated appropriately for medical, psychological, or social disorders. Such instances of effective treatment, if they exist, would fail to distinguish the Wayward Minor statute from criminal legislation generally."[62] The court found the "central fallacy" in the argument was that the statute afforded *parens patriae* care rather than punishment: "the statute fails to require any course of treatment at all. Specifically, there is no assurance that wayward minors will be given special treatment substantially distinguishable from that accorded to criminals and reasonably related to the condition upon which the adjudication of waywardness is based."[63]

## § 11.05  APPEALS

Although the United States Supreme Court has never held that juveniles, nor adult offenders for that matter, have a constitutional right to appeal questionable aspects of their adjudications or dispositions, almost all states statutorily provide for judicial review of orders of juvenile court judges.[1] While many statutes permit parents as well as the juvenile to appeal, parents cannot block an appeal if the juvenile wishes to bring his case to the attention of the appropriate appellate court.[2]

---

[60] Gesicki v. Oswald, 336 F. Supp. at 376.

[61] The court explained:

> The penal character of the Wayward Minor statute is clearly indicated by several factors. It is important to distinguish the now-expired Wayward Minor statute at issue in this litigation from New York's statutory scheme for treating juvenile offenders. Except where jurisdiction in cases of unusually serious crimes is transferred to the adult courts, all offenses committed by minors under the age of 16 in New York are heard by the Family Courts. These juvenile offenders may not be incarcerated in an adult prison, and the provisions conferring jurisdiction on the Family Courts in these juvenile cases is contained in the Family Court Act, not in the Criminal Code.
>
> By contrast, the Wayward Minor statute permits the incarceration of those adjudicated under it in any of the correctional institutions maintained by the State of New York for the incarceration of adult criminals, the statute itself is contained in the Criminal Code, and trials are conducted in courts of general criminal jurisdiction. Confinement in an adult prison may continue for as long as three years.

*Id.* at 377–78. For a discussion of the court's conclusion that the disposition in *Gesicki* was punitive, see Gardner, *supra* § 7.02, note 10, at 841–42.

[62] Gesicki v. Oswald, 336 F. Supp. at 377.

[63] *Id.* at 378–79.

[1] Davis, *supra* § 2.02, note 9, at 6-51 to 6-52.

[2] *Id.* at 6-52.

Some states permit appeals only from orders of disposition.[3] Most states, however, permit appeals of all "final" orders, including adjudications.[4] Interlocutory orders are generally not appealable.[5] Thus, decisions waiving jurisdiction to criminal court are not appealable.[6]

In addition to direct appeal, juvenile court orders are subject to collateral attack. Review is available under common law writs of mandamus, prohibition, error, certiorari, and coram nobis as well as under modern postconviction relief statutes.[7]

---

[3] *Id.* at 6-53.

[4] *Id.*

[5] *Id.*

[6] *Id.*

[7] *Id.* at 6-57.

# Chapter 12
# THE FUTURE OF THE JUVENILE JUSTICE SYSTEM

## § 12.01  OVERVIEW

The juvenile justice system faces an uncertain future. With the waning of the rehabilitative ideal in the area of delinquency in many jurisdictions,[1] the juvenile justice system is in the process of reinventing itself in terms of theoretical considerations traditionally associated with the criminal justice system or even, perhaps, of merging altogether into that system. In the status offense context, rehabilitating troubled youngsters remains the primary purpose for asserting juvenile court jurisdiction. To the extent that this goal is unattainable or at least unattained, the wisdom of continued employment of status offense jurisdiction is a matter of serious debate, even for those who see a need for protecting children through judicial intervention.

## § 12.02  DELINQUENCY

As has been discussed throughout earlier Chapters of this text, a variety of considerations presently call into question the continued viability of the traditional model of juvenile court jurisdiction in delinquency cases. For many observers, the historical *parens patriae* foundations of delinquency jurisdiction have drastically eroded[1] due to the coalescence of several factors including 1) the criminalization of the adjudication process by the United States Supreme Court;[2] 2) a perception that the juvenile justice system has failed in achieving its traditional goal of rehabilitating delinquent offenders;[3] 3) a recognition that serious juvenile crime is increasing;[4] and 4) an emerging body of social science data suggesting that adolescents are not significantly different (*i.e.*, less competent, less mature) from adults. These factors call into question the necessity and wisdom of affording special *parens patriae* treatment for adolescent offenders.[5] It must be noted that all of these factors entail empirically controversial conclusions. As a consequence, informed opinion does not universally recognize the need to abandon traditional understandings and rethink the premises of delinquency jurisdiction.[6]

Some who see *parens patriae* principles as no longer supporting, or at least exclusively supporting, juvenile court jurisdiction in the delinquency context favor maintaining a separate system for juvenile offenders, but base that system on punitive and preventive detention rationales. Proponents of such models routinely

---

[1] *See supra* § 11.03[B]; *see also* P. Holland & W. Mlyniec, *Whatever Happened to the Right to Treatment?: The Modern Quest for a Historical Promise*, 68 Temp. L. Rev. 1791, 1811–16 (1995).

[1] *See, e.g.*, Feld, *supra* § 11.03, note 6; F. Sherman, *Thoughts on a Contextual View of Juvenile Justice Reform Drawn from Narratives of Youth*, 68 Temp. L. Rev. 1837, 1838–40 (1995).

[2] *See supra* § 7.03.

[3] *See* Gardner, *supra* § 7.02, note 29, at 131.

[4] *See* Sherman & Talley, *supra* § 11.03, note 208, at 891.

[5] *See supra* § 1.02[B]. *But see* E. Cauffman & L. Steinberg, *The Cognitive and Affective Influences on Adolescent Decision-Making*, 68 Temp. L. Rev. 1763 (1995) (suggesting that adolescents and adults *do* differ somewhat in decision-making behavior).

[6] *See, e.g.*, Rosenberg, *supra* § 7.02, note 35.

favor increased use of incarcerative dispositions, based on, and proportional to, the offense committed, for fixed periods, generally shorter in length, however, than those imposed against adults who commit the same offense.[7]

Somewhat surprisingly, many commentators who favor punishing juvenile offenders also favor abolishing juvenile court jurisdiction and disposing of juvenile cases within the criminal justice system.[8] The argument follows that once *parens patriae* principles are abandoned as the theoretical support for juvenile justice, the system has lost its *raison d'etre*. Proponents of this approach often argue that the youth of the offender can be accommodated within the criminal justice system by adopting a policy of scaled-down punishments for minors, should such be desirable.[9] Moreover, youthful offenders would arguably benefit from increased availability of the infancy defense in criminal courts as well as from the procedural advantage of trial by jury.[10]

Proponents of retaining a separate system of punitive juvenile justice argue that the supposed advantages of the criminal system could be embodied in the juvenile system if it simply made the infancy defense and jury determinations available in delinquency adjudications.[11] Moreover, to the extent that juvenile offenders are not as culpable as similarly situated adults for their offenses, retaining a separate system of punitive juvenile justice is arguably desirable because it may visit less stigma upon those whom it adjudicates "delinquent" than is conveyed towards those labeled "criminal," whether they be adults or juveniles who are "waived" to adult court.[12]

Policy makers thus face crucial decisions in developing strategies to deal with the problem of juvenile crime. The shape of such strategies depends to a considerable degree on how juvenile rights are understood. At one extreme, policy makers may see all juveniles as possessors of protectionist rights and thus decide to retain the traditional *parens patriae* model. At the other extreme, they may see at least some juvenile offenders as full-fledged responsible persons who thus should be held fully accountable for their criminal offenses. As a third, and perhaps more realistic alternative, policy makers may increasingly attempt to reconcile both protectionist and personhood theories in fashioning responses to juvenile crime. This alternative recognizes that young people are entitled to a degree of protection even though they function, to a degree at least, as responsible persons.[13]

---

[7] See Feld, *supra* note 1, at 842–47, 852–54, for a discussion of states adopting this approach.

[8] For references to commentators favoring abolishing juvenile courts, see Gardner, *supra* note 3, at 132 and Sherman, *supra* note 1, at 1840–41 n.13.

[9] *See, e.g.*, Feld, *supra* § 7.02, note 35, at 723–24.

[10] *Id.*

[11] *See, e.g.*, Gardner, *supra* note 3; *see also* G. Melton, *Taking* Gault *Seriously: Toward a New Juvenile Court*, 68 NEB. L. REV. 146, 150 (1989) (arguing for retaining juvenile courts but increasing their attention to due process rights of juveniles).

[12] *See* Gardner, *supra* note 3, at 148–51.

[13] *Id.* Note that none of the new models of punitive juvenile justice have totally abandoned the interest in helping or rehabilitating juvenile offenders. Holland & Mlyniec, *supra* § 12.01, note 1, at 1812–16. See *supra* § 2.04 for discussion of a theory of rights integrating aspects of both protectionist and personhood theories.

## § 12.03 STATUS OFFENSES

Traditionally, *parens patriae* provided the theoretical underpinnings of both delinquency and status offense jurisdiction. While juvenile court interventions in delinquency cases are now commonly justified in many jurisdictions in terms of additional or different considerations, *parens patriae* continues to provide the virtually ubiquitous theoretical basis for status offense jurisdiction.[1] In status offense cases, juvenile courts employ mechanisms aimed at engaging children in activities deemed beneficial to them, such as regular school attendance. The courts also provide responses aimed at discouraging conduct considered potentially harmful to the child such as running away from home or acting "waywardly" or "immorally." Thus, exercise of status offense jurisdiction is by its nature premised on the view that the courts will impose dispositions that are "good," or "necessary," for the welfare of the child.

Because status offense jurisdiction is inherently paternalistic, it is linked to the protectionist theory of rights. For protectionists, exercise of status offense jurisdiction is desirable so long as the courts in fact provide needed help to troubled children. Therefore, for protectionists, the question of whether juvenile courts should continue to intervene in the status offense context is essentially an empirical matter.

On the other hand, status offense jurisdiction, if asserted over competent adolescent persons, appears theoretically at odds with the personhood theory of rights. On that view, such persons are entitled to be free from paternalistic state interventions.[2] This view of juvenile rights is reflected in the position of the Juvenile Justice Standards advocating the abolition of status offense jurisdiction.[3] While no jurisdiction has yet to make this move, it may someday occur, especially in light of the emerging trend towards holding juveniles at least partially responsible persons when they commit criminal offenses.

As with delinquency matters, policy makers face difficult questions as they ponder the future of status offense jurisdiction in juvenile court. Sound answers to these questions depend on a clear understanding of the rights of children in relation to their parents and the state as well as an awareness of how the juvenile justice system operates and the extent to which it delivers on its promise to help children in need.

---

[1] *See supra* § 11.04[C], [D].

[2] *See supra* § 2.03.

[3] *See supra* § 8.04, note 31 and accompanying text.

# TABLE OF CASES

[References are to pages.]

[References are to pages.]

[References are to pages.]

[References are to pages.]

[References are to pages.]

[References are to pages.]

[References are to pages.]

# Y

# Z

# INDEX

[References are to pages.]

[References are to pages.]

[References are to pages.]

[References are to pages.]

[References are to pages.]

[References are to pages.]